Gift upon Gift

Princeton Theological Monograph Series

K. C. Hanson, Charles M. Collier, D. Christopher Spinks,
and Robin Parry, Series Editors

Recent volumes in the series:

Randall W. Reed
*A Clash of Ideologies: Marxism, Liberation Theology,
and Apocalypticism in New Testament Studies*

Donald E. Gowan
The Bible on Forgiveness

Myk Habets
The Anointed Son: A Trinitarian Spirit Christology

David H. Nikkel
Radical Embodiment

Jeff B. Pool
*God's Wounds: Hermeneutic of the Christian Symbol
of Divine Suffering, Volume Two: Evil and Divine Suffering*

William A. Tooman
*Transforming Visions: Transformations of Text, Tradition,
and Theology in Ezekiel*

Poul F. Guttesen
*Leaning Into the Future: The Kingdom of God in the Theology
of Jürgen Moltmann and the Book of Revelation*

Christopher W. Skinner
*John and Thomas—Gospels in Conflict?: Johannine Characterization
and the Thomas Question*

David Paul Parris
Reception Theory and Biblical Hermeneutics

Gift upon Gift
Covenant through Word in the Gospel of John

SHERRI BROWN

☙PICKWICK *Publications* · Eugene, Oregon

GIFT UPON GIFT
Covenant through Word in the Gospel of John

Princeton Theological Monograph Series 144

Copyright © 2010 Sherri Brown. All rights reserved. Except for brief quotations in critical publications or reviews, no part of this book may be reproduced in any manner without prior written permission from the publisher. Write: Permissions, Wipf and Stock Publishers, 199 W. 8th Ave., Suite 3, Eugene, OR 97401.

Pickwick Publications
An Imprint of Wipf and Stock Publishers
199 W. 8th Ave., Suite 3
Eugene, OR 97401

www.wipfandstock.com

ISBN 13: 978-1-60899-391-8

Cataloging-in-Publication data:

Brown, Sherri.

    Gift upon gift : covenant through word in the gospel of John / Sherri Brown, with a foreword by Francis J. Moloney, SDB.

    Princeton Theological Monograph Series 144

    xxiv + 266 p.; 23 cm. Includes bibliographical references.

    ISBN 13: 978-1-60899-391-8

    1. Bible. N.T. John—Criticism, interpretation, etc. 2. Covenants—Biblical teaching. I. Title. II. Series.

BS413.C41 B76 2010

Manufactured in the U.S.A.

This work is dedicated to my family in all its extended shapes, sizes, and flavors. It is dedicated first and foremost to my parents, Pat and Billie Brown, and my siblings, Tricia and Patrick. Without their love, support, and humor I could never have made it this far. This product of years of study, struggle, and reflection is also dedicated to my larger family, including the Salesians of Don Bosco of the Australian province. I owe an immeasurable debt to all those at the Province Centre in Melbourne, especially Frs. Peter, Paul, Tim, and Joe, and my dear friend Trish. Their generosity, hospitality, faith, and koala-finding skills sustained me through the most productive days. It goes without saying that I never could have completed this task without the guidance, counsel, and occasional hammer dropping of Frank Moloney, my friend, mentor, and all-around guru. These things have been written for all of you.

From his fullness we have all received gift upon gift, because while the law was given through Moses, the gift of truth came through Jesus Christ.

—John 1:16–17

Contents

Foreword / ix

Preface / xiii

Abbreviations / xv

1. The Gospel of John and the Covenant Metaphor / 1

    Covenant in the Gospel of John / 1

    A Literary Approach to the Study of Covenant in the Gospel of John / 11

    Studying John through the Prism of Dialogue: The Gospel's Dramatic Nature / 15

    Covenant as the Guiding Literary Paradigm of the Gospel of John / 21

2. Covenant in Scripture / 23

    Covenant in the Old Testament / 24

    Key Covenantal Texts in the Old Testament / 39

    Conclusion: Characteristics of the Old Testament Covenant Relationship / 64

3. John and Scripture: Beginnings and Endings / 68

    The Structure of the Gospel / 68

    John as Evangelist and Writer of Scripture / 70

    Endings: The Conclusion of the Body of the Gospel (20:30–31) / 75

    Beginnings: The Prologue to the Body of the Gospel (1:1–18) / 78

    John the Baptist: The Prologue Embodied in the Gospel Action (1:19–34) / 95

    Discipleship and the Teaching of the Son of Man / 103

    The Hope of Israel: The Dialectic of Fulfillment / 105

4 Covenantal Dialogue in John 2–4 / 108

   The Catechetical Journey from Cana to Cana (John 2–4) / 108
   The Dialogue of Covenant in John 2–4 / 136

5 Covenantal Dialogue in John 5–12 / 141

   The Feasts of Israel (John 5–10) / 142
   Moving to Glory (John 11–12) / 172
   The Dialogue of Covenant in John 5–12 / 175

6 Covenantal Dialogue in John 13–20 / 180

   The Last Discourse (John 13–17) / 181
   The Passion: The Covenantal Dialogue of the Cross (John 18–19) / 190
   The Resurrection of the Word (John 20) / 224
   The Dialogue of Covenant in John 13–20 / 225

7 Community and Covenant: Gift upon Gift / 230

   Epilogue: The Covenant for the Community of Believers (John 21) / 232
   Covenant as a Guiding Literary Paradigm / 236
   Covenant through Word in the Gospel of John / 243

Bibliography / 251

Foreword

Johannine scholarship has come a long way since the mid-nineteenth century. As a critical approach to the Bible took hold within the European (read German) universities at that time, the Fourth Gospel was relegated to a backwater. The passion of these early critics was history. They worked tirelessly to discover, from the many available manuscripts, what was the most authentic and original version of the biblical text. They dug deep into the texts themselves in an attempt to discover the "sources" of the books as we have them. Especially important in this quest were the sources for the Pentateuch, and the sources for the Synoptic Gospels, and the most reliable sources for the discovery of the life of Jesus *exactly as it had happened*. Finally, they sought to discover the authentic and historically verifiable contours of the life and person of Jesus of Nazareth. The Gospel of John had no place in this hard-nosed world. Critics leapt upon Clement of Alexandria's description of the Fourth Gospel as "the spiritual Gospel," and regarded it as mystical, a late example of the development of a certain form of "catholic" theology, and thus irrelevant for their pursuits.

None of these concerns have disappeared from biblical scholarship. Indeed, they must remain part of the toolbox of any serious scholar. They are certainly present in the study that follows. Of course, subsequent research has shown that disregard for genuine historical reminiscence in the Gospel of John was foolish. Interestingly, however, perhaps the most significant single contribution to the restoration of the Fourth Gospel to the scholar's desk came from the most creative historical critic of the twentieth century, Rudolf Bultmann. His commentary on the Gospel of John, first published in 1943, established John—along with Paul (in his later *Theology of the New Testament*)—as a creative theological genius. Although interest in Bultmann's commentary has waned in recent decades, his flawed but brilliant reading of this fascinating text continues to inspire much in Johannine scholarship.

The work that follows has little to do with Bultmann's commentary, much less with his understanding of John's sources and his reconstruction of the "original" Johannine text. However, it continues the Bultmannian tradition by arguing that the Gospel of John is a coherent and sophisticated literary and theological unity. For Bultmann, this literary and theological sophistication was the work of the Evangelist (using his earlier material coming from a Signs Source and some Gnostic discourse material). For Dr. Sherri Brown, it is to be found at every turn in the Johannine way of telling a familiar story. A product of her own time, she is more interested in the narrative as it was first accepted in the Christian church, and as it has come down to us. However, her study recognizes the important truth that even the narrative critics must devote time, energy, and attention to historical context. It is dishonest to interpret narrative without situating it in a world where subtle narrative readings would have made sense. Text without context is pretext!

Brown has written a work that looks back upon a long history of Johannine scholarship and suggests a new paradigm for a reading of the text itself, situating it in a Christian community late in the first Christian century. Her points of departure are not new. Since the mid-twentieth century voices have been raised in articles and occasional monographs that the theme of covenant was crucial to a correct reading of John (e.g., Malatesta, Simoens, Schneiders, Chennattu). More recently, but prior to Brown's work, a strong case has been made that the author of the Fourth Gospel deliberately situated his "book" side by side with all books that formed Israel's sacred Scripture, consciously bringing them to their "end" (the Johannine *telos*: D. Moody Smith, Moloney).

The unique contribution of this study is its focus upon a literary and rhetorical background provided by ancient drama, and the dialogues that are crucial to that form of communication, as a pointer to the structure and theology of the Johannine dialogues. Much attention has been given to the Johannine discourse material, but a feature of the Fourth Gospel is the lengthy dialogues that have no parallel in the Synoptic tradition. Only in John do single characters (or a group made into a character, as with the Johannine "Jews") engage in lengthy discussions with Jesus (John the Baptist, the mother of Jesus, the Samaritan woman, the man born blind, "the Jews," Pilate). However, in the ancient dramas the prologue to the work sets the theme for the dialogues that follow. Brown's analysis of the Johannine prologue (1:1–18) demonstrates convincingly the centrality of the theme of covenant on this first page of the story and the dialogues that follow.

Her work on the role of ancient drama and the structure and meaning of covenant is enlightening, but it is her application of these elements to the interpretation of the Johannine dialogues, in the light of her reading of the prologue, that is most informative. One of the features of this study is Brown's bold attempt to read what must be regarded as the most difficult dialogue in early Christian literature as both Scripture and covenant: the dialogue between Jesus and "the Jews" in John 7–8. A response to the anxiety and pain that has emerged among scholars when they are faced by this slanging match where one is accused of illegitimacy (see 8:41) and the other is accused of being a child of the devil (see 8:44) is but one of the rich rewards resulting from a careful reading of the study that follows.

Throughout, however, Brown is not only concerned with the particular passage or dialogue under consideration. She keeps the literary and theological fabric of the Fourth Gospel as a whole in her sights at all times. She necessarily asks what relevance telling the story of Jesus *in this way* might have had for a Christian community at the end of the first Christian century, and, like all good scholarship done within the context of the Christian church, she asks us what it means when the life of Jesus is presented as an invitation to covenant, and simultaneously an invitation to recognize that in the story of Jesus found in the Gospel of John the sacred Scriptures of Israel and Christianity have come to completion.

Francis J. Moloney, SDB
Australian Catholic University
Melbourne

Preface

> There is, indeed, a truth, a practicality, a value, even a grandeur in this Johannine love within the household of faith. I confess a certain enthusiasm for it, and on occasion would gladly discourse at length on its merits. But we understand the Fourth Gospel very slightly yet, and we shall never understand it at all until we get into the way of seeing it steadily and seeing it whole, an *und für sich*. Most of our writers about it cannot forget the Synoptics as they peruse its pages, and consciously or unconsciously wrest it either into a false consonance with them or into a dissonance not less false, in either case to their own destruction. We must learn to be content with uniqueness here, and let the Gospel say what it will, whether or no its words are congenial to our modern temper. . . . But [John] has something of his own to tell us, if only we will be quiet and stop trying to make him repeat the revelation of Paul and Peter and Mark. When shall we give him an ear?
>
> —Clayton R. Bowen on "Love in the Fourth Gospel," 1933

The study that follows is my attempt to join the ranks of scholarship on the Gospel according to John and give my ear to the Fourth Evangelist and his particular telling of the story of Jesus Christ. This project sprung from a doctoral seminar with Professor Francis J. Moloney at The Catholic University of America in 2003. At that time I challenged myself to exegete the dialogue between Jesus and his mother at the wedding feast in Cana. The rest, as they say, is history. This study convinced me that the concept of the OT covenant metaphor is integral to the Gospel, though the evangelist never uses the term itself. I am certainly not alone in this reading or in the various hermeneutics that contribute to this understanding of the Fourth Evangelist, and I happily build upon the work of my predecessors. My contribution is to suggest that the covenant metaphor is indeed the very literary fabric with which the evangelist weaves the entirety of his story. I employ scholarship on the notion that the evangelist understood himself to be writing Scripture—the culmination of the story of Israel—and used the conventions of ancient drama to recount the force of the movements of dialogues across the Gospel. These dialogues, I suggest, are in turn revealed to be symbolic of the covenantal challenge of Jesus the Christ and potential responses to that challenge of living in covenant relationship with God through Jesus. I hope my passion for this Gospel contributes to the understanding of the unique voice of John the Evangelist.

This book is a revised version of my doctoral dissertation, completed at CUA in 2007. Like most of us who achieve the completion of this process, I managed only with the support of my own community of believers. Those who knew, even when I doubted, that this could be done, was worth being done, and should be done by me, are many, and they supported me in innumerable ways. I want to thank the members of my dissertation committee, Francis T. Gignac and Frank J. Matera, for their time, teaching, and thoughtful critiques of my work. Both my work and I are better for it. I must also thank my fellow *Moloneyschule* members for being the best friends, scholars, classmates, and colleagues I could ask for during this period in my life: Dr. Kelly Iverson, Dr. Christopher Skinner, Dr. Gregg Morrison, and Rev. Daniel Claire. It seems there was no problem we couldn't solve or pedagogy we couldn't rewrite over a beer—or two.

I would also like to thank my students and colleagues both inside and outside of CUA who gave me ideas, kind words, good humor, a kick into gear, and/or a job(!) when I needed it. Brian Shanley, OP, and Kurt Pritzl, OP, were very important to me during this time. The folks in St. Meinrad School of Theology's Permanent Deacon Formation Program, in Education Parish Service at Trinity University, and at Wesley Theological Seminary were also invaluable as I developed as a scholar and teacher in this period. You all were the best I could have hoped for.

I would also like to thank K. C. Hanson and the editorial staff at Pickwick Publications and Wipf and Stock for publishing this book in the Princeton Theological Monograph Series.

This work is dedicated to my family in its various manifestations. I thanked you there and I thank you again here. My parents and siblings have sustained me in many ways, and I love them for it. In particular, I have given and will continue to give my *Doktorvater* Francis J. Moloney, SDB, my gratitude, respect, and love, as well as a number of my less endearing qualities. I do hope that is okay with you Frank, because you've got the job for life, whether you want it or not. You all are the reason this study was possible and this book is now complete.

Abbreviations

AB	Anchor Bible
ABD	*The Anchor Bible Dictionary*, edited by David Noel Freedman; 6 vols. (New York: Doubleday, 1992)
ABR	*Australian Biblical Review*
ABRL	Anchor Bible Reference Library
A.J.	*Antiquitates judaicae*
AnBib	Analecta Biblica
Apoc. Abr.	*Apocalypse of Abraham*
AsSeign	*Assemblées du Seigneur*
ASV	American Standard Version
AThR	*Anglican Theological Review*
B&L	Bible & Liberation Series
Bar	*Baruch*
BASOR	*Bulletin of the American Schools of Oriental Research*
BBC	Broadman Bible Commentary
BDAG	Bauer, Walter, Frederick W. Danker, W. F. Arndt, and F. W. Gingrich, *Greek-English Lexicon of the New Testament and Other Early Christian Literature*; 3rd ed. (Chicago: University of Chicaco Press, 2000)
BDF	Blass, Friedrich, and Albert Debrunner, *A Greek Grammar of the New Testament and Other Early Christian Literature*, translated and revised by Robert W. Funk (Chicago: University of Chicago Press, 2000)
Ber.	*Berakhot*
BETL	Bibliotheca Ephemeridum theologicarum Lovaniensium

Bib	*Biblica*
BIS	Biblical Interpretation Series
BLS	Bible and Literature Series
BNTC	Black's New Testament Commentaries
BSac	*Bibliotheca Sacra*
BTB	*Biblical Theology Bulletin*
BZ	*Biblische Zeistschrift*
CahRB	Cahiers de la Revue biblique
CBET	Contributions to Biblical Exegesis and Theology
CBQ	*Catholic Biblical Quarterly*
CBQMS	Catholic Biblical Quarterly Monograph Series
CD	*Damascus Document*
COL	Christian Origins Library
CurTM	*Currents in Theology and Mission*
DRev	*Downside Review*
EBib	Études bibliques
Eccl. Rab.	*Ecclesiastes Rabbah*
ER	*The Encyclopedia of Religion*, edited by Mircea Eliade; 16 vols (New York: MacMillan, 1987)
EstBib	*Estudios Bíblicos*
ETL	*Ephemerides Theologicae Lovanienses*
EuD	*Euntes Docete*
EvQ	*Evangelical Quarterly*
ExpTim	*Expository Times*
FB	Forschung zur Bibel
FFNT	Foundations and Facets: New Testament
FM	*Faith and Mission*
FRLANT	Forschungen zur Religion und Literatur des Alten und Neuen Testaments

GBSNT	Guides to Biblical Scholarship: New Testament Series
Gen. Rab.	*Genesis Rabbah*
HBibS	Herders biblische Studien
HSM	Harvard Semitic Monographs
HTKNT	Herders theologischer Kommentar zum Neuen Testament
HTR	*Harvard Theological Review*
IBS	*Irish Biblical Studies*
ICC	International Critical Commentary
Imm	*Immanuel*
Int	*Interpretation*
JAOS	*Journal of the American Oriental Society*
JBL	*Journal of Biblical Literature*
JNSL	*Journal of Northwest Semitic Languages*
Jos. Asen.	*Joseph and Asenath*
JPSLJC	Jewish Publication Society Library of Jewish Classics
JR	*Journal of Religion*
JSNT	*Journal for the Study of the New Testament*
JSNTSup	Journal for the Study of the New Testament: Supplement Series
JSOTSup	Journal for the Study of the Old Testament: Supplement Series
JTS	*Journal of Theological Studies*
JTSA	*Journal of Theology for Southern Africa*
Jub.	*Jubilees*
KJV	King James Version
LB	*Linguistica biblica*
LD	Lectio Divina

LSJ	Liddell, Henry George, Robert Scott, and Henry Stuart Jones, *A Greek-English Lexicon*; 9th ed. (Oxford: Clarendon, 1996)
LTP	*Laval théologique et philosophique*
LV	*Lumen Vitae*
Mid.	*Middot*
MLSB	Museum Lessianum: Section biblique
NA27	Novum Testamentum Graece, Nestle-Aland, 27th ed.
NAB	New American Bible
NCB	New Century Bible
NEchtB	Neue Echter Bible
Neot	*Neotestamentica*
NIB	The New Interpreter's Bible
NIV	New International Version
NovT	*Novum Testamentum*
NovTSup	Novum Testamentum Supplements
NRSV	New Revised Standard Version
NTD	Das Neue Testament Deutsch
NTL	New Testament Library
NTS	*New Testament Studies*
NTTRU	*New Testament Textual Research Update*
NTTS	New Testament Tools and Studies
OBT	Overtures to Biblical Theology
OTL	Old Testament Library
Pes.	*Pesahim*
RB	*Revue biblique*
RechBib	Recherches bibliques
RevExp	*Review and Expositor*
RNT	Regensburger Neues Testament
RSR	*Recherches de science religieuse*

RSV	Revised Standard Version
RTD	Regenssburger Neues Testament
RTR	*The Reformed Theological Review*
Sal	*Salesianum*
Sanh.	*Sanhedrin*
SBF	Studium Biblicum Franciscanum
SBL	Society of Biblical Literature
SBLDS	Society of Biblical Literature Dissertation Series
SBLMS	Society of Biblical Literature Monograph Series
SBLRBS	Society of Biblical Literature Resources for Biblical Study
SBLSymS	Society of Biblical Literature Symposium Series
Scr	*Scripture*
SE	*Studia evangelica*
Semeia	*Semeia*
Sheq.	*Sheqalim*
SNTSMS	Society for New Testament Studies Monograph Series
Song Rab.	*Song of Songs Rabbah*
SP	Sacra Pagina
ST	*Studia theologica*
Suk.	*Sukkah*
T. Levi	*Testament of Levi*
TD	Theologischen Dissertationen
TDNT	*Theological Dictionary of the New Testament*, edited by Gerhard Kittel and Gerhard Friedrich, translated by Geoffrey W. Bromiley; 10 vols. (Grand Rapids: Eerdmans, 1964–76)
TDOT	*Theological Dictionary of the Old Testament*, edited by G. Johannes Botterweck and Helmer Ringgren, translated by Geoffrey W. Bromiley et al.; 14 vols. (Grand Rapids: Eerdmans, 1974–2004)

TLZ	*Theologische Literaturzeitung*
TS	*Theological Studies*
TTE	*The Theological Educator*
TW	*Theologie und Wirklichkeit*
TynBul	*Tyndale Bulletin*
TZ	*Theologische Zeitschrift*
UBT	Understanding Biblical Themes
VT	*Vetus Testamentum*
WBC	Word Biblical Commentary
WMANT	Wissenschaftliche Monographien zum Alten und Neuen Testament
WUNT	Wissenschaftliche Untersuchungen zum Neuen Testament
WW	*Word and World*
ZNW	*Zeitschrift für die neutestamentliche Wissenschaft und die Kunde der älteren Kirche*

1

The Gospel of John and the Covenant Metaphor

THE JOHANNINE STORY OF JESUS IS A CAREFULLY CRAFTED LITERARY treatise theologically underpinned by discourse on covenant and Scripture. Through his Gospel the Fourth Evangelist provides catechesis to a believing community on the nature of its faith in the God of Israel's ongoing covenant with the created order. The purpose of the present study is to take the recent work on covenant in the Gospel according to John a step further by examining the entirety of the Gospel through a narrative lens that focuses on several key dialogues spanning John's story of Jesus. Studying the whole of the Gospel through the prism of dialogue will shed light upon the evangelist's intention for these complex interactions on both the narrative level and the covenantal-discourse level of the Fourth Gospel. This study therefore attempts to uncover a new paradigm for reading John against the background of covenant. By grasping this theological fabric of the Gospel, the richness of its dialogue and imagery is allowed to have its full voice in terms of covenant fulfillment and the enduring commitment of God to a believing people.

This chapter will introduce the topic of the study by surveying the secondary literature on covenant in the Gospel according to John. The chapter will then proceed by outlining the literary and dialogical methodology that will undergird the study in order to lay the foundation for a systematic analysis of covenant as the guiding literary paradigm of the narrative.

Covenant in the Gospel of John

We now embark upon our exploration of how OT covenantal narrative themes emerge in the revelatory story of the Fourth Evangelist. We begin by surveying the issue in contemporary biblical scholarship, then look ahead to the study of covenant as the guiding literary paradigm of the Gospel of John.

Contemporary Scholarship

In the 1970s Edward Malatesta raised the question of covenant in the Johannine literature by studying the syntactic use of the verbal constructions "to abide in" and "to be in" in the First Letter of John, in *Interiority and Covenant: An Exegetical Study of the εἶναι ἐν and μένειν ἐν Expressions in 1 John*. His groundbreaking work was followed and expanded upon first by Yves Simoens in the 1980s in *La Gloire d'aimer: Structures stylistiques et interprétatives dans le Discours de la Cène*, then by Sandra Schneiders in the 1990s in *Written That You May Believe: Encountering Jesus in the Fourth Gospel*. In recent years, Rekha Chennattu studied covenant formulae in the discipleship material in the Gospel, particularly the discourse of John 13–17, in her doctoral dissertation published as *Johannine Discipleship as a Covenant Relationship*.[1] These works will comprise the following overview of the literature.

Edward Malatesta

Edward Malatesta's pioneering 1974 doctoral dissertation delved fully, for the first time, into the covenant motif in the Johannine literature.[2] He focuses on the interiority expressions εἶναι ἐν and μένειν ἐν and their resonance of the OT new covenant themes as expressed particularly in the prophetic oracles of Jeremiah and Ezekiel. Although he is concerned primarily with an exegetical analysis of the First Letter of John, he grounds his exploration in the literary characteristics of interiority expressions in both 1 John and the Fourth Gospel.[3]

---

1. A less considerable work that will not be analyzed in the development of the literature but that remains noteworthy for its focus on the covenant theme and the Johannine community is J. W. Pryor, *John, Evangelist of the Covenant People*.

2. Notable works upon which he builds are de La Potterie, *Verité dans Saint Jean*; Kennedy, "Covenant-Conception," 23–26, and "Significance and Range of the Covenant-Conception," 385–410; Boismard, "Connaissance de Dieu," 365–91, and "Je ferai avec vous une alliance nouvelle," 94–109.

3. Malatesta, *Interiority and Covenant*, 27–36.

Methodologically, he claims a Johannine hermeneutic grounded in interiority:

> The chief characteristic of the Johannine understanding of Christianity is precisely the awareness that the intimate relationship between Jesus, the Father and the Spirit establishes, maintains and develops the communion of the members of the Christian community with Jesus, the Spirit and the Father. Moreover, according to John, the communion of Christians with each other and their relationship to the world are grounded in their communion with God.[4]

From this vantage point, he can assert the two interiority expressions under consideration: εἶναι ἐν (denoting the richness of existence) and μένειν ἐν (denoting the concept of abiding in terms of "inward, enduring personal communion"). He further asserts that the preposition ἐν "is precisely the element that converts both verbs into words describing an interior way of being and remaining" and makes both expressions relational and therefore covenantal.[5] Malatesta's research finds these interiority expressions throughout the Gospel but concentrated in the last discourse (John 13–17). Further, the last interiority expression in the Gospel "highlights the glorified Jesus as being in His disciples."[6]

Malatesta then turns to an examination of these interiority expressions in the OT, beginning first with the MT, then turning to the LXX.[7] Once this contextualization is complete, he analyzes the covenantal aspect of these occurrences as a preparation for Johannine usage.[8] Beginning with covenant formulae in the OT, he focuses on the concept of the divine indwelling. He notes that nine OT new covenant texts contain some or all of five essential themes: the covenant formula, the interior renewal of the nation or of individuals, the reunification of Israel, blessings, an announcement of the definitive covenant (Deut 30:1–10; Jer 24:5–7; 31:31–34; 32:37–41; Ezek 11:14–21; 16:53–63; 36:2–35;

---

4. Ibid., 6.

5. Ibid., 24–27.

6. Ibid., 32. See John 17:26 for this final occurrence. The expressions occur in full form 29 times, and an additional 17 times where the verb is to be understood within the verbless clause.

7. Ibid., 42–64.

8. Ibid., 60–77.

37:21–28).⁹ What comes to the fore in this study is the explicit interiorization/interior renewal aspect of the new covenant texts in Jeremiah and Ezekiel. While the Jeremiah texts manifest "an interiorization of the Law, knowledge of God, and forgiveness of sins," the Ezekiel texts reveal God's promises of "another heart and a new spirit."¹⁰ He concludes that the major OT themes related to covenant, and particularly to the interiorization of the new covenant, are: (1) the heart, (2) the Spirit as related to indwelling, (3) the union of wisdom with the just, and (4) observance of the commandments.¹¹

The remainder of Malatesta's important study (and the bulk of the work) is devoted to a close exegesis of 1 John in light of interiority and covenant. However, his contribution to and, in many ways, initiation of the development of covenant literature on the Gospel according to John is invaluable.

Yves Simoens

Several years later, in 1981, Yves Simoens published *La Gloire d'aimer: Structures stylistiques et interprétatives dans le Discours de la Cène*, the first significant work focused on the covenant theme in the Gospel of John itself. As the title suggests, this work is devoted entirely to a structural analysis of the last discourse in John 13–17. Simoens suggests that a covenant genre is present in this scene more so than, and even to the exclusion of, the traditionally accepted farewell discourse type.

After a thorough survey of the state of the question with regard to the structure and integrity of John 13–17, Simoens argues for the narrative unity and coherence of these chapters by establishing a chiastic structure as follows:

---

9. Ibid., 68–69. Here Malatesta cites de la Fuente, "Cumplimento," 293–311.

10. Malatesta, *Interiority and Covenant*, 69–70.

11. Ibid., 70–77. His detailed textual analysis reinforces my own narrative-critical reading of the latter Prophets. See chapter 2 for my discussion.

A   13:1–38   *Agapè*: Glorification
 B   14:1–31   Encouragement; *Agapè*-garde de la parole; Départ
  C   15:1–11   Demeurer; Joie
   D   15:12–17   *Agapè* mutuelle
  C′   15:18—16:3 Haine du monde; Persecution-
                   Exclusion par ignorance
 B′   16:4–33   Départ; Joie; Encouragement
A′   17:1–26   Glorification: *Agapè*

In this analysis, 15:12–17 and the covenantal notion of mutuality in love form the fulcrum of the chiasm.[12]

Drawing upon the work of Jean L'Hour for the essential elements of the covenant form, Simoens proceeds to substantiate a claim that these chapters are covenantal in genre rather than a farewell scene.[13] He claims that John 13–17 comprise a reformulation of OT covenant tradition by asserting that this discourse is modeled on the literary structure of the OT covenantal document *par excellence*, the book of Deuteronomy.[14] The comparative analysis is illustrated as follows:[15]

Covenant Form	I Historical Prologue	II Great Commandment	III Stipulations	IV Blessings and Curses	V Canticle
Deuteronomy	1:1—4:40	4:44—11:32	12:1—26:15	26:16—30:20	32–33
John	13	14	15:1—16:3	16:4–33	17

Further, Simoens claims, the correspondence of these five components of the covenantal form are repeated in the final prayer of chapter 17 itself: a historical prologue in vv. 1–5, a great commandment in vv. 6–11, stipulations in vv. 12–19, blessings and curses in vv. 20–23, and a closing canticle in vv. 24–26.

Although he has now collapsed his seven-part chiastic structure of the last discourse into this five-part covenantal form, Simoens contin-

---

12. Simoens, *Gloire d'aimer*, 52–80; italics original. See esp. the charts on 77–79.

13. Ibid., 200–50. See also L'Hour, *Morale de l'alliance*.

14. Simoens (*Gloire d'aimer*, 203) grapples with and adapts Lacomara's work on Deuteronomy and John 13–17. See Lacomara, "Deuteronomy and the Farewell Discourse," 64–84.

15. Simoens, *Gloire d'aimer*, 204–5.

ues to find the central assertion of "stipulation" to be a call for mutual love among the disciples (15:12–17 are now the central verses of the 15:1—16:3 covenantal stipulation section). Thus, the OT covenantal form of the book of Deuteronomy provides the model for the Fourth Evangelist's understanding of the new covenant and its call to love through the gift of the Holy Spirit.[16]

Sandra Schneiders

In the 1990s, Sandra Schneiders published what quickly became a standard text for the study of the Gospel of John: *Written That You May Believe: Encountering Jesus in the Fourth Gospel*. In it she determined to "engage the biblical text through rigorously critical study undertaken in the context of living faith."[17] Her project "is an engagement of the text which is rooted *simultaneously* and *equally* in the faith of the Christian community, past and present, and in the best critical biblical scholarship."[18] She thus places herself firmly in the stead of her *Doktorvater*, Edward Malatesta, coupling critical exegesis with faith commitment in an effort to make such scholarship "meaningful."[19] The work contains fourteen chapters, a number of which appeared elsewhere as exegetical articles, divided into three parts. The first part introduces the reader to the Gospel and the background necessary for approaching it, while the second part is constituted by interpretive chapters that probe deeper into the text. The final chapter, comprising the third part, synthesizes the foregoing with a provocative hypothesis on the authorship of the Fourth Gospel.

Although Schneiders's work does not deal specifically with covenant as a genre or thematic form, her scholarship opens up the Fourth Evangelist's self-understanding as a writer of sacred Scripture. By way of introductory "synthetic treatments of the Fourth Gospel as a whole," she intends to plunge "readers into the Johannine world, immersing them

---

16. Ibid., 204.

17. Schneiders, *Written That You May Believe*, 1. Originally published in 1999, she produced a revised and expanded edition of this work in 2003, from which this overview is drawn.

18. Ibid., 1–2. She accepts the term "sapiential" as capturing the essence of her approach, following the self-description of Bruno Barnhart in his commentary (italics in the original). See Barnhart, *Good Wine*.

19. Schneiders, *Written That You May Believe*, xi.

in the powerful literary techniques, unique perspective on Jesus, community ethos, theological stance, and spiritual sensibility that pervade this Gospel so that they develop a 'feel' for this very different Gospel."[20] In this vein, she finds that the evangelist provides the reader the hermeneutical key to his story of Jesus at the close of the body of the narrative (John 20:30–31).[21] As she unpacks these verses, Schneiders presents her approach to the evangelist's understanding of the nature both of Jesus and of his own mission as teller of that story:[22]

1. The Gospel is Selective and Unique
2. The Text is the Locus of Revelatory Encounter
3. The Text is Written for Its Contemporary Readers
4. The Purpose of the Encounter: That You May Believe
5. The Object of Believing: Jesus Who Is Messiah and Son of God
6. The Fruit of Believing: That You May Have Life in His Name.

John 20:30–31, then, provides the key to understanding the spirituality and theology of the Gospel as a whole.

From this foundation, Schneiders can assert that, for this evangelist, Jesus becomes the hermeneutical key to the fullness of the meaning of the Jewish Scriptures. Throughout the text, John "alludes to Old Testament themes, motifs, events, characters, or even collations of texts without citing them exactly."[23] In this way, the reader steeped in the Jewish scriptural tradition can encounter the real depth of the Gospel itself. It is at this point that Schneiders can begin to point to the numerous evocations of the OT covenant relationship that run through the Gospel. She affirms:

> Scholars have pointed out the ubiquity in John of the themes of the new creation, new covenant, and new Israel. Jesus is present-

---

20. Ibid., 3.

21. "Now Jesus did many other signs in the presence of his disciples, which are not written in this book. But these are written that you may [continue to] believe that Jesus is the Messiah, the Son of God, and that through believing you may have life in his name." Hence the title of Schneiders's work, *Written that You May Believe*, 9.

22. For what follows, see ibid., 9–15.

23. Ibid., 35. She points to John 5:39 for her assertion of Jesus as hermeneutical key and bases her affirmations here on the classic work of Freed, *Old Testament Quotations*.

ed in myriad ways as the new Moses, who feeds the people in the wilderness, gives the new law of love, and above all incarnates the presence of God among the people as light of the world. A major motif of the Fourth Gospel is that Jesus replaces for Christians the law, temple, Sabbath, and feasts with himself.[24]

The central assertion that can be gleaned from this discussion is that, according to Schneiders, John's Gospel "does not merely *contain* symbols; it is itself symbolic."[25] Jesus is the incarnation of God, the Word made flesh, and the Gospel text is the literary symbol of Jesus, where he can be encountered in an unmediated way. The narrative is thus essentially revelatory, the very notion of which connotes mutuality in relationship, a core covenantal theme. To conclude the overview of Schneiders's contribution to the development of this literature, we return to her assessment of her own project in so far as it accords with that of the Fourth Evangelist:

> The integral interpretation of any biblical text is the process of engaging it in such a way that it can function as locus and mediator of transformative encounter with the living God. In this process of interpreting the New Testament as Sacred Scripture we experience and claim it as the Christian classic par excellence: the revelatory text.[26]

Rekha Chennattu

The work of Rekha Chennattu provides the most extensive examination of the covenant motif in the Johannine literature to date. Her doctoral dissertation, published in 2006 as *Johannine Discipleship as a Covenant Relationship*, explores key discipleship texts throughout the Gospel (1:35–51; 13–17; and 20–21) in search of a paradigm for the nature of such discipleship in the Johannine community. After a survey of recent scholarship (1970–2000), Chennattu develops a discipleship motif based upon a narrative exegesis of the call stories of John 1:35–51 within its literary context.[27] Building upon the discipleship work of her predecessors and a critical assessment of Simoens's groundbreaking

---

24. Schneiders, *Written That You May Believe*, 35–36.
25. Ibid., 36.
26. Ibid., 148.
27. Ibid., 1–40.

work on covenant in the last discourse (John 13–17), she uncovers an OT covenant motif in the call to discipleship. She bases her claims upon the introduction of the abiding motif (μένω), the concept of Jesus as Messiah, the call of the disciple to witness, the naming/renaming aspect of the calls, and the very foundation of discipleship in promise.[28]

Chennattu then turns to a broad exploration of covenant in the OT, including its origin, historical development, meaning, nature, and forms. The focus eventually centers on covenant-making rituals in Israelite traditions, where she examines what she finds to be the essential elements of an OT covenant relationship.[29] She discerns an election motif, a notion of mutual belonging underscored by the presence of YHWH and the covenantal concepts of knowledge, witness, peace, promises, as well as the call to love and keep the commandments. After assessing Simoens's work and affirming the OT background for the Johannine covenant motif, Chennattu studies the structure of John 13–17 in terms of literary function and this established covenant motif.[30] She determines that "the structure and content of John 13–17 are analogous in function to the covenant renewal ceremony found in Joshua 24."[31] She concludes:

> The covenant motif of chapters 13–17 is well integrated into the literary context of chapters 1–12. The disciples are initiated into a covenant relationship in 1:35–51. The narrative section of 2–12 calls the disciples to decision and thus functions as a hortatory preparation for the covenant renewal in 13–17. The whole process culminates in Jesus' prayer that seals the new covenant instituted by Jesus, surpassing the covenant under Moses as well as former covenant traditions. The rapid overview demonstrates how narratives and discourses in chapters 2–17 are intimately connected by the covenant motifs that run across the gospel.[32]

In these early chapters, Chennattu situates Johannine discipleship, as manifested in John 13–17 in particular, within "the broad OT theme of the covenant motif and the narrower world of its Johannine literary

---

28. Ibid., 41–49.
29. Ibid., 57–66.
30. Ibid., 81–87.
31. Ibid., 81 n. 129.
32. Ibid., 88.

context."³³ She then turns to a more thorough exegesis of chapters 13–17 in terms of an OT covenant renewal form. The structure she uncovers flows along the following broadly drawn lines:

13:1–38	Jesus and the Disciples Gathered Together for the Farewell Meal
14:1–31	The Promise of God's Indwelling Presence and Guidance
15:1–17	A Call to Abide and Keep the Commandments
15:18—16:24	Jesus' Warning of the Consequences of Discipleship
16:25–33	The Disciples' Profession of Faith
17:1–26	A Prayer Consecrating the Covenant Community of the Disciples

She has already established that the structure of this last discourse is roughly analogous to the covenant renewal ceremony in Joshua 24.³⁴ At this point she examines the discourse, focusing selectively on the established covenant and discipleship motifs. What emerges, she claims, is a paradigm of a new covenant relationship with the disciples.

> In sum, the covenant themes—election, intimate abiding relationship, indwelling presence, keeping God's commandments, and mutual knowledge—run through the discipleship discourses in 13–17 and provide the theological definition of what it means to be a disciple of Jesus. The evangelist presents the paradigm of discipleship in terms of a covenant relationship that mirrors the mutuality, reciprocity, and intimacy of the Father-Son relationship revealed to the disciples in Jesus' life, mission, and death.... The evangelist takes the OT covenant metaphor, redefines and broadens its prospect, and applies it to the relationship between God and the new covenant community of Jesus' disciples.³⁵

Chennattu goes on to establish covenant/discipleship motifs in John 20–21, reclaiming John 21 as "an integral part of the final redactor's design of the unfolding story of Jesus" in the process.³⁶ Her basic contention is that while the passion narrative of John 18–19 brings the story of Jesus to its climax, it is John 20–21 that brings the disciples' story to a close and establishes the new covenant community. She structures the chapters as follows:

---

33. Ibid.
34. Ibid., 68–69. See chapter 2 for an analysis of Joshua 24.
35. Schneiders, *Written That You May Believe*, 139.
36. Ibid., 140.

20:1–18	Reclaiming the Covenant Relationship of the Disciples
20:19–31	Empowering the New Covenant Community
21:1–25	Constituting the New Covenant Community

Here she is able to assert that what "was programmatically promised in chapters 13–17 is now effectively actualized in chapters 20–21."[37] Discipleship in and of Jesus constitutes the foundation of a new community (i.e., the Johannine community) in terms of a redefined OT (i.e., new) covenant.

In the final chapter of her study, Chennattu establishes the centrality of the covenant motif as a crucial feature of first-century Judaism and thus the impetus behind the evangelist's understanding and integration of covenant as the paradigm for discipleship. She concludes, "Amid the sociopastoral and theological identity crises of the Johannine community perceived as a deviant group within synagogue Judaism of post-70 C.E., the paradigm of discipleship as a covenant relationship redefines the community as the chosen people of God and consolidates the group as a distinct social and religious community."[38]

With the conclusion of this survey of scholarship on various aspects of the covenant metaphor in the Gospel of John, we can turn to the manner by which the present study will examine the Fourth Evangelist's integration of this important OT symbolic presentation of God's relationship with the created order.

A Literary Approach to the Study of Covenant in the Gospel of John

Debating the value of scholarship in recent years that incorporates literary scholarship into biblical criticism, Mieke Bal concludes that, since the Bible is undeniably a founding text of Western culture, it is "both totally religious, whatever that may mean, and totally literary."[39] She goes on to assert: "*Reading* is the term that can help undermine the false certainties, truths, positivity of both disciplines [of biblical and literary scholarship]. For the better of both."[40] Her comments reflect the growing

---

37. Ibid., 179.
38. Ibid., 211.
39. Bal, *Anti-Covenant*, 11.
40. Ibid. For a fully developed treatment of Bal's interpretive stance and theory of narrative criticism, see Bal, *Narratology*.

interest in the Bible as literature that has spawned both new theories of biblical interpretation as well as the refinement of traditional approaches.[41] Further, the narrative nature of a large portion of biblical material has led to the development of narrative criticism as a hermeneutical method by which both the text and the impact of that text upon the reader may be studied in terms of poetics and narrative art.[42] In his classic statement advocating a more holistic literary approach to the study of biblical narrative, Meir Sternberg focuses on the unity of the final form of the biblical authors' presentation of God's story:

> Traditional speculations about documents and sources and twice-told tales have now piled up so high on the altar of genesis as to obscure the one remarkable fact in sight, which bears on poetics. Granting the confusion of variants that went into the making of the Bible, the fact remains that the finished discourse never introduces them as variants, but rather strings them together into continuous action.[43]

Biblical scholar Adela Yarbro Collins insists, however, that these literary methods must be used to supplement (not replace) study of the original historical context of the text: "Whatever tension there may be between literary- and historical-critical methods, the two approaches are complementary."[44] An integration of the more traditional historical-critical, or diachronic, method with these synchronic approaches that focus on the storytelling world in the text can allow for a fuller understanding of both text and context.

---

41. See, e.g., Alter and Kermode, eds., *Literary Guide to the Bible*; and Prickett, *Words and the Word*.

42. For information on poetics and narrative structure, see Abbott, *Cambridge Introduction to Narrative*; Chatman, *Story and Discourse*; Rimmon-Kenan, *Narrative Fiction*; Booth, *Rhetoric of Fiction*. For a survey of the development of the study of biblical narrative, see Gerhart, "Restoration of Biblical Narrative"; Alter, *Art of Biblical Narrative*; Sternberg, *Poetics of Biblical Narrative*; Berlin, *Poetics and Interpretation*; Bar-Efrat, *Narrative Art in the Bible*. For a basic introduction to the development of narrative criticism, see Powell, *What Is Narrative Criticism?*

43. Sternberg, *Poetics of Biblical Narrative*, 127.

44. Collins, "Narrative, History and Gospel," 153. She prefaces this conclusion by the statement that "if, as I am convinced, all meaning is context bound, the original context and meaning have a certain normative character. I suggest that Biblical theologians are not only mediators between genres. They are also mediators between historical periods" (150).

In his introductory work on biblical narrative criticism, Mark Allen Powell articulates four basic components of the larger field of literary criticism as it works in conjunction with historical criticism. These characteristics are thus also fundamental to the narratological methodology of the present study in general, and to the current issue of the development of the covenant metaphor from a narrative perspective in particular.[45]

1. Literary criticism focuses on the final form of the text. Without denying the potential stages in the development of the finished text, a focus on the final form interprets a narrative as it stands now, and for its original readers.

2. Literary criticism emphasizes the overall unity of the text. Biblical narratives are viewed as coherent wholes. Literary analysis searches for internal connections that give insight to the larger discourse of given narratives.

3. Literary criticism understands the text as an end in itself. The immediate goal of literary criticism is to understand a story as told, giving full voice to the manner in which it is told. Powell notes that "whatever insight is obtained will be found in the encounter of the reader with the text itself."[46]

4. Literary criticism is based upon speech-act models of communication. The philosophical bases for narrative criticism are derived from communication theory whereby every act of communication involves three components: a sender, a message, and a receiver. "In literature, the sender may be identified with the author, the message with the text, and the receiver with the reader."[47] The text, therefore, is a medium through which a message is passed from the author to the reader (or listener in an oral culture).

---

45. For the characteristics that follow, see Powell, *What Is Narrative Criticism*, 6–10.

46. Ibid., 8.

47. Ibid., 8–9. Here, Powell is following the speech-act model proposed by Roman Jakobson in *Language in Literature*. See also Chatman, *Story and Discourse*, 161–66. The basic communication model is: Author → Text → Reader.

Choosing narrative as the mode of that communication, then, is itself part of the message. Telling a story resonates with the lived experience of readers and allows these readers to identify with and/or distance themselves from various aspects of and characters in the story. Further, within the narrative, authors choose the specific events to be shared, how they will be narrated, and in what order, so that these authors can best communicate the message as they intend it to be received. Literary critic Menakhem Perry articulates the significance of plot order:

> The literary text, like any verbal text, is received by the reader through a process of "concretization." Its verbal elements appear one *after* another, and its semantic complexes (e.g., scenes, ideas, characters, plot, value-judgments) build up "cumulatively," through adjustments and readjustments. That a literary text cannot yield its information all at once is not just an unfortunate consequence of the linear character of language. Literary texts may effectively utilize the fact that their material is grasped successively; this is at times a central factor in determining their meanings. The ordering and distribution of the elements in a text may exercise considerable influence on the nature, not only of the *reading process*, but of the *resultant whole* as well: a rearrangement of the components may result in the activation of alternative potentialities in them and in the structuring of a recognizably different whole.[48]

Thus, the way in which an author tells his or her story is determinative of its meaning.

Much more could be said about literary criticism in general and narrative criticism in particular, but that is beyond the scope of the present study. This brief overview serves to lay the groundwork for a more detailed introduction of the particular dialogical approach that will buttress the methodology for a hermeneutic of covenant in the Gospel of John. A final point that segues into the next section is provided by literary scholar Frank Kermode in his study of the prologue of the Fourth Gospel:

> All the evangelists insist that we take an interest in stories, an insistence we neglect when we pick the stories apart in trying to decide which of them is earliest, nearest to the actual event. So that in a sense the critic who attends to story and leaves aside

---

48. Perry, "Literary Dynamics," 35.

questions of history is attending to the first demand the evangelists make.[49]

Studying John through the Prism of Dialogue: The Gospel's Dramatic Nature

In the prologue to his Gospel narrative, "John offers us something which, though it relates events, is much closer [than narrative] to being a theological discourse. Yet the difference should not be exaggerated. For . . . discourse is typical of John."[50] In her comparative investigation of the prologue of the Gospel of John, Morna Hooker explains:

> The bulk of the rest of John's gospel—until we come to the passion narrative—is theological discourse, held together by a slight narrative framework: his material is essentially a brief account of certain activities of Jesus, together with lengthy theological comment on the significance of those activities, usually in the mouth of Jesus himself. In the Prologue, the order is reversed: we have theological statements, with a couple of references to John the Baptist to "anchor" what is being said in history. Yet the juxtaposition of historical narrative and theological interpretation is in many ways similar to the rest of the gospel.[51]

This juxtaposition of historical narrative and discourse is so pronounced in the Johannine story of Jesus that a number of scholars over the past century have suggested a relationship between the Fourth Gospel and

---

49. Kermode, "St. John as Poet," 5. Kermode is speaking in hyperbole here to make his point. Although I certainly do not take the position that all historical questions should be "left aside," his general thrust is thought provoking and insightful.

50. Hooker, "Johannine Prologue," 41. In this assessment, Hooker is comparing the Johannine prologue to that of the Gospel of Mark.

51. Ibid., 41. I do not agree with Hooker's characterization of the Gospel's narrative framework as "slight." In fact, as the present study will reflect, I find that the Fourth Evangelist provides an intricately woven narrative in which to present his message. Nonetheless, in these comments Hooker rightly pinpoints the integration of the prologue with the body of the narrative. She follows up incisively, "Controversy regarding the Johannine Prologue has so concentrated on the question of the 'poetic' style that it has perhaps been overlooked that as far as form and content is concerned, we might well expect John to write a prologue in this way." I am incorporating her insights into a launching point for a discussion of the dialogical (in her words, "theological discourse") nature of the Gospel as a whole.

ancient drama. A brief discussion of this investigation will flesh out the hermeneutic operative for the present study.

William Domeris opens his study of the dramatic nature of the Gospel of John by quoting the words with which Euripides brings *Alcestis* to a close. Domeris notes that, like Euripides, the Fourth Evangelist, in the closing verses of his work (21:24–25), "brings to our notice the incredible act of God, the realization of the impossible and like the great dramatist he too makes use of a dramatic form of presentation." Writing in 1983, Domeris offers a study that examines the Gospel's structure, characters, and format. He claims that the "continuous use of direct speech, the naming of the speakers and the ease with which the Gospel can be reproduced in dramatic form suggest that John has deliberately fashioned his Gospel after the model of the Greek dramas and particularly the Tragedies."[52] His brief article is detailed and comprehensive, but Domeris is by no means the first modern scholar to suggest this dramatic flavor.

In 1907 Francis R. Montgomery Hitchcock was an early voice to compare the plot of the Gospel with the conventions of Greek tragedy.[53] In 1925, Robert H. Strachan put forth a more detailed study of the Gospel's structure in terms of the form of works written for performance.[54] The following decade, Clayton R. Bowen went so far as to claim that the Fourth Gospel is not a narrative at all but "a miscellany of material conceived dramatically, passages, dialogues, monologue, sketches of setting, of characters, of exits and entrances, of time and place and such like."[55] Bowen's study concluded that the canonical form of the Gospel was merely a draft, a pageant work in progress. These early studies all have a somewhat negative tone, as these writers attempted to explain the form and content of this Gospel (always in comparison to the Synoptic Gospels) in terms of historical value. In 1948, C. Milo Connick published a more positive study that attended to basic dramatic techniques such as artistic form, concentrated action, irony, time and place indications, and dialogue patterns.[56] He concluded that while "the Gospel cannot be regarded as drama (since it was not designed to

52. Domeris, "Johannine Drama," 29–30.
53. Hitchcock, "Dramatic Development."
54. Strachan, *Fourth Evangelist*.
55. Bowen, "Fourth Gospel as Dramatic Material," 295.
56. Connick, "Dramatic Character of the Fourth Gospel."

be performed by actors on the stage), its dramatic character is undeniable." Further, he asserted that the "dramatic character of this Gospel is a datum which must be given due weight before judgments are reached regarding such problems as the historicity and anti-Jewish character of this Gospel."[57]

Some thirty-five years later, Domeris continued this increasing interest as he sketched his own comparison. He notes that the scenes in John are "self-contained, held together by the sense of movement towards the destiny of Jesus," and yet thematic questions "like the problem of unbelief, judgment and related ethical issues" introduced early on arise at various moments over the course of the Gospel and thereby allow for a sense of overall unity. This, says Domeris, "is what one would expect in a Greek drama."[58] Some of the answers to these questions are found in the discourses of Jesus, "while the crucial question of the identity of Jesus finds its answer also in the confessions of various individuals" who come into contact with him. Jesus thus takes the leading role, almost always standing at center stage, though the various minor characters share the spotlight from time to time in dialogue, only to "quickly vanish into the shadows to be replaced by another" as attention remains riveted on Jesus.[59] His discourses are punctuated by leading questions that break them into dialogues and so reveal the evangelist's dramatic intentions.[60] These dialogues and their resulting crises and confessions move the drama inexorably toward "the hour" of Jesus' glorification.[61]

Speech as Action in the Gospel of John

These studies on dramatic character all highlight one phenomenon in particular: speech is action in this story of the gospel event. Much of what *happens* in the Gospel according to John happens when Jesus of Nazareth is in dialogue with other characters in the story. Thus much

---

57. Ibid., 169.

58. Domeris, "Johannine Drama," 31.

59. Ibid., 31, 32.

60. Ibid., 33.

61. Throughout this study, the term "dialogue" is used in the dramatic sense to indicate that two or more people are speaking to each other in an ongoing verbal interaction where speech constitutes the primary action of the scene. See Brant, *Dialogue and Drama*, esp. 74–158.

can be gleaned from studying the Gospel through the prism of dialogue. The image of a prism is particularly helpful here, as these dialogues are truly multifaceted. On the narrative level, the evangelist does indeed advance his story of Jesus through these dialogical interactions. At the same time, on the "discourse" or "meta-narrative" level, the evangelist employs these dialogues symbolically to present Jesus as the revelatory incarnate word of God and to illustrate how the children of God are to respond in relationship with that word.[62]

As noted above, in recent years, a number of scholars have included a focus on one or another of the dramatic features of John's Gospel.[63] In the twenty-first century, Jo-Ann A. Brant has concentrated particularly on the elements of Greek tragedy in the Fourth Gospel. She articulates that her objective "is to unmask the skilled artistry of the gospel, designed to produce a compelling rendition of the story of Jesus capable of finding an audience in a world where Homeric epics and Greek tragedies were still read."[64] The model for the production of the Gospel in the first century that she presupposes is the performance of Greek and Roman tragedies "in the form of readings to an audience in a private home."[65] Therefore, although not intended for the stage, "much of the form is that of performance text," and attention to this form results in the recognition of much of the content as "tragic mimesis—the poetic representation of action and people."[66] Working in conversation with scholars of dramatic criticism as well as with the Greek and Roman tragedies themselves, Brant provides extensive discussion of speech as action, observing that the "prominent role that dialogue and direct speech play in the Fourth Gospel calls for attention to the capacity of language to perform multiple functions in one literary context." She therefore explores the way that language works in the Gospel in a man-

---

62. For more on the metanarratives of the Gospel of John, see Reinhartz, *Word in the World*.

63. See, e.g., Nicholson, *Death as Departure*; Stibbe, *John as Storyteller*; Tovey, *Narrative Art and Act*.

64. Brant, *Dialogue and Drama*, 6–7.

65. Ibid., 15. A recent monograph by M. L. Coloe provides an intriguing correlative study to this notion of Christian households developing through shared liturgy and praxis. She suggests that "the symbolism of the household [in the Gospel of John] may provide insight into the spirituality of the Johannine community." Coloe, *Dwelling in the Household of God*, 200–201.

66. Brant, *Dialogue and Drama*, 8.

ner comparable to theatrical discourse by discussing speech as gesture and speech as deed.[67] The following presentation summarizes the elements prevalent in the dialogues of the Fourth Gospel.

SPEECH AS GESTURE

In the three-part typology of artificial language (icon, index, symbol), dramatic texts rely heavily upon index. An index is any sign that refers to objects denoted by being affected by those objects.[68] The use of indices in the Gospel of John includes the following six aspects.

1. *Deixis* is identified as language used to point to subjectivity, temporality, spatiality and modality, particularly personal and demonstrative pronouns and adverbs such as "here" and "now." Employing this type of language serves to attract attention and identify contextual elements.

2. *Indices of Movement* consist of language in dialogue that refer to movement while that action is carried out. These indices serve in lieu of stage directions in order to facilitate the interpretation of the plot.

3. *Indices of Setting* consist of language that points to objects, temporal setting, and physical setting. These indices serve to describe the place inhabited by the characters as well as space that lies beyond the current sphere of activity.

4. *Ambiguous Indices of Conflict* refer to any language that can both mislead and clarify. These are used to generate conflict, including when the protagonist uses deceptive or ambiguous language

---

67. Ibid., 75. The following material relies on Brant's detailed analysis (ibid., 77–149). She notes her indebtedness to John Austin's theory of speech-acts whereby in "the act of saying something, utterances can be invested with an illocutionary force designed to have an effect upon the person or persons to whom the utterance is directed or to effect a change of some sort." For more on speech-act theory, see Austin, *How to Do Things with Words*. For a study of speech-act theory in practice with narrative and reader-response criticism of the Gospel of John as a literary speech-act, see Botha, *Jesus and the Samaritan Woman*.

68. Brant, *Dialogue and Drama*, 78. The category of icon, "which includes metaphor, consists of signs that bear resemblance to that which they signify. A symbol denotes its referent "through the association of ideas that may be arbitrary or conventional and may require some sort of interpreter in order for the connection to be made." These categories have traditionally received a great deal of attention in Johannine scholarship.

that can fit both the world of the antagonists and the world of the speaker, such that the antagonists believe they are talking about the same reality when they actually are not.

5. *Redundant Narration* is a technique wherein the narrator uses language that refers to objects, time, and place, which is then also used by the characters in dialogue (usually repeated verbatim). This technique serves to confirm the veracity or integrity of those characters.

6. *Reported Action* is language used by characters to report events rather than having events staged or narrated. This technique serves to bring the action of the plot into dialogue and thereby involves the perspectives of the characters.

Speech as Deed

The verbal gestures of the protagonist that interpret reality often collide with those of other characters; thus conflict develops and speech becomes the principal action of the drama. Jesus, as the protagonist of the Gospel, uses words to achieve his ends by provoking responses and challenging characters to take action, thereby moving the plot forward.[69] The following three dramatic speech patterns are prevalent in the Gospel according to John.

1. *Antithesis* refers to language that organizes a speech through strong rhetorical rhythm rather than idea exchange. This type of language gives the illusion of natural flows of thought and enacts the conflict that constitutes the drama and arouses strong opposing reactions from interlocutors.

2. *Flyting* is the technical term for language and literary scenes that demonstrate prowess through a verbal exchange as a show of wits and provocation. Flyting often exploits the different meanings of words for subtlety and cleverness and includes insults, curses, boasts, riddles, miniature stories, and especially irony. The merit of each onslaught is measured by whether the verbal parrying remains within the limits of the facts, and is determined by the audience/readers.

---

69. Ibid., 114–15. See also Elam, *Semiotics of Theatre and Drama*, 103–91.

3. *The Formal Debate* (ἀγών) consists of complex language and literary scenes that are forensic in nature and resonate a trial structure. These dramatic patterns include accusations of legal infractions, testimonies, scrutiny of witnesses, and the rendering of judgment. A formal debate can organize both the plot and the experience of the audience or readers whereby they come away urged to render a judgment of their own.

The characteristics of these forms of indicative language and these patterns of speech-action in the plot, in concert with an appreciation of the overall dramatic flavor of the narrative, provide valuable tools for exegesis of the Fourth Gospel. These tools will augment the examination of key dialogues over the course of the narrative in the context of the evangelist's use of the OT covenant metaphor to underpin the theological fabric of the good news he writes to a community living in what it understands to be the revelation of God in the Christ event.

Covenant as the Guiding Literary Paradigm of the Gospel of John

A gradual uncovering of the important biblical component of covenant as background to the Johannine writings has begun in the last fifty years. At the same time, the landscape of biblical criticism in general has shifted. In recent decades, building upon the acquisitions of historical criticism, the discipline of narrative criticism has emerged in the field of biblical scholarship as an approach that integrates the historical approach with a focus on the final form of the text that preserves its sacred nature. Recent scholarship has therefore begun to reassert an emphasis on the thematic unity and end product of the Fourth Gospel.[70] To this point, however, there has been no systematic study of the Gospel according to John as a narrative whole with particular concern for this emerging question of covenant as a guiding literary paradigm. Further, the previous studies focused primarily on the narrator's storytelling technique and the discourse material of the Gospel. Crucial and sometimes enigmatic dialogues throughout the Gospel have been left largely unexamined in this regard.

---

70. See Culpepper, *Anatomy of the Fourth Gospel*; Moloney, *John*, and *Gospel of John: Text and Context*.

The present study will proceed to examine the central role of covenant in the narrative uncovering of the Gospel of John, with a focus on the dialogical nature of the revelatory process. This effort will incorporate an overview of the OT covenant metaphor, provided in the following chapter. Recent work on the Gospel of John as Scripture, particularly that of Francis J. Moloney, who suggests that the Fourth Evangelist understood himself to be writing Scripture based upon the narrator's use of fulfillment language in summary statements across the Gospel, will comprise the first part of chapter 3.[71] A study of beginnings and endings in terms of the narrative's frame will follow, laying the groundwork for a close study of several crucial dialogical interactions over the course of the narrative to elucidate the evangelist's covenant-fulfillment literary paradigm in his presentation of the Gospel. Although any of the dialogues of the Gospel narrative could be examined in terms of this covenantal underpinning, the dialogues examined in the following chapters present various points on the continuum of response to Jesus that span the breadth of the narrative. Chapter 4 will focus on the positive interaction between Jesus and his mother at the wedding feast at Cana (John 2:1–12), while chapter 5 will examine the intensely negative exchange between Jesus and "the Jews" at the temple during the Feast of Tabernacles (John 7–8).[72] Chapter 6 will present the overall flow of the second half of the Gospel in general and the passion narrative (John 18–19) in particular, and highlight the highly ambivalent response of Pilate to both Jesus and "the Jews" in the dialogue on the nature of kingship and truth (18:28—19:16a). Chapter 7 will conclude this study with a focus on the community commission of Peter and the Beloved Disciple that looks to a future in covenantal leadership and followership as narrated in the epilogue (John 21). The evangelist's readers may be able to find themselves on the journeys of these various individuals and groups, respond in their own decision of belief in the covenantal word of Jesus, and thereby find a place amidst the Johannine community, the new covenant children of God.

---

71. See Moloney, "Gospel of John as Scripture"; Labahn, "Between Tradition and Literary Art"; Scholtissek, *In ihm sein und bleiben*; Smith, "When Did the Gospels Become Scripture?"

72. Throughout this study, I will enclose the term "the Jews" in quotation marks to denote that the term is not used to indicate the Jewish people generally. The Fourth Evangelist uses the term to indicate the opposing side of the christological debate about Jesus. See the discussion in Moloney, *John*, 9–11.

2

Covenant in Scripture

THE METAPHOR OF COVENANT IS THE PRIMARY MEANS BY WHICH THE biblical authors in the Old Testament express the special relationship between God and God's creation in general, and God's chosen people Israel in particular. Both the texts that narrate the story of Israel and its relationship with God and the prophetic literature that communicates God's will and summons Israel to live rightly in this relationship are replete with accounts of and references to God's covenantal activity in the world. In addition to detailed recounting of covenant-making and covenant-renewing rituals and ceremonies, this literature preserves the broader themes and symbolism of the covenant metaphor. These storytellers and prophets integrate this language into their larger works in order to share their message of life in unique relationship with God, even when the term "covenant" does not appear. The Prophets in particular rarely use the word itself, even as they pepper their works with calls to covenant relationship. Likewise, this term does not appear in the Gospel according to John. Nonetheless, the recent scholarship surveyed in the previous chapter suggests that, like his scriptural predecessors, this evangelist incorporated the metaphor of covenant in the telling of his Gospel. Without ever using the word itself, the Fourth Evangelist weaves the thematic language and symbolism of covenant throughout his story of God's activity in the world in Jesus as a literary technique to draw his readers into his sacred narrative of true relationship with God.

This chapter will reinforce the foundation of covenant as the guiding literary paradigm of the Gospel of John by examining the nature of covenant in key texts in the Scripture of Israel. In this way we can begin to feel the texture of the literary fabric that the Fourth Evangelist used in composing his account of the Gospel story on behalf of his community of readers.

Covenant in the Old Testament

At its root, a covenant is defined as "an agreement enacted between two parties in which one or both make promises under oath to perform or refrain from certain actions stipulated in advance."[1] It has long been accepted in OT scholarship that the primary means by which one can understand the relationship between God and Israel as expressed in the Scriptures of Israel is in terms of covenant.[2] The question still arises, however, as to when in the history of Israel as a nation did this self-understanding develop. The corresponding question can be asked on the literary level with regard to the compositional history of Israel's Scriptures. Volumes have been written on the subject. For the purposes of the present study, two perspectives can be traced briefly by way of background information. A historical perspective provides context for the world behind the text of the Jewish Scriptures through study of the historical formation of Israel as a nation and religious people. A narrative perspective offers insight into the origin and development of the tradition in the text of the Jewish Scriptures themselves as a product of the lived experience of the people of Israel. This conceptual foundation will lead to a closer analysis of key covenantal texts in the body of the Scripture, which in turn will result in the manifestation of a number of overarching themes that return again and again in the OT covenant relationship.

The Development of the Covenantal Tradition: The Historical Perspective

Based on the work of the great nineteenth-century scholar Julius Wellhausen, a long-established maxim of historical critics holds that covenantal theology was not fully developed in Israel until the time of the Babylonian exile, as the Israelites came to terms with the loss

---

1. Mendenhall and Herion, "Covenant," 1179.
2. See the discussion in McCarthy, *Old Testament Covenant*.

of their temple and nationhood.³ As recently as the 1980s, the work of Ernest Nicholson argued that the century-long discussion had come full circle in that it was no longer deniable that the beginnings of covenant theology were to be found in the oracles of the eighth-century prophets, again proposed in terms of exile, in this case the Assyrian exile of the northern tribes and the impending threat of the same in the south.⁴ Little credence is given to any notion of a covenant between YHWH and the children of Israel as forming the backbone of the people from its beginnings. Literarily, with regard to source criticism, this historical conclusion is reflected in the idea that the covenantal concept could not have originated earlier than the Deuteronomist strand of the Pentateuch narrative and in the work of the Deuteronomistic historian. Further, the locus of covenant ideology is placed primarily in the exilic Priestly thread of the narrative.⁵

In the twentieth century, an alternative position began to take hold, beginning with the publication of Walther Eichrodt's *Theologie des Alten Testaments* in the 1930s.⁶ This far-reaching study argued that the history of Israel itself, as well as the composition of its Scripture, was constructed entirely around the covenant theme. Initially greeted with widespread criticism, his position was largely vindicated, at least in principle, by the discovery of a significant body of archaeological data regarding the treaty-making formulae and rituals of the ancient world. These data were interpreted and presented in the groundbreaking studies of George Mendenhall and Klaus Baltzer, who argued that the covenant forms present in the OT are to a crucial extent modeled on the ancient Hittite suzerainty treaties and therefore would have been employed during the age of that empire in the second millennium BC.⁷

This general position was initially advanced and further refined by Delbert Hillers and David Noel Freedman. In his sweeping literary study, Hillers follows Mendenhall by tracing the developing covenant

---

3. Wellhausen, *Prolegomena to the History of Israel*.

4. Nicholson, *God and His People*. In this vein, see also the important work of McCarthy, *Treaty and Covenant*. He is followed by his student Kalluveettil with *Declaration and Covenant*.

5. See the discussion of McKenzie, *Covenant*, 4–24.

6. See the bibliography for the English edition.

7. Mendenhall, *Law and Covenant in Israel*; Baltzer, *Covenant Formulary*.

motif in the OT narrative through the lens of what he calls "the history of a biblical idea."[8] Freedman's work is more specific in advocating the second millennium treaty-type basis for Israel's covenant tradition. Although he warns that it does not constitute a "universal key to the Scriptures," he does definitively assert:

> It can therefore be affirmed that the covenant principle is intrinsic to the biblical material and that it defines the relationship of God to his people. Further, the term "covenant" itself was consciously applied by the Israelites to their relationship with Yahweh, from the earliest times.[9]

Recently, Frank Moore Cross has advocated this position by linking the West Semitic tribal society concept of *kinship-in-law* to the covenantal basis of earliest Israel.[10] He claims that the social organization of these tribal groups, including the children of Israel, was grounded in kinship. "Kinship relations defined the rights and obligations, the duties, status, and privileges of tribal members, and kinship terminology provided the only language for expressing legal, political, and religious institutions."[11] The kinship group conceived of itself as having one life; literally shared flesh and blood (see Gen 29:14, 37:27; 2 Sam 5:1; Judg 9:1–4). Therefore, to the kinship group, the family, fell the obligations of protection (military and otherwise), promoting social welfare, and redemption (גְּאֻלָּה). The duties of the "redeemer," or גֹּאֵל, include avenging the blood of a kinsman, buying back property sold by a poor kinsman, redeeming the kinsman sold into debt slavery, and securing the line of a deceased near kinsman by marrying his widow.[12] Thus, according to Cross, the idiom of family (מִשְׁפָּחָה), love (אַהֲבָה), loyalty (חֶסֶד), and truth/fidelity (אֱמֶת) is intrinsically the idiom of kinship and covenant. This social organization further gave tribal peoples the language to express their religious affiliation, the words with which to relate to their god. For Israel, YHWH was the *Divine Kinsman*.[13]

---

8. Hillers, *Covenant*.
9. Freedman, "Divine Commitment," 419–31.
10. Cross, *Epic to Canon*, 3–21.
11. Ibid., 3.
12. Ibid., 4–5. See Num 35:19–27; Lev 25:25–33, 48–49; Ruth 3:9, 12–13; 4:1–14.
13. Ibid., 6–7. See Gen 12:3: the Divine Kinsman blesses those who bless his kindred and curses those who curse his kindred.

As tribal societies grew and became more complex, developing into tribal leagues or confederations, the concept of *kinship-in-law* comes into play. Marriage, adoption, and covenants between individuals and groups, often with the deity as witness and bound with covenant oaths, are the primary means by which outsiders—non-blood kin—are incorporated into the kinship family. In this way outsiders were "grafted onto the genealogies" and "kinship-in-law became kinship-in-flesh."[14] Therefore, the very foundation of the tribal confederation is one of covenantal kinship. Indeed, Cross argues:

> The failure to recognize the rootage of the institution of covenant and covenant obligations in the structures of kinship societies has led to confusion and even gross distortion in the scholarly discussion of the term bérît, "covenant," and in the description of early Israelite religion.[15]

Cross's concern is that the fullness of both mutuality and binding legal obligation is not stripped from the covenantal formation of the Israelite tribal federation, as he considers Wellhausen and his followers such as Nicholson and McCarthy to have done. Rather, covenant should be upheld as the very root of the earliest kinship-based society of the people of Israel. YHWH adopts Israel as a "son" and is understood as "father," enters into marriage with the "bride" Israel, is called "husband," and swears covenantal oaths taking on the mutual obligations of kinship. In this way Israel, from the foundational tribal era of Moses, in fact became the עַם יהוה, the people (kindred) of YHWH.[16] Cross argues that this covenantal kinship basis and its accompanying institutions flourished in Israel throughout the tribal era but waned in the early days of the monarchy, somewhat displaced by royal theology and its institutions. Late in the monarchy and through the exile and postexilic era, however, a "revival of covenantal ideology, law, and cultic practice" began to arise. What can be seen in the schools of the Deuteronomist and Priestly writers, then, is a "stalwart effort to reconstruct and resurrect the covenantal institutions of the 'Mosaic Age,' that is, of the era of

---

14. Ibid., 7. The full discussion is found on pp. 7–11. See 1 Sam 7:14; 18:1–3; Ps 2:7; Isa 9:5.

15. Ibid., 15.

16. Cross, *Epic to Canon*, 12–13.

the league." This was an idyllic aim to which they were, in large part, successful.[17]

The two positions traced only briefly in this section offer extensive, if somewhat conflicting, insight into the historical context of the formation of the people of Israel and the composition of their self-understanding in terms of sacred texts. The final product of this complex compositional history, however, tells its own story.

The Development of the Covenantal Tradition: A Narrative Perspective

An alternative perspective on the biblical developments of the covenant metaphor in the story of Israel and God's work in creation focuses on the final form of the sacred texts, however complex their compositional history.[18] This narrative must be given its due, for this is the story that was alive and binding for the Fourth Evangelist.

On the narrative level, the concept of God working in history in covenantal relationship with creation is present from the beginning in God's word of creation (Gen 1:3) and develops in stages across the breadth of the Scripture texts. The very fact that the foundations of Israel are understood in terms of its role as God's chosen people and are preserved as its story indicate an underlying covenantal basis. Further, the beginning of this story tells of God's word of creation. God literally spoke creation into being (1:1—2:4a). Communication thus becomes the basis of relationship, and relationship becomes the basis of God's interaction with creation. On the narrative level, then, the seeds of covenantal theology are planted with creation and are manifest in God's people with God's word to Adam (2:16-17). God gives Adam life and

---

17. Ibid., 19–21.

18. It is interesting to note that even Mendenhall, who advocates the earliest, Mosaic dating, for the rise of the covenant formulae in the history of Israel, understands the earliest covenant texts in the OT *narrative*, i.e., the Noah and Abraham texts in Gen 6–9 and 12–22, respectively, to be representative of the breakdown of the covenant form evidenced in the later (postexilic) Priestly stratum of authorship. See Mendenhall, "Covenant," 1188–90. From a *narrative* perspective, however, these covenant texts serve as introductions, founding events upon which the later, more elaborate covenant stories, especially the Sinai covenant of Exod 19–24, build. In this way the OT narrative tells a story wherein God's covenantal relationship with creation develops and becomes more complex through history.

food and shelter, then culminates the covenant in the gift of community with the creation of his partner the woman (2:18–25). In return, God demands obedience. When Adam fails in disobedience and the perfect union of that relationship is broken (3:1–24), the re-establishment of right relationship with God becomes the guiding force of the rest of the story of the Hebrew Scriptures. Covenant, then, is the guiding literary and theological paradigm of the entire Hebrew Bible.

What begins in the narrative of Genesis 1–3 as a covenant-like relationship between God and all humankind through the first human being, Adam, suffers through what is characterized as Adam's disobedience to that covenant. The narrative is careful to illustrate, however, that God never breaks fidelity to his promises. Even as Adam and Eve lose their right to Eden, God clothes and prepares them for the life they have chosen (3:21). Humankind expands (Gen 4), and the ensuing chapters follow the righteous line of God in terms of the corresponding expansion of sin (4:1—11:32).

Genesis 6–9 tells the story of Noah and God's work in creation to begin anew. In the flood narrative the word "covenant" first appears (Hebrew: בְּרִית; Greek: διαθήκη) as God promises to establish his covenant with Noah (6:18) and eventually promises never again to wipe out all of creation regardless of the spread of sin (9:10–11). This is ultimately a covenant between God and the created order, and the mark of this covenant is what has come to be known as the rainbow (9:12–17). God's covenantal relationship with humankind, however, needs more story, as the early chapters of Genesis close with the confusion and scattering of humankind following the attempted construction of the tower of Babel (11:1–9). This scattering symbolizes the radical break in the covenantal relationship between God and humankind as the opposite of the unity for which it was created. There is a distinctive gap in the narrative here as the pace accelerates and several hundred years are crossed by way of genealogy (11:10–32). This gap in the narrative symbolizes the gap between God and humankind as God looks to restore the covenant with a chosen people through one man.

Genesis 12:1 marks God's choice of Abraham (initially called Abram) and the first iteration of God's promise to him. The next eleven chapters narrate Abraham's journey of faith as he comes to terms with this covenantal relationship (Gen 12–22). The stories of his successes are interspersed with his failings before God as Abraham makes his way. The journey is marked by the narration of God's covenant with Abraham in Genesis 15 and 17, each time more detailed, more expansive, and more compelling. This is ultimately a covenant between God and the family of this one man. The familial nature of the covenant is symbolized in the mark of circumcision that becomes the signifier of kindred relationship (17:9–14).[19] Abraham cannot fully accept the covenant until he has made his way before God, and it is not until God calls him by name in Genesis 22:1 that Abraham can fully respond. God's command here is the most difficult thus far, but Abraham finally responds without mediation or qualification and is rewarded for his faith (22:9–19). The blood of the sacrifice seals the covenant.

From this point forward in the biblical narrative, there is always a call and response necessary for the establishment of the covenant with God. This covenant—both its promises and its demands—only expands as Israel grows from a people, the children of Israel, into a nation (Gen 32—Exod 18). Exodus 19–24 provides the extensive narrative of the final step. Crucial to the sealing of this covenant is God's offer, "Now therefore, if you will obey my voice and keep my covenant, you shall be my own possession among all the peoples" (19:5). And it is just an offer, not operative until the people respond, "All that the Lord has spoken, we will do" (19:8). The bulk of the rest of the Torah is consumed with God telling his people all that they must do (Exodus 20 through Deuteronomy). For their part, the people struggle with the covenant's demands, but the Law is provided as the gift that guides the people into right relationship with God.

Across the rest of Israel's Scriptures, this is the covenant that is operative. For this reason, Joshua calls the confederation of Israelite tribes to a covenant renewal ceremony at Shechem after the successful conquest of the promised land of Canaan (Josh 24). It is thus the demands of the Sinai covenant that determine the success or failure of both Israel as a whole and the lives of its individual people. Literarily, through the Prophets it is the covenant to which the people are called. Even after restoration from exile, it is this covenant that marks Ezra's reorganization and administration of the people (Neh 8–10). The char-

---

19. The ancient rite of circumcision, perhaps originally connected to marriage or rite of passage to adulthood, is here transferred to early childhood so as to become a sign of God's everlasting covenant with Abraham and his descendants, a mark of membership in the covenant family.

acterization of God becomes more and more distant—God no longer walks in the garden with his people (Gen 3:8)—but God's fidelity to this covenant never wavers. Even into the latest literature of the OT, in the apocalyptic visions of Daniel where God is acting in the heavenly realm, God is always characterized as having the final word (Dan 7–12). And this final word, much like the first words, will be one of creation. Those who stand fast and remain faithful will rise at the appointed time into new life (Dan 12:1–13). God's covenant abides.

In order to elucidate this overview, the components of the covenant traditions as evidenced in Israel's Scriptures can be examined in terms of both types and forms.

Types of Covenants in the Old Testament

Although varying in form, three fundamental types of covenants are found in the OT. Covenants between God and human beings and/or creation generally are mentioned in the narrative overview above with pertinent examples provided. Present also are covenants between human parties. Examples include those between Abraham and Abimelech (Gen 21:22–34), between Laban and Jacob (Gen 31:43–55), and between David and Jonathan (1 Sam 18:1–9; 20:1–42; 23:18). Finally, evidence can be found in the OT of covenants between humans or God and nonhumans, i.e., animals or inanimate objects.[20] The present study is concerned primarily with covenants between God and human beings, although the covenants between human parties seem to be modeled on the former and will therefore also offer insight into the Fourth Evangelist's mine of theological symbolism, imagery, and language.

A basic component of the covenants between God and human beings in the OT is that one party of the covenant (God) is vastly more knowledgeable, more powerful, and more "sighted" than the other (human[s]). In every instance, God *knows*, can *do*, and can *see* things in creation and history that the human parties do not and cannot. This "constant feature" of the covenantal relationship between God and hu-

---

20. Chennattu, *Johannine Discipleship*, 52. In her discussion of this type of OT covenant (see esp. 52 n. 13), Chennattu includes Job's covenants with stones (Job 5:23), his eyes (31:1), and Leviathan (40:28), as well as the covenants made between the leaders of Jerusalem and death (Isa 28:15, 18), YHWH and day and night (Jer 33:20, 25), and YHWH and the beasts (Ezek 34:25; Hos 2:20).

mankind, according to David Noel Freedman, gives this type of biblical covenant a particular character that is unparalleled in the ancient world.[21] Therefore God is always the initiating agent of these covenants. Likewise, this gives God encompassing *authority* in this relationship, while the human participants are always called to some form of *obedience*. There is always a binding of promise and/or service at play.

While varying greatly in detail and even in purpose, the covenants between God and humans can be further classified into two kinds: what Freedman calls "covenants of human obligation" and "covenants of divine commitment." He explains:

> In one series, which corresponds generally to the pattern of the Hittite suzerainty or vassal treaties, the terms or stipulations are imposed upon the human party in what may be called a covenant of human obligation. In the other series the roles are reversed: God takes upon himself certain obligations. Since these agreements also proceed from the divine initiative, we cannot speak of the human imposition of terms upon God. Rather, we may call this type a covenant of divine commitment.[22]

The paradigmatic example of the covenant of human obligation is the people-forming event at Mount Sinai where Moses mediates the covenant between God and Israel (Exod 19–24). The renewals of this covenant through the rest of the OT are necessarily also of this kind, including those at Shechem (Josh 24) and Jerusalem after the exile (Neh 8–10). The primary example of the covenant of divine commitment is revealed in God's relationship with Abraham, and particularly in the covenantal activity in Genesis 15. This type is also found prior to this narrative section in God's interaction with Noah (Gen 6–9), as well as in God's later covenant with David (2 Sam 7).

In terms of form, these two types of covenants between God and human beings can be discussed in reverse order to reflect the narrative development of the OT text.

---

21. Freedman, "Divine Commitment," 420. He uses the umbrella term "superior" for God's role in these covenants, but I prefer the more descriptive and active qualities of God's knowledge, power, and sight that become operative for the Fourth Evangelist.

22. Ibid., 420.

Covenant Forms in the Old Testament

In the case of the covenant of divine commitment, God offers a promise of blessing, binding the human recipient to God's protection and plan for creation in history, based upon the obedient response-in-action of the chosen one.[23] In the case of Noah (Gen 6–9), he obediently builds the ark God requests, and the covenant promised in 6:9–22 (see v. 18) becomes a reality in 9:8–17 (see v. 9). No further (future) acts of this kind are required; the covenant is based on obedient response in the form of physical action. In the case of Abraham, his story begins in earnest at Genesis 12:1. In this case, God says, "Go . . . to the land I will show you," and follows with the promise of blessing. Genesis 12:4 states, "So Abram went." The call and response-in-action are immediate and clear. Abraham's journey has only just begun here, and the divine covenant with him is far more complex than that with Noah. The covenantal context does not come to the fore until Genesis 15, but the form is the same: God gives a call to action, and Abraham responds precisely as commanded. In both of these instances, however, the biblical author gives little evidence as to *why* God chooses these particular potential covenant partners. Noah is described as "righteous" and "blameless in his generation" (Gen 6:9), but Abraham (Abram at this point) is not characterized personally at all prior to God's call. Righteousness is, however, later reckoned to him (Gen 15:6), as the story becomes explicitly covenantal and Abraham takes the next step of not only acting in accordance with, but also believing, God's promises. The story of the Davidic covenant shows a further development in the faith-based activity of the human participant that precedes the divine covenantal promise. David's story begins at 1 Samuel 16, and he has proven his obedience in action and faith time and again when his narrative reaches Nathan's oracle at 2 Samuel 7. What is clear in all these cases, however, is that "the divine commitment is unilateral and unconditional, without obligations made on the human party."[24] The form seems to be:

1. Call to action and promise of covenant on the part of God;
2. Response-in-action on the part of the human; and

---

23. McCarthy refers to these as "promissory covenants" (*Old Testament Covenant*, 32, 37, 46–49).
24. Freedman, "Divine Commitment," 425.

3. Making of an eternal covenant, creating an enduring bond between God and the human being along with his progeny.²⁵

The form of the second covenant type, Freedman's covenant of human obligation, is more complex and variable. For our purposes, we can discuss the one form most often advocated for these types, the suzerainty treaty, as the "essential covenant pattern," and outline how several biblical examples may fit this form.²⁶

George Mendenhall's pioneering study of international treaties extant from the Hittite Empire of 1450–1200 BC as they correlate with the OT covenant form has long been given primacy of place in the developing field of OT covenant studies.²⁷ Due to what he suspects are fortunate "accidents of transmission or excavation," adequate source material is available for studying treaty material contemporaneous and interactive with the pre-Mosaic and Mosaic periods of Israel.²⁸ Building upon the work of V. Korosec, he discusses the two general types of treaties found in these documents: the suzerainty treaty and the parity treaty.²⁹ Arguing that the suzerainty treaty is the basic form, Mendenhall focuses on its structure, noting that its primary purpose is to establish "a firm relationship of mutual support between the two parties (especially military support)."³⁰

---

25. God's "covenant in peace" with Phinehas (Num 25) is also often given as an example of the covenant of divine commitment. Here, God had relayed the command to Moses to have impaled the people of Israel who had "yoked themselves to the Baal of Peor." Phinehas, grandson of "Aaron the priest" takes it upon himself, in his zeal for the Lord, to impale a blatant abuser. God rewards his "zealous" response-in-action by making "a covenant of perpetual priesthood" with his descendents, what later tradition understands to be the formation of the Zadokkite priesthood. In this case, God did not chose Phinehas, as with Noah and Abraham. He gave the general command, and Phinehas in effect chose himself by his obedient response. God, however, is still the initiator and sole obligant of the enduring bond.

26. See Freedman, "Divine Commitment," 427.

27. Mendenhall, *Law and Covenant*, 24–50.

28. Ibid., 27–28.

29. For this background material, see Korosec, *Hethitische Staatsverträge*.

30. Mendenhall, *Law and Covenant*, 29–30. Mendenhall explains that the suzerainty treaty is a one-way treaty presented by a superior (the suzerain) to an underling (the potential vassal) offering protection qualified by stipulations that the latter chooses to accept or reject. The parity treaty is a two-way treaty offering mutual benefit as qualified by stipulations to which both parties must agree. Therefore, Mendenhall argues that a parity treaty is, in essence, two suzerainty treaties between equals in opposite directions. For this reason, he focuses his research on the suzerainty treaty.

Examination of the text of the Hittite suzerainty treaty reveals a six-part structure to which Mendenhall projects three additional response components. The form is:

1. Preamble (identification of the author of the covenant and his attributes);
2. Historical Prologue (description of the previous relations of the two parties);
3. Stipulations (often referred to as "the words," this section constitutes the detail of the obligations imposed upon and accepted by the vassal as well as the interests of the suzerain protected by the covenant);
4. Provision for Deposit in the Temple and Periodic Public Reading;
5. List of Gods as Witnesses; and
6. Curses and Blessing Formula (indication that the sanctions are religious).

To this basic text Mendenhall presumes:

7. A formal oath by which the vassal pledged obedience;
8. Some sort of solemn ceremony; and
9. Some form for initiating procedure against a rebellious vassal (breach of covenant).[31]

It is the fullness of this formula that, according to Mendenhall and others, provides the foundation upon which the covenants in Israelite traditions of the OT are envisioned and built.[32]

The text of the covenant narrative at Sinai is the focus of Mendenhall's study, particularly the Decalogue of Exodus 20.[33] As with suzerainty treaties, the two parties are by no means equal: the "suzerain" (in this case YHWH) offers his terms, and the "vassal" (in this

---

31. Ibid., 32–35.

32. So Baltzer, Hillers, Freedman, and Cross. See above for the sketch of this argument as well as the relevant bibliographic references.

33. A fundamental observation is that the biblical authors use the same term, בְּרִית (*berit*), for this covenant as they do for covenants between kings. See 1 Kgs 15:19; 20:34.

case Israel) determines if this is in its best interest and, if so, swears to the terms. Exodus 20:1–2a would constitute the preamble, identifying YHWH sufficiently as "your God." Verse 2b would provide the historical prologue, albeit a brief one—the Exodus itself providing all the background necessary for the current covenant offer. The actual Decalogue (vv. 3–17) supplies the stipulations of the treaty. To have one lord is the principal command in the treaty, as here in the Ten Commandments. Building upon Mendenhall's work, Hillers notes that casting the "stipulations" in negative form is appropriate because, as in the suzerainty treaty, "certain acts are intolerable if there is to be any covenant with God, or any life together as his people—murder, theft, adultery, perjury, and so on—but once these forbidden areas have been fenced off, the rest of their affairs are for them to manage."[34] As in the Hittite form, there is no formal obligation presented on YHWH's part in the covenant offer itself. There is no part 4, provision for deposit and public reading) contained in this narrative; but Scripture itself bears out that this is indeed what was practiced.[35] Likewise there is no explicit part 5, list of gods as witnesses, present. Hillers points out that this section could hardly be expected to survive the transfer of the treaty form to the religious sphere where YHWH, *the* God to be covenanted, takes on the role of the suzerain.[36] Verses 18–26 round out this chapter as well as this portion of the covenant-making narrative by pointing to parts 4 and 5, and implicitly invoking part 6, the blessings and in particular the curses that follow from the completed covenant. It will not be until the end of Exodus 24 that ritual action brings to a close the covenant-making process.[37]

Joshua 24 records the first renewal of the Sinai covenant between God and the twelve tribes of Israel at Shechem. This narrative of the biblical covenant-making process also reflects a pattern resonant of extrabiblical suzerainty treaties.[38] In the definitive formation of the twelve-tribe league at this ancient religious site, an act is recounted

---

34. Hillers, *Covenant*, 50.

35. The ark of the covenant was eventually constructed to house the tablets of the Decalogue (Exod 25), and the renewal ceremonies in the times of Joshua, Josiah, and Ezra bear out the practice of public reading (see Josh 24; 2 Kgs 23; Neh 8–10).

36. Hillers, *Covenant*, 52–53.

37. See the analysis of Exod 19–24 below for more detail.

38. For more detail, see Hillers, *Covenant*, 58–66.

that is so decisive as to beget a tradition of periodic covenant renewal.[39] Joshua 24:1 recounts the gathering of "all the tribes of Israel," and v. 2a identifies "the God of Israel" in the typical pronouncement formula of a preamble (part 1).[40] A far lengthier historical prologue (part 2) than that offered at Sinai begins at v. 2b and runs through v. 13. No detail of stipulations (part 3) is given, for Joshua stresses only service to YHWH to the exclusion of all other gods, i.e., the First Commandment.[41] A call to obedience and decision is interjected in vv. 14–15, followed by the people's positive response in an oath formula in vv. 16–18. A variation of a curse formula (part 6) can be seen in vv. 19–20 as Joshua warns of the consequences for making this covenant, but the people reiterate their determination in v. 21. In vv. 22–23 the people are called as witnesses to themselves and their covenant (part 5), and the people articulate their acceptance a third time in v. 24. The covenant is completed in v. 25, where stipulations are given further allusion; and the covenant is deposited (part 4) in vv. 26–28, concluding the renewal narrative.[42]

A final biblical example of the suzerainty treaty form in Israelite traditions lies in the fullness of the book of Deuteronomy, "the biblical document of the covenant *par excellence.*"[43] Delbert Hillers builds upon the work of W. L. Moran and claims, "The size of the book makes it hard to see its framework on a first reading, but once this outline is extracted, any reader can at once detect the impress of the covenant form."[44] Providing indicators for the parts of the suzerainty treaty form, his outline is:

---

39. For a detailed discussion, see Wright, *Shechem*, esp. 123–38.
40. See Mendenhall, *Law and Covenant*, 41–44, for this analysis of the structure of Josh 24.
41. Hillers, *Covenant*, 62.
42. See the analysis of Joshua 24 below for more detail.
43. See Moran, "Love of God in Deuteronomy," esp. 82. See further a positive response to this study in McCarthy, "Notes on the Love of God in Deuteronomy."
44. Hillers, *Covenant*, 150.

1:1—4:43	The History of God's Dealing with Israel (parts 1 and 2)
4:44—26:19	Covenant and Commandments (Stipulations, part 3)
5:1-33	The Decalogue
6:1—11:32	Exhortation on Keeping the Covenant
12:1—26:19	Laws Issuing from the Covenant
27:1-26	Covenant Ceremony (Deposit and Provision for Public Reading, part 4; no part 5 is narrated)
28:1-69	Blessings and Curses (part 6)
29:1—34:12	Mosaic Speeches Concluding the Book

Distinctive about Deuteronomy's presentation of Israel's covenant relationship with God are several terms that reflect ancient covenantal concepts, including the characteristic designation of Israel עַם סְגֻלָּה God's "peculiar people" or "treasured possession," the notion of "walking after" a god to denote worshiping or serving, and, most significantly and pervasively, the concepts of knowing (from the Hebrew ידע) and loving (from the Hebrew אהב) to denote both obedience and, further, loyalty and devotion "with the whole heart."[45] Hillers ventures to claim that love here "is in part the language of emotion, in part the language of international law."[46] Therefore, in addition to the book of Deuteronomy's paradigmatic covenant status, it is also the "biblical document *par excellence* of love," thus giving us "the mother lode of much other influential biblical teaching about love for God."[47]

It is important to note that nowhere in the OT is the complete structure of the Hittite suzerainty treaty reflected precisely. The absence of this exact text form, along with the fact that this treaty type does not explain YHWH's *concern* for Israel's welfare, has led some scholars to disavow completely this formulaic basis.[48] We must not, however, throw the proverbial baby out with the bathwater. Direct imitation is not the only means by which one can appreciate and adopt existing norms or forms. Nor should we assume that tribal Israel was too primitive to have known of or have creatively adapted international covenant customs of its surrounding culture.[49] It has long been accepted that covenant "is the central expression of the distinctive faith of Israel as 'the people of

---

45. Moran, "Love of God," 83–87, here 87.
46. Hillers, *Covenant*, 154.
47. Moran, "Love of God," 82; then Hillers, *Covenant*, 152.
48. So Nicholson, McCarthy, and McKenzie.
49. So Wellhausen. See above for discussion and bibliographic information.

Yahweh,' children of God by adoption and free decision rather than by nature or necessity."[50] That the peoples of the tribal era also had the ability to adopt and reformulate existing customs creatively to share their lived experience, their *story*, and reflect just this "distinctive" worldview must also be substantially vindicated.[51] In his advocacy of the underlying suzerainty treaty form for the biblical idea of Israel's covenant with God, Hillers fittingly concludes, "Even though these resemble formal texts of covenants at some points, they are most exactly described as *narratives of how a treaty with God was made*."[52]

Key Covenantal Texts in the Old Testament

Key covenantal narratives of the OT can now be examined along the established guidelines of type and form so that we may garner the fundamental themes and essential elements that constitute the covenantal relationship that underpins the story of God's working in history. What follows is not close exegesis in the technical sense, but rather a more broadly drawn narrative interpretation of the Scriptures that were intimately known to the Fourth Evangelist because they comprised the integral symbolic and theological components of his first-century Jewish worldview. They told the story of Israel—*his* story—in the order of God's plan for creation. We will thus trace the developing covenantal tradition in the historical order that would have been known to the evangelist, leaving off at a point in the story where he could have found himself picking it up again.

The Noachic Covenant: Genesis 6–9

The book of Genesis can be divided in the broadest sense into two parts. It begins with an account of the primordial history of the known world. This narrative takes up the first eleven chapters of the book. The text then moves into the more specific account of the ancestry of the people of Israel with the patriarchal narratives of Genesis 12–50. This first section, the primordial history, is the basis for everything that follows in the Bible. The narratives in these early chapters provide the impetus

50. Nicholson, *God and His People*, viii.
51. See Cross, *Epic to Canon*, 3–21.
52. Hillers, *Covenant*, 47. Emphasis added.

for the rest of the final form of the story. Thus, Genesis 1–11 is often called, in particularly Christian terminology, the prologue to salvation history. As is common knowledge, the biblical lands are part of the earliest inhabited regions of the world. The biblical setting is larger than Palestine, however. The geographical canvas for the saga of salvation history is known as the Fertile Crescent: a narrow arc of land stretching from the Persian Gulf to Egypt. The water resources in this area make life possible along the edge of a vast desert area, and it was in this cradle of civilization that biblical history began.

The story of Noah and his experience of covenant with God makes up the bulk of Genesis 6–9. The narrative slows down here after moving rapidly through a number of generations of the history of humankind by way of genealogy (Gen 5). These chapters are all but unanimously considered a composite account of two ancient sources (the Yahwist and the Priestly) not preserved consecutively but intricately intertwined to present one continuous story.[53] Genesis 6 opens with a strange and provocative story of the spread of humankind that is consonant with the multiplication of evil across the earth (6:1–4). Verse 5 then provides God's reasoning for the coming deluge: "the inclination of the thoughts of their hearts" was "evil." Humankind (הָאָדָם), to whom the earth (הָאֲדָמָה) was given and whose inclination was to be for God, focused only on evil. God regretted this climactic move of creation, and his heart was aggrieved (over against the heart of humankind that had become turned toward evil and, thus, away from God). Therefore God determined to "un-create" all animate beings. But Noah "found favor" in the eyes of YHWH (v. 8), ensuring that "re-creation" would follow God's anguished "un-creation."

Noah is characterized immediately as a father who is "righteous," "blameless," and who "walked with God" (vv. 9–10). Creation generally is then given further characterization as filled with חָמָס, a technical legal term typically translated as "violence" but more astutely rendered

---

53. Again, this is a narrative interpretation of the final form of the text, the story that would have been known to the Fourth Evangelist. Therefore, for the purposes of this study, source criticism is not integral. Thus, no further word will be offered on this matter; rather the final narrative will be examined. For a discussion of the interconnectedness of the ancient sources in the biblical account of the flood, see Brueggemann, *Genesis*, 73–88; Skinner, *Genesis*, i–lxv, 148–81; Speiser, *Genesis*, 48–63; Westermann, *Genesis*, 1:1–69, 384–487; von Rad, *Genesis*, 24–29, 116–34.

"lawlessness."[54] Noah's character as described in 6:9–10 is apparently all the rationale necessary for God first to choose to create the earth anew, then to choose Noah as the one through whom to save the best of what was already created. God begins to speak directly to Noah at 6:13 and his determination and directive run through v. 21. God opens by giving Noah his reasoning and his intent (destruction, v. 13), then begins his instruction to Noah by way of an imperative ("Make an ark," vv. 14–16). He then clarifies his plan: "For my part, I am going to bring a flood" to destroy what is on the earth, "but I will establish my covenant with you" (v. 18; see vv. 17–21). The first occurrence of "covenant" (בְּרִית) in the OT is found here in the mouth of God through his directive to Noah. God follows his intent to establish a covenant with Noah, with detailed directions of all that Noah must do in order to bring it about (vv. 18–21). For his part, "Noah did this; he did all that God commanded him" (v. 22).

Noah says nothing in response to God. In fact, Noah has no direct speech anywhere in this narrative. What is determinative for Noah is his response-in-action, his obedience. God says, "Make," and Noah not only "makes" but "does" all that God tells him to "do." The author uses the same Hebrew verb root in every instance (עשׂה) to emphasize Noah's thoroughgoing obedience. Then God likewise does as promised, loosening the dome created on the second day (see Gen 1) and allowing the waters of the deep and the heavens to burst forth (7:11).

Genesis 7–8 details the flood itself; then God begins to speak to Noah again at 8:15. Once more God opens with a command; this time it is "Go out" (v. 16). The re-creation is to begin as the animate beings preserved on the ark are to "be fruitful and multiply on the earth" (see 1:22, 28). Verse 8:18 recounts that Noah once again responds in full obedience to God's call, "So Noah went out" (note again the same Hebrew root in vv. 16 and 18, יצא). This second response-in-action is followed by Noah's first initiating action as he builds an altar and offers a burnt sacrifice to God (v. 20). As a direct result of the "soothing odor," God speaks from his heart once again, and once again because of the inherent evil in the heart of humankind God determines to take action (8:21; see 6:5–6). This time, however, God determines to fulfill his promise to establish a covenant: never again to doom the earth (הָאֲדָמָה) because of humankind (הָאָדָם).

---

54. Speiser, *Genesis*, 51.

God gives his blessing to Noah as well as his imperative for fertility (9:1; see 1:28). The sanctity of life, particularly human life, is affirmed, however limited and transient.[55] The focus of Genesis 9 then turns to God's covenant with Noah (vv. 8–17). What was promised before the flood comes to fruition as part of the re-creative communication. God speaks with the emphatic, "And I am establishing my covenant with you" (v. 9). God makes his covenant with Noah and his offspring, but not only with humankind; rather with all of the re-created order (v. 10). The covenant is eternal and creation will never again be destroyed (v. 11). God then offers the bow in the sky as a sign for both creation and himself to mark the eternal nature of the covenant with creation and God's determination to maintain relationship with it (vv. 12–17).

Noah, the primary human character of this account, is silent throughout. God initiates all the action and does all the speaking. Noah's response is in his action, and by his obedient action he accepts God's word of covenant and lives his life in accord with that relationship, thus facilitating God's covenant with all creation.

The Abrahamic Covenant: Genesis 12–22

The second part of the book of Genesis, chapters 12–50, forms the bulk of the narrative and covers the ancestral period of the history of Israel. There is a significant break in the narrative here. The story moves forward several hundred years by way of a genealogy (11:10–32). The break in the narrative is symbolic of the radical break in the relationship between God and God's creation that occurred, narratively, in the confusion of languages and the ultimate scattering of the people resulting from the tower of Babel story (11:1–9). From this point forward God will never again walk with his creation in the garden, or anywhere else for that matter. The distance between God and his creation only grows. And with that distance, sin also grows. The characterization of the fearsome and awesome power of God also expands.

The narrative of the ancestral period begins with a man called Abram, whom God eventually renames Abraham. The Abraham cycle of stories begins at Genesis 12 and runs through Genesis 23. According to 11:27–32, Abraham's family came from "Ur of the Chaldees," a city in

---

55. Ibid., 58–59.

the southern Euphrates valley. From there they migrated northwest to Haran, which biblical tradition treats as Abraham's homeland.[56]

Genesis 12:1–3 is traditionally understood to recount the call of Abraham. After several centuries of apparent silence, God calls out to one person: "Now YHWH said to Abram, 'Go . . .'" (12:1). And that one person responds, taking his family and all that he owns with him: "So Abram went . . ." (12: 4). Once again the narrative recounts God's call in terms of command, and the chosen one's response-in-action in terms of precise obedience. And for his obedience Abram receives the assurance of blessing: a great nation and a great name (12:2), along with the covenantal obligation of blessing and cursing (v. 3). After the radical break with all creation at Genesis 11, God chooses to work in terms of individual faith and practice. From this action, we find the new basis for a people of God. In response to God's call at Genesis 12, Abram moves his wife, Sarai, and his nephew, Lot, to Canaan. In Canaan Abraham receives a divine promise: "to your descendents I will give this land . . ." (12:7).[57] He then continues southwest through the Negev desert and into Egypt. He finally returns to settle near Hebron upon the repetition of God's promise (13:14–18). From this point, he is presented as a semi-nomad in the central hill country of Palestine.

We cannot do justice to the fullness of Abraham's story here, but crucial for the present study is not only God's covenant of divine commitment to Abraham, but also the journey—of both body and spirit—that is integral to the content and the purpose of that covenantal relationship. On the narrative level, God's covenant with Abraham grows as Abraham grows. His movement, therefore, is not only physical but spiritual as well, as he moves from pure response-in-action accompanied by a faith riddled with doubt, to response-in-action that is grounded in the fullness of faith. This doubt overtakes Abraham immediately following the promises of 12:1–9, as he endangers Sarah, the promised matriarch, to the hands of Pharaoh (12:10–20). Abraham's doubt continues to hinder his faith even as he continues to respond in action. Thus, his is a move

---

56. For more detailed exegesis of Gen 12–23, see Brueggemann, *Genesis*, 105–203; Skinner, *Genesis*, 240–339; Speiser, *Genesis*, 85–173; von Rad, *Genesis*, 158–250; Westermann, *Genesis*, 2:123–376.

57. Both the religious significance of Shechem and the future interaction with the Canaanites are alluded to here in 12:6.

from strict obedience to obedience in faith—and this is what is eventually reckoned as righteousness. On this journey we now continue.

In language that resonates covenantal oath formulae, the narrative recounts how Abraham separates from Lot, after which God shows Abraham the land that will be given to him and his offspring (13:14–18). This passage confirms both Abraham's obedient action and God's commitment to the divine promise. Abraham was commanded to go to the land that God "will show" him (12:1) and, now that Abraham is there, God does indeed show him in expansive moves. God once again commands Abraham to go (13:17), and Abraham complies (v. 18). This new act of obedience is followed immediately by Abraham's overwhelming success in rescuing Lot from eastern kings, exemplifying his ability, as heir to the blessing, to protect his people and overcome his enemies (14:1–24). The proof of this blessing, and Abraham's acknowledgment of it, bring him to the first full expression of God's covenantal action (15:1–21).

God's divine commitment in this narrative episode is revealed in two components: the promise of progeny (15:1–6) and the promise of the land (15:7–21). God appears to Abraham this time in a vision to reassure him of his reward (v. 1). What is exceptional about this account is that for the first time in the covenant development of the biblical narrative, the human party responds to God verbally (vv. 2–3). Further, Abraham enters into full dialogue with God by expressing his doubt about God's ability to carry out his promise, given the reality of his aging situation. Even more remarkably, God responds not in anger, but in the openness of relationship in communication, bringing Abraham outside and giving the visual confirmation of the stars as the gauge by which his offspring will be numbered (vv. 4–5). Abraham then takes the first step from mere obedience in action to active obedience in faith when "he believed" YHWH. And here God first credits him with "righteousness" (v. 6), and proceeds to the issue of land.

In language that will be echoed at Sinai, God solemnly affirms that it was he who brought Abraham from land of the Chaldeans and into the promised land of Canaan (v. 7).[58] God reasserts the intended gift of this land, but Abraham, in his burgeoning agency as recipient of God's covenant, demurs. He wonders how he will know this will come to be (v. 8). Again, God responds positively to Abraham's assertion, and pro-

---

58. Freedman, "Divine Commitment," 422–23.

vides a ritual sacrifice to seal the covenantal oath (vv. 9–21).[59] As the ritual begins, it is to this knowledge that God speaks, "Know this for certain..." (vv. 13–16). A flaming torch passes through the cut pieces of the halved animals and God formally swears an oath of covenant (vv. 17–21).

This is not the end of Abraham's journey, however. The very next chapter describes the doubt that persists when Abraham "hearkened to the voice" of another human being, in this case Sarai (16:2), when he has been called time and again to "hearken to the voice" of God. This leads to strife in the family and the endangering of Abraham's own child (16:3–6). God must intervene, rectifying the wrong done to Hagar, saving the unborn child, and presenting the child with a divine commitment of his own (vv. 7–16). God then goes to Abraham and recommits them both to the covenanted promises.[60]

In form, the covenantal narrative in Genesis 17 is much the same as the text of Genesis 15. God is the primary agent, choosing and addressing Abraham, identifying himself and giving command (17:1). The covenantal nature of the encounter is stated explicitly and promise of progeny is reiterated immediately (v. 2). Abraham is renamed in the process to represent this divine commitment (vv. 3–5). The nature of the covenant as eternal is clarified and the promise of land is once again brought to bear (vv. 6–8). What is distinctive in this episode is the sign of the covenant that God introduces in vv. 9–14: circumcision will henceforth mark God's covenant with Abraham and all that are his. It is, however, simply an identifying mark; it does not effect the divine commitment.[61] Sarai, too, is renamed and the child from her womb is identified as Isaac (vv. 15–21). Thus, with regard to the narrative, the covenant develops further. Its sheer magnitude comes to the fore. When God finishes speaking, he departs (v. 22). The theophany is over. Abraham's agency as a participant is reduced; he simply receives the promise in silent awe (see v. 3 for Abraham's posture throughout the theophany).

---

59. See Jer 34:8–22 for a similar covenant sealing ceremony. "Cutting a covenant" in this way was an ancient practice of oath taking.

60. I am well aware that the covenant narratives preserved in Gen 15 and 17 are generally considered to be varying traditions of the same event (from J and P, respectively). On the narrative level, however, we see the ups and downs of Abraham's journey of faith, and it is this final form that is pertinent. This is one of many examples where the interplay of varying traditions has produced a striking final narrative.

61. Freedman, "Divine Commitment," 425.

His ensuing action, however, is once again one of full obedience, as he takes Ishmael and his entire household to be circumcised (vv. 23-27).

Abraham's agency is then reasserted in the following chapters as he shows hospitality to representatives of YHWH (18:1-15) and intercedes actively on behalf of Sodom and Gomorrah (18:16-33). Abraham's past doubt must be resolved, however, and the second account of the endangerment of Sarah (20:1-18) as well as the second account of strife over Hagar and Ishmael (21:1-21) test Abraham's mettle. This portion of his journey is resolved in his handling of the Abimelech dispute (introduced in Gen 20) when Abraham becomes the covenant initiator and lives peacefully as an alien in a foreign land, calling on the name of YHWH (21:22-34).

Abraham's journey comes to its climax at Genesis 22. His winding path of growth and development over the last ten chapters of narrative has been building to this ultimate point of decision where "God puts Abraham to the test" (22:1), and Abraham must confront not only his own true nature but also that of the God with whom he is covenanted.[62] In this encounter God, for the first time in their relationship, calls Abraham by name (v. 1). In fact, Abraham is called three times by three different characters denoting the crucial nature of his role: first by God ("Abraham!," v. 1), then by Isaac ("my Father!," v. 7), and finally by the angel of YHWH ("Abraham!," v. 11). Each time Abraham answers in the same, most fundamental, manner: הִנֵּנִי. With this simple particle of existence, best translated consistently as "Here I am," Abraham places himself directly before God in an unmediated way. This brief episode thus "embodies what is perhaps the profoundest personal experience in all the recorded history" of the OT.[63]

With the command to sacrifice his "only son" (אֶת־בִּנְךָ אֶת־יְחִידְךָ), the beloved son of the promise, God puts Abraham, who has been so obedient in action, to the ultimate test of faith. For his part, Abraham responds in word as well as deed, exemplifying that his faith in God's promise has finally matured with his obedience. By raising his hand to kill his son, Abraham's journey of faith reaches its goal and he is rewarded: "For now I know that you fear God ..." (v. 12). Isaac is spared (as is

---

62. See Søren Kierkegaard's brilliant thought project preserved in *Fear and Trembling* for an insightful presentation of the "leap of faith" Abraham must take here if he is to go forward in covenant with God.

63. See Speiser, *Genesis*, 164.

Abraham) and a ram is given for the sacrifice. It is this sacrifice, the result of Abraham passing God's test, that ultimately seals God's covenant of commitment to Abraham. The final reassurance of the covenant is offered (vv. 15–19). Abraham's story quickly and unremarkably comes to a close, and his place in God's covenantal action in history assured.

The Sinai Covenant: Exodus 19–24

The locus of the narrative of the Sinai covenant is contained in Exodus 19–24. This story can be broadly structured in four parts:

19:1–25	Preparation for the Covenant: Suggestion and Response
20:1–21	The Decalogue and the Fear of God
20:22—23:33	The Covenant Collection: The Beginnings of the Stipulations
24:1–11	The People Accept the Covenant

It is the second part, the giving of the Decalogue itself, that reflects the covenant form, but this covenant is incomplete without the response and ritual of the final segment (Exod 24); therefore a brief discussion of the full event will be presented.

Exodus 19:1 marks the arrival at Sinai as the day of "the third new moon" after the children of Israel departed Egypt. The literary unit of 19:3–6 marks the solemnity of the occasion in liturgical style. The unit is marked by the prophetic "Thus you shall say . . ." (v. 3), and "These are the words . . ." (v. 6). Moses ascends the mountain for the first time, where God commands him to address the people on his behalf as the one who delivered them from the Egyptians "on eagles' wings" (v. 4). In this manner Moses is to offer a covenant to Israel (vv. 5–6), specifically, "If you obey my voice and keep my covenant, you shall be my treasured people." In the few words of this solemn introduction, it becomes clear that this covenant is strikingly different from those that God has established thus far. God explicitly uses a mediator (Moses) to offer a *conditional* covenant to an entire people, and has them respond first by word and then, only when the covenant is sealed, by deed.

On the narrative level, this is a development and expansion of the covenantal nature of God's relationship with the children of Israel. The divine commitment remains, but the human obligation in word and deed, i.e., in *relationship*, comes to the fore. The human component becomes operative. Thus regardless of God's fidelity, the covenant can be broken. The people must "obey the voice" of God and "keep the covenant"; they must remain in active relationship with God and God alone.[64] Moses does as he is commanded, and the people respond positively in full voice. Verse 8 recounts, "The people answered together as they said: 'All that YHWH has said, we will do.'" The people are then instructed to consecrate themselves for two days to prepare themselves, for "on the third day the Lord will come down upon Mount Sinai in the sight of all the people" (v. 11). The theophany occurs on the third day as promised (vv. 16–25).

The purpose of the consecration and theophany is so that God may initiate the covenant-making process through the giving of his words. The bulk of Exodus 20 is devoted to the narration of these ten words, the Decalogue, in covenant form. In structure, the following components are apparent: a preamble that identifies YHWH as the covenant-giver (vv. 1–2a), a brief historical prologue (v. 2b), and stipulations of the covenant in terms of apodictic law (vv. 3–17, the Decalogue itself). Their role as witness to the covenant theophany strikes fear in the people, leading them to ask Moses to take an official role as covenant mediator, formalizing his role as God's prophet (vv. 18–19). For his part, Moses agrees; he urges the people not to fear but to understand the curses that are integral to the covenant relationship (vv. 20–21).

Moses then draws near to God to receive further instruction, resulting in the largely casuistic law that makes up 20:22—23:19, typically called the Covenant Collection or "book of the covenant" (24:7). This collection begins and ends with legislation regarding ritual and the worship of God (20:22–26; 23:10–19), so that all social interaction as the people of YHWH is framed in worship. The last portion of this section recounts God's role in the covenant as military leader and protector of the people (23:20–33), grounded in the first commandment that YHWH be their God alone (23:33; see 20:3).

Exodus 24:1–11 narrates the completion and ratification of the covenant in two rituals. Contingent upon the completion of the covenant seems to be the twofold reiteration of the people's commitment to exclusive relationship with God through keeping the covenant stipulations laid before them in the Decalogue. Following YHWH's command,

---

64. Abraham "hearkened to the voice" of another on occasion and caused his own stumbling on his journey, but his covenant was never at stake. In the conditional nature of this covenant, God presents its maintenance as dependent on this very obedience.

Moses returns to the people and lays out all the statutes and ordinances of YHWH (vv. 1–3a). They respond for the second time, again in one voice, "All the words that YHWH has said, we will do" (v. 3b; see 19:8). Moses then commits the words to writing. The following morning he presents a sacrifice of burnt offerings and reads "the book of the covenant" to all the people (vv. 4–7a). The people then respond for the third time, finally committing themselves in full, "All that YHWH has said we will do, and we will be obedient" (v. 7b). The final verses of this narrative present the two rituals by which the covenant is sealed. This likely reflects two ancient traditions of a single event, but on the narrative level we are provided with two means of covenant ritual, one with the people as a whole, and one with their representative leaders.[65] The blood of the sacrifice offered to God is dashed on all the people (v. 8), reflecting "the ancient belief that sacrificial blood has the power to bring together two parties in a sacred covenant."[66] Then Moses and the leaders of the people went up the mountain where "they beheld God, and they ate and drank" (vv. 9–11), thus giving evidence that sharing a common meal was an accepted means of sealing a covenant.

Here for the first time in the biblical narrative the human parties of a covenant with God make explicit their conscious commitment of *obedience* to YHWH, rendering them full participants, active agents, in this covenantal relationship.

The Covenant Renewal at Shechem: Joshua 24

The book of Joshua describes the conquest of Canaan, the land promised first to Abraham and then to the children of Israel at Sinai, in epic pageantry. The tribal assembly at Shechem was a covenant-making event, in terms of a renewal of the Sinai covenant, of crucial importance to the creation of a unified people. In fact, some argue that this is the most important chapter in the Bible for the history of Israel.[67] Following the covenant form outlined above, this narrative is structured as follows:

---

65. Again we see the interplay of sources combined by the narrator to form a striking final narrative.

66. Anderson, Bishop, and Newman, *Understanding the Old Testament*, 84. See Gen 15:7–21; Jer 34:18–19.

67. Ibid., 131. See above for my analysis of Joshua 24 in terms of the suzerainty treaty form. For the dialogical structure and literary unity of Joshua 24, see Giblin, "Structural Patterns."

24:1–2a	The Preamble of the Covenant Renewal
24:2b–13	Recitation of the Historical Relations between God and Israel
24:14–24	Call to Decision in Obedience and Response of Total Allegiance
24:25–28	A Ceremony Sealing the Covenant

Through this covenant-making process, the covenant at Sinai was made contemporaneous with the conquest generation. By reaffirming the Sinai covenant, the people rendered themselves personal participants in that same covenant.

Joshua 23 recounts the farewell speech of Joshua himself. Therefore, bringing the tribes together in covenant renewal to form a confederation is Joshua's final act as prophetic leader of the people of God. The final verses of Joshua, in chapter 24, recount Joshua's death and the faithfulness of Israel that he facilitated. When Joshua gathers "all the tribes of Israel to Shechem . . . before God" (v. 1) and initiates the address "Thus says YHWH" (v. 2a), he places himself in the role of prophetic messenger and spokesman for God. He then moves between the first and third persons, varying when he speaks on his own behalf and when he speaks for God.[68]

At 24:2b, Joshua begins to recite the sacred history of Israel, dwelling on God's action on Israel's behalf in the exodus and the wilderness (vv. 5–10, a summary of Exodus through Numbers), but beginning with the divine promises to the patriarchs (vv. 2b–4, a summary of Gen 12–50). The inclusion of the patriarchs could be an indication that the tribal assembly included peoples who did not take part in the exodus but did trace their kinship back to the patriarchs and thus to those covenantal promises.[69] The rehearsal of YHWH's relations with the people, all in the I-Thou pattern of God's saving action, concludes with the events of the conquest (vv. 11–13).[70] The purpose of the recitation comes in the call to decision to the current generation that follows immediately and replaces the stipulations of the secular treaty form.

Verses 14–24 are marked, as are all the covenant-making passages, by imperative and response. Joshua begins to speak on his own

---

68. Note the shift here from Exod 19–24, when God spoke directly. Following the people's plea there that Moses speak for God, to abate their fear God no longer speaks directly to his people, but is mediated by his prophets, in this case Joshua.

69. Anderson, Bishop, and Newman, *Understanding the Old Testament*, 132; Hillers, *Covenant*, 59.

70. See Mendenhall, *Law and Covenant*, 41.

behalf here, and in the two verses that make up his initial challenge (vv. 14–15) he presents five imperatives that signify the locus of this event: fear YHWH (יִרְאוּ אֶת־יְהוָה, v. 14), serve him (וְעִבְדוּ אֹתוֹ, v. 14 [twice]), put away other gods (וְהָסִירוּ אֶת־אֱלֹהִים, v. 14), and choose (בַּחֲרוּ, v. 15) YHWH as God. The first commandment of Sinai is here reiterated in terms of service. YHWH has already chosen Israel; it is now for Israel in the form of the tribal confederation to respond with their choice for YHWH. And the people do so: in vv. 16–18 they provide their initial choice of service in terms of what YHWH has done for them in the exodus. This superficial response is not enough, and Joshua emphasizes the commandment by indicating the curses that are inherent in the covenantal relationship (vv. 19–20). The people then respond a second time by offering an unqualified vow to service (v. 21), to which Joshua demands affirmation by witness, asserting for the third time the need to abide by the first commandment (vv. 22–23). The people can then give their third and final response to the call, affirming their determination to *serve* YHWH by finally also vowing their obedience: "YHWH our God we will serve, and him we will obey" (v. 24; see Exod 24:7).

It is only with the three-part response to God's offer of covenant, grounded in obedience, that the covenant renewal can be completed by way of a ceremonial ritual (vv. 25–28). The statutes and ordinances of the covenant made were written "in the book of the Torah of God" and deposited in a sanctuary to YHWH as witness to the covenant renewal (vv. 25–27). Joshua then dismisses the people to their tribal inheritances, made possible through their recommitment to the "inherited" covenant of their ancestors rendered alive and active in their own time (v. 28).

The Davidic Covenant: 2 Samuel 7

The story of David, the shepherd-turned-king of the united kingdom of Israel, spans the books of Samuel and continues into the first chapters of the books of Kings. David enters the narrative of Israel's history at 1 Samuel 16 as a boy tending his father's flock in Bethlehem, but even at the first mention of his name the reader begins to understand the powerful role he will have in the national and religious developments to come: "And Samuel took the horn of oil, and anointed him in the midst of his brothers; and the Spirit of YHWH came mightily upon David from that day forward" (v. 13). David's rise to power is swift and direct from the moment he enters public life, first as a musician in King Saul's court, then as the king's armor bearer and the champion who slays the Philistine Goliath. His special relationship with God is foreshadowed even in these early verses. By the time David becomes king (2 Sam 2), and certainly by the time of David's death (2 Kgs 2), this relationship has become one of the most complex and intricately drawn in all of Israel's Scriptures.[71] God's interaction with David takes the explicit form of a divine promise, in terms of temple and dynasty, at 2 Samuel 7.

Following Freedman's categories, the covenantal relationship that is formed between YHWH and David at 2 Samuel 7 can be understood as the final OT narrative of a covenant of divine commitment in the vein of those with Noah and Abraham.[72] As such it is unconditional and unprovoked.[73] Of these three narratives it is the most brief, yet it shows an advancement in complexity of form. David's initiative for temple building is presented as providing the impetus for God to make this covenant, rather than God's own plan for humankind. There is also no direct dialogue or interaction of any kind between God and David in this passage. Rather Nathan, God's prophetic spokesperson, serves as the intermediary of the divine promise itself. Even David's response of praise is presented as a prayer, as opposed to direct conversation. Nonetheless, God promises to bless David and his descendants in terms of their very personal relationship and lends authority to his claim for the loyalty of all the tribes.[74]

The text of 2 Samuel 7 can be divided broadly into two parts, with vv. 1–17 comprising the divine promise and vv. 18–29 making up David's prayerful response. The passage begins on a transitional note— "And it happened when the king was dwelling in his house and YHWH

---

71. For detailed exegesis of 1–2 Sam, see McCarter, *I Samuel* and *II Samuel*; and Alter, *David Story*.

72. Freedman, "Divine Commitment and Human Obligation," 421, 426. The term "covenant" is not used explicitly here, but where this event is remembered in the Psalms, the term בְּרִית does characterize the nature of this divine promise. See Pss 89 and 132.

73. As is often considered in modern scholarship, the Davidic covenant is reiterated in the Psalms as conditional (see Pss 89 and 132). Since the present study focuses on narrative, these texts will not be discussed here. For a helpful discussion of the "many repercussions in biblical literature" of the Davidic covenant, including the Psalms, see Kruse, "David's Covenant." For our purposes, it is the covenantal nature of God's relationship with David in terms of temple and dynasty and the symbolism and imagery that provides for the Fourth Evangelist that is significant, not its conditionality.

74. Matthews, *Old Testament Turning Points*, 96.

had granted him respite all around from his enemies . . ." (v. 1)—that links this to the previous chapters that established David as king and led to the ensconcing of the Ark of the Covenant in Jerusalem.[75] These first verses also introduce the theme of "dwelling" (יָשַׁב), which will run through this passage, such that the concepts of "house" and "dynasty" (the Hebrew בַּיִת in both cases) can be interwoven to make up the divine promise. In this way this episode also introduces the succession narrative that begins at 2 Samuel 9 and runs through the first chapters of 1 Kings. Thus chapter 7 along with chapter 8 provides a fulcrum to the David story that highlights his personal relationship with God and his role as God's anointed king.

The prophet Nathan enters the narrative for the first time in 2 Sam 7:2 but is quickly established as a true spokesman for God when "the word of YHWH" comes to him (v. 4) and the prophetic discourse begins with the messenger formula of "Thus says YHWH" (v. 5).[76] All of vv. 4–7 serves as a preamble of sorts to the divine promise, coming closest of all the covenants of divine commitment to part 1 of the form of the suzerainty treaty. These verses identify YHWH, David's deity, as the same God of the exodus and thus of all of the people Israel. YHWH also confirms the dwelling presence of his name in the tabernacle since the days of the Sinai covenant (vv. 6–7). Likewise, vv. 8–9a reads like the historical prologue (part 2) of the Hittite treaties. In these lines God recites the past deeds performed on David's behalf specifically, and identifies David as both a shepherd and as YHWH's chosen prince over his people Israel. The divine promise of future glory and unmatched greatness in name is outlined in vv. 9b–11, including a reaffirmation of a land for the people in which they may live in peace and security.[77] Any similarity to the suzerainty treaty form fades here as the crux of the promise, a dynasty for David (v. 11), is followed not by stipulations but rather by the assurance of the establishment of an everlasting relationship (vv. 12–16). David is promised offspring (v. 12) who will build a house for YHWH (v. 13) and whose relationship with YHWH is likened to a father-son kinship of obedience and discipline (v. 14) as well as steadfast love (חֶסֶד, v. 15) and blessing. In his role as prophet, Nathan speaks "all these words" to David (v. 17).

75. Alter, *David Story*, 231.
76. Ibid., 232.
77. Matthews, *Old Testament Turning Points*, 97.

The second part of 2 Samuel 7 begins with David entering the tent in which the Ark of the Covenant has been placed after receiving Nathan's oracle, where he "sat before YHWH" (v. 18). The verb translated here as "sat" (יָשַׁב) is identical with the verb that opened the chapter and can also indicate "to dwell," thus establishing a parallel with the first part of the chapter and reinforcing the themes of dwelling and house.[78] In a liturgical style David extols the greatness and uniqueness of God, who has made the divine presence known through his word (vv. 21–22). David then recounts God's redeeming action on Israel's behalf through the exodus, when the people were set aside in God's name (vv. 23–24). With this prayer we see a further development from the Noah and Abraham accounts, as David explicitly accepts God's covenantal promise, including the blessing and obedience that entails (vv. 25–29). Robert Alter notes that the "fondness of biblical prose for thematic key words is especially prominent in the grand theological performance that is David's prayer, in which the key words function as formal rhetorical motifs."[79] These key themes include "speaking" (through the word of promise and revelation), "house" (in terms of dynasty and the dwelling presence of God), "blessing," and "forever," all of which can be included in the covenantal discourse of the OT.

The Covenant Texts in the Prophets: Hosea, Isaiah, Jeremiah, and Ezekiel

An exegesis of each occurrence of a covenantal text in each prophet is beyond the scope of this study. The primary concern here is to bring to light the OT covenantal background of the Fourth Evangelist's particular language and symbolism. The early literary Prophets do not make much use of the actual term בְּרִית in their oracles, which could lead one to believe that the idea of covenant as the primary means by which one can understand the relationship between God and Israel was either unknown to the Prophets (i.e., not yet developed) or had been largely abandoned by them.[80] The twentieth-century research on the Hittite treaties introduced above, however, has shed new light on the broad

---

78. Alter, *David Story*, 234.
79. Ibid., 235.
80. Hillers, *Covenant*, 120.

range of the verb "to know" in international relations, which, like the covenant form, can be transferred to the religious realm of Israel, and particularly to the language and imagery of the Israelite Prophets. This language of "knowing God" also commonly appears in prophetic texts that reflect the literary pattern of the lawsuit of God, or covenant lawsuit (as seen in, e.g., Hos 4:1–3; Mic 6:1–8; and Jer 2:4–13).[81] We will follow the work Herbert Huffmon, and later Delbert Hillers, on the treaty background of the Hebrew verb "to know" (ידע), to discuss several texts that highlight this covenantal aspect, facilitating a closer look at several key prophetic uses of covenantal imagery.[82]

Herbert Huffmon was the first to demonstrate that the Hebrew verb ידע bore an additional aspect to its already broad literal and figurative range of "to perceive or understand," "to recognize or come to the knowledge of," "to distinguish good and evil or be wise," or "to know sexually."[83] Based upon his research of ancient Near Eastern treaties, Huffmon gleans an additional technical sense of "to recognize a legal relationship," "to recognize treaty stipulations as binding," or "to enter into a binding agreement."[84] He goes on to assert that both the OT covenant narratives as well as Israel's Prophets use the verb ידע in the very same senses, with the added dimension of the intimacy of the religious realm.[85]

A prime example of this covenantal usage is found in the earliest literary prophet of the OT, the eighth-century missionary to the Northern Kingdom, Amos. Speaking on behalf of God, he avows:

> Hear this word that YHWH has spoken against you, O people of Israel, against the whole family that I brought up out of the land of Egypt: You only have I known [יְדַעְתִּי] of all the families of the earth; therefore I will punish you for all your iniquities. (Amos 3:1–2)

With direct reference to the Exodus, YHWH alludes to the covenantal bond that followed at Sinai, connecting his "knowledge" of Israel with

---

81. Huffmon, "Covenant Lawsuit in the Prophets"; McCarthy, *Old Testament Covenant*, 35–40.

82. Huffmon, "Treaty Background" and "Further Note on the Treaty Background"; Hillers, *Covenant*, 120–42.

83. See Botterweck, "ידע."

84. Huffmon, "Treaty Background," 31, 33, 36.

85. Ibid., 31.

their becoming his particular people in the wilderness. The "therefore" in this passage stems from the apparent failure to acknowledge the binding covenant relationship. YHWH is thus invoking the covenantal curses. An example from Isaiah connects the failure of knowledge of God with the exile:

> Therefore my people go into exile for want of [literally, "from a wearing out of"] knowledge [דַּעַת]; their honored men are dying of hunger, and their multitude is parched with thirst. (Isa 5:13)

Huffmon again relates the "lack of knowledge" asserted here directly to a failure of Israel's covenant obligations.[86] Hillers, following Huffmon, affirms the significance of this lexical feature for the two interpretive outcomes it produces:

> The first is ... the gain in understanding [of] what the Old Testament means by "knowing God." This kind of knowledge of God is primarily unmystical and unintellectual. It is not acquired by protracted study or contemplation, or by admission to the secrets of some esoteric lore. Instead it is shown in a life of performance of God's will.... The second ... is that we see a connection between prophetic language and thought and the terminology associated with treaty relationships. Even if the word *covenant* is not prominently on display in their writings, the complex of ideas associated with covenant is present as an invisible framework, in this case forming the foundation for one of their principal concerns, the knowledge of God.[87]

The eighth-century prophet Hosea has long been associated with his use of covenant language and imagery. Although he is primarily remembered for speaking of his own marriage as a metaphor for God's covenant marriage with Israel, he also makes extensive use of the verb ידע in this same manner of pointing to the mutual covenantal obligations of YHWH and Israel. The literary work that bears Hosea's name is structured broadly in two parts. Chapters 1–3 contain the covenantal imagery of Hosea's marriage, while chapters 4–14 consist of prophetic speeches that fall into two components, each initiated by legal indictments of Israel for breach of covenant (4:1; 12:2) and concluded by the hopeful imagery of restoration (11:1–11; 14:1–7). Although much can

---

86. Ibid., 37.

87. Hillers, *Covenant*, 123–24.

be gleaned from the covenant metaphor of the first section of Hosea's work, it is the second, larger section that, building upon the covenant relationship established in the first section, is replete with imagery of knowledge and covenant obligation.[88]

The opening lines of Hosea 4 make a direct connection between knowledge of God and faithfulness to the Sinai covenant:

> Hear the word of YHWH, O people of Israel; for YHWH has a lawsuit [רִיב] against the inhabitants of the land. There is no faithfulness [truth: אֱמֶת] or loyalty [steadfast love: חֶסֶד], and no knowledge [דַּעַת] of God in the land. Swearing, lying, and murder, and stealing and adultery break out; bloodshed follows bloodshed. Therefore the land mourns, and all who live in it weaken; together with the wild animals and the birds of the air, even the fish of the sea are perishing. (Hos 4:1–3)

A full five of the Ten Commandments are mentioned, and the resulting "therefore" that connects the mourning and weakening and perishing confirms the curses of the covenant breach. Knowledge of God is the required response to God's saving act and the resulting covenant bond. "The lack of such knowledge had led to the loss of any reality in the role of being the covenant people."[89] YHWH goes on with his indictment:

> My people are destroyed for lack of knowledge; because you have rejected knowledge, I reject you from being a priest to me. And since you have forgotten the law [תּוֹרַת] of your God, I also will forget your children.... They shall eat, but not be satisfied; they shall play the whore, but not multiply; because they have forsaken YHWH to devote themselves to whoredom. Wine and new wine take away the understanding. (4:6, 10–11)

Note the cursing of the covenant-sealing action of eating and drinking as well as the removal of the covenant blessing of fertility that accompany the people's failure to remember (i.e., practice, live, "walk in") the Torah of God in the Sinai covenant.

Just what is it that YHWH requires? Hosea clarifies God's role as well as God's demands on the people as he begins to conclude his work:

---

88. For more information on the marriage bond as a symbol of God's covenant relationship with Israel, see Kruger, "Israel, the Harlot"; Mays, *Hosea*, 21–60.

89. Mays, *Hosea*, 69.

> I am YHWH your God from the land of Egypt; you know [תֵּדָע] no God but me, and besides me there is no savior. It was I who knew you [יְדַעְתִּיךָ] in the wilderness, in the land of drought. (Hos 13:4–5)

The covenant bond is intimate and exclusive, and the people's ongoing knowledge of it and walking in it will continue to be their salvation.

> I will heal their faithlessness; I will love them freely, for my anger has turned from them.... Whoever is wise, let him understand these things; whoever is discerning, let him know [וְיֵדָעֵם] them; for the ways of YHWH are right, and the upright walk in them, but transgressors stumble in them. (Hos 14:4, 9)

The seventh- and sixth-century prophets Jeremiah and Ezekiel build upon this symbolism as well as this covenantal use of the verb ידע. God's relationship with Israel was intimate, grounded in its Sinai role as God's particular people, and his demand in return was absolute fidelity.[90] Again, knowledge of God is closely related to the people's conduct as well as to their feelings, their disposition. In describing the hope for the future repentance of the people, Jeremiah reports, "I will give them a heart to know [לָדַעַת] that I am YHWH; and they shall be my people and I will be their God, for they shall return to me with their whole heart (24:7). Of course, Jeremiah's famous "new covenant" passage is probably the most telling—and the most beautiful—example of God's desire for the knowledge of the people in terms of their heart as well as their walk:

> See, the days are coming, says YHWH, when I will make a new covenant [בְּרִית חֲדָשָׁה] with the house of Israel and the house of Judah, not like the covenant [כַּבְּרִית] which I made with their fathers when I took them by the hand to bring them out of the land of Egypt, my covenant [אֶת־בְּרִיתִי] which they broke, though I was their husband, says YHWH. But this is the covenant [הַבְּרִית] which I will make with the house of Israel after those days, says YHWH: I will put my law [תּוֹרָתִי] within them, and I will write it upon their hearts; and I will be their God, and they shall be my people. And no longer shall each man teach his neighbor and each his brother, saying, "Know YHWH [דְּעוּ אֶת־יְהוָה]," for they shall all know me [יֵדְעוּ אוֹתִי], from the least of them to the greatest, says YHWH; for I will forgive their iniquity, and I will remember their sin no more. (Jer 31:31–34)

---

90. Heschel, *Prophets*, 59–60.

What is particularly striking about this passage is not just the connection between knowing God and living in covenant with God, but the direct identification of the Sinai covenant with knowledge of God as well as the promise of a new covenant, built upon the old, which will be expressed and lived in a distinctive way.

The prophet Ezekiel is a unique witness among the classical prophets, for he is a prophet of the exile. Expelled from his home in the first wave of deportations of 597 BC, this Judean priest was called by God in Babylon to speak first of the coming final devastation, then of the hope for coming restoration. In this vein Ezekiel understands the knowledge of God to be fundamental to understanding both God's covenantal relationship with Israel as well as God's plan for its future. In fact, he uses a form of the phrase "[they] shall know that I am YHWH" (וְיָדְעוּ כִּי־אֲנִי יְהוָה) some sixty-two times in the work that bears his name, in prophesying both cursing and blessing upon Israel for her covenantal obligation to God. Through Ezekiel, God tells of the coming curse of the exile for Israel's covenant breach:

> And *they shall know that I am YHWH*, when I disperse them among the nations and scatter them through the countries. But I will let a few of them escape from the sword, from famine and pestilence, that they may confess all their abominations among the nations where they go, and *may know that I am YHWH*. (Ezek 12:15–16; emphasis added)

Yet, when the foretold destruction comes to pass and the exile has brought the fullness of Israel's knowledge to bear, Ezekiel's prophecy turns to peace and hope. YHWH then begins to characterize himself as the good shepherd of his scattered people:

> I myself will be the shepherd of my sheep, and I will make them lie down, says the Lord YHWH. I will seek the lost, and I will bring back the strayed, and I will bind up the crippled, and I will strengthen the weak, and the fat and the strong I will watch over; I will feed them in justice. (Ezek 34:15–16)

The intimacy of God's covenantal relationship with Israel remains integral in this new image, and the knowledge of God is still the fundamental manner by which covenantal obligations are both lived and expressed. The shepherding of the lost and scattered people will enable YHWH to establish his covenant anew, again in a distinctive way:

> I will make with them a covenant of peace [בְּרִית שָׁלוֹם] and banish wild beasts from the land, so that they may dwell securely in the wilderness and sleep in the woods. And I will make them and the places round about my hill a blessing; and I will send down the showers in their season; they shall be showers of blessing. And the trees of the field shall yield their fruit, and the earth shall yield its increase, and they shall be secure in their land; and *they shall know that I am YHWH*, when I break the bars of their yoke, and deliver them from the hand of those who enslaved them . . . and none shall make them afraid. And I will provide for them prosperous plantations so that they shall no more be consumed with hunger in the land, and no longer suffer the reproach of the nations. And *they shall know that I, YHWH their God, am with them*, and that they, the house of Israel, are my people, says the Lord YHWH. And you are my sheep, the sheep of my pasture, and I am your God, says the Lord YHWH. (Ezek 34:25–31; emphasis added)

Like Jeremiah before him, Ezekiel believed the covenant that God will establish with his people in the future will have a distinctive character, yet be built solidly upon the old. This "new" covenant of "peace" will encompass both the action and the very being of those counted among his sheep, yet remain lived intimately in the knowledge of God.

In addition to this usage by the Prophets of the verb "to know" (ידע) as the language of the OT covenant metaphor, a survey of the prophetic texts also reveals that the concept of "truth" informs the symbolic language of the covenant relationship between God and Israel. Forms of the term אֱמֶת are found throughout the prophetic literature to signify the origin and nature of this relationship as well as the fidelity inherent in maintaining it.

"Truth" is the language of the basis of God's covenant. Through the prophet Jeremiah, God recounts the establishment of the covenant. "For I planted you as a choice vine, from the seed of truth (אֱמֶת, Jer 2:21). "Truth" is also the language of living in covenant relationship with God. Through the prophet Zechariah, YHWH commands the people: "Render true judgments [אֱמֶת מִשְׁפָּט], show kindness and mercy [וְחֶסֶד וְרַחֲמִים] to one another, do not oppress the widow, the orphan, the alien, or the poor; and do not devise evil in your hearts against one another" (Zech 7:9–10; see also 8:16–17). Likewise, YHWH commands the people to express their worship with the simple command, "Love truth and peace" (וְהָאֱמֶת וְהַשָּׁלוֹם אֱהָבוּ, Zech 8:19). The covenant of life that YHWH gives those to whom he has chosen is described in Malachi in these terms of faithfulness:

> My covenant with him was a covenant of life and well-being [בְּרִיתִי הָיְתָה אִתּוֹ הַחַיִּים], which I gave him; this called for reverence, and he revered me and stood in awe of my name. True instruction [תּוֹרַת אֱמֶת] was in his mouth, and no wrong was found on his lips. He walked with me in integrity and uprightness, and he turned many from iniquity. (Mal 2:5–6)

The Prophets also teach that the lack of truth is tantamount to a breach of covenant with YHWH. Hosea couples the lack of truth with the lack of knowledge in bringing the covenant lawsuit against Israel: "Hear the word of YHWH, O people of Israel; for YHWH has an indictment against the inhabitants of the land. There is no faithfulness or loyalty [אֵין־אֱמֶת וְאֵין־חֶסֶד], and no knowledge of God in the land" (Hos 4:1). The prophet Isaiah likewise describes life in the land of Israel in breach of covenant as the failure of truth: "Justice is turned back, and righteousness stands at a distance; for truth stumbles in the public square [כִּי־כָשְׁלָה בָרְחוֹב אֱמֶת], and uprightness cannot enter. Truth is lacking [הָאֱמֶת נֶעְדֶּרֶת], and whoever turns from evil is despoiled" (Isa 59:14–15; see also 48:1). The failure, even death, of truth is also a fundamental component of Jeremiah's characterization of the breach of covenant. YHWH has Jeremiah say to the people, "This is the nation that did not obey the voice of YHWH their God, and did not accept discipline. Truth has perished [אָבְדָה הָאֱמוּנָה], it is cut off from their lips (Jer 7:28; see also 5:1–3; 9:3–5).

Finally, the Prophets also incorporate the language of truth into their message of restoration and covenant renewal that will follow the people's repentance and recommitment to their relationship with YHWH. Through the prophet Jeremiah, YHWH speaks of the blessing of the restoration of the covenant:

> If you return, O Israel, says YHWH, if you return to me, if you remove your abominations from my presence, and do not waver, and if you swear, "As YHWH lives!" in truth [אֱמֶת], in justice, and in uprightness, then nations shall be blessed by him, and by him they shall boast. (Jer 4:1–2)

The prophet Isaiah likewise characterizes the repentant remnant of Israel as restoring its covenant relationship to YHWH in truth: "On that day the remnant of Israel and the survivors of the house of Jacob will no more lean on the one who struck them, but will lean on YHWH, the Holy One of Israel, in truth" (בֶּאֱמֶת, Isa 10:20; see also 43:9). Isaiah summarizes both the character of God and the character of the new covenant with the restored Israel in this concept of faithfulness and truth. This is the blessing of living with God in covenant love, knowledge, and fidelity:

> Then whoever invokes a blessing in the land shall bless by the God of truth, and whoever takes an oath in the land shall swear by the God of truth; because the former troubles are forgotten and are hidden from my sight. (Isa 65:16)

The Covenant Renewal at Jerusalem: Nehemiah 8–10

Nehemiah 8 records that Ezra read a book of the Law in the hearing of all Jerusalem. This could be the first reading of the Torah as we now have it.[91] Most importantly, Nehemiah 10 recounts that Ezra organized a formal ratification of the covenant of Moses after the Feast of Tabernacles. Later Jewish tradition considered Ezra a second Moses, attributing the definitive editing of the Torah to him. For this reason, these chapters warrant a closer look, since they provide the most contemporaneous covenant renewal tradition to the Fourth Evangelist's own time and place.[92]

Ezra-Nehemiah is the biblical account of the promised postexilic return and restoration. It can be broadly structured in three parts: the introductory edict of return and response (Ezra 1); the fullness of Israel's response and restoration (Ezra 2—Neh 7); and the celebration of reconstruction and restoration (Neh 8–13). The large second section can be further structured as a three-stage response, framed by lists of returnees (Ezra 2 and Neh 7). The first stage presents the

---

91. Myers, *Ezra-Nehemiah*, lix. For an exegesis of Neh 8–10, see also Blenkinsopp, *Ezra-Nehemiah*, 282–319; Throntveit, *Ezra-Nehemiah*, 96–111; Williamson, *Ezra, Nehemiah*, 277–340.

92. Dating the composition of the final form of Ezra-Nehemiah is difficult, but a strong consensus points to ca. 400 BC. See Myers, *Ezra-Nehemiah*, lviii–lxxi. Although the canonical status of the Hebrew Bible in general was still in process at the time of the Fourth Evangelist, and the Writings in particular were in flux with regard to their being understood as "Scripture," the oral tradition of the Ezra-Nehemiah narrative would have been in circulation in first-century Palestine.

reconstruction of the temple (Ezra 3–6), the second recounts the mission of Ezra and the initial formation of the community according to Torah (Ezra 7–10), and the third stage completes the reconstruction of Jerusalem under the leadership of Nehemiah (Neh 1–6). Nehemiah 8–13 narrates the celebration of this restoration, with Nehemiah 8–10 focusing on the reading of the Torah and the people's recommitment to covenant with God.

Restoration culminates in the momentous event of reading and implementing the Torah in Nehemiah 8, thus paralleling the events at Sinai (Exod 19–24) with regard to the formation of the community as the people of God. All the people gathered and "told the scribe Ezra to bring the book of the Torah of Moses, which YHWH had given Israel" (v. 1b). The initiative of the people is presented as the impetus behind the reading and renewal, thus indicating that the "book of the Torah" is understood as the document of the covenant with God. Accordingly, all the people rise when Ezra opens the book in veneration of God's presence in the book itself (v. 5). The narrative is careful to assert the people's full understanding of the Torah they heard (v. 8), as well as their verbal assent to the blessing of God (v. 6). The people then eat and drink in rejoicing "because they understood the words" (v. 12). The Torah is then implemented in the celebration of the Festival of Tabernacles as prescribed for that time (vv. 13–18).

Nehemiah 9–10 then presents the covenant renewal itself in terms of confession (Neh 9) and commitment (Neh 10). After the eating and drinking that signified their joy in chapter 8, the people turn to fasting for the preparation of the spirit (9:1–5). The communal prayer that provides the forum for confession recites the historical experience of Israel as the people of God. Verses 7–31 provide a summary of the traditions preserved from Genesis through the exile, with particular emphasis on the Exodus and Sinai traditions of covenant (vv. 9–23), all in the form of a prayer. The people acknowledge the steadfast love of God (חֶסֶד) as the integral component of his covenant-keeping character (הָאֵל הַגָּדוֹל הַגִּבּוֹר וְהַנּוֹרָא שׁוֹמֵר הַבְּרִית) in their climactic plea for continued protection in relationship (v. 32; see vv. 32–37). The people then close their prayer by confirming their commitment to covenant renewal with God in writing (v. 38). The document is affirmed by signatories on behalf of the entire people (10:1–27), and the communal pledge of commitment reflects the stipulations of covenantal behavior that the people take upon themselves (10:28–39).

Two notable points arise from this account of postexilic covenant renewal. The first is that, although resonances of covenant-making forms are present throughout the narrative—including public reading, recitation of the historical relationship between God and his people, a form of stipulations (in terms of voluntary obligation), and witness to the seal of the covenant—on the whole this covenant renewal narrative does not follow a form we have seen before in the biblical narrative. The second point is correlative to the first: in this case the entire impetus for renewal is the motivation of the people. God is not an active agent in this account. We have come to the opposite extreme from the Noachic covenant where Noah was the silent responder to God's directive for action. Here the people of Israel take on the full role of renewal instigator, bearing all the consequences of their decision and actions. They do all the talking. As a people they have long ago been "chosen," God's presence is a given, and God's covenant-making and covenant-keeping character of love and loyalty in relationship is well known. What has been missing through the exile is the people's obedient response in action to the covenantal promises of Torah. This is the situation that is remedied in Nehemiah 8–10.

Conclusion: Characteristics of the Old Testament Covenant Relationship

Through this literary reading of the covenantal narrative preserved in the OT, five fundamental characteristics of the essence of biblical covenant texts and the covenantal relationship these texts emanate can be articulated. The first and most fundamental characteristic is the aspect of *chosenness*.[93] In the biblical narratives of God's covenantal interaction with humankind, God is always the primary agent: God determines to make the covenant, and God chooses the person or people through whom he will implement his plan for creation. Further, the allegiance

---

93. I am deliberately avoiding use of the term "election" here in favor of "chosenness." Essentially, the biblical narrative asserts the sovereignty of God and his will to choose those human beings through whom God will carry out his plan for creation. The so-called doctrine of election is developed in the OT particularly in Deuteronomy. See esp. Weinfeld, *Deuteronomy 1–11*, 60–62.

to which God calls those covenant participants is always exclusive. Whether the covenant text is a narrative of divine commitment or of human obligation, God is the one who initiates the covenantal activity and the human participants are those chosen. Even in the later covenant renewals, especially Nehemiah 8–10 where God does not play an active role, the people respond to and make alive and current their ancestral experience of this chosenness. These renewals reinforce the continual call and response dynamic (i.e., choice for God) inherent in the relationship.[94]

The second element characteristic of the OT covenant relationship is the offer of *covenantal promises*. Those chosen by God to participate in covenant relationship are made promises as part and parcel of establishing that particular obligation. In the earlier (in terms of biblical chronology) covenants of divine commitment (Noah: Gen 6–9; Abraham: Gen 12–22), God's promises are straightforward and direct. Yet, even in the covenants of human obligation, where the promises are conditional and couched formulaically in terms of blessing and cursing, the primary covenantal benefit to the human participants is the promise of becoming, remaining, or renewing their role as God's "particular people" or "treasured possession."[95] The covenant is the act of sealing the promise and accepting these mutual roles.

The third characteristic that manifests from a literary rehearsal of the biblical narrative is the corollary human response to the first two characteristic covenantal moves on God's part: *covenantal obedience in action*. In the narratives of Noah and Abraham, it is not necessary for the chosen recipients of God's covenantal promises to speak to— to interact with—God in any way; they must simply act in accordance with God's imperative. Beginning with Abraham, however, as we move through biblical history, the human response becomes more complex as the human relationship with God develops. The response shifts from the physical alone to both the physical and the spiritual, as indicated by verbal interaction with God. Humankind's disposition before God and in relationship with God becomes more significant as the world it inhabits becomes more complex. By the end of the OT covenant history (Neh 8–10, and evidenced in the book of Daniel), the human response effectively takes the lead role in the covenant narrative over from God's

---

94. See Nicholson, *God and His People*, 147–48.
95. Ibid., 210.

initiating activity. In every chapter of this narrative, however, the fundamental quality of the response remains the same: obedience. Ultimately, as long as "the community is obedient to [the covenant] terms, the relationship will be maintained and the blessings associated with the covenant will be provided."[96] Full, unmediated obedience to God's imperative, be it physical or a complex integration of the physical and the spiritual/verbal, is demanded both to establish and to renew covenantal relationship with God.

The first three articulated characteristics of the OT covenant relationship each build upon the former to establish the relationship itself. Taken together, these three characteristics and the resultant relationship they form make possible the fourth characteristic: *the abiding presence of God* in creation and in the midst of human life. In the covenants of divine commitment, Noah and Abraham both built altars as loci for encountering and worshiping YHWH at crucial points in the unveiling and fulfilling of covenantal promises (see Gen 8:20; 12:7, 8; 13:18; 22:9). The covenantal law ensuing from the first covenant of human obligation, the Sinai treaty (Exodus 19–24), demanded the construction of the tabernacle as the dwelling place for God in the people's midst. God gives the people the command, "And let them make me a sanctuary, that I may dwell in their midst" (25:8). From upon that mercy seat, says God, "There I will meet with you" (25:22). The foremost benefit of the covenant is the binding relationship that facilitates YHWH's presence.[97] This *shekinah*, or dwelling presence, of God in the midst of his covenanted people becomes of primary concern from this point forward, and in the days of Solomon results in the construction of the temple that becomes the focus of Israelite worship. Alongside the recommitment of the people in obedient relationship, the very impetus behind the covenant renewal ceremonies in the days of Joshua (Josh 24) and Ezra (Neh 8–10) is ensuring this presence of God.

Articulating the final characteristic of the OT covenant relationship in many ways brings us to the purpose of the entire activity: making God known in creation. The fifth basic characteristic is the *knowledge of God*. As evidenced in the overview above, it is the prophets to whom we

---

96. Freedman, "Divine Commitment and Human Obligation," 428. He goes on to note that "at stipulated intervals (every seven years, according to Deut 31:9–13) the people of Israel will renew their pledge of obedience."

97. McKenzie, *Covenant*, 50–51.

are indebted for bringing this aspect of the covenantal relationship into focus. The covenant as articulated in the promises of God establishes the manner by which God knows his chosen people and, as articulated in the stipulations of the Ten Commandments, establishes the manner by which those same people may know God. This knowledge (דַּעַת) includes understanding God's binding loyalty (in terms of steadfast love, חֶסֶד) and faithfulness (in terms of truth, אֱמֶת) in kinship with his people (see Hos 4:1–3).[98] The flourishing of this knowledge of God made possible through the dynamic of daily living in covenantal obedience breathes life into the relationship between God and his people. Likewise, however, the failure or wearing out of this knowledge (see Isa 5:13) threatens the very existence of the covenantal relationship, and thereby the existence of the people of God. To live in the truth of the love and knowledge of God, then, is the fundamental purpose and the overarching hope of the OT covenant relationship.

The themes gleaned from a narrative review of the OT covenant texts provide the language used to articulate this hope and its resulting lived experience in the literary expression of this covenantal relationship between God and humankind. The language of knowledge, love, truth, and familial kinship in the context of Israel's Scripture is thus the language of covenant. The OT covenantal texts and the celebrations that recall God's covenantal and saving action in the past and render that action present in the current community provide the symbolism for ongoing use of the covenant metaphor. It is from this rich storehouse that the Fourth Evangelist could draw to express his story of Jesus as the revelation of God's new covenant activity in creation on behalf of humankind, the children of God.

---

98. See Cross, *Epic to Canon*, 3–20; de Menezes, *Voices from Beyond*, 110–13.

3

John and Scripture

Beginnings and Endings

IN HER WORK ON BEGINNINGS AND ENDINGS IN NT NARRATIVE, MORNA Hooker notes that there is "frequently a literary and thematic connection between the beginning and end of a composition. Tidy endings often take us back to where we began: a skilful use of what the literary critics call *inclusio* reminds us that it was, after all, the writer's purpose all along to lead us to precisely this point."[1] Through a focus on his own choice of beginnings and endings, the Fourth Evangelist's understanding of Scripture and his role in writing Scripture in light of the Christ event will be established in this chapter. The spotlight will rest upon the prologue (1:1–18) as well as the ending of the body of the Gospel (20:30–31). Based upon the established speech-action nature of the Gospel, John the Baptist's role in 1:19–34 will then serve as the first dialogical study as the prologue is embodied in this crucial character.

The Structure of the Gospel

A first step toward a closer examination of this Gospel narrative is to assess the basic structure of its plot. The almost universal approach to structuring the Gospel according to John nowadays is first to note four fundamental components.[2] A prologue (1:1–18) is followed by the body of the Gospel, which is presented in two sections: the public ministry

---

1. Hooker, *Endings*, 3. See also Hooker, *Beginnings*.
2. An alternative approach in contemporary scholarship views the Gospel in its entirety as one large chiasm or series of chiasms. See Ellis, *Genius of John*; and Mlakuzhyil, *Christocentric Literary Structure*. One must beware of pan-chiastic scholarship, however. See Lund, *Chiasmus in the New Testament*. People probably did speak, write, and think in chiasms, but John does not necessarily respond to the rigors of this form across the book.

of Jesus, commonly referred to as the Book of Signs (1:19—12:50); and the departure of Jesus, which includes a last discourse, the passion, and post-resurrection appearances, commonly referred to as the Book of Glory (13:1—20:31). The conclusion to the body of the Gospel is then followed by an epilogue (21:1-25).[3] In order to arrive at this roadmap for entering the narrative world of the Fourth Gospel, we look for textual markers that serve as signposts along the way. The prologue (1:1-18) provides the clear words of an insider—the infallible narrator who communicates to the readers everything they need to know to begin the Gospel. John 1:19 starts the story itself, yet at 13:1 something different happens. Readers are provided at 13:1 almost a new prologue to the period of private ministry and departure that flows through to 20:29, with the final verses (20:30-31) serving as a conclusion to the body of the Gospel—a first ending. But then we read John 21. No extant manuscripts appear without it, so it is not an addendum in any secondary sense. Any analysis of the final form of the Gospel must incorporate the narrative of John 21 as an integral component of this story that looks to the future of the community formed by the narrative.

In John 1:1—20:31 the evangelist gives a very powerful and cohesive narrative to show the reader how a community is to survive. John leaves a history in the absence of Jesus ("Come and see;" "Blessed are those who have not seen and yet have come to believe" [1:39; 20:29]). If, as will be established in the following section, the evangelist understood himself to be writing Scripture (γραφή, see 20:9-10, 30-31), then this book is aimed at readers who have not seen and yet believe that they may be summoned to belief and go on believing. In John 21 the evangelist provides a continuation of the community and a sign for how it is to go on. The epilogue provides a basis for leadership, institutionalization, and the church that is not addressed in chapters 1-20. The fishing expedition and the dialogue between Jesus and Peter provide the models for the church, the pastor, and the witness, for all who believe for all time.

---

3. For detailed exposition of this basic structure, see Brown, *John*, cxxxviii–cxlvi. For a slightly different plot mapping built upon the journey motif in the Gospel, see Segovia, "Journey(s) of the Word."

John as Evangelist and Writer of Scripture

That John is an evangelist is undisputed. He has written a Gospel to proclaim his understanding of the good news of the Christ event. To say that John is a writer of Scripture is a separate claim. The Gospel of John has achieved canonical status in the Christian tradition and is accepted as Scripture by practicing Christians universally. Delineation as "canonical" thus presumes scriptural status. The term "Scripture" delineates "texts that are revered as especially sacred and authoritative."[4] The term "canon" denotes the delimitation of such texts. Therefore, the Fourth Evangelist is also rightly understood as a writer of Scripture. To posit that this evangelist *understood himself* to be writing Scripture, however, is another matter altogether. Yet it is this assertion that is fundamental to the thesis that the evangelist used the covenant metaphor as the literary and theological fabric of his version of the good news.

Biblical scholarship has generally taken the position that the NT authors did not think of themselves as writers of Scripture, claiming the occasional nature of these documents to be prohibitive of any sort of "sacred and authoritative" import to their compositional design.[5] Dwight Moody Smith, however, has sought to re-open this discussion particularly with regard to the Gospel narratives.[6] Smith notes the following by way of introduction:

> Significantly, "canon" (κανών) is not used of sacred writings in the NT, but "scripture" (γραφή) of course is. In most, but not all, cases, "scripture" refers to what Christians call the Old Testament. The existence of scripture as well as canon implies the existence of a religious community that accords status and authority to certain texts. It goes without saying that the community in question believes that such status and authority actually belong to, adhere in, the text because of its subject matter, God in relation to human beings.[7]

---

4. Graham, "Scripture," 33.

5. See, e.g., von Campenhausen, *Formation of the Christian Bible*, 122.

6. See the publication of his 1999 presidential address to the Society of Biblical Literature: Smith, "Gospels Become Scripture." For further discussion of the intertestamental period and the writing of Scripture, see Obermann, *Christologische Erfüllung*, 409–22.

7. Smith, "Gospels Become Scripture," 4.

Smith goes on to argue the case for the Synoptic evangelists as self-conscious writers of Scripture, though he does not find himself able to make as strong a claim for the Fourth Evangelist.[8] He does, however, assert:

> John continues to go its separate way, rooted in the ancient biblical narrative but affirming in ways different from Matthew and Luke that the narrative comes to a theological climax and end with Jesus. Jesus' τετέλεσται from the cross means that the narrative is finished as well.[9]

John's Gospel is indeed "rooted in the ancient biblical narrative."[10] Further, the evangelist gives evidence within his story, both grammatically and symbolically, that he understands himself to be recording the next segment of the biblical narrative, i.e., to be writing Scripture. Through his recent narrative analysis that builds on Smith's suggestions, Francis J. Moloney argues that the Fourth Evangelist "brings *the biblical narrative* to an end" for the subsequent Johannine tradition through this Gospel and thereby lays "explicit claim to be writing γραφή."[11] In what follows we will briefly discuss Moloney's thesis and suggest how these claims form the basis for the present study of the evangelist's literary motif of covenant fulfillment and completion.[12]

Fulfillment Language and the Composition of Scripture

In the first half of the Gospel, seven direct citations from the OT appear, each in correlation with a revelatory moment in Jesus' public ministry. As Jesus labors in dialogue with "the Jews" openly (ἐν παρρεσία; see, e.g., 7:4) throughout his public ministry, these citations serve to estab-

---

8. Ibid., 7–15.

9. Ibid., 14.

10. For a sample of more detailed studies of the interrelationship of the Gospel of John and the narrative of the OT, see, e.g., Barrett, "Old Testament"; Hanson, *Prophetic Gospel*; Manns, *Jean*; Westermann, *John*.

11. Moloney, "Gospel of John as Scripture," 456.

12. In his article, Moloney acknowledges the substantial influence of several foundational studies, including Obermann, *Christologische Erfüllung*; and Faure, "Alttestamentlichen Zitate." For more recent work, he further points to Klauck, "Geschrieben, erfüllt, vollendet"; Labahn, "Jesus und die Autorität"; Scholtissek, "'Geschrieben in diesem Buch."

lish who Jesus is—within the scope of the biblical narrative.[13] They are provided either without introduction, or following some form of the verbal expression ἐστίν γεγραμμένον. In 1:23 (with no introduction), John the Baptist suggests that Jesus is Lord. In 2:17, the disciples remember Scripture (with introduction) as it points to the body of Jesus as the temple. In 6:31 and 6:45, Scripture is used (with introduction) by both "the Jews" and Jesus in the context of his claim to be the living bread. In 10:34 (with introduction), Jesus refers to Scripture in establishing his claim to be Son of God.[14] In 12:13 (without introduction) and 12:15 (with introduction) the narrator provides the scriptural basis for the acclamation of the kingship of Jesus. However, with the arrival of "the Greeks" in Jerusalem and their request to see Jesus (12:20–22), and amid rising discontent, Jesus announces that "the hour" that has been drawing ever nearer since the advent of his ministry (2:5) "has come for the Son of Man to be glorified" (12:23). With the arrival of the hour of Jesus' glorification, his imminent crucifixion comes to the fore of the narrative.[15] He begins to close his open teaching by proclaiming, "Now is the judgment of this world. . . . And I, when I am lifted up from the earth, will draw all people to myself" (12:31–32). The narrator affirms, "He said this to show by what death he was to die" (12:33), and this manner of grounding the gospel story in the scriptural narrative likewise draws to a close.

As Jesus turns toward the cross, the evangelist turns to specific fulfillment language in terms of Scripture to elucidate his actions. Jesus departs from the crowds, and the reader is told explicitly for the first time that their unbelief, which would result in his being lifted up, was so "that the word of the prophet Isaiah might be fulfilled" (ἵνα ὁ λόγος Ἡσαΐου τοῦ προφήτου πληρωθῇ, 12:38–40). The narrator then claims that the two statements of Isaiah recounted here (see Isa 53:1; 6:10) were uttered

---

13. Again, the term "the Jews" is enclosed in quotation marks in this study to indicate that the evangelist uses the term primarily to refer to the christological opponents of Jesus rather than to a distinct ethnic group.

14. In this same discourse, Jesus confirms that "the Scripture cannot be broken" (οὐν δύναται λυθῆναι ἡ γραφή, 10:45), a remarkable statement given his revelatory proclamation of current action in history through him.

15. Moloney, "Gospel of John as Scripture," 458. For more on the "hour" of the Son of Man, see Moloney, *Johannine Son of Man*, 161–85. Regarding Moloney's correlation of the lifting up on the cross and the revelation of the glory of God, see Moloney, "Telling God's Story."

initially by the prophet because he saw the glory of Jesus (12:41). Thus the evangelist begins a pattern that will intensify across the second half of the Gospel which points to the relationship between the cross of Jesus and the fulfillment of Scripture. Five further citations from the OT occur in the narrative, each of them reinforcing the fulfillment of Scripture. In the midst of Jesus' last discourse (John 13–17), Judas's betrayal comes to pass "that the Scripture may be fulfilled (ἵνα ἡ γραφὴ πληρωθῇ, 13:18), prompting Jesus to explain that the hatred meted out against him "is to fulfill the word that is written in their law" (ἵνα πληρωθῇ ὁ λόγος ἐν τῷ νόμῳ αὐτῶν γεγραμμένος, 15:25). Fulfillment language intensifies through the passion narrative (John 18–19), and three times during the crucifixion scene OT Scripture is quoted in terms of fulfillment in Jesus' being lifted up (as a king on a cross in 19:24; as the Passover lamb in 19:36; and as the one pierced in 19:37). This fulfillment process climaxes at the moment of Jesus' death through a passage based on Ps 69:21 (Ps 68:22 LXX) and a shift in word choice that emphasizes the teleological moment of the glorification of God. "After this, when Jesus knew that all was now finished [ὅτι ἤδη πάντα τετέλεσται], in order that the Scripture might be fulfilled [ἵνα τελειωθῇ ἡ γραφή], he said, 'I thirst' . . . When Jesus had received the wine, he said, 'It is finished' [τετέλεσται]. Then he bowed his head and gave up his spirit" (19:28–30). The verbs τελέω and τελειόω denote "to fulfill, perfect, bring to final accomplishment."[16] Thus, through the life and death of Jesus Christ, the λόγος (12:38; 15:35) / γραφή (13:18; 19:24, 28, 36) of the OT "not only continues to be narrated in the Gospel of John; it comes to its completion, its fulfillment, its τέλος as the promise of Jesus' words is fulfilled."[17] Moloney goes on to discuss the further fulfillment language, notably where Jesus' own word (λόγος) is fulfilled, thereby further correlating the very word of Jesus with Scripture (17:12, 18:9, 32). Jesus is the word of God (1:1–2) made flesh (1:14–18) who continues to utter the word of God, coalescing with ἡ γραφή such that by his death Scripture is fulfilled.[18]

The final movement in this claim that the writer of the Gospel of John understood himself to be writing Scripture focuses on the further

---

16. BDAG, s.vv. τελέω, τελειόω. See also Moloney, "Gospel of John as Scripture," 459.

17. Ibid., 460. See also Obermann, *Christologische Erfüllung*, 325–30, 350–64.

18. Moloney, "Gospel of John as Scripture," 460–62.

Johannine uses of ἡ γραφή.[19] On three occasions, the term occurs in the discourses of Jesus as he affirms the Jewish Scriptures (5:39; 7:38; 10:35). On only one occasion is the term found in the mouth of others, where the people rightly interpret Scripture but fail to see that Jesus fulfills the promise of the Christ of which they speak (7:42). The final two occurrences of ἡ γραφή appear in information recounted by the narrator and, in large part, serve to frame the body of the Gospel narrative (2:22, 20:9). Both instances concern the disciples and their developing knowledge of Jesus as the Christ and his word as Scripture that comes to completion only after the resurrection.[20] Taken together, this frame reinforces the proposal that this author regarded his story of Jesus as the fulfillment of Scripture; and the Scripture that is written to perfect this knowledge shared by the initial disciples and handed on to all future generations is this very Gospel.

Recent scholarship on the Fourth Evangelist's self-understanding as an author of Scripture is crucial to the present study because it provides a response to the *why* question: if, as this study intends to show, the evangelist made use of the OT covenant metaphor as a guiding narrative motif evinced through both symbolism and dialogue, why would he do so? What would be the purpose of such a literary technique? The answer lies in this established mission not only to continue the biblical story but, further, to bring it to an end, even its τέλος, through his γραφή of the narrative of Jesus Christ. Since, as discussed in the preceding chapter, the metaphor of covenant is the primary concept that characterizes and unifies OT literature and particularly the biblical *narrative* of Israel, God's covenantal relationship with creation in general and the children of God in particular (see 1:12) is the fundamental means by which the evangelist can resonate the word of Scripture and the Johannine community can be drawn into the sacred narrative of that Scripture. In the culmination of his argument, Moloney asserts:

> The use of "fulfillment" language in the second half of the Gospel, culminating in 19:28–30, shows that the author claims to have brought the story of Israel's Scripture to an end. As this

---

19. Ibid., 463–66.

20. For more detail on this sort of reading of John 2:22, see Moloney, "Reading John 2:13–22." For a like-minded assessment of John 20:9 and greater detail on John 20 in general, see Byrne, "Faith of the Beloved Disciple." This study stands counter to the negative assessment put forth in O'Brien, "Written That You May Believe."

is the case, the story the evangelist tells, heard and read by later generations, is ἡ γραφή: the completion of Israel's Scripture. Indeed, as he closes his Gospel account, he tells all who have heard and read the Scripture of the Johannine Gospel that it has been *written* precisely for that purpose (20:30–31).[21]

It is to a closer look at the conclusion to the body of the Gospel that we now turn.

Endings: The Conclusion of the Body of the Gospel (20:30–31)

Chapter 20 of John's Gospel begins to bring his story to a close with several accounts of appearances of the resurrected Jesus. Given the evangelist's understanding of the "lifting up" of Jesus through his crucifixion (3:14; 8:28; 12:32) as the ultimate glorification that "finishes" his mission in the world (19:30), one might wonder at the necessity for explicit resurrection encounters; but the evangelist is concerned to continue to fulfill the word that Jesus spoke during his earthly ministry.[22] Through his interactions with the disciples in 20:1–29, Jesus fulfills his promises to return to them (14:18–19; 16:16); and they are able to begin to understand the Scripture of the word of Jesus about the raising of the temple of his body (2:19–22). As the journey of the disciples begins to reach its τέλος, the evangelist, as author, can then turn to the readers to bring them to their own cruces of faith decision.

The vast majority of scholars posit John 20:30–31 as the conclusion to the body of the Gospel, with John 21 following as an epilogue.[23] In these verses the evangelist provides his philosophy of writing (v. 30) and the purpose of what he has written (v. 31):

---

21. Moloney, "Gospel of John as Scripture," 466.

22. Hooker, *Endings*, 68. For a brief discussion of potential sources for John 20 and its literary relationship to the Synoptic resurrection accounts, see Lindars, "Composition of John 20."

23. See, e.g., Carson, *John*, 660–63; Lagrange, *Saint Jean*, 520; Moloney, *John* 542–44. For a discussion of the possibility that these verses constituted the original conclusion to the Gospel as a whole, with John 21 a later appendix, see Brown, *John*, 2:1057–61. For a modern commentator who does not discuss 20:30–31 in terms of a conclusion, see Hoskyns, *Fourth Gospel*, 550. For an alternative view, that 20:30–31 forms the opening frame of a larger conclusion movement, see Segovia, "Final Farewell of Jesus."

> Of course Jesus also did many other signs in the presence of his disciples that have not been written in this book; but these are written that you may go on believing that Jesus is the Christ, the Son of God, and that by believing you may have life in his name.[24]

In v. 30, the narrator shares with the reader that the telling of the activity that signifies who Jesus is was not exhausted by his story. Rather, the evangelist has chosen from the wealth of traditions about Jesus in crafting his narrative. Here he uses his preferred term for Jesus' miraculous activity, σημεῖα, "signs." The choice of this term is particularly pointed for the signifying role this activity carries throughout the Gospel. The term also resonates with the evangelist's intended readers as it harks back to the "signs" of Moses on behalf of YHWH during the exodus narrative (Exod 4:8, 9, 17, 28, 30; 7:3; 10:1, 2), as well as YHWH's own action to signify his glory in the Sinai wilderness (Num 14:11, 22; Deut 4:34; 6:22; 7:19; 11:3; 16:38; 26:8; 29:3; 31:13, 17; 34:11).[25] In v. 31, he confirms that this was done not only for literary but also for theological purposes.

At this crucial moment, the evangelist returns to his focus on γραφή. He confirms his purpose in terms of what "is written" (γέγραπται). New Testament Greek scholar Daniel Wallace notes: "This common introductory formula to OT quotations seems to be used to emphasize that the written word still exists. Although just beyond the reach of grammar, the exegetical and theological significance of this seems to be ... that of present and binding authority."[26] In a footnote, Wallace pointedly explains that "γέγραπται is used ethically and eschatologically. That is, it introduces both commands that are still binding (e.g., Matt 4:4, 7, 10; 21:13; Luke 2:23; 19:46; John 8:17; Acts 23:5; 1 Cor 1:31; 9:9; 1 Pet

---

24. For translating μέν οὖν as "of course," see Brown, *John*, 2:1054. For translating Ἰησοῦς as the subject and ὁ χριστός as the predicate nominative convertible proposition of v. 31, see Wallace, *Greek Grammar*, 46–47. Wallace argues persuasively against D. A. Carson's position in favor "the Messiah" as subject and "Jesus" as predicate nominative. The exegetical significance of this decision is apparent in the coming paragraphs. For Carson's position, see "Purpose of the Fourth Gospel," esp. 642–44.

25. I follow the majority opinion that the "signs" here refer to the Johannine Gospel story as a whole rather than just the resurrection appearances. See Brown, *John* 2:1055; Lincoln, *Saint John*, 506; Moloney, *John*, 544; Schnackenburg, *St. John*, 3:337. D. A. Carson is not convinced; see *John*, 661. For an extensive survey and discussion of the research, see van Belle, "Meaning."

26. Wallace, *Greek Grammar*, 576.

1:16) and fulfilled prophecy (e.g., Matt 2:5; 11:10; 26:24; Mark 1:2; 9:12; Luke 3:4; Acts 1:20; 13:33; Rom 9:33; 11:26)." But then he ponders the fact that the "usage of γέγραπται in John 20:31 is somewhat unusual in that it does not introduce a quotation from the OT but a concluding remark about the Gospel itself."[27] As argued above, the Fourth Evangelist uses this scriptural formula in this "unusual" way precisely because he understands his writing of this Gospel narrative that has provided his readership both binding commands and the articulation of fulfilled prophecy as part of, and quite possibly the τέλος of, the γραφή, of the story of God's action in the world.[28]

By way of two final or "telic" ἵνα clauses, the evangelist affirms his purpose for his community of readers.[29] A famous textual difficulty initiates the telling of this purpose: ἵνα πιστεύ[σ]ητε. Early manuscripts attest both the present subjunctive and the aorist subjunctive of the verb "to believe" (πιστεύω).[30] The translation provided above opts for the present subjunctive, the exegetical force of which is that the evangelist is writing that his community of believers, who are making their own journeys of faith which include facing doubt, opposition, and rejection, "may go on believing."[31] The second ἵνα clause provides both the content ("that Jesus is the Christ, the Son of God") and the result ("life in his name") for that ongoing action of believing. Regardless of the mainstream social, cultural, and theological categories of the world that have put them out, the Johannine community of readers have chosen the path that fulfills Scripture and gives the true gift of life.

In terms of "invitations to discipleship," this ending to the body of the Gospel of John opens the door for its readers to situate themselves

---

27. Ibid., 576 n. 14.

28. See Moloney, *John*, 544. In this verse, Moloney continues to build upon the work of Obermann, *Christologische Erfüllung*, esp. 418–22.

29. For the syntax of the ἵνα clauses, see Wallace, *Greek Grammar*, 472. For the use of these clauses in Johannine literature for community instruction, see Riesenfeld, "Zu den johanneischen hina-Sätzen."

30. For more detailed textual criticism regarding the relatively evenly divided support for both πιστεύητε and πιστεύσητε, see Metzger, *Textual Commentary*, 219–20.

31. So Brown, *John* 2:1056; Lincoln, *Saint John*, 506–7; Moloney, *John* 544; Schnackenburg, *St. John*, 3:337–38. For more detail see the article by Fee, "On the Text and Meaning." This assertion opposes the position of those who see this Gospel as primarily a missionary tract; see Carson, "Syntactical and Text-Critical Observations"; van Unnik, "Purpose"; Robinson, "Destination and Purpose."

as the disciples of Jesus whose belief is affirmed and reaffirmed as they journey through "life in his name" (20:31). "The book may have come to a tidy end, but John does not expect us to put the book back on our shelves with a sigh of satisfaction and the thought that this was a good story: this is meant to be the kind of book that changes lives."[32] The epilogue, John 21, is a portrait of how that can happen.[33] Yet this ending to the Gospel's main narrative makes any sense at all only in terms of its beginning (1:1–18).

Beginnings: The Prologue to the Body of the Gospel (1:1–18)

As a first page, the prologue is fundamental to the narrative structure of the Gospel.[34] Scholars have argued over its placement, some claiming it to be the last part of the Gospel to take definitive shape after a long history of development within the community.[35] Nonetheless, its positioning must be understood as part of the author's strategy, even the threshold for the narrative to come.[36] The reader comes to the body of the Gospel provided with the information in the prologue—information only the narrator and the reader have. Though the reader may not fully understand the enigmatic philosophical ideas and motifs of the prologue, these are precisely what create the tension that begs the question of *how* concerning God's action in the world. The subsequent narrative "shows" what the prologue "tells."[37]

---

32. Hooker, *Endings*, 74. The subtitle to Hooker's book is "Invitations to Discipleship."

33. For my more detailed discussion of John 21, see chapter 7.

34. Moloney, *Belief in the Word*, 23.

35. For a survey, see Brown, *John*, 1:21–23. For a stalwart argument of the prologue's unity with the rest of the Gospel, see Barrett, *St. John*, 125–26. Barrett says, in *Prologue*, 27, "The Prologue is not a jig-saw puzzle but one piece of solid theological writing. See also Barrett, *John and Judaism*, 20–35.

36. See the provocative literary analysis in Kermode, "St John as Poet."

37. "Showing" and "telling" are the means by which narratives reveal character. See Booth, *Rhetoric of Fiction*, 3–9. Tom Thatcher elaborates: "'Telling' occurs when the narrator makes direct evaluative statements or gives information not normally available in the readers' experience. 'Showing' occurs when the narrator offers selective information about the actions of the characters and allows readers to draw conclusions from them. By combining 'telling' and 'showing' the author enables readers to develop 'both intrinsic and contextual knowledge' of the characters" (Thatcher, "Jesus, Judas, and Peter," 435). See also Harvey, *Character and the Novel*, 32.

There is a strong use of parallelism to structure the poetic language of the prologue.[38] Robert Alter has argued that highly structured epic poetry was the accepted oral and literary expression of polytheistic religions. Thus, the biblical authors' choice of prose narrative to tell their stories is a conscious break from this custom in an effort to say something different, "to transform storytelling" from the realm of the "ritual" to the well-trod "wayward paths of human freedom."[39] The Fourth Evangelist's use of the poetic prologue as a foundation for his Gospel that suddenly and definitively breaks into prose narrative can thus be understood as a reflection of his theological perspective. The incarnation of the Word suddenly and definitively turns the custom and "truth" of the world on its ear. The "epic qualities" of these verses "establish an ordered system of relationships between God, his Word, his creation, and its history."[40] The narrative then unsettles that order, as events do not occur as the prologue readers expect; for this is the story of God's self-revelation in history.[41]

The structure of the eighteen verses of the prologue is elusive. Numerous attempts have been made to capture the fullness of this poetic prelude.[42] For example, Marc Lacan submits that a useful metaphor in grasping the flow of this introductory hymn is that of waves on the beach during the incoming tide.[43] Each wave is made up of essentially the same substance, and yet each rhythmic onslaught moves a little further, presenting itself with more clarity and complexity. In this flow, the prologue is presented in three waves, with each wave carrying a surge of symbolism and theological detail the reader must have at hand to embark upon a reading of the Gospel itself. The waves in this compelling image are delineated as vv. 1–5: The Word in God becomes the Light of

---

38. See de la Potterie, "Structure du Prologue"; Lacan, "Prologue de Saint Jean"; Rissi, "John 1:1–18."

39. Alter, *Art of Biblical Narrative*, 23–46, esp. 26.

40. Moloney, *Belief in the Word*, 24.

41. Ibid.

42. For several recent scholarly claims, as well as her own complex mapping, see Coloe, "Structure of the Johannine Prologue." See also Giblin, "Two Complementary Literary Structures"; Irigoin, "Composition Rythmique."

43. Lacan, "Prologue." This metaphor is adopted by Moloney, *Belief in the Word*, see esp. 23–27.

the World; vv. 6–14: The Incarnation of the Word; and, vv. 15–18: The Revealer: The Only Son Turned toward the Father.[44]

For the purposes of this study, the work of Alan Culpepper on the prologue proves most insightful as well as most provocative.[45] Recognizing the complexity of these eighteen verses, Culpepper acknowledges that more than one structuring technique may well be in play in the prologue. Thus, any diagram of it should be open to the fluidity of the evangelist's style since "perfect symmetry or adherence to the identifiable pattern" should not be expected and various literary techniques are often not mutually exclusive.[46] Nonetheless, Culpepper finds himself convinced that the underlying framework of the Johannine prologue is the chiasm. Therefore, he determines to build upon the work of his predecessors and isolate both the flow and the pivot of the prologue, the latter of which he finds at v. 12b: ἔδωκεν αὐτοῖς ἐξουσίαν τέκνα θεοῦ γενέσθαι.[47]

In this vein Culpepper reviews the literature of both those who find chiasms in the Johannine prologue and elsewhere in the Bible as well as of those who are far more hesitant to acknowledge widespread occurrence throughout the biblical literature and use in the prologue in particular.[48] Finding himself firmly in the scholarly tradition of those who see a chiastic structure to the prologue, Culpepper nonetheless notes that each of these scholars "fixes the centre of the structure differently." He thus concludes that the "diversity among writers who are oth-

---

44. For this structuring pattern, see de la Potterie, "Structure du Prologue," 359–67.

45. Culpepper, "Pivot." D. A. Carson likewise sees Culpepper's as the most persuasive structure of the prologue presented to date; see Carson, *John*, 13.

46. Culpepper, "Pivot," 8. In n. 35, Culpepper defers to the work of C. H. Talbert: "Imperfections of form are the rule in antiquity. . . . It was, moreover, a stated rule that perfect symmetry was to be avoided (e.g. Horace, *On the Art of Poetry*, 347 ff.; Longinus, *On the Sublime*, 33, I; Demetrius, *On Style*, 5, 250)." For more detail, see Talbert, "Artistry and Theology."

47. Quoting W. C. van Unnik tongue in cheek, Culpepper fears the upshot of his study will be "the new things he said were not true and the true things he said were not new" ("Pivot," 1). See van Unnik, "Purpose of St John's Gospel," 383. Even so, Culpepper determines to refine the scholarship detailed in the following works: Lund, "Influence of Chiasmus" and *Chiasmus in the New Testament*; Boismard, *St John's Prologue*; Lamarche, "Prologue de Jean"; Feuillet, *Prologue du Quatrième Évangile*; Hull, *John*.

48. Culpepper, "Pivot," 2–6. Note that this study was published in 1980; thus the literature survey does not cover more recent attempts at the chiastic structure of the prologue. For those who eschew the notion of a chiasm in the prologue, Culpepper mentions Brown, *John*, 1:23; Bultmann, *John*, 15 n. 1.

erwise basically in agreement on the structure of the prologue indicates that the centre of the proposed chiasm needs to be studied further."[49] To do so, he clarifies the definition of a chiasm as "a placing crosswise" that "may comprise whole passages as well as single sentences, that often there are inversions of *similar ideas* rather than *identical terms*, and that in addition to chiastic structures in which there is no middle term (ABB´A´) there are chiasms at whose centre is a single, central line (ABCB´A´)."[50]

Culpepper then investigates the prologue to the Gospel of John for evidence of a chiastic structure based upon the analysis of the corresponding elements by way of three overarching criteria: (1) language—primarily the occurrence/repetition of catchwords; (2) conceptual parallels; and (3) content—in terms of the theme or themes of each pericope.[51] As noted above, Culpepper concludes that the evangelist presents the prologue in an extended chiasm with seven corresponding elements that turns on the pivot of v. 12b. The crux of the prologue, and thus the focus of the narrative the prologue introduces, is the mission of the Word of God who "gives them" (those who receive him) "power to become children of God."

An outline of Culpepper's proposed structure is followed by a discussion of the prologue itself based on this presentation.

---

49. Culpepper, "Pivot," 4–5. Regarding a pivot, the scholarship lines up as Lund: v. 13; Boismard: vv. 12–13; Lamarche: vv. 10–13; Fueillet: no pivot, vv. 10–11 balance vv. 12–13; and Hull: vv. 11–12.

50. Ibid., 7. In this definition, Culpepper refers explicitly to both Lund, *Chiasmus*, 31; and Clark, "Criteria for Identifying Chiasm."

51. Culpepper, "Pivot," 8. See pp. 9–17 for the analysis and p. 16 for a diagram of the criteria and evidence for the chiasm. The remainder of the study focuses on the significance of the pivot (v. 12b).

```
A    vv. 1-2
   B    v. 3
      C    vv. 4-5
         D    vv. 6-8
            E    vv. 9-10
               F    v. 11
                  G    v. 12a
                     H    v. 12b
                  G′   v. 12c
               F′   v. 13
            E′   v. 14
         D′   v. 15
      C′   v. 16
   B′   v. 17
A′   v. 18
```

Werner Kelber remarks that "[b]oth in life and in literature beginnings are consequential, but risky undertakings." He then goes on to discuss the Fourth Gospel's beginning: "Transcendental and earthly beginnings, this double gesture of centering and decentering, constitute the prologue's program which creates the central predicament for the subsequent narrative."[52] Similarly, Morna Hooker suggests that beginnings are the manners by which our evangelists present the key to understanding all that follows.[53] This view of the function of the prologue coupled with Culpepper's basic map will serve as the guide through which we can examine the key the Fourth Evangelist provides to open the passageway into his Gospel.

In the Beginning Was the Word (vv. 1–11)

The first words of the prologue, and thus of the entire Gospel, ἐν ἀρχῇ, are identical with the opening words of Genesis in the LXX. They serve to bring the Fourth Evangelist's first readers "to the beginning," not only of this narrative but to the beginnings of their sacred narrative of history, when God literally spoke creation into existence (Gen 1).[54] By

52. W. H. Kelber, "Birth of a Beginning," 121.

53. Hooker, *Beginnings*, xiii. For detail of the Johannine prologue as the key to the Gospel, see pp. 64–83.

54. For a detailed study of the prologue, esp. 1:1–5, as a targumic exposition of Gen 1:1–5, see Borgen, "Targumic Character of the Prologue" and "Logos Was the True Light." Borgen argues that "John i. 1–5 is the basic exposition of Gen. i. 1–5, while John

resonating this shared story of God's action in history, the evangelist firmly grounds his story in the realm of the sacred Scripture of Israel. This literary intention is furthered with the fullness of the initial clause: ἐν ἀρχῇ ἦν ὁ λόγος. The use of *logos* terminology here has been much discussed, and can be rooted in the Jewish wisdom tradition as well as the Hellenistic philosophical tradition.[55] The evangelist's choice of it here allows for rich and varied symbolism, evoking God's revelation in Torah as well as the broader voice of the sages through the cultural milieu.[56] On the narrative level, however, it allows for a fundamental identification of the *logos* with the creative activity of God. The "word" that is introduced here corresponds with God's very word of creation in the beginning.[57]

---

i. 6ff. elaborates upon terms and phrases from John i. 1–5" ("Targumic Character of the Prologue," 291). In this vein, Daniel Boyarin reads "the first five verses as a coherent, pre-existent logos manifesting a particular *Gattung*, a synagogue homily of the Proem variety, and having a particular *Sitz im Leben* which the latter thirteen verses expand and comment upon. . . . In this text we find not a hymn, but a midrash; that is, not a poem, but a narrative, a *chronologically* ordered text" (Boyarin, "Gospel of the Memra," 267). I fully concur with Boyarin's position here. He seems to understand this position to preclude a chiastic structure for the prologue (see ibid., 267 n. 94), on the presupposition that chiasms are restricted to poetry. The literature on chiasms, however, shows that they can be used liberally in narrative as well. Therefore, I see no reason that a text, in this case the Johannine prologue, cannot be both chiastic and chronological in presentation.

55. For a detailed discussion, see Tobin, "Prologue of John."

56. In his provocative study Derek Tovey suggests that *logos* "in the opening verse of John's Gospel functions as a nonsequential sequence-signal (as well as a character-substitute) which prompts the reader to ask, 'What Word?' and to wonder as to the identity of this mysterious figure. And because the implied author quickly raises the expectation of the reader that this Word is a human character, the question is more likely to be framed, '*Who* is this Word?'" (Tovey, "Narrative Strategies in the Prologue," 141). The audience thus becomes determinative of the formative background of the *logos* concept.

57. In his study of the relation of the Johannine Logos to the *Memra* of the Palestinian Targum, Daniel Boyarin notes that "the strongest possible reading of the *Memra* is that it is not a mere name, but an actual divine entity, or mediator." He later concludes that "the *Memra* performs many, if not all, of the functions of the Logos of Christian Logos theology (as well as of Wisdom), and an a priori case can be made, therefore, for some kind of connection between these two, after all, etymologically cognate entities in non-rabbinic Judaism" ("Gospel of the Memra," 255–57). Citing conclusive evidence for the connection of the targumic *Memra* and the *Logos* of John, Boyarin concludes "an actual point of origin for the term *Memra* as derived from an interpretation of Gen 1:3. One could almost say that "I am" is a name for the *Memra* from this targumic text" (259). See also McNamara, "Logos of the Fourth Gospel"; and G. Anderson, "Interpretation

The staircase parallelism that proceeds in v. 1 picks up the introduction of the *logos* and affirms that the λόγος ἦν πρὸς τὸν θεόν. The eternal nature of the word is indicated here with the imperfect form of εἰμί, which is contrasted with all that is created or comes to be (ἐγένετο) in vv. 3, 6, and 10. What is most notable in this second step of the first verse, however, is the use of the preposition πρός to link the existence of the Word with God. Although typically translated as "with," the power of this preposition is found in the connotation of its literal translation as "to" or "toward." In its eternal state of being the Word is turned toward God. This image indicates an inherent relationality between the *logos* and God that is reinforced in the final step of this first staircase: καὶ θεὸς ἦν ὁ λόγος. The definite article preceding λόγος and absent from θεός indicates the former is the subject and the latter the predicate. The predicate appears first to continue the staircase parallelism and allow for the fullness of the syntax to claim and "what God was, the Word was."[58] "As a being independent of God, its Originator, the Logos of the prologue is primordially oriented toward union with God."[59] The expansiveness of this first verse prepares readers for God's revelatory action in the story to come.[60] The second verse reflects a second layer of parallelism as it succinctly reiterates and affirms the claims of the first verse: "This one was in the beginning toward God" (οὗτος ἦν ἐν ἀρχῇ πρὸς τὸν θεόν, v. 2).[61]

---

of Genesis 1:1."

58. For this relational reading of v.1, see Moloney, *Belief in the Word*, 28. See also Delebecque, *Jean*, 143.

59. Waetjen, "Logos," 265. This study thoroughly discusses the presentation of the *logos* in the prologue and the narrative impact of this concept on the Gospel as a whole.

60. C. K. Barrett rather famously comments on John 1:1, "John intends that the whole of his gospel shall be read in the light of this verse. The deeds and words of Jesus are the deeds and words of God; if this be not true the book is blasphemous" (*St. John*, 156).

61. Derek Tovey would concur with my strong translation of οὗτος as *this one*. He writes, "As a demonstrative, it functions as a kind of literary 'index finger' . . . which points the reader back to the . . . character-substitute encountered in the metaphor of 'the Word' in verse one. It will also be used to place this character-substitute in juxtaposition with another character about to be introduced; and finally to link the character Jesus with the metaphor of 'the Word', as well as another major metaphor, that of 'the Light'" ("Narrative Strategies," 141). For my discussion of deictic language in the Fourth Gospel, see chapter 1.

Verses 3–5 push the chiasm of the prologue forward by further presenting the nature and role of the *logos* as the vehicle for creation (v. 3) who is the giver of life (v. 4) who stands fast in the darkness lighting the way for humankind (vv. 4–5). Verse 3 emphasizes (as does its counterpart v. 17) what "came to be" (ἐγένετο) through the as-yet-unnamed *logos*, who himself always existed (ἦν, v. 1). The Word's affirmed role in all creation is foundational for understanding him as the giver of "life" and "light." The evangelist introduces these themes of life, light, and its corresponding darkness, which will play out across the rest of the narrative but also continue an exposition of Genesis 1 that resonates the eternal creative force of God.[62] The final words of v. 5 further hint at the conflict to come between the Word as giver of light (Gen 1:3–5) and the darkness that exists among the people who are the caretakers of God's creation (Gen 1:26–30). The reader is told in regard to the shining light, the darkness οὐ κατέλαβεν. This verb can carry the sense of "overcome" in the physical sense as well as "receive" in the sense of "comprehend."[63] Thus, a physical threat is implicated, as well as the notion of the Word already in the world, in the form of Torah, which has not been fully understood.[64] This statement leads directly to the introduction of John the Baptist, the one who comes to give testimony, and also becomes part of the driving force toward the crux of the entire prologue.

Verses 6–8 form the next segment of the prologue's chiasm and introduce the first human being (ἄνθρωπος) into the story, a man named John (v. 6).[65] This human being is articulated as having come to be (ἐγένετο), in distinction to the eternally existing *logos*. In the same breath, however, the evangelist describes him as "sent from God" (ἀπεσταλμένος παρὰ θεοῦ), making him the only fully human character

---

62. Culpepper, "Pivot," 11.
63. BDAG, s.v. καταλαμβάνω.
64. Boyarin, "Gospel of the Memra," 272.
65. These verses, along with their counterpart in v.15, interject a prose style quite strikingly into the fluid hymn-like poetry of the rest of the prologue, leading many to argue they are interpolations to the *Vorlage* of the prologue. J. A. T. Robinson, e.g., bluntly referred to these verses as "rude interruptions" ("Relation of the Prologue"). For a brief discussion as well as her own succinct argument to the contrary that sees these verses as an integral connection to the body of the narrative, see Hooker, "John the Baptist and the Johannine Prologue." Culpepper concurs and argues that the double articulation of John and his role is further evidence of the chiastic presentation of the prologue ("Pivot," 12–13).

in the narrative to be identified as such. John, then, is special: he is sent into the world from God with a mission. Readers are alerted right away that this man can be trusted. His mission is to testify (vv. 7-8). John is to bear witness (μαρτυρήσῃ) to the light of the eternal *logos* identified in v. 4. As the witness sent from God, everything that John says about Jesus can be trusted as true.[66] Through the introduction of John and his role, the evangelist also introduces the concept of belief in the Word.[67] Verse 8 carefully clarifies the distinction between John the human witness and the light, but his role is crucial: to point to the light and thus facilitate the process of faith (ἵνα πάντες πιστεύσωσιν δι' αὐτοῦ, v. 7).

Verses 9-10 flow out of the final words of vv. 6-8 and return focus to the light, now further characterized by way of truth: τὸ φῶς τὸ ἀληθινόν (v. 9). The true light whose enlightening reign reaches everyone was coming into the world. The incarnation foreshadowed here comes to pass in the counterpart to these verses, v. 14. The imminent conflict of the Gospel story, however, is also reaffirmed, this time in terms of knowledge (v. 10; see v. 8). The very world of which the light was instrumental in creating (ὁ κόσμος δι' αὐτοῦ ἐγένετο) did not know him (ὁ κόσμος αὐτὸν οὐκ ἔγνω). The imperfect ἦν indicates that the *logos* (characterized as light) was already in the world. This could be a further identification of the *logos* with Torah, making these verses a reference to the giving of Torah to Israel and Israel's failure to understand the fullness of its implications for relationship with God.[68] This identification, made in terms of knowledge, brings aspects of the language and symbolism (knowledge and Torah) of covenant into the prologue's presentation of the person and mission of the *logos*.

Verse 11, although a distinctive movement in the prologue's chiasm in its own right, provides powerful parallelism to this disconnect between the light and the world through the intimate language of "his

---

66. See my analysis below. As is commonly noticed, John is not referred to as "the Baptist" in the Fourth Gospel, as his role in this narrative is as a "witness." I will, however, often refer to him by his accepted title in order to distinguish him from the Gospel's traditional author.

67. As is also commonly noticed, "belief" as a noun (πίστις) does not occur in the Fourth Gospel, but forms of the verb πιστεύω/πιστεύομαι occur regularly and often (98 times). Thus, faith in the Gospel of John is always an action and is rightly described in terms of a process, or better, a journey.

68. Boyarin, "Gospel of the Memra," 277. See also Dodd, *Interpretation*, 271, 295; and Barrett, *St. John*, 136.

own" (οἱ ἴδιοι αὐτόν). The *logos*, instrumental giver of life and light in intimate relationship with God, comes into what is his own and is not received by his own people. Giving, receiving, and rejecting in relationship thus become the operative interactivity of the incarnation of the Word.

The Children of God: The Chiastic Center of the Prologue (v. 12)

At v. 12 the reader arrives at the pivot of the prologue (v. 12b, marked H) and the hinges upon which the pivot turns (vv. 12a and 12c, marked G and G′).[69] Put another way, the force of the entire prologue is poised on the fulcrum of the mission of the Word "to give them power to become children of God."[70] The balance of the three phrases of v. 12 can be lost in English translations that present v. 12c in apposition to v. 12a, and thus directly following the initiating reference "but to those who received him" (so RSV, NRSV, NIV). In effect, however, the evangelist's Greek syntax allows the central assertion of the Word's giving action to be framed by the introduction (v. 12a) and description (v. 12c) of the potential recipients of the gift of the Word. In v. 12a the nominative builds upon those to whom the Word came (οἱ ἴδιοι, v. 11), v. 12b properly delineates the indirect object of the power the word gives (αὐτοῖς) in the dative, and v. 12c characterizes "them" as "those who believe in his name" likewise in the dative (τοῖς πιστεύουσιν). Verses 12a and 12c are thus corresponding phrases that hinge the core assertion of v. 12b.[71]

This central assertion, the giving to those who receive the Word the power to become children of God, is understood to be the crux

---

69. The discussion of this verse is based on the position detailed in Culpepper, "Pivot," 15–17.

70. In delineating the "laws of chiastic structures," Lund (*Chiasmus*, 46) claims that the "very core of the message is found in the central line." Although Ernst Käsemann's analysis of the prologue takes a very different approach to the one presented here, he too identifies this verse as the climax: "Verse 12 specifies the gift which is his to bestow and the goal of his redeeming effectiveness" ("Structure and Purpose of the Prologue," 151–52).

71. For the correspondence of these phrases, see also Brown, *John*, 1:10.

of the prologue's message to the reader. Therefore, this core must also profoundly affect the corresponding elements that provide the balance of the prologue's message.[72] Ernst Käsemann asserts that the "establishment of sonship to God through the Son of God is the eschatological end of all God's dealings with the world, the goal of the Creator and Creation." Thus v. 12 "could be regarded as the culmination of the whole ... [of] what was achieved by the manifestation of the Revealer."[73] Thus, this expressed aim will affect the articulation of every statement that follows. This effect is already apparent in v. 12. The claim is that those who receive the Word will be given the power to become children of God, but how does one go about receiving him in order to achieve this status? By believing in his name (v. 12c). The remainder of the prologue can thus be studied in this vein, the consequence of which will be to shed light on what it means to become "children of God" and how this could be the *telos* of John's Gospel.

Gift upon Gift: The Word Became Flesh and Dwelt among Us (vv. 13–18)

Those who believed received the Word and thereby received a gift in return, the power to become children of God. Verse 13 stands in apposition to v. 12 and also corresponds antithetically to v. 11. The Word's own did not receive him. Verse 13 continues the *how* of v. 12c. If v. 12c describes the role of the receivers in this relationship, then v. 13 describes the role of God and the *how* of becoming God's children. Three standard (human) ways how this could happen are listed negatively by way of dismissal, followed by the positive assertion that children of God are indeed born of God (ἀλλ' ἐκ θεοῦ ἐγεννήθησαν). Natural descent, ordinary human sexual desire, and the husband's will do not avail, for

---

72. The correspondence of receiving the Word to becoming children of God also suggests that "while Israel, which had been given the Torah, nevertheless rejected the Logos, some others, not necessarily Israel by virtue of flesh-and-blood parentage, became children of God via their receiving of the *Logos Asarkos*" (Boyarin, "Gospel of the Memra," 278). See also Dodd, *Interpretation*, 271.

73. Käsemann, "Structure and Purpose," 152. Although I do not concur with Käsemann's overall interpretation of the prologue as an example of early Christian Gnosticism, his insights on v. 12 are striking and extend beyond this theological perspective.

spiritual birth comes from above.⁷⁴ This notion is more fully articulated in the discourse of John 3 but introduced here in terms of the mission of the Word. Because of the coming of the Word into the world and the rejection by οἱ ἴδιοι, "heritage and race" are rendered irrelevant to birth from God and the "privilege of becoming the covenant people of God" also changes forever.⁷⁵

Concluding this initial characterization of the children of God, the evangelist returns to what God did to make this possible. Verses 9–10 revealed that the Word, characterized as "the true light," was "coming into the world." Corresponding to this proclamation, v. 14 majestically announces how this happened, who the *logos* becomes, and what he gives in the process:

> And the Word became flesh and pitched his tent among us, and we beheld his glory, the glory as of a father's only son, full of the gift which is truth.

Scholars who oppose any proposed chiastic structure to the prologue typically point to this verse describing the glory of the incarnation of the eternal *logos* as the climax of the hymn.⁷⁶ These words are powerful indeed, and their impact should not be minimized. With regard to the flow of the prologue, they announce an event long coming, made possible by the plan of God to re-envision the covenant people as children of spiritual, not human, birth. In his influential study of the prologue to John with reference to the Palestinian Targum, Daniel Boyarin affirms this point:

---

74. Carson, *John*, 126. Raymond Brown questions the use of αἱμάτων in the plural to mean natural descent. Although the mixture of bloods was understood to be the natural process of procreation, it was typically rendered in the singular. Lacking a better interpretation, however, Brown concludes this must have been the evangelist's intention. He notes that θελήματος σάρκος must indicate "lust" and θελήματος ἀνδρός refers to the culturally accepted leadership of the husband in such family matters. For his discussion, see Brown, *John*, 1:11. Frank Kermode, in his examination of the axioms of "being" and "becoming" in the prologue, notes that "we meet in v. 13 a paradoxical style of becoming (of birth) which is actually a form of being: being born not of the stuff of becoming, being born into being" ("St John as Poet," 10).

75. Carson, *John*, 126. See also Pryor, "Covenant and Community," 48. This phenomenon is discussed in detail in the analysis of John 8 in chapter 5.

76. Among others, see Bultmann, *John*, 60; Käsemann, "Structure and Purpose," 159; Beasley-Murray, *John*, 4–9; Barrett, *St. John*, 149–50; Moloney, *Belief in the Word*, 25–27.

> In light of this hypothesized close relationship between Palestinian Memra and Logos, I would like to propose that what marks the Fourth Gospel as a new departure in the history of Judaism is not to be found in its Logos theology at all but in its incarnational Christology, and that that very historical departure, or rather advent, is iconically symbolized in the narrative itself. When the text announces in v. 14 that "the Word became flesh," that announcement is an iconic representation of the moment that the Christian narrative begins to diverge from the Jewish Koine and form its own nascent Christian kerygma.[77]

Boyarin goes on to explain:

> On the formal or literary level . . . when v. 14 announces the Incarnation, there has been a history that has prepared the way for that moment without, however, anticipating it and spoiling the drama. On the theological level, the Prologue now presents us with a clear account of the preexistent Logos and the reason for the Incarnation. On the level of the history of religions, we see that this preexistent Logos, i.e., the preexistent Logos upon which the Fourth Gospel is founded, in every sense, is a Jewish Logos, and the continuity of Johannine religion with the Judaism of its day is assured.[78]

Just as God's action in the Sinai covenant and the giving of the Torah changed the nature of God's relationship with creation, the incarnation of the Word, while very much in accord with that history, once again decisively alters the manner by which creation can relate to God. The narrator leaves no doubt as to the full humanity of the incarnate Word with the use of σάρξ to describe this inbreaking of God's action.

---

77. Boyarin, "Gospel of the Memra," 261. I further concur with Boyarin that the prologue is "a well-integrated narrative that bridges the temporal gap between the pre-existent Logos and the Incarnation as the story of the Gospel" (267). But whereas he reads the presentation as vv. 6–18 narrating a christological interpretation of vv. 1–5, which themselves are a typically "Jewish" midrash of Gen 1:1-5 (271), I follow Culpepper's understanding of the narrative of the prologue turning on the pivot of v. 12b and the determination of giving all who receive the Word the power to become children of God. The incarnation of the Word results from God's plan as articulated at v. 12b. Boyarin suggests v. 14 marks the departure from "perfectly unexceptional non-Christian Jewish thought" (265), whereas I claim that this departure of the incarnation became necessary and imminent at the proclamation of v. 12b. Boyarin is responding to Dodd, Bultmann, and Haenchen here, which I certainly appreciate. See Dodd, *Interpretation*, esp. 269–81; Bultmann, *John*, esp. 21–22; and Haenchen, *John*, esp. 126–36.

78. Boyarin, "Gospel of the Memra," 268.

Further, the exodus event and the covenant-making time in the wilderness at Sinai are brought to mind with the action of ἐσκήνωσεν. The verb σκηνόω means literally to "pitch a tent," and the form here is generally translated as "dwelt." The evangelist's verb choice, however, resonates with Exodus 33–40, where God renews the covenant with Israel mediated by Moses and the people are told to make a tent (the tabernacle, σκηνή,) so that God can dwell among them. After a lengthy description of the Tabernacle and its construction, Exodus 40 recounts the erection of the Tabernacle and the placement of the tablets of the Law in the Holy of Holies, laid within the Ark of the Covenant. Depicting the incarnation of the Word in terms of the שְׁכִינָה (shekinah), or dwelling presence of YHWH, thus also preserves his divinity as a new presence of God and site of God's covenantal activity in creation.[79]

The enfleshed *logos* dwelt "among us" (ἐν ἡμῖν). The narration shifts to the first-person plural as the narrator speaks inclusively from the perspective of the children of God.[80] "We have beheld his glory," the visible and powerful manifestation of God that likewise harks back to the revelation of the glory of God to Moses on Mount Sinai (Exod 34:15–16).[81] Verse 14d explicitly describes the glory of the incarnate Word in the context of a father's only son: δόξαν ὡς μονογενοῦς παρὰ πατρός. This phrase introduces the evangelist's characteristic christological formulation and offers a very human image of the "incomparably privileged status" of the incarnate Word as "the only son" of God as father, ensuring that "Jesus' status and glory in relation to God are viewed as unique."[82]

Verse 14e then concludes this powerful statement by further describing the incarnate Word and at the same time continuing the

---

79. Brown, *John*, 1:32–33. Here Brown further notes that in the rabbinic literature the term שְׁכִינָה (shekinah) is used "as a surrogate for Yahweh in His dealings" with humankind as "a way of preserving God's transcendence." See Exod 25:8; 29:46; Zech 2:14 for forms of the verb שכן in terms of YHWH's dwelling. Note that the Hebrew verb and its noun derivative have the same consonants as the Greek verb the evangelist uses: ἐσκήνωσεν, from the verb σκηνοω and corresponding to the noun σκηνή, σ, κ, ν. This resonation would not be lost on the evangelist's first readers and listeners.

80. This inclusive narration also serves to draw the reader into the potentiality of becoming part of that group. For a discussion, see Bowen, "Notes on the Fourth Gospel," 22.

81. Brown, *John*, 1:34. Morna Hooker reads the entirety of John 1:14–18 as a midrash on Exod 33–34. See Hooker, "Johannine Prologue," 53–56.

82. Lincoln, *Saint John*, 105. For a discussion of the translation of μονογενοῦς as *only son*, see Moody, "God's Only Son."

articulation of *how* he gives believers power to become children of God (v. 12b). The incarnated Word is full of χάριτος ("grace") and ἀληθείας ("truth").[83] Most scholars simply understand this phrase as descriptive and take the juxtaposition of χάρις and ἀλήθεια as expressing the OT covenant love of God, reflecting the common OT pairing of חֶסֶד וֶאֱמֶת.[84] This reading has much to commend it, but the biggest hindrance to accepting it fully is the evangelist's use of χάρις.[85] Thus, without precluding a reflection of pure covenant love, a more satisfying interpretation is needed. Francis J. Moloney suggests just such a solution that both takes seriously the careful diction of πλήρης χάριτος καὶ ἀληθείας and allows for the continuing articulation of the mission of the Word now incarnate. Noting that much exegetical speculation on this phrase has been inappropriately influenced by the use of this term in Pauline theology, Moloney observes that the expression occurs in the Fourth Gospel only in the prologue, and the "Fourth Gospel must be allowed to have its own use of this word."[86] By translating χάριτος, which appears in the genitive, with its more widely held denotation of "a kindness, a manifestation of good will, a gift, an unexpected favor," and reading the καί as epexegetical, thus allowing the second term, ἀληθείας, also in the genitive, to explain the first, the phrase is rendered more clearly as "full of a gift which is truth."[87] Thus the Word, giver of light and life, now incarnate, is filled with a new gift, truth. The giving and receiving of this gift of truth is intimately connected to the power to become children of God (v. 12b) and thus to the crux of the mission of the incarnate Word.[88] The remainder of

---

83. Like Brown (*John*, 1:14), I read the nominative πλήρης as modifying ὁ λόγος, though it is often used indeclinably; against Carson who takes the expression as a modifier of δόξαν (*John*, 130).

84. See Exod 34:6. Raymond Brown, e.g., espouses this notion: "The theme of enduring covenant love ... fits in well with the Tabernacle and glory references.... The great exhibition of the enduring covenant love of God in the OT took place at Sinai, the same setting where the Tabernacle became the dwelling for God's glory. So now the supreme exhibition of God's love is the incarnate Word, Jesus Christ, the new Tabernacle of divine glory" (*John*, 1:14, 35). For a more recent commentator who also follows this line, see Lincoln, *Saint John*, 105.

85. Brown himself notes the difficulty (*John*, 1:14).

86. Moloney, *John*, 45. See further his discussion on p. 39.

87. Ibid., 45. See LSJ, s.v. χάρις; BDF §442.9, 16.

88. In his exposition of the prologue that focuses on v. 14, Andrew Osborn asserts that the NT use of the word means much more than the restricted "modern" notion of

the prologue returns to where it began by continuing to elucidate this gift, integrating it into the life and being of the enfleshed Word.

This incarnate Word is then firmly grounded in history as the narrator returns to John, the human witness sent by God (vv. 6–8), whose testimony readers can trust (v. 15). In this role, John provides the first direct speech about the Word and the first direct speech of the Gospel. To assert both the correspondence of this verse to vv. 6–8 as well as the trustworthy nature of John's message, the evangelist places in the mouth of John the narrator's major verbs about him, and has him repeat them in this "riddle-like formula," thereby confirming in direct speech what the narrator claimed for him.[89] John testifies that the Word is "the one who comes" (ἐρχόμενος) after him temporally, but ranks before him. Returning to the imperfect tense of vv. 1–2, John explains that this is so "because he was before me." With this historical grounding and temporal designation in place, as well as the corresponding element to John's initial witness (vv. 6–8), the prologue surges forward with the mission of the Word.

In v. 16, the narrator picks up from v. 14 by way of explanation, determined both by the return to the first person plural ("we have all received") and the reference to the "fullness" of the gift of the Word incarnate (τοῦ πληρώματος αὐτοῦ). The narrator continues to speak in the collective voice of the children of God as he details the process of God's action in creation in terms of their reception of God's gifts. Retaining the earlier understanding of χάρις as "gift," what God has done through the enfleshed Word is give the gift (that is truth) upon a gift: χάριν ἀντὶ χάριτος.[90]

---

truth in utterance: "It refers to that truth in character which not only leads to truth in speech, but manifests integrity in action, together with a firm belief in that which is real and true as opposed to vanity and hypocrisy" ("Word Became Flesh," 46). In OT terms, this would also entail the unified relationship with God that is produced by covenantal obedience.

89. Staley, "Structure of John's Prologue," 252. Thus, John is the readers' accurate witness, but not the true light. Robert Alter discusses this phenomenon of the role of direct speech in Hebrew narrative: "Phrases or whole sentences first stated by the narrator do not reveal their full significance until they are repeated, whether faithfully or with distortions, in direct speech by one or more of the characters" (*Art of Biblical Narrative*, 182).

90. I continue to follow Moloney here for the rendering of χάρις. See *John*, 46. He notes that typically the difficult preposition ἀντί has been translated as *upon* to render the idea of a superabundance of grace, and that this translation is question-

The nature of the new gift has been introduced in v. 14 and the nature of the first gift has been behind the very characterization of the Word in vv. 1–5, but both are illuminated in v. 17: "For the law [ὁ νόμος] was given [ἐδόθη] through Moses, the gift which is truth [ἡ χάρις καὶ ἡ ἀλήθεια] came to be through Jesus Christ." The aorist passive of δίδωμι is read as a divine passive; thus the law was a gift from God, and the reference to Moses ensures that the covenantal gift of Torah resonates through this proclamation. The gift which is truth came to be (ἐγένετο), harking directly back to v. 14 (ὁ λόγος σάρξ ἐγένετο). Thus, this gift of truth was given through the incarnation of the Word, who is finally identified in history as Jesus Christ. This gift of truth is likewise a gift of God that acts in history in covenant with creation. Moloney asserts, "One cannot 'replace' the other. One prolongs and perfects the never-ending graciousness of God. The gift of the Law is perfected in the gift of the incarnation."[91] This understanding renders the evangelist's presentation of the person and mission of Jesus Christ (the Word that gives the gift of truth) covenantal. The giving of the gift of the Law was God's covenantal activity at Sinai. The incarnation of the Word that is full of the gift which is truth is God's covenantal activity in Jesus.

The final verse of the prologue, v. 18, returns to the beginning (v. 1–2) while elucidating the relationship of Jesus as "only son" to the Father who is turned toward that Father, now in history.[92] It is that one who makes God known (ἐξηγήσατο), and in this way gives humankind the ability to become children of God (v. 12b). This is indeed a new covenantal move in history, but the gift of truth in no way supersedes the gift of the Law, for this is the Word made flesh. As Boyarin concludes, "Of course, for the Evangelist, the Incarnation supplements the Torah—that much is explicit—but, for John, it is only because the *Logos Ensarkos* is a better teacher, a better exegete than the *Logos Asarkos*—

---

able. For more detail, see Edwards, "*Charin anti charitos*." Although I concur with this position, I retain the English "upon" in an effort include the full range of meaning here, since ἀντί could denote "instead of," "for," or even "in behalf of" in addition to the stricter "instead of" (see BDAG, s.v. ἀντί). I am attempting to avert any reference to replacement or supersessionism, as this hermeneutic is a tragic misreading of the Fourth Gospel. As Boyarin asserts, "Jesus comes to fulfill the mission of Moses, not to displace it" ("Gospel of the *Memra*," 280). Boyarin in turn references the evidence in Suggit, "John XVII. 17."

91. Moloney, *John*, 46.

92. For a full discussion of this reading, see Moloney, "John 1:18."

ἐκεῖνος ἐξηγήσατο—that the Incarnation takes place."[93] Morna Hooker likewise points to the same phenomenon:

> There is therefore not only a partial antithesis between Christ and Moses, there is also an antithesis between Christians and Moses, who are both recipients of the revelation. So it is we (v. 14) who have seen his glory, and the glory is that of the Logos; it is we (v. 16) who have received χάριν ἀντὶ χάριτος. This double theme—Christ as the revelation of God's glory, and as the fulfillment of the Torah, to which Moses only pointed forward—is the theme of the rest of the gospel.[94]

The remainder of the Gospel will narrate the *how* of the covenantal claim that the prologue introduces. In essence, the new covenant gives the power to become children of God, which comes to pass in the receiving of the gift that is truth as revealed by the Word incarnate, Jesus Christ the only son who is in perfect relationship to God the Father.

John the Baptist: The Prologue Embodied in the Gospel Action (1:19–34)

We have concluded this extended investigation of the frame of the Fourth Gospel, the evangelist's endings and beginnings. We focused on his self-understanding as a writer of Scripture as well as his scriptural claim of Jesus Christ as the incarnate Word who fulfills the Torah of the Sinai covenant and gives a new covenant, the gift of truth, to those who would be children of God. We can now turn to the presentation of the body of the Gospel. The bridge from the prologue to this action of the body of the Gospel is manifested in the human witness sent from God, named John. He becomes the embodiment of the prologue as he continues to give valuable information about the person of Jesus as well as about the story to come, now in the form of dialogues with other human characters.

The function of the prologue in the Gospel of John, as it is in all four Gospels and Greek literature in general, is to give a synthesis of the story to come, to communicate to readers at the onset just who Jesus is and what he has done. This sort of pronouncement is done deliber-

---

93. Boyarin, "Gospel of the Memra," 284.
94. Hooker, "Johannine Prologue and the Messianic Secret," 55.

ately, and never more powerfully than in John 1:1–18. Throughout the rest of his Gospel, the Fourth Evangelist recounts sustained narratives, pushed forward through dialogical interaction, between Jesus and various individuals—the disciples, the crowd, "the Jews," Nicodemus, etc. In this Gospel, the reader participates in a deliberate literary device of misunderstanding. Jesus makes a theological or existential statement, his dialogue partners misunderstand and respond on a literal or practical level, and Jesus then seeks to bring them along and push them past what they think they know to a more profound knowledge of God and God's action in Jesus.[95] The revelatory impetus of this story is thus the in-breaking of God into human history. The misunderstanding is rooted in this in-breaking and always occurs because the characters have not read the prologue. Only the reader and the storyteller know the prologue. Thus, this is a narrative technique to draw the reader into the narrative world of the evangelist as an insider.

The prologue tells the reader the *who* and the *what* of the events at hand, but leaves open the *how*. The story itself is necessary to understand how it all happens. The prologue gives readers everything they need to know to make the right decisions and judgments about Jesus all along the way of the story. The evangelist, therefore, is primarily concerned with *the reader* and not the characters of the story. There are three places where the narrator plays an intrusive role: 1:1–18; 19:35; and 20:30–31, leading readers along with footnotes to shape the reading.[96] John the Baptist, introduced by the narrator so strongly as the human witness sent from God in the prologue, then opens the narrative as the first character in the story with dialogical force. Since the narrator placed the readers' didactic trust in this man named John, this character, upon entering the story (and even launching the story) thus becomes the prologue embodied. He is the one character who always witnesses accurately to the Word made flesh, just as he was sent to do. His first dialogue at 1:19–28, followed by the monologue of 1:29–34 and coupled with his final initial witness in 1:35–37, provide readers

---

95. The prime early example of this is the encounter between Jesus and Nicodemus (3:1–21). Jesus instructs Nicodemus that he must be born ἄνωθην ("from above"). He misunderstands and asks how a man can enter his mother's womb again (δεύτερον, "a second time"). Readers learn early on that when the evangelist uses words with the potential for double meanings, they are best served to take *both* as intended.

96. The first and third of these have been discussed; the second will be discussed in chapter 6.

the grounds from which to form decisions about the characters in the narrative, and about their own belief in the Word.

Testimony Declared

All of 1:19–37 occurs over the course of three consecutive days (1:29, 35) during which John testifies just as the prologue articulates he was sent to do. The detail of John's witness over this three-day progression directly parallels the pattern set forth in vv. 6–8. On day one John declares he is not the light (vv. 19–28), on day two he witnesses positively to the light (vv. 29–34), and on day three people begin to believe through him (all of vv. 35–42 make up day three; the Baptist's role concludes at v. 37).[97] On the first day John is approached by a delegation from Jerusalem and finds himself in dialogue with them over his identity. His task at this point is largely to assert their misconceptions about who he is and what he is doing, and thus his initial testimony is largely negative.

The opening of v. 19 directly connects the action of the day at hand with information provided in the prologue: "And this is the testimony [ἡ μαρτυρία] given by John." Both the demonstrative pronoun and the subject noun are indices that point back to John's mission as stated in the prologue and focus readers' attention to the beginning of the action proper. John is first interrogated by a delegation "sent from Jerusalem." The one who is sent from God (ἀπεσταλμένος παρὰ θεοῦ, v. 6) is confronted by "the Jews" sent from Jerusalem (ἀπέστειλαν . . . ἐξ Ἱεροσολύμων, v. 19). That they are identified as "priests and Levites" alerts readers that they will be interested in John's activity as it pertains to ritual purity and the purification rites that he may be initiating. They approach him with the question that will mark these first days, and indeed, the first part of the body of the Gospel: "Who are you?"[98] Again their use of a pronoun in direct speech, this time the personal pronoun σύ, lends emphasis and focuses attention on the person of John and the identity in question.

---

97. Dodd, *Historical Tradition*, 248. So also Brown, *John*, 1:45; and van der Merwe, "Historical and Theological Significance," 273n18. This view stands in opposition to that of Staley, who sees an ironic tension between the portrayal of John in the prologue and in 1:19–28 (*Print's First Kiss*, 76–77).

98. The Jerusalem delegation asks John this question here at 1:19, then again at 1:22. This question of identity is put in various ways to Jesus or to others about Jesus throughout his public ministry (see 5:12, 8:25, 9:13–41, and 12:34).

The beginning of John's testimony is a response that characterizes what he is not. "He confessed, and did not deny it, but confessed, 'I am not the Christ'" (v. 20). The narrator's strong pleonastic introductory formula of John's first direct speech correlates the content of the testimony (ἡ μαρτυρία, v. 19) with the act of confessing (ὁμολόγησεν, v. 20). When confronted with official interrogation, the witness can choose to confess or deny his identity and self-understanding, and John chooses to confess.[99] The recitative ὅτι marks John's first statement. In response to their general question, "σὺ τίς εἶ;" marked only by the deictic pronoun σύ, John chooses to turn the dialogue to the question of Christology.[100] He asserts, "I am not the Christ." Using his own deictic pronoun ἐγώ, John points negatively to his own subjectivity in a manner that will correspond to the positive claim that Jesus will make time and again over the course of the Gospel.[101] This first response is the most expansive denial that the Baptist will provide his interrogators in this interaction.

The delegation continues with its quest for identification with the question "What then?" (τί οὖν; v. 21). Even as they take the lead suggesting possible titular claims, dialogically they continue to point emphatically to the subjectivity of John's role with the personal pronoun: σὺ Ἠλίας εἶ; . . . ὁ προφήτης εἶ σύ; ("Are you Elijah? . . . Are you the prophet?"). With his unambiguous christological refutation in v. 20, the Baptist's succeeding denials progress more concisely, cutting short any designs his interlocutors' may have for information or even the dialogical upper hand: "And he said, 'I am not' . . . And he answered, 'No.'"[102] With the

99. Moloney (*John*, 58) further correlates this act of confessing with the Johannine community readership's situation where "uncompromising confession of Jesus as the Messiah was leading to exclusion from the synagogue." The verb ὁμολογέω appears elsewhere in the Fourth Gospel only at 9:22 and 12:42, "in which some form of exclusion from the synagogue is at stake."

100. Although historically it is likely that questions of the Baptist's messianic claims had circulated and thus specifically spurred this delegation (see Barrett, *St. John*, 172), the rhetorical force of giving John the agency of turning the dialogue to the question of Christology allows the evangelist to affirm the Baptist's role as the witness sent from God.

101. ἐγώ εἰμι. . . See 4:26; 6:20, 35, 41, 48, 51; 8:12, 18, 24, 28, 58; 10:7, 9, 11, 14; 11:25; 13:19; 14:6; 15:1, 5; 18:5, 8. So Barrett, *St. John*, 172. For more detail on the negative christological nature of the Baptist's assertion and how it affects the later positive claims by Jesus, see Freed, "Ego Eimi in John 1:20."

102. For discussion of the Jewish expectations for the eschatological figures of the Messiah, Elijah, and the prophet (like Moses) and their relationship to one another, see Brown, *John*, 1:46–50. Regardless of the conception of him in Christian tradition,

transitional conjunction οὖν of v. 22, a favorite of the evangelist, one can then almost feel the frustration of the interrogators as they find themselves where they began: "What are you?"[103] They must have an answer "for those who sent us," but they concede all identification power, and thus the dialogical lead, to John: "What do you say about yourself?"

Only then does John testify positively as to who he is by accepting the role of the Isaian voice (ἔφη ἐγὼ φωνὴ βοῶντος ἐν τῇ ἐρήμῳ, v. 23; see Isa 40:3).[104] All four canonical Gospels agree in giving John the Baptist this Isaian voice (Mark 1:3; Matt 3:3; Luke 3:4), but unlike the Synoptic Evangelists who narrate this identification, the Fourth Evangelist allows John the witnessing agency to give voice to his own self-identification. The Baptist "says" (ἔφη) that he is the "voice" (φωνή) "crying out in the wilderness" in order to prepare the people to "make straight the way of the Lord."[105] He allies his own voice with that in the book of the prophet Isaiah and finally positively asserts his testimonial role.

Raymond Brown notes that the passage in Isaiah refers to the role of the angels, by leveling hills and filling valleys, to prepare the way in the wilderness for the children of Israel to return to Palestine from the Babylonian captivity. By contrast, "John the Baptist is to prepare a road, not for God's people to return to the promised land, but for God to come to His people."[106] However, the two contexts are not mutually exclusive. Brown himself continues, "His baptizing and preaching in the desert was opening up the hearts of men, leveling their pride, filling their emptiness, and thus preparing them for God's intervention." As the human link between the prologue and the narrative of the Gospel, John also prepares a way for the new children of Israel to receive the Word and come to the promised gift of truth, thereby becoming children of God (see vv. 35–37).

---

the Baptist gives no indication of having thought himself in the role of Elijah. See Robinson, "Elijah, John and Jesus."

103. With regard to the conjunction, Wallace (*Greek Grammar*, 674) notes that the "transitional force of οὖν sometimes comes close to the inferential force, as here." See other occurrences in John 2:18, 20; 3:25; 4:33, 46; 5:19; 6:60, 67; 7:25, 28, 33, 35, 40; 8:13, 21, 22, 25, 31, 57; 9:10, 16.

104. For a detailed study John's quotation and the LXX of Isa 40:3, see Menken, "Quotation."

105. For a contrast of the "voice" (φωνή,) of John and the "word" (λόγος) of Jesus, see Cullmann, *Christology*, 260.

106. Brown, *John*, 1:50.

Verse 24 provides an interlude to the dialogue of this first day. By way of a periphrastic perfect passive the narrator states that a second delegation "had been sent from the Pharisees."[107] Archibald Robertson notes that "John does, as a matter of fact, use the past perfect [pluperfect] more frequently than do the Synoptists. He uses it to take the reader 'behind the scenes' and often throws it in by way of parenthesis."[108] This backgrounding technique allies readers with the narrator, who continues to share information that will aid their understanding and decision making. Narratively, this aside also allies the Pharisees with "'the Jews from Jerusalem'" (v. 19), who will often be identified throughout the rest of the story as the opponents of Jesus and his christological mission (2:18–20; 5:10–18; 6:41–59; 7:11–53; 8:20–59; 10:19–42; 18:31—19:42).[109] Therefore, the full range of the opposition to the good news is laid out on this first day.

The delegation initiates one further dialogue exchange in v. 25. Repeating the Baptist's three-part denial of vv. 20–21, they ask him why, then, he is baptizing. This first reference to baptism indicates indirectly what prompted the delegation in the first place. John's practice of baptizing must have brought him to the attention of the Jerusalem authorities and has now given him the opportunity to fulfill his particular testimonial role in this Gospel narrative. By way of another use of the deictic conjunction οὖν, inferential in force, the interrogators question why, if John the Baptist does not claim any recognizable eschatological identity of the messianic era, he is performing an eschatological act of purification like baptism.[110] Although there is no sound first-century evidence apart from the Gospel that links the practice of baptism to these eschatological roles, the question does serve to keep the christological issue before the readers.[111]

---

107. Wallace, *Greek Grammar*, 585.

108. Robertson, *Grammar of the Greek New Testament*, 904–5.

109. Because of the textual instability of this verse, a number of scholars have argued that v. 24 is an indicator of the gospel's literary prehistory and suggest that a second delegation is indicated here. The historical question is that priest and Levites would typically belong to the Sadducees and would scarcely have partnered with Pharisees to send forth a delegation. See Bultmann, *John*, 58; Boismard, "Traditions Johanniques"; and van Iersal, "Tradition und Redaktion." See the general discussion in Brown, *John*, 1:67–71.

110. Brown, *John*, 1:51.

111. Moloney, *John*, 51–53.

John's response affirms his baptizing role, even as he continues to witness to the one who is coming after him (ἐγὼ ὁ βαπτίζω ἐν ὕδατι … ὁ ὀπίσω μου ἐρχόμενος, vv. 26–27). Again with the deictic use of the pronoun ἐγώ, the Baptist points first to what he does do (baptize), then to what he is not. The task of untying "the strap of the sandal" was given to the lowliest in the hierarchy of a master's slaves, and the Baptist disclaims his worthiness even to perform that task.[112] The strength of this image is magnified by John's claim that the one who is coming is already standing among them, and they do not know him (ὑμεῖς οὐκ οἴδατε). John's apocalyptic allusion to the hidden one to come emphasizes what the interrogators "do not know" and the Messiah they will be hard-pressed to recognize and receive in the narrative to come.

The first day concludes by geographically situating these events in "Bethany across the Jordan" (v. 28). Closing an episode with this sort of index of setting is common in the Fourth Gospel (2:12; 4:54; 6:59; 8:20; 9:54) as the evangelist draws the readers into the place inhabited by the characters and points them to space beyond the current sphere of activity. The imperfect periphrastic introduced by the subordinating conjunction (ὅπου) confirms that John's declaration of the testimony he was sent to impart was marked by his ongoing activity of baptizing.[113]

Testimony Fulfilled

John's witness continues in terms of fulfillment the very next day (τῇ ἐπαύριον, v. 29) as he points verbally to the promised coming one (ἐρχόμενος, v. 27) as he sees Jesus coming toward him (ἐρχόμενον πρὸς αὐτόν). The first day's testimonial dialogue becomes a monologue on this second day of promise fulfillment. John's interlocutors have faded from the scene and John bears witness to any and all who would hear. He begins his testimony with the deictic interjection ἴδε, which verbally points to Jesus, "here!" He then gives Jesus the title "Lamb of God" and the mission "who takes away the sin of the world," which link the human being Jesus, who has finally come onto the scene of the Gospel drama, with the divine *logos* of the prologue. He is the Lamb "of God" who has come into the "world" (see vv. 1–2, 9–10). Since readers trust the witness

---

112. Ibid., 58.

113. For the use of the imperfect periphrastic, see Wallace, *Greek Grammar*, 648; and Barrett, *St. John*, 10, 175.

of John, he now also indicates a correlation between the Jesus the Lamb's role in "taking away sin," with Jesus the incarnate Word's stated mission of giving the gift of truth that empowers receivers to become children of God (see vv. 12, 14, 17). Questions about John's intention with this title, which appears here and in v. 35 but is otherwise unknown in the Gospel narratives, have generated a great deal of scholarship.[114] The consensus is that John's lamb image falls in line with his apocalyptic outlook of the conquering lamb who brings judgment. In the context of the Fourth Gospel narrative, however, John's pointing to Jesus as the Lamb of God becomes particularly poignant as both the characters in the story and the readers of the story experience the passion. Jesus is condemned at the moment the paschal lambs are being sacrificed (19:14) and led to the slaughter like the lamb who is the suffering servant of Isaiah 53:7. So much of the story to come is indicated in this first sight of Jesus by the Baptist and the witness that encounter evokes, that the full meaning of his title for Jesus must be allowed.[115]

John the Baptist grounds this testimony of fulfillment by referring to and repeating verbatim his witness from the prologue ("This is the one of whom I said . . . ," v. 30; see v. 15). Again, John is the one merely human character who bridges the omniscient introduction of the prologue into the discrete narrative of the body of the Gospel. Both the demonstrative pronoun that points to Jesus (οὗτος) and the personal pronoun that points back to himself (ἐγώ) provide deixis that strengthen these verbal connections. The one sent by God to witness comes to embody that prologue as he continues to give information that transcends the space, time, and culture of the story world and keeps the reader apprised of God's action in the world.

John's testimony continues on this second day through vv. 31–34. The issue of human knowledge that he first mentioned on day one (v. 26) comes up again as John now affirms the limits of his own powers of perception (vv. 31, 33). He acknowledges that his entire ministry of baptism (v. 31) is in order that through the movement of the Spirit (in the form of a dove, v. 32) he might hear the word of the one who sent him and recognize Jesus as the coming one who will baptize with the

---

114. For an extensive overview of the scholarship on this title as well as his own conclusions, see C. W. Skinner, "Another Look."

115. See Brown, "Three Quotations," 292.

Holy Spirit (v. 33).¹¹⁶ John is then able to initiate God's revelation in Jesus (v. 31). With these statements affirming his own role and alluding to the role of Jesus in God's plan, John can also conclude this second day's witness with the strong statement that he understands that he is fulfilling the mission God sent him to complete even as his testimonial promise of the first day is fulfilled in the coming of Jesus: "And I myself have seen and have testified that this is the Son of God" (v. 34). Speaking again in the perfect (κἀγὼ ἑώρακα καὶ μεμαρτύρηκα), the Baptist brings focus to the completion of this portion of his duty. Jesus is the Son of God who has broken into the world and who will transcend all human expectations for his mission. "This second day of preparation for the gift of the *doxa* further informs the reader of the story, but not the other characters *in the story*, of *who* Jesus is and *what* he does. The question of how all this takes place becomes more urgent."¹¹⁷

Discipleship and the Teaching of the Son of Man

Day three of the Fourth Gospel (τῇ ἐπαύριον, v. 35) begins with John again, this time standing in partnership with two of his disciples. His introductory testimony declared and fulfilled, John now bridges the narrative into the ministry of Jesus as he verbally points his disciples (λέγει, ἴδε) to Jesus whom he sees walking by. He links this day's testimony to his previous witness by using his title of choice for Jesus and his mission: ὁ ἀμνὸς τοῦ θεοῦ ("the Lamb of God," v. 36; see his opening statement of day two at v. 29). This designation from their first teacher becomes a direction for these two disciples as they in turn follow Jesus (ἠκολούθησαν τῷ Ἰησοῦ, v. 37). John the Baptist, his mission complete (see vv. 6–8), now fades from the scene as the readers turn with the disciples along the path of John's verbal index finger and follow along on the journey of these disciples as they participate in the mission of Jesus.

---

116. By not reporting the actual baptism, the evangelist maintains focus on the Baptist's role as witness and Jesus' burgeoning role as mediator of God's covenant through the Spirit. For more on Jesus as the one who baptizes with the Holy Spirit, see Brown, *John*, 1:51–54; and "Three Quotations," 294–95.

117. Moloney, *John*, 53–54. Note the twofold connection between the Baptist's confession of his own status and his twofold statement that he did know the revealer to Israel (1:31–33).

For his part, Jesus takes up the mantle of control of the dialogue, which he will guide and maintain for the rest of the Gospel, and initiates conversation with his new followers (v. 38). His first direct speech of the Gospel will mark his questioning discourse to all who would listen and follow him for the rest of his earthly ministry and beyond: "What are you seeking" (τί ζητεῖτε)? The disciples respond positively yet firmly within their Jewish religious and cultural categories, "Rabbi (which translated means 'Teacher') where do you abide?" The narrator's translational aside further clarifies the limits of their initial perception. And yet their question of abiding (ποῦ μένεις;) will indeed be answered, as Jesus will have much to teach them about where he and they are ultimately to abide (see the discourse of John 13–17). Jesus responds with an ambiguous openness that paves the way for the theological pushing that will characterize following him as well as the new sights and insights with which followers who become receivers will be rewarded: "Come and you will see" (v. 39).

The disciple named Andrew continues this ingathering by finding and bringing in his brother (v. 40).[118] Upon hearing Andrew's claim of finding the Messiah, his brother Simon joins them and is immediately renamed Kephas (translated Peter) by Jesus (vv. 41–42). Day four (vv. 43–51) commences (τῇ ἐπαύριον, v. 43) with a trip to Galilee, and the gathering of eager disciples continues as they heap titles upon Jesus, however firmly trenched within their own cultural expectations. This series of "findings" culminates in v. 49 when Nathanael replies, "Rabbi, you are the Son of God! You are the King of Israel!"[119] Jesus must then stop and begin to reorient their vision to the mission at hand.

> Jesus answered, "Do you believe because I told you that I saw you under the fig tree? You will see greater things than these." And he said to him, "Amen, amen I say to you, you will see heaven opened and the angels of God ascending and descending upon the Son of Man." (vv. 50–51)

---

118. Much has been surmised about the pointed anonymity of the second disciple. For an overview, see Neirynck, "Anonymous Disciple."

119. Jesus finds Philip in 1:43, and Philip says "we have found" in v. 45. This is an early indication of the limited nature of the disciples' belief. From this point until Jesus ends their speculation in 1:50–51, they fail to recognize that Jesus is "from God" or "of God," as the reader knows from the prologue.

In the Gospel of John, Jesus employs the designation "the Son of Man" to highlight that he is the earthly one who comes from God. In referring to himself as the Son of Man, then, Jesus underscores that he, in all of his humanity, is the point of communication between heaven and earth (v. 51).[120] In all their titles of respect for Jesus the disciples have not yet come to identify Jesus as the one turned toward God in intimate relationship both from the beginning (v. 1) and now in history (v. 18). With the acclamation of Nathanael as the Israelite without duplicity (v. 47), Jesus turns the image of Jacob, who would become Israel, onto himself and claims that he, Jesus, will be the new Jacob's ladder (v. 51; see Gen 28:12–17). The Son of Man is the new ladder and gateway to heaven, and he will be the new communication of God in and to the world. Jesus stops Nathanael and the rest of his neophyte disciples with this almost harsh word so that they can begin to open themselves to the new action of God in history that is at hand.[121]

The first chapter of the Gospel thus comes to a close. John has witnessed to Jesus as the Lamb of God and Son of God (vv. 29, 34, 36). Discipleship in the Fourth Gospel has been illustrated as being and abiding (μένω) with Jesus (v. 38).[122] Both the disciples and readers are ripe for the revelation of God in Jesus, the Son of Man. Andrew Kelly and Francis J. Moloney, in their study of the experience of God in the Fourth Gospel, offer an observation that provides a fitting coda to this investigation of the opening days of the Gospel journey (1:19–51):

> In the remainder of the Gospel's first chapter, all the actors in the unfolding drama are present: John the Baptist (1:19–33), the God who has sent the Baptist and spoken to him (1:33), the Holy Spirit (1:32–33), Moses and the prophets (1:45), the disciples (1:35–51), "the Jews" (1:19)—and, of course, the evan-

---

120. For detail on the OT messianic and apocalyptic underpinnings of the dialogue between Jesus and Nathanael, see Koester, "Messianic Exegesis"; Neyrey, "Jacob Allusions"; Rowland, "John 1:51."

121. This presentation relies on the somewhat minority position of F. J. Moloney and his insight into the Son of Man in the Fourth Gospel and the particular introductory role 1:50–51 has in establishing the title that Jesus chooses to fit the earthly mission that will lead to his glorification by God the Father. For his most recent articulation of this reading, see Moloney, *John: Text and Context*, 66–92. The chapter entitled "The Johannine Son of Man Revisited" reviews and nuances his position from over 30 years of scholarship. For his initial treatment, see Moloney, *Johannine Son of Man*, esp. 23–41.

122. Coloe, *Household of God*, 39.

gelist himself. In a quite literal sense, John the Baptist sets the stage on which the drama will be enacted, and the experience of God will occur.[123]

The Hope of Israel: The Dialectic of Fulfillment

The movement of the beginning of the body of John's Gospel (1:19–51) is most clearly delineated by the temporal markers that push the story forward through a flurry of activity across the span of a first week (τῇ ἐπαύριον, vv. 29, 35, 43; then καὶ τῇ ἡμέρᾳ τῇ τρίτῃ, 2:1).[124] Thus, 1:19–28 narrates day one, 1:29–34 narrates day two, 1:35–42 narrates day three, 1:43–51 narrates day four, followed by a distinctive three-day gap before the narration picks up again (2:1). This temporal structuring is often seen as the week of a new creation.[125] The primary thematic problem with this interpretation of the structure is that creation is not much of a motif in this Gospel; revelation is. If the cue is taken rather from Exodus 19:15–16 ("on the third day ..."), then the first four days plus the three-day narrative gap does not point to creation but is instead a direct reference to the theophanic revelation on Sinai that results in God's covenant with Israel.[126] As discussed above, the first three days show the Baptist living out everything claimed about him in the prologue, and he is the only one in the Gospel who always gets it right about Jesus. John the Baptist is the prologue embodied, and he thus accurately portrays his own role (on day one) and points to Jesus as the Lamb of God and the Son of God (on day two). In days three and four, the gathering disciples begin to heap titles onto Jesus, but none of these titles go far enough—they all remain in the religious and political categories within which the disciples are comfortable. Jesus constantly

---

123. Kelly and Moloney, *Experiencing God*, 61–62.

124. For more detail, see Saxby, "Time-Scheme."

125. Boismard is the most famous advocate of this position. See, e.g., *Baptême à Cana*, esp. 14–15; and *Jean*. See also Barrosse, "Seven Days"; and Trudinger, "Seven Days."

126. See Moloney, *John*, 50–63. The *Mekilta on Exodus* in the rabbinic literature presents explicit instructions on how the people are to spend four days preparing prior to the three days of preparation for the ancient celebration of Pentecost, the commemoration of the gift of the Law on Sinai. For a Hebrew/English edition, see Lauterbach, ed., *Mekilta de-Rabbi Ishmael*. For a broader scholarly discussion, see Potin, *Fête juive de la Pentecôte*.

explodes comfortable categories. Thus, at the end of day four Jesus rebuffs Nathanael for his signs-based faith and prepares them all for the revelatory process to come in terms of his own role as the Son of Man (1:50–51).

Raymond Brown has noted that "John is a gospel of encounters." He points to several key interactions over the course of the narrative: "Nicodemus, the Samaritan woman at the well, the cripple at Bethesda, the man born blind, Mary and Martha, and even Pilate," and notes that these characters "one after another" make "their entrance onto the Johannine stage to encounter Jesus, the light come into the world; and in so doing they have judged themselves by whether or not they continue to come to the light or turn away and prefer darkness (Jn 3:19–21)."[127] In the encounters examined in the chapters to come, Jesus interacts in dialogue with several different types of characters as he first initiates then strives to fulfill his mission in the world. The nature of his mission as introduced in the prologue and heralded by John the Baptist is to give the covenantal gift of truth in the glory of God. This mission puts Jesus in tension with the prevailing authorities, both political and theological, of his own contemporary Jewish cultural milieu. The evangelist wants to show, however, that this is not to say that the mission and identity of Jesus are in conflict with Israel's Scripture or its own story of covenantal relationship with God. Rather, the good news of the Christ event is that the biblical narrative is brought to its fulfillment in Jesus, and all those who believe in the word of Jesus, who receive the gift of truth, are given the power to become children of God.

The dialectic sparked by the word of Jesus creates dramatic dialogical interactions that actively move his story to its fulfillment on the cross that glorifies both God and the Son and produces a new covenantal community of God's children who have received the Word. We now turn to the early portion of Jesus' public ministry, narrated in John 2–4, and to the first dialogical encounter where this process of covenantal challenging takes place, at a wedding feast in the town of Cana in Galilee (2:1–12).

---

127 Brown, "Resurrection in John 20."

4

Covenantal Dialogue in John 2–4

In this chapter we will analyze the first narrative unit of the Gospel, a catechetical journey "from Cana to Cana" (John 2–4). Our focus will rest upon the dialogue between Jesus and his mother at the wedding feast in Cana (2:1-12). This exchange initiates the dialogical underpinnings of the covenantal fabric of the Gospel narrative. The complex though ultimately positive interaction between Jesus and his mother inaugurates his public ministry and in the process presents the paradigm for discipleship before the hour of his glorification. In the remainder of the chapter we will move through the journey of catechesis of belief in the Word along with Jesus and his disciples. We will also note how Jesus' dialogue shifts in the second Cana encounter, this time with a royal official, and brings this section to a close.

The Catechetical Journey from Cana to Cana (John 2–4)

John 2:1-12 is a Janus-like passage in that it looks back to the first week of Jesus' public appearances and ahead to the return to Cana and the evangelist's confirmation of the first and second signs. Readers participate in Jesus' travel from Cana to Cana but also have the discipleship episodes of 1:19-51 at the forefront of their consciousness. At the close of the first days, the reader cannot help but feel that the disciples are coming to an authentic faith and an understanding of Johannine Christology. But then the reader encounters Jesus' semi-reprimand of Nathanael.[1] This is the hermeneutic of the Gospel: whenever people seem to come to a solid articulation of faith, Jesus engages them in

---

1. See the discussion of this reading of Jesus' word to Nathanael in 1:50–51 in chapter 3.

dialogue and, using verbal indices of conflict, challenges them to go further. But if the disciples need to go further, where must they go? The evangelist answers this question across the narrative journey from Cana to Cana, providing an early Christian catechesis on authentic faith.

The Covenantal Dialogue at the Wedding Feast (2:1–12)

In the Gospel of John, the public ministry of Jesus of Nazareth is fully inaugurated at a wedding feast at Cana in Galilee (2:1). Through this vivid narrative the evangelist introduces symbols and signs that will mark not only the nature of this ministry but the essence of the messiahship of the *logos* so eloquently introduced in the prologue (1:1–18). Themes of revelation, messianic feast, water, wine, signs, the hour, and the glory of the Son are all manifest in this single event. This first sign (2:11) therefore looks back to the first days of Jesus' public appearances (2:1; see 1:19–51)—even to the very ἀρχή (beginning: 2:11; see 1:1)—while at once preparing the way for the fullness of his ministry and passion (2:3–10; see 19:25–30).

The masterful brevity of this passage is compounded by the complex dialogue between the major characters. From its opening words, the symbolism of the scene points invariably to the revelation with which it ends. The content of that revelation is brought about by word and covenant, however cryptic to the modern reader. The catechetical nature of the narrative becomes clearer, however, once the evangelist's self-understanding as a writer of γραφή—Scripture—is brought to bear. John writes to the believer who knows the story so that his community of readers "may go on believing" that Jesus is the Christ, the Son of God (20:30–31).[2] The evangelist writes to affirm and deepen their faith in the good news, the gift of truth, that Jesus brought into the world (1:14, 17), and it is the dialogical catechesis of belief in the Word of that story that drives the narrative. The revelation of the nature of that belief begins at a wedding feast in a town called Cana, in Galilee.

---

2. For the basis of this position, see the reading of John's statement of purpose at 20:30–31 established in chapter 3 reading the present subjunctive of πιστεύομαι.

Structure of the Passage

The verses that narrate the beginning of the signs that Jesus performs throughout his public ministry, and the first of two signs set in Cana of Galilee (2:1-12; 4:46-54), open with the temporal designation καὶ τῇ ἡμέρᾳ τῇ τρίτῃ ("on the third day," 2:1). This is the most explicit temporal designation thus far in the Gospel and marks a clear break in the narrative.[3] The narrator's sudden silence on intervening days alerts the reader that something new and distinctive is about to take place. Following on this temporal marker, the first two verses set the stage for the action at hand and bring all the relevant characters onto the scene, either explicitly or implicitly. The reader is told directly that Jesus, his mother, and his disciples were invited to a wedding celebration. The establishment of a wedding feast indirectly provides for the presence of supporting characters, including servants, a chief steward, and a bridegroom, who will be necessary for the full effect of the sign.[4]

The action of the scene begins with the dialogue between Jesus and his mother that makes up vv. 3-5. Their speech alternates with the verses both instigated (v. 3) and concluded (v. 5) by the mother of Jesus. For his part, Jesus speaks for the first time in this setting, and the only time to his mother, in these verses (v. 4). After her final words to the servants, she fades from the scene, not to return until the final exit (v. 12).

Once the mother of Jesus redirects the focus to the servants, the scene is further detailed (v. 6) in order to set up Jesus' response to this dialogue (vv. 7-8). The action intensifies and is marked by imperative and response as the servants act silently in accordance with the word of Jesus. At this point, Jesus himself fades from the scene and the servants remain as implied, and still silent, witnesses. The chief steward then enters the scene for the first time and takes over the spotlight (vv. 9-10). The reader is informed indirectly that a sign has occurred. The chief steward, for his part, turns to another silent character, the bridegroom, to expound unwittingly upon the symbolism of the event. Verse

---

3. The more general τῇ ἐπαύριον has served as the primary textual marker thus far (1:29, 35, 43).

4. This technique of gathering major characters in a theologically conducive setting in order to add symbolic discourse to the subsequent narrative episode is a regular Johannine practice; see 3:22-25; 4:5-7; 4:46; 5:1-3; 6:1-4; 7:1-2, 9-10; 8:2-3; 10:22-23; 11:1.

11 resolves the action and clarifies the function of the event as well as its effect on specific characters in the narrative, "his disciples."

Verse 12 is properly a bridge passage that at once wraps up the preceding episode and pushes the narrative forward. Commentators therefore differ as to the inclusion of this verse in the pericope.[5] Some point to the quasi-temporal marker μετὰ τοῦτο as an indication of a break in the narrative. But this is not the vague and far more common μετὰ ταῦτα, which can be rendered "after these things" and does clearly mark narrative shifts.[6] Rather, the use of the neuter singular demonstrative τοῦτο ("after this") specifically relates the activity at hand with the action that precedes it, while looking ahead to what comes next.[7] Taken together with v. 11, these verses provide a frame for the narrative whereby all the major characters regroup and move forward, though arguably changed, and yet in a communion of sorts. The mission and ministries of these characters will play out over the course of the Gospel. Following this line, the passage is structured as follows:

vv. 1–2 The Wedding Feast: Introduction, Character, and Setting
    vv. 3–5 Jesus and His Mother: Dialogue and Covenant
    vv. 6–8 Jesus and the Servants: Imperative and Response
    vv. 9–10 The Chief Steward and the Bridegroom: Result and Reaction
vv. 11–12 Jesus, His Mother, Brothers, and Disciples: Revelation and Resolution

This structure will serve as the basis for the following exegetical analysis. That exegesis will pinpoint how this passage functions in the shape of the larger Gospel narrative. At this point it is sufficient to understand this Cana story as the inauguration of the public ministry of Jesus as well as the impetus behind the general understanding of this ministry as "The Book of Signs" (1:19—12:50).[8] More immediately, this

---

5. Those who understand 2:1–12 as a narrative unit include Barrett, *St. John*; Bultmann, *John*; Lindars, *John*; Smith, *John*; Moloney, *Belief in the Word* and *John*; and Talbert, *Reading John*. Carson, *John*; and Schnackenburg, *St. John*; understand v. 12 as part of the following pericope. Brown, *John*, also restricts this passage to 2:1–11 but understands v. 12 as a stand-alone transitional unit.

6. See John 3:22, 5:1, 5:14, 6:1, 7:1, 13:7, 21:1.

7. This construction also occurs in John 11:7, 11:11, pushing forward the narration of the raising of Lazarus. The only other time it occurs in the Gospel is at 19:28 immediately following the only other interaction between Jesus and his mother, where it marks the climax of the crucifixion scene.

8. For a discussion of "The Book of Signs" as such, see Brown, *John*, 1:cxxxvii–cxliv,

passage is the starting point of a cycle of catechetic stories that manifest "from Cana to Cana" (2:1—4:54) and turn on an understanding of belief in the "word" of Jesus.[9] As such, many more or less elaborate attempts have been made to discover a source behind this account.[10] Because of its rich christological tone, few suggest any historical value for the text.[11] The analysis to which we now turn, however, examines the passage in light of the narrative within which it is placed and the effect it has both on the story itself and on the ones who read that story as their own.

Exegetical Analysis

The first days of Jesus' public life were focused on the testimony of John the Baptist and the gathering of the first disciples (1:19–51). Jesus' almost harsh word to Nathanael brought an abrupt close to what had been a seemingly perfect time of discovery and anticipation on the part of the disciples (1:50). The entire ministry of John the Baptist had pointed to Jesus as the *logos* set forth in the prologue (1:1-2, 19–37). The gathering disciples, however, seem trapped in the categories of their Jewish religious and cultural milieu. All the titles they give to Jesus are restricted to this worldview. Thus, regardless of their earnest zeal to find and follow "him of whom Moses in the law and also the prophets wrote" (1:45), their eyes were not yet opened to the glory of the *logos*.

With the unexpected promise of the powerful image of the angels of God ascending and descending upon him that Jesus puts forth immediately after the harsh word, he also articulates the title that will fit his earthly mission, the Son of Man (1:51). This statement creates a palpable tension whereby both the disciples and the readers (who have read the prologue but are nonetheless affected by the eagerness of the

---

41.

9. See Moloney, *John*, 63–163; and *Belief in the Word*, 77–191.

10. The results range from the standard "signs source" theory (see Schnackenburg, *St. John*, 1:323–25) to the Dionysian pagan feasts (see Bultmann, *John*, 113–15) to a re-created Synoptic parable (see Lindars, *John*, 123–33).

11. Brown, *John*, 1:101. But in opposition to this position, Carson suggests that "we have long eclipsed the day when we may allow ourselves to think that the only account that has any pretension of being of historical value is the one where the writer is theologically disinterested in what he or she is writing" (*John*, 167). He further suggests, and I concur as my exegesis will show, that the background of this passage is the OT itself, mediated through first-century Judaism.

disciples) are ripe for revelation. With this tension in the air, Jesus and his disciples arrive in Cana.

The Wedding Feast: Introduction, Character, and Setting (vv. 1–2)

The first verses set the scene for the narrative to come, and the opening phrase provides the key to the nature of that narrative. The narrator suddenly switches both the setting and the tone with the temporal marker. The reader is thus alerted that something new is at hand. The previous indices of setting in the narrative have been pointed but far less specific. The τῇ ἐπαύριον . . . τῇ ἐπαύριον . . . τῇ ἐπαύριον ("the next day [1:29] . . . the next day [1:35] . . . the next day" [1: 43]) that moved the narrative forward in the first days are now replaced with the fully articulated καὶ τῇ ἡμέρᾳ τῇ τρίτῃ ("and on the third day"). Given the prophetic word that immediately precedes this temporal shift (1:51), the conjunction καί, which has not introduced these markers thus far, is almost resultative in effect.[12] That the story has suddenly jumped ahead to "the third day" creates a narrative gap that further alerts the reader.

On a symbolic level the designation "on the third day" resonates the experience of God's revelation at Sinai narrated in Exodus 19.[13] In that event, "On the third new moon after the people of Israel had gone forth out of the land of Egypt, on that day they came into the wilderness of Sinai" (v. 1). When presented with the opportunity to become God's "own possession among all peoples" if they make a covenant with God (v. 5), the people respond without qualification, "All that the Lord has spoken we will do" (v. 8). In response, God says to Moses, "Go to the people and consecrate them today and tomorrow, and let them wash their garments, and be ready by the third day; for on the third day the Lord will come down upon Mount Sinai in the sight of all the people" (vv. 10–11). Exodus 19:16–25 narrate the promised revelation of the glory of God, while Exodus 20 further details the content of the cov-

---

12. The use of καί to introduce a result from what precedes is found in Matt 5:15, 23:32; Mark 8:34; 2 Cor 11:9; Heb 3:19; 1 John 3:19. The English gloss would be, e.g., "and then . . ." or "and so . . ." (BDAG, s.v. καί).

13. For this symbolism I rely on the work of Moloney, *John*, 66. Scholars often put forth the resurrection as the primary referent of this symbolism. Although I agree that such imagery could be in the air of this narration, it is only secondary to the primary symbolism of the revelation at Sinai; see the exegetical analysis below. See also Coloe, *Household of God*, 39–58; and Serra, "Tradizioni della teofania sinaitica."

enant established beginning with the Decalogue. Marking the narrative of the wedding feast at Cana "on the third day" brings the revelatory event of the covenant at Sinai to the fore as its guiding force.

What happens on this third day is "a wedding feast in Cana, Galilee."[14] This image of a marriage feast summons up further biblical images, this time of the messianic era and its fullness signified by wine and abundance (Amos 9:13–14; Hos 2:19–20, 14:7; Isa 25:6–8, 54:4–8, 62:4–5; Jer 2:2, 31:12; Song of Songs).[15] The wedding celebration itself would have lasted seven days (Judg 14:12; Tob 11:19), but the festivities began with a procession in which the bridegroom's friends brought the bride to the groom's house where the entire party gathered for a wedding supper.[16] There, in the midst of this celebration, was "the mother of Jesus."

Although she is never named, the mother of Jesus is given primacy of place as the first character introduced in this passage, indicative of her role in the events to come. In fact, her designation as "mother" by the narrator (four times in these twelve verses, then four additional times in her only other scene in the narrative, the crucifixion at 19:25–27) is set in relief against how Jesus eventually addresses her as "woman" (here in v. 4, and again at the crucifixion in 19:26). How her characterization as woman and mother affects the message of the Gospel remains to be seen, but for the moment her role as "the mother of Jesus" drives this episode forward.[17] The narrator then advises that her son Jesus, along with his disciples, was also invited to the wedding.[18] Thus, the major

---

14. This town is mentioned only in John, and is connected to Nathanael in 21:2. There are two possible locations for the town in Galilee, but the more likely is Khirbet Qana, about nine miles north of Nazareth. Designating it "in Galilee" could simply be to distinguish it from the Cana (Kanah) near Tyre mentioned in Joshua 19:28 while connecting it to Jesus' chosen destination in 1:43. See Lindars, *John*, 128; Brown, *John*, 1:98.

15. Brown, *John*, 1:104–5; Moloney, *John*, 66.

16. Brown, *John*, 1:97–98. For detail on Second Temple Jewish marriage customs, see Collins, "Marriage, Divorce, and Family." A helpful summary in the context of John 2–4 is found in Coloe, *Household of God*, 29–37, 53–58.

17. See Moloney, *Mary*, 31–50, for an insightful discussion of this characterization in the Fourth Gospel.

18. Wallace (*Greek Grammar*, 401) observes how this picture can be rendered as the disciples "merely tagging along while all of the action centers on Jesus." This image has been exploited by some to indicate that the disciples were not invited, and their presence is what leads to the wine crisis that follows; see Moloney, *John*, 71 (who sees

characters are assembled and the stage is set through notions of a messianic banquet and the revelation of the glory of God by means of word and covenant. The action begins as Jesus encounters his mother in this environment.

Jesus and his Mother: Dialogue and Covenant (vv. 3–5)

The genitive absolute καὶ ὑστερήσαντος οἴνου quickly puts forth the problem and provides the motivation for the dialogue between Jesus and his mother.[19] The "wine" for the wedding feast "ran out," putting the bridegroom in a potentially shameful position.[20] Although the narrator has explained the situation, which is to be understood as a social crisis, the evangelist then employs the speech-as-action techniques of reported action and redundant narration in order to focus the scene and bring the mother of Jesus to center stage. The mother of Jesus says (λέγει) to him (πρὸς αὐτόν) simply, "They have no wine."[21] By having his mother report the event to Jesus, rather than staging it, the evangelist brings the action of the plot into dialogue.[22] Not just the event, but

---

no textual evidence for such); Bultmann, *John*, 115 (who calls such a suggestion "grotesque"). The idiomatic usage of the construction coupled with the narrator's silence on any such implication would preclude the idea.

19. The opening phrase of v. 3 provides the impetus for the action of the rest of the scene. Three variations of this setting are attested. The two alternate readings offer background and a "common-sense" justification for the crisis at hand, while the present reading simply states the problem. Although one can imagine a scribe replacing or elaborating upon this skimpy description in order to smooth the narration and relieve the characters of any responsibility for the crisis, the reverse (replacing clear exposition with something more cryptic) is not so easily conceived. Coupled with the strong, broad-based attestation for the shorter reading, the text of NA27 is accepted as original.

20. Schnackenburg (*St. John*, 1:327) notes that "[c]are was taken to provide enough wine" at such festivities "which was freely poured." Carson (*John*, 169) further asserts that running out of wine "would be a dreadful embarrassment in a 'shame' culture." For more detail on the honor/shame social dictates as they affect this passage, see Williams, "Mother of Jesus." Although such imagery is certainly present, I am not asserting that the honor/shame paradigm is the guiding metaphor of this narrative. Rather, these cultural norms provide the basic framework for the revelation of the true δόξα.

21. Note the narrator's switch to the historical present as the action intensifies.

22. Regarding dramatic technique, Brant (*Dialogue and Drama*, 89) calls this line of direct speech an index of movement and observes that "the Johannine propensity to let characters' speech represent the world behind the text can be meteoric in speed and effect." Therefore, these "simple words accomplish much more than gesture to what is

the perspectives of Jesus and his mother as well are brought into play. Although the details of their relationship have not been narrated, she speaks to him with the full authority and intimacy that a mother-son relationship would merit.[23]

His mother's brief statement, however, only magnifies the tension. Most commentators take for granted that she is requesting a miracle from her son, or, at the very least, is requesting something from him.[24] But this is not so. She simply makes a statement, "They have no wine."[25] Moreover, she virtually repeats what the narrator has just stated. Although it may seem to be repetitive in the context of the narrative, Colleen Conway understands this repetition as a clue to the unique construction of her character. "Unlike any other character in the narrative, apart from Jesus, she shares insight with the narrator. She is the character who perceives the problem and makes it known to Jesus."[26] This technique of redundant narration confirms for readers the veracity and integrity of the mother of Jesus. Readers are provided evidence that she can be trusted and looked to for guidance in responding to Jesus. Furthermore, if the messianic era is marked by a wedding banquet and an abundance of wine (Amos 9:13–14; Hos 2:19–20, 14:7; Isa 25:6–8, 54:4–8, 62:4–5; Jer 2:2, 31:12; Song of Songs), her direct testimony of the lack of wine highlights this symbolism and makes known the perceived deficit at hand. Therefore, she introduces what will become a Johannine

---

happening at the moment." See chapter 1 for an overview of the dramatic techniques Brant identifies in the Gospel.

23. Although the narrator makes explicit neither why his mother is concerned about the situation nor what she expects from Jesus, an apocryphal tradition holds that "Mary was the aunt of the bridegroom, whom an early 3rd century Latin preface identifies as John the son of Zebedee" (Brown, *John*, 1:98). He goes on to say that this "is to be associated with the tradition that Salome, wife of Zebedee and mother of John, was Mary's sister, a relationship which makes John the cousin of Jesus." On the narrative level, she certainly shows familial concern and authority and could be turning to Jesus in the same light. For a discussion of the first-century Palestinian social dictates that could be behind her involvement, see Williams, "Mother of Jesus."

24. For a discussion of the scholarship on Mary's role in this passage, see Maccini, *Her Testimony Is True*, 98–117.

25. Contrast her interaction with Jesus (direct speech) to that of the official who approaches him upon his return to Cana (4:46). The narrator relates that he "asked him to come down and heal his son...."

26. Conway, *Men and Women*, 72. Although this insight is extremely helpful, she too asserts that Jesus understands his mother's comment as a request, a conclusion that is not a logical necessity.

theme of reinterpretation and fulfillment, of both Jewish expectations and the feasts through which those expectations are remembered and experienced.²⁷ This makes Jesus' response to his mother's statement all the more incisive: τί ἐμοὶ καὶ σοί, γύναι; οὔπω ἥκει ἡ ὥρα μου.

The question Jesus puts to his mother has been described as one of the most difficult phrases of the Fourth Gospel.²⁸ The full reply, the only thing Jesus says to her in this passage, presents a twofold response, each side of which has been deemed problematic in the context of the narrative. His first words are ambivalent and followed by an apparent non sequitur about his "hour." That he then proceeds to do something about her statement only intensifies the ambiguity. The verbless clause τί ἐμοὶ καὶ σοί is a translation of the Hebrew idiom מה לי ולך, which is rendered literally in English, "What (is) to me and to you?" The expression is terse even in Hebrew and Greek, and its harshness cannot be mediated even by the most earnest attempts to soften it.²⁹ The deictic personal pronouns ἐμοί and σοί, act as a verbal index finger pointing to the subjective involvement of Jesus and his mother. Addressing his mother with the vocative γύναι ("woman") adds to the intensity of his first words of the scene.³⁰

The idiom τί ἐμοὶ καὶ σοί appears in the LXX four times.³¹ Judges 11:12 reads, "Then Jephthah sent messengers to the king of the Ammonites and said, 'τί ἐμοὶ καὶ σοί, that you have come to me to fight against my land?'" Likewise, 2 Chronicles 35:21 reads, "But he [Neco] sent envoys to him [Josiah], saying, 'τί ἐμοὶ καὶ σοί, king of Judah? I am not coming against you this day, but against the house with which I am at war; and God has commanded me to make haste. Cease opposing God, who is with me, lest he destroy you.'"³² In 2 Kings 3:13 Elisha responds to the kings' request for prophecy by saying, "τί ἐμοὶ καὶ σοί; Go to the prophets of your father and the prophets of your mother." On

---

27. Grassi, "Wedding at Cana."

28. Conway, *Men and Women*, 72.

29. See Maynard, "TI EMOI KAI SOI."

30. Despite Bultmann's efforts (*John*, 116), Schnackenburg claims that in the Semitic world such an address to one's mother is "unusual and astonishing" (*St. John*, 1:328).

31. The same idiom with variations in number appears two more times: "And the king said τί ἐμοὶ καὶ ὑμῖν, sons of Zeriah?" (2 Sam 16:10) and "And David said, "τί ἐμοὶ καὶ ὑμῖν, sons of Zeruiah, that you should this day be adversaries to me?" (2 Sam 19:22).

32. Josiah does not cease and is killed in the subsequent battle.

a more personal level, 1 Kings 17:18 tells of a woman's address to Elijah when her son falls ill shortly after he arrives among her household: "τί ἐμοὶ καὶ σοί, O man of God? You have come to me to bring my sin to remembrance, and to cause the death of my son!" In the NT, the idiom in either the singular or the plural appears in Mark 1:24 and its parallel in Luke 4:34, and in Mark 5:7 and its parallels in Matthew 8:29 and Luke 8:28. In each of these instances, a demon or a person possessed by a demon addresses Jesus in this way. In each occurrence of this idiom in biblical literature, therefore, a crisis is at hand, and the addressee's response to it determines the future of both parties.

Most commentators take this collective evidence to indicate that the idiom itself is negative, thus often rendering it "What do you have against me?" or more colloquially "What's it to me or you?" (the implied answer being "Nothing!").[33] This understanding indicates at the least simple disengagement, and at most outright hostility.[34] Thus, Jesus' response to his mother becomes not only harsh, but also a sharp rebuke. Since most commentators also take her statement as a request, it follows that with this rebuke Jesus also rebuffs his mother's request to somehow remedy the situation, miraculously or otherwise. Scholars are then left to reconcile the fact that Jesus proceeds almost immediately to do just that. What happens here? Is he convinced by her rejoinder? But she does not even address him. Rather, she turns to "the servants" and says simply, "Whatever he might say to you, do." Is he moved to action by her faith in him? This is more likely, but it still implies that the will of Jesus, and thereby the will of God, is subject to human demands. Further, there is no implication in the text that this is what happens.

The force of the dialogue becomes far less problematic when Jesus' mother's opening comment is properly understood not as a request of any kind but as a symbolic statement signaling that the people are bereft of the essential components for the messianic wedding banquet within the further symbolic context of Pentecost—the revelation of the glory of God. Jesus' response must then be considered as something other than a rebuff, since no request was made of him. Grammatically, the

---

33. BDAG goes so far as to offer the gloss, "What have I to do with you? What have we in common? Leave me alone! Never mind!" (s.v. ἐγώ). This seems to over-read the grammar.

34. See Conway, *Men and Women*, 72–73, for a discussion of this perspective. See also Brown, *John*, 1:99.

construction of the idiom is a dative of possession, whereby the dative substantive (ἐμοὶ καὶ σοί) possesses the noun to which it is related (τί).[35] In this light a more nuanced translation would be "What belongs [or "is common"] to me and to you?" The force of this construction is to emphasize the object possessed, in this case the interrogative τί.[36]

The question then becomes, what is between the two of them, if anything? If the presumption of negativity is set aside, a second look at the biblical evidence for this idiomatic expression will shed some light. In each of the cases mentioned where warring kings are involved, the *what* can be expressed in terms of binding agreements or treaties. Therefore the answer to the question could involve alliance as much as it could antipathy. On the more personal level, the *what* of this expression seems to invoke the idea of covenant in terms of relationship. The demoniacs who address Jesus in this way point to the nature of their relationship in the spiritual realm, the implication in this case being a desire for a policy of noninvolvement. When Elisha uses it to the kings who have approached him, he follows by suggesting they go instead to the prophets of their ancestors—with whom they presumably have some established relationship or covenant. He then decides to help them after all, based on his relationship with the king of Judah. When the woman with the dying son uses this idiom in addressing Elijah, she too goes on to speak of the quality of their relationship and what may be between them. Elijah, for his part, responds by healing her son.[37] Some sort of mutual obligation and promise is always set forth—a covenantal

---

35. Wallace, *Greek Grammar*, 149–51. The usage, though not especially common, occurs with copulative verbs such as εἰμί (which is understood in the verbless clause that makes up this idiom). For the elliptical use of τί, see BDF §299.3.

36. Wallace, *Greek Grammar*, 150–51. Wallace acknowledges that the idiomatic nature of this expression is problematic beyond grammatical classification, but nonetheless affirms the construction, thereby eschewing the "leave me alone!" idea.

37. "And he said to her, 'Give me your son.' And he took him from her bosom, and carried him up into the upper chamber, where he lodged, and laid him upon his own bed. And he cried to the Lord, 'O Lord my God, hast thou brought calamity even upon the widow with whom I sojourn, by slaying her son?' Then he stretched himself upon the child three times, and cried to the Lord, 'O Lord my God, let this child's soul come into him again.' And the Lord hearkened to the voice of Elijah; and the soul of the child came into him again, and he revived. And Elijah took the child, and brought him down from the upper chamber into the house, and delivered him to his mother; and Elijah said, 'See, your son lives.' And the woman said to Elijah, 'Now I know that you are a man of God, and that the word of the Lord in your mouth is truth.'" 1 Kgs 17:19–24.

challenge. The respondent's decision to accept or reject the covenant proffered determines the action that follows.

Given the established symbolic context of revelation and the covenant at Sinai, this idea of idiomatic covenantal language begins to make sense of the interaction between Jesus and his mother at the wedding feast. She makes known to him the deficiency of wine; he responds with a sharp idiom of covenantal challenge. But what is the nature of this covenant? The second part of Jesus' response seems to indicate what it is not: "my hour has not yet come."

With this statement, the theme of "the hour" is introduced to the Gospel. Jesus' cryptic references to his hour will drive his entire public ministry (4:21, 23; 5:25, 28; 7:30; 8:20), and its arrival (12:23, 27) will mark the turning point of the Gospel (13:1), the content of his passion ("Father, the hour has come; glorify your Son that the Son may glorify you," 17:1), and the future of his church (19:27).[38] With this statement in 2:4 in response to his mother's declaration of the lack of wine, Jesus signifies that the hour of his full glorification has not yet arrived and that part of his covenant will have to wait for its full expression (see 19:25–27).

The mother of Jesus accepts this without qualification. Her next words confirm her acceptance and indicate the role that she will take. Resonating the words of the children of Israel at Sinai, and again at the ritual that seals the covenant, "All that the Lord said, we will do" (πάντα ὅσα εἶπεν ὁ θεός ποιήσομεν [LXX], Exod 19:8; see also 24:3, 7), she turns to the servants and says, "whatever he might say to you, do" (ὅ τι ἂν λέγῃ ὑμῖν ποιήσατε, v. 5). She accepts his challenge just as the children of Israel accepted the covenant at Sinai, and with her imperative sets in motion the revelation. Her role fulfilled for the moment, she fades from the scene.[39]

Jesus and the Servants: Imperative and Response (vv. 6–8)

The narrator now returns to detail the scene further with a noteworthy description of "six stone water jars" that were there "for the purifica-

---

38. Not all commentators read 19:25–27 as a symbolic establishment of the church. For support of this interpretation, see Barrett, *St. John*, 552; Brown, *John*, 2:923; Moloney, *John*, 504; and *Mary*, 31–50. For the analysis of this passage, see chapter 6.

39. She withdraws to return in a way that recalls Cana in 19:25–27, by way of the literary "bridge" 16:21.

tion rites of the Jews." The days of preparation and purification that preceded the revelation of the glory of God on the third day are brought back to mind. Jars such as these were crucial to follow these purification requirements.[40] Because of their necessary size they were often embedded in the ground, and they were typically made of earthenware.[41] But earthen jars could contract impurity and would have to be broken; therefore stone jars, which would not, were particularly treasured.[42] Scholars disagree, however, on the symbolic value of numbering them as six. Raymond Brown argues that most attempts at such delineation are farfetched.[43] But, given the care of the detail and that the evangelist chose to number them at all, some openness to symbolism must be granted. The number six is typically understood in relation to the number seven, the number of perfection. That their number falls short of perfection is consistent with the lack of wine already established. Thus their number could be a hint that the former covenantal gift (that of the Law) is to be perfected.[44]

The theme of water will return throughout the Gospel (chapters 3–7, 9, 19), but is introduced here in terms of abundance, since each stone jar held "twenty or thirty gallons." The Greek μετρητής is a liquid measure of about forty liters, or nine to ten gallons.[45] Two or three measures, then, can be rendered "twenty or thirty gallons." There are six jars—this is a massive amount of water.

The remaining verses of this section are marked by imperative and response. The servants introduced by the mother respond to her command by further obedience to the commanding word of Jesus (vv. 7–8).[46] As silent doers of the word, they implicitly partake of the covenant established by the voiced interaction between Jesus and his mother. The rest of this episode, then, is a continual acting out of this

---

40. See Lev 11:29–38.
41. Schnackenburg, *St. John*, 1:332.
42. Lev 11:35; Brown, *John*, 1:100.
43. Brown, *John*, 1:100; Lindars, *John*, 130.
44. Moloney, *John*, 68. In this understanding he points back to the prologue at 1:16–17.
45. BDAG, s.v. μετρητής.
46. Brant (*Dialogue and Drama*, 87) classifies Jesus' speech in this segment as indices of movement: "Jesus' directions to the servants at the wedding at Cana indicate their actions, some of which, but not all, the narrator reiterates."

doing of the word of Jesus. He speaks to them in command to "fill the water jars," and they "filled them to the top." The evangelist provides another example of redundant narration, this time direct speech (γεμίσατε) followed by narration (ἐγέμισαν αὐτάς) to confirm the right response of the servants. This rare construction ἕως ἄνω ("to the top") reinforces both their obedience and the perfecting abundance of the event to come.[47] Jesus then says to them once again in command, "Draw the water now and bring it to the head steward," and "they brought it." Again the redundant narration of Jesus' direct speech (ἀντλήσατε νῦν καὶ φέρετε … οἱ δὲ ἤνεγκαν) confirms the obedient participation of the servants as they act out covenantal relationship initiated by the mother of Jesus. The word of Jesus and the responsive action of the servants thereby resolves, or in Johannine terminology "perfects," the perceived deficiency of the wedding feast.

The Chief Steward and the Bridegroom: Result and Reaction (vv. 9–10)

With his last command Jesus introduces the next new character to the scene, ὁ ἀρχιτρίκλινος, "the chief steward." This term has as its primary reference "the slave who was responsible for managing a banquet."[48] Because of the nature of his dialogue in this passage, his role may be more elevated—that of a "master of the feast" or a "guest chosen to run the affair because he is on familiar terms with the bridegroom."[49] Regardless, his role in this narrative is to verify the sign which, it should be noted, is not described. Through indices of movement in direct speech it is, rather, experienced.

With the narrative turn to the head steward, Jesus himself fades from the spotlight for the moment. The characters who bridge the narrative this time are "the servants" who bring what they have drawn from the jars. The chief steward "tasted the water become wine" (τὸ ὕδωρ οἶνον γεγενημένον) and immediately "called the bridegroom" to confirm the abundance of wine, the miraculous nature of which he has no knowledge. It is "the servants" who have full knowledge of the event (οἱ δὲ διάκονοι ᾔδεισαν οἱ ἠντληκότες τὸ ὕδωρ). They are still silent but nonetheless

---

47. See 2 Chr 26:8, the only other biblical occurrence of this phrase.

48. Thus, "headwaiter" or "butler." It is derived from the term τρίκλινος, a banquet room with three couches. BDAG, s.v. ἀρχιτρίκλινος.

49. BDAG, ibid.; Brown, *John*, 1:100. See Sir 32:1.

witnesses to the sign. They can attest that what the chief steward says to the bridegroom is profoundly true, even though his own understanding remains at the superficial level of his own categorical worldview. As doers of the word who know the true nature of the sign at hand as well as who is responsible for it, the servants become models with whom readers can identify.

"Everyone serves the good wine first and after they get drunk, an inferior one; but you have kept the good wine until now."[50] Attempts have been made to find evidence of a rule of some sort in first-century banquets that everyone followed and that this bridegroom has broken.[51] Such investigations miss the point of the proclamation in the advancement of the narrative.[52] The chief steward speaks of τὸν καλὸν οἶνον twice in his statement. Placing the adjective in the first attributive position on both occasions, the chief steward notes the goodness of the wine in what he understands to be the exceptional act of the bridegroom.[53] By mistakenly crediting the bridegroom with this extraordinary (though not miraculous in his eyes) act (and emphatically so with the articulation of the deictic personal pronoun σύ), the words of the chief steward further evoke images of the messianic wedding banquet through which the bridegroom inaugurates the messianic age with an abundance of wine. The dramatic irony is, of course, that the true bridegroom is only just beginning to reveal himself (2:11; 3:23–36).[54]

---

50. Note that the Greek behind what has been translated here as *everyone* is in fact the more pointed πᾶς ἄνθρωπος, which emphasizes activity and reactivity of human beings, in contrast to that of Jesus.

51. See Bultmann, *John*, 118; Barrett, *St. John*, 102.

52. Brown (*John*, 1:100) affirms such attempts are silly, and suggests the evangelist is merely putting forth a "type of shrewd practice that is common to human nature" that elucidates the event.

53. Wallace, *Greek Grammar*, 306. Note also the present of what "everyone does," emphasizing the timeless nature of a human practice that has been suddenly preempted (ibid., 524).

54. Attempts to identify Jesus with the bridegroom on the narrative level in this passage miss the point of the messianic symbolism on the discourse level. Such imagery does open the door for this identification in 3:22–33.

Jesus, His Mother, and His Disciples: Revelation and Resolution (vv. 11–12)

The narrator returns to summarize the event and affirm its effects on several characters. "Jesus did this as the beginning of the signs in Cana, Galilee."[55] The evangelist is not simply emphasizing the power of Jesus but his sovereignty as well. Jesus is the one whose word has the power to initiate covenant, made apparent through signs. Verse 11b-c then follows this proclamation with elaborative result clauses. Further, the action that follows the first clause (ἐφανέρωσεν τὴν δόξαν αὐτοῦ) given in the aorist tense (καὶ ἐπίστευσαν εἰς αὐτὸν οἱ μαθηταὶ αὐτοῦ) has an ingressive aspect that is best expressed in English by the idea that Jesus "revealed his glory, and his disciples began to believe in him."

With the second clause of this verse, the evangelist makes clear the nature of the covenant in the time before the arrival of "the hour." It is manifested through "signs" and its purpose is to begin the revelation of "his glory" (τὴν δόξαν αὐτοῦ). The sight of the *doxa* here continues to correlate this scene with the covenant text of Exodus 19 where the sight of the *kebôd* at Sinai reveals the presence of God in that covenant-making scene. The full manifestation of the *doxa* of God cannot be known until "the hour" arrives and God becomes the agent of the revelation. Here Jesus begins his participation in that glory so that his disciples may begin to believe in him.

This last clause highlights something that may have eluded the reader's attention thus far. The disciples, who were present with Jesus at his arrival in Cana (2:2), are mentioned again for the first time since the action began. They have apparently been standing by all along and, like the servants, have become silent witnesses to the sign. Unlike the servants, however, they are merely observers at this stage. They have yet to become doers of the word. At this point, they are just becoming

---

55. The syntax and diction of this clause (ταύτην ἐποίησεν ἀρχὴν τῶν σημείον ὁ Ἰησοῦς ἐν Κανὰ τῆς Γαλιλαίας) is curious, resulting in two variant readings. Translators have rendered it in English a number of ways, emphasizing one aspect or another. The RSV reads, "This, the first of his signs, Jesus did"; the NAB, "Jesus did this as the beginning of his signs"; the NIV, "This, the first of his miraculous signs, Jesus performed"; the KJV, "This beginning of miracles did Jesus"; the ASV, "This beginning of his signs did Jesus"; the NRSV "Jesus did this, the first of his signs." Note that although the absence of the definite article before ἀρχήν is crucial in understanding the syntax of the Greek, it must be provided in the English for smoothness without changing the force of the original.

believers. And, unlike the mother of Jesus, they are farther still from perceiving the fullness of the covenant that is integral to believing. This process of becoming is a journey for the disciples that will span the rest of the Gospel. At Cana, it has only just begun.

The final verse of this passage brings the major characters back together and introduces the brothers of Jesus to the Gospel.[56] Their unbelief, over against the developing belief of the disciples, will come into play at a later stage (7:1–10). These last verses taken together form an inclusio with vv. 1–2 and bridge the narrative to the next events in Jesus' ministry. This group, however changed both physically and spiritually by the events at Cana, moves forward into Capernaum and ever closer to "the hour" that will, readers have every reason to believe, change everything.

Conclusion: The Covenant of the Believer at the Wedding Feast at Cana

The narrative of the wedding feast at Cana captures in twelve verses the essence of the beginnings of the ministry of Jesus depicted in the

---

56. The text of the final verse of this pericope is ambiguous in presenting the group that moves on to Capernaum with Jesus. That his mother traveled with him is uncontested. However, the rest of the company seems to have been unclear. Codex Sinaiticus has "his mother and his brothers" were with him. Codex Regius indicates that both "the brothers and the disciples" were present but does not relate those groups to Jesus with the genitive pronoun. Codex Vaticanus, Codex Athous Laurae, P75 and the first hand of P66 all read "the brothers and his disciples," while the broadest spectrum of witnesses attest "his brothers and his disciples" (the corrector's hand of P66, Codex Alexandrinus, Codex Koridethi, both Family 1 and 13, the Byzantine Majority, 33, and all the Latin and Syriac versions; Codex Cyprius and the Freer Codex also follow this reading, but posit "and his disciples" before "and his mother"). Although the weight of the external evidence lends to this last reading, it provides a curious band of travelers and does not easily explain the existence of the others. Note that "brothers" of some sort are always attested although this is the only group not previously mentioned in the narrative. This does not preclude the authenticity of their presence. The mother of Jesus was also unmentioned prior to 2:1, where she arrives on the scene with full narrative force as a major character in the ensuing episode. Their presence therefore must have been original, but just who they were comes into question. Some scholars assert this must be a synonym for "the disciples" and therefore posit the reading of Sinaiticus as original and giving rise to the others, but there is no internal evidence to support this. Metzger (*Textual Commentary*, 173) argues that the last reading does account for the rise of the others but acknowledges the weight of the evidence that does not include the first genitive pronoun by enclosing it in square brackets. This is the reading that has also been accepted for the present study.

Gospel of John. The stark dialogue and vivid imagery allow the evangelist to introduce the symbolic framework of the rest of the earthly ministry of Jesus and to foreshadow the hour of the glory of God. The essence of this symbolic framework is covenant, the nature of which is made manifest through belief in the word and revelation. The archetype for this covenant is presented through the dialogue between Jesus and his mother and the relationship that is established.

Her presentation as both woman and mother further characterizes both this covenant and the vocation of the believer once the hour arrives. It is the woman whose character Jesus holds up as their model: "When a woman is in travail she has pain, because her hour has come; but when she gives birth to a child, she no longer remembers the anguish, for joy that a child has been born into the world" (16:21). Further, every time Jesus approaches and interacts with one he calls "woman" throughout the rest of his ministry, the covenant with this first woman will be called to mind. When Jesus says to the Samaritan at the well, "Woman, believe me, the hour is coming when neither on this mountain nor in Jerusalem will you worship the Father" (4:21), or to Mary Magdalene at the empty tomb, "Woman, why are you weeping? Whom do you seek?" (20:15), the reader is reminded of the covenant with the woman who first believed without seeing any signs and wonders, who believed foremost in the word of Jesus.

The Rest of the Journey

The fullness of this first portion of Jesus' public ministry, the so-called Cana to Cana narrative (2:1—4:54), provides the Johannine catechesis on the nature of authentic faith. The two signs at Cana in Galilee that form the beginning and ending of this teaching are the literary frames of the journey of faith.[57] The physical movement between these two events mirrors the theological journey whereby Jesus brings the Word to the universal community of potential receivers and believers. The Cana to Cana narrative thus offers a catechesis on the universal possibility of a journey of faith. This is what everyone goes through on their birth from above (3:1–21) and journey of spiritual existence. Note that the noun

---

57. For an exploration of how minor characters are employed to develop the journey of belief in the Gospel of John, including the mother of Jesus (2:1–12, 19:25–27) and the royal official (4:43–54), see Howard, "Significance of Minor Characters."

"faith" never appears in John's Gospel, but the verb "to believe" or "to have faith" appears over sixty times.[58] Faith is an action. It is dynamic and communicative, and whenever Jesus' dialogue partners think they "have" it and have arrived, Jesus verbally challenges them to go further. There is also a constant tension in the expectation and acceptance of "signs faith." The revelation of God in Jesus must always be anchored in the historical event of the cross and the glorification that can only be revealed upon the belief in that word of Jesus.

The flow of this narrative can be mapped as follows:[59]

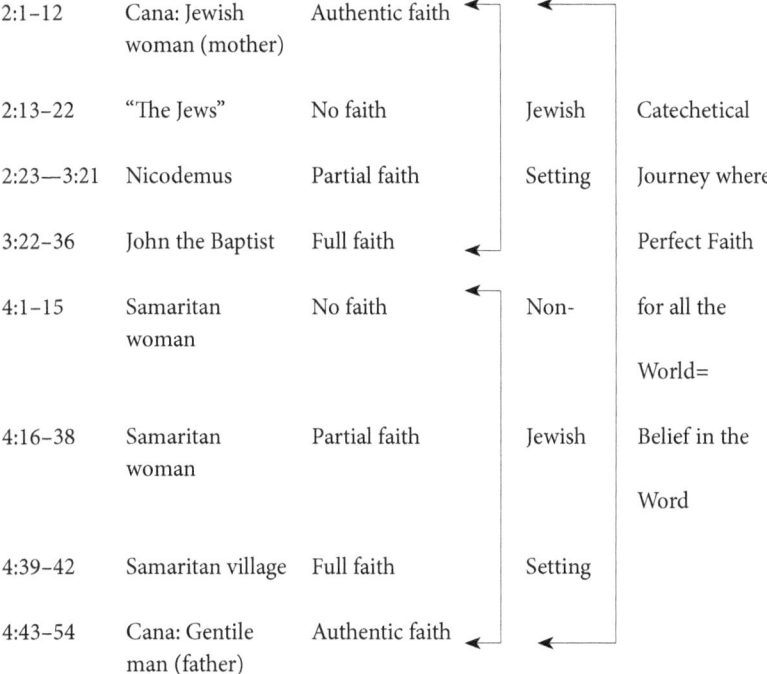

In the remainder of this chapter we will briefly discuss two more of these encounters along the way: the final scene in Jewish territory, focusing on the relationship between Jesus and John the Baptist (3:22–

---

58. See John 1:7, 12, 50; 2:11, 22; 3:12, 15, 18, 36; 4:21, 39, 41, 48, 50, 53; 5:24, 38, 44, 46; 6:29, 35, 40, 47, 64, 69; 7:5, 31, 38, 48; 8:24, 30, 45; 9:18, 35, 38; 10:25, 37, 42; 11:15, 25, 40, 42, 45, 48; 12:11, 36, 42, 44, 46; 13:19; 14:1, 10, 29; 16:9, 27, 30; 17:8, 20; 19:35; 20:8, 25, 29, 31.

59. For this narrative flow, I rely on the work of Moloney, "Cana to Cana"; *Belief in the Word*, 77–191; and *John*, 63–164.

35); and the final episode of the section, following Jesus' movement through non-Jewish territory and focusing on the interaction of Jesus and the royal official (4:43–54). These episodes are affected by whence we have come and will affect where we are going in the examination of covenantal dialogue in the Gospel of John.

The Prologue Embodied Reprise: The Faith of John the Baptist (3:22–35)

At the conclusion of his time at the wedding feast in Cana, Jesus and his entourage went down to Capernaum and remained there a few days (2:12). When the feast of the Passover drew near, he went up to Jerusalem, where his demonstration against commerce in the temple area brought him into his first confrontational dialogue with "the Jews" there (2:13–22). Although "the Jews" reject the word of Jesus about the temple and consider his role nonsensical (v. 20), the dialogue has the positive effect on the disciples of remaining with them, such that "after he was raised from the dead, ... they believed [ἐπίστευσαν] the Scripture [τῇ γραφῇ] and the word [τῷ λόγῳ] that Jesus had spoken" (v. 22). The narrator's comment about the knowledge and faith of Jesus (vv. 23–25) leads into an extended dialogue instigated by Nicodemus, "a leader of the Jews" (3:1–21). The naïve questioning by Nicodemus provides Jesus the opportunity for discourse about heavenly things, including God's love and plan for the world and the role of the Son of Man in that plan (3:11–16). The episode concludes without resolution for Nicodemus. For the rest of his story, the reader must press on (see 7:45–52; 19:38–42). The scene ends with Jesus' final words hanging in the air: "But the one who does the truth comes to the light, so that one's deeds might be shown as labored in God" (3:21).

After these things (Μετὰ ταῦτα) Jesus and his disciples move from Jerusalem to the Judean countryside, where they spend some time baptizing (3:22). As in the first verses of the Cana scene, key characters are gathered in 3:22–24 into a temporal and spatial setting that provides the impetus and motivation for the dialogue that follows (see 2:1–2). Jesus and his disciples are participating in a baptizing ministry (v. 22). John was likewise continuing his own baptizing ministry "at Aenon near Salim," where both people and water were abundant (v. 23). The narrator then informs readers that "John had not yet been thrown into prison" (v. 24). Through this last index of setting, the narrator points beyond the space inhabited by the characters in the narrative, indeed beyond what he will ever narrate. Yet with this one aside, he provides both historical and temporal grounding for the event at hand and alludes to the entirety of the rest of the Baptist's story. By assuming that readers are intimately familiar with the end of the Baptist's story, the narrator exchanges a knowing nod with his readers and punctuates this final scene of the martyr *par excellence*.

A debate (ζήτησις) arises between the disciples of John and "a Jew" regarding purification (v. 25).[60] Although no details of this controversy are provided, it spurs John's disciples to come to him with concern over the increasingly successful baptizing ministry of Jesus. It is difficult to connect the narrator's indication of a debate regarding "purification" (καθαρισμοῦ) directly with the ensuing question of baptism.[61] This conflict creates a narrative tension that intensifies attention both on the question itself and on the Baptist's coming response. John's disciples address him as "Rabbi" and inform him that "the one who was with you across the Jordan, to whom you witnessed [σὺ μεμαρτύρηκας], look [ἴδε], this one [οὗτος] is baptizing and all are going to him" (v. 26). The deictic use of the personal and demonstrative pronouns coupled with the deictic interjection ἴδε emphasizes the contrasting subjects of John and Jesus, while illustrating the disciples' anxiety over the situation. The

60. The only serious textual difficulty of this scene is found here at the end of v. 25. Whereas a number of manuscripts, including Alexandrinus, Vaticanus, the corrector's hand of Sinaiticus, and P75 among others read "with a Jew," a number of other important manuscripts, including the first hand of Sinaiticus, Koridethi, and P66, among others attest the plural. If the singular is original it would be the only occurrence in John's Gospel, which uses the plural often. However, even the plural never occurs without the definite article, rendering "the Jews." In dealing with this textual instability, a tradition has arisen in scholarship that the original reading was Ἰησοῦ, such that the controversy arose between John's disciples and Jesus. For a recent survey and avocation of this position, see Pryor, "John the Baptist." Such speculation, however, is made without any evidence, internal or external. The singular is the *lectio difficilior* and is accepted as original. The singular Ἰουδαίου connects this off-stage interlocutor with the region of Judea where both parties are located, (see Schnackenburg, *St. John*, 1:413–14) without directly connecting him with "the Jews" of Jerusalem who serve as the primary opponents of Jesus.

61. See Brown, *John*, 1:151–52; and Moloney, *John*, 109, for brief discussions. The real issue seems to be the debate that has arisen, more so than its content. Neyrey and Rohrbaugh ("He Must Increase") thus suggest translating the term strongly as "controversy" or "conflict" as the issue for the disciples of John is one of envy because of a culturally conditioned response to "limited good" in a "zero-sum" world.

hyperbolic πάντες ("all") confirms the Baptist's ministry is declining noticeably. John continues his persistent defiance of human norms by responding counter-culturally and offering his final witness to Jesus.[62]

The pleonastic ἀπεκρίθη Ἰωάννης καὶ εἶπεν ("John answered and said") highlights the solemn definitiveness of the Baptist's response.[63] He begins by speaking not of Jesus directly but of the sovereignty of God. A human being is able to receive only what is given from heaven (v. 27). As presented in the prologue, John highlights the gift-giving prerogative of God and the receiving power of humankind (1:12, 16–17). Resonating his first witness to the Jewish delegation, John calls his own disciples to be his witnesses, and repeats, "I am not the Messiah" (οὐκ εἰμὶ ἐγὼ ὁ Χριστός, v. 28; 1:20). He goes on to affirm, "Rather,'I was sent before that one'" (ἀλλ' ὅτι Ἀπεσταλμένος εἰμὶ ἔμπροσθεν ἐκείνου). The one proclaimed in the prologue to be sent to witness to the light (1:6–8; see 3:21) continues to witness to his role. By using the demonstrative pronoun ἐκεῖνος, John points not just to ὁ Χριστός (the grammatical referent of the pronoun), but also to the one he verbally pointed to those first days (1:29, 35–36) thereby linking the expected Messiah with the one (Jesus, v. 22) whose ministry is now in question.

John then turns to the messianic imagery of marriage and applies the role of the friend of the bridegroom (ὁ φίλος τοῦ νυμφίου) as a metaphor for his role in the events at hand (v. 29). As the friend, he rejoices at the success of bridegroom.[64] John is the voice of one crying in the wilderness (1:23) who witnesses to the one coming, whom he now characterizes with the messianic image of the bridegroom. He is not the voice of the bridegroom (τὴν φωνὴν τοῦ νυμφίου, v. 29). Therefore as the

62. Neyrey and Rohrbaugh (ibid.) make much of how countercultural John and his response are as he steps outside the "limited-good" culture and, although he acknowledges it, refuses to play the "zero-sum game." Jesus' increasing success and renown does not diminish John's role, rather, it affirms his merit.

63. Moloney, *John*, 109. This Semitic rendering is often used by the Fourth Evangelist.

64. For a helpful discussion of the role of the friend of the bridegroom in the wedding festivities as well as the Baptist's use of this metaphor to point to himself, see Coloe, *Household of God*, 25–37. John the Baptist uses a common social custom to illustrate that by accepting the role of the bridegroom's friend, he is stepping outside just such cultural norms of competition and limited good in his refusal to be envious of the ministry of Jesus. See Neyrey and Rohrbaugh, "He Must Increase." Just as there is no competition for the bride between the bridegroom and the friend, there can be no competition between John the Baptist and Jesus.

friend "who stands and listens for him," rather than being envious, or in any way concerned, he "rejoices greatly" (χαρᾷ χαίρει) on account of that voice. John can then proclaim, "So this joy of mine is fulfilled" (ἡ χαρὰ ἡ ἐμὴ πεπλήρωται). The deictic language that John uses points to the emphatic finality of his current witness, now referring directly to Jesus: "It is necessary for that one (ἐκεῖνον) to increase, but me (ἐμέ) to decrease." Contrary to first-century Palestinian religious or cultural expectations of one whose ministry has achieved as John's has until now, he willingly yields to Jesus' expanding ministry. John explodes convention precisely because his role lies outside human bounds, so that his very decline in the face of Jesus' increase means that his duty is complete and his role fulfilled.

The final words of this scene, and the final verses of this journey through Jewish territory, expand upon the role and experience of the one who comes from above (3:31–36; see the geographical shift in 4:1–4). Although this reflection can be understood as a progression from the Baptist's words in v. 30, scholars have debated from whose lips they are uttered in the context of the narrative. The present study understands vv. 31–36 as a final discourse by the narrator to summarize and conclude this first leg of the journey from Cana to Cana.[65] From the immediate context, vv. 31–32 affirms why Jesus must increase, and also rejects the concern of John's disciples, who can be included in those who belong "to the earth" and speak about "earthly things." At the same time, these condemning words also apply to "the Jews" who rejected Jesus (2:18–22), as well as to Nicodemus who has not yet let go of earthly categories and concerns (3:1–21). Verses 33–34 reiterate key positive actions introduced in the prologue and manifested in the narrative thus far: witnessing (μαρτυρεῖ, v. 33), giving (δίδωσιν, v. 34), and receiving (λαμβάνει, v. 33). The trustworthiness of the one sent from God is affirmed (ὃν γὰρ ἀπέστειλεν ὁ θεὸς τὰ ῥήματα τοῦ θεοῦ λαλεῖ, v. 34), and

---

65. Those who understand vv. 31–36 to be a continuation of the Baptist's speech include Barrett, *St. John*, 224–25; and Wilson, "Integrity of John 3:22–36." For the argument that these words come from Jesus (by way of a rearrangement of the text), see Schnackenburg, "Situationsgelösten Redestücke." For a position that asserts these verses come from the lips of Jesus but are placed here by the evangelist as a summary statement, see Brown, *John*, 1:159–60; Dodd, *Interpretation*, 309. Those who understand these verses as a final reflection of the narrator include Lagrange, *Saint Jean*, 96; Carson, *John*, 212–14; Moloney, *John*, 104–13. Moloney argues for the thematic unity of all 2:1—3:36.

whoever receives his witness seals that God is true (ὁ θεὸς ἀληθής ἐστιν, v. 33). Verse 35 introduces the love of God for the Son as the relationship of the Father to the Son (ὁ πατὴρ ἀγαπᾷ τὸν υἱόν). Because of this familial relationship, the Father has given all things to the Son (v. 35). The words and actions of Jesus in the story thus far, and in the fullness of the Gospel to come, flow from this relationship.[66]

Verse 36 closes this section by providing the choice this gift of God puts before the world. Believing in the Son is the decision that confers eternal life (ὁ πιστεύων εἰς τὸν υἱὸν ἔχει ζωὴν αἰώνιον), while the alternative to believing is characterized not as disbelief but as disobedience. The one who disobeys (ὁ ἀπειθῶν) chooses not life but abides in the wrath of God (ἡ ὀργὴ τοῦ θεοῦ μένει ἐπ᾽ αὐτόν). Edward Malatesta has shown that "abiding" is intrinsic covenantal language in John.[67] In the OT the "wrath of YHWH" is used in Exodus 32:10–12 to describe God's reaction to Israel's covenantal disobedience as the people turn to the golden calf (see also Deut 9:19), as well as in the Prophets to describe YHWH's judgment upon Israel's turning from its covenantal relationship with God (see, e.g., Isa 9:19; Jer 7:20; 30:24; 44:6; Ezek 5:13; 7:8; 20:8; 38:19; Hos 13:11; Mic 5:15; Zech 7:12). Just as Israel's covenant obligations to YHWH were based on obedience, the Fourth Evangelist uses the activity of disobeying to narrate the action of all who do not believe the Son and therefore do not receive the gift of God. The gift of truth, from the God who is true (v. 33), confers life (v. 36; see 1:4). This is the covenantal activity of the Son that is increasing in 3:22–36, even as John the Baptist's witness completes and, his role fulfilled, he must decrease (3:29–30).

The Return to Cana: The Healing of the Official's Son (4:46–54)

Jesus' journey with his disciples continues, now through a conscious decision to leave Judea and return to Galilee by way of Samaria (4:1–4). The remainder of the journey from Cana to Cana thus moves through territory outside the world of Judaism. After an extended discussion with a Samaritan woman at a well that is presented in two movements (4:5–15 and 4:16–30), Jesus has a brief interlude with his disciples alone

---

66. Moloney, *John*, 112.
67. Malatesta, *Interiority and Covenant*. See the overview in chapter 1.

(4:31–38). Jesus' time in Samaria closes in 4:39–42 with many of the Samaritan villagers believing in Jesus, first on the witness of the woman (v. 39) and then because of his own word (v. 41). The evangelist's purposes in this journey, which provides for a discourse on who Jesus is and the progression of individual witness and group faith, are made clear in the final declaration of the Samaritan villagers as they reflect upon their experience of the word of Jesus: "We know [οἴδαμεν] that this one [οὗτος] is truly the savior of the world" (ἀληθῶς ὁ σωτὴρ τοῦ κόσμου, v. 42). The word of Jesus is now proclaimed effective for all the world. With this pronouncement in the air, Jesus returns to Galilee.

As he has in previous events (2:1–2; 3:22–24; 4:1:6), the narrator sets the scene temporally and geographically, reflecting with the readers upon where they have been while at once providing the impetus for the event at hand.[68] Verses 43–45 bridge the narrative out of Samaria and into Galilee (v. 43), recalling the events at the Passover festival in Jerusalem (v. 45; 2:13–25) and mentioning the notoriety Jesus has achieved as word of him and his actions spreads through the countryside with the returning Galileans. In the midst of this setting, the narrator inserts a traditional saying attributed to Jesus himself (αὐτός . . . Ἰησοῦς) regarding a prophet's lack of honor in his own country (v. 44).[69] It is difficult to situate this saying within the context of Jesus moving, after two successfully received days in Samaria, into Galilee where he is also welcomed (v. 45). By relating this bit of information here, however, the narrator achieves two things. First, he punctuates the reality that with John's witness complete, it is now Jesus who must give voice to testimony (αὐτὸς γὰρ Ἰησοῦς ἐμαρτύρησεν, v. 45; see 5:31, 36; 7:7; 8:14, 18; 10:25; 13:21; 18:37). Second, the narrator signals that this sort of welcome based on signs and bold acts may not be the authentic faith that the prophetic figure of Jesus truly desires. Readers are alerted to the notion that in the events to come, this sort of faith understanding may be corrected. Verse 46 then introduces the scene itself and heightens this alert by locating Jesus in Cana and harking back to the authentic

---

68. These verses provide a commentary on the story this far. See Dodd, *Historical Tradition*, 238–41.

69. See Mark 6:4; Matt 13:57; Luke 4:24; 13:33–34. For a more detailed discussion of this verse, see Pryor, "John 4:44"; Moloney, *John*, 151; Reim, "John IV.44"; Sturch, "'PATRIS' of Jesus"; Willemse, "Patrie de Jésus."

faith that brought about the beginnings of his ministry.⁷⁰ Finally, the other major character in this scene is introduced: a certain royal official (τις βασιλικὸς); and the motivation for the scene is set: his son lay ill in Capernaum.⁷¹

The crux of the encounter between Jesus and the royal official is recounted in vv. 47–50. Although the title "royal official" could identify either a Jew or a Gentile, the context of this dialogue, as it concludes Jesus' journey through the world outside of Judaism as well as the evangelist's tendency to explicitly identify Jewish characters, suggests that readers are to understand him as a Gentile.⁷² The narrator explains that upon hearing that Jesus had returned from Judea to Galilee, the official went out and asked (ἠρώτα) Jesus to go down (to Capernaum) and "heal his son" (ἰάσηται αὐτοῦ τὸν υἱόν), for he was about to die (v. 47).

The next three verses recount the dialogue between Jesus and the official in direct speech, this time instigated and concluded by Jesus. The similarity between this encounter and that of Jesus' first visit to Cana is notable (2:1–12). In the present passage, the primary dialogue falls again into three parts, beginning and ending by the word of Jesus with his interlocutor providing the central assertion. In the first Cana event, the primary dialogue was instigated and carried forward by his mother, with Jesus' covenantal challenge holding her statement and response together. But resonation need not result in direct imitation. What we see here is a progression in the discourse based upon the fullness of the journey from Cana to Cana.⁷³

Jesus then (οὖν) responds to the official's entreaty with another provocative challenge: "Unless you see signs and wonders, you will not

---

70. Schnackenburg ("Traditionsgeschichte") suggests this verse would have introduced the traditional miracle story that the Fourth Evangelist incorporates into his narrative here. For a survey of the discussion of the relationship of this passage to the Q account of the centurion (Matt 8:5–13; Luke 7:1–10) see Neirynck, "John 4,46–54."

71. Readers will remember that Capernaum is where Jesus and his entourage abided for many days (2:12) following the first sign in Cana where he revealed his glory (2:11). Some scholars understand 4:46–54 as an introductory scene to 5:1–47. See, e.g., Feuillet, "Signification théologique." Although this scene does bridge the narrative out of this first journey, indicators such as v. 46 mark this event primarily as a return to Cana that completes the journey and illustrates the progress of Jesus' ministry.

72. See the discussion and survey of scholarship in Mead, "Basilikos in John 4.46–53"; and Moloney, *John*, 160–61.

73. Although I do not agree with his conclusions, C. H. Giblin ("Suggestion, Negative Response") insightfully details this progression over the course of the narrative.

believe" (v. 48). The deictic conjunction οὖν coordinates Jesus' statement with the official's request for a healing sign. The narrator has recounted the official's act of requesting (v. 47), and since Jesus has not been characterized as a physician of any sort, readers must understand this entreaty, as does Jesus, in terms of "signs and wonders." This again is a progression from the first Cana story, for now it is Jesus' renown that has led this official from the larger world to him. For his part, Jesus challenges the interlocutor to articulate what it is he really wants, and what it is he truly believes. He challenges the official beyond signs and wonders. But Jesus directs his verbal challenging not just to the official. He accuses "you people" of not believing (οὐ μὴ πιστεύσητε) without seeing signs and wonders. His statement in the plural extends beyond the official who faces him to the Galileans who stand behind this dialogue as festive hangers-on (v. 45).[74]

The royal official responds to Jesus' harsh words in the face of his dire need by, instead of retreating, taking a verbal step closer to Jesus. Κύριε, he says, "come down before my boy [τὸ παιδίον μου] dies" (v. 49). His response to the word of Jesus is now recounted in direct speech. He refers to the child the narrator described as "his son" (αὐτοῦ τὸν υἱόν, v. 47) as "my boy" (τὸ παιδίον μου, v. 49). This designation referring to his sick child would begin to humanize him even to the most skeptical reader.[75] His verbal approach to Jesus in response to the word of challenge is rejoined by Jesus in command form. Using the present imperative, Jesus tells him to "go [πορεύου], your son will live" (v. 50).[76] For his part the official, now further humanized as "the man" (ὁ ἄνθρωπος), began to believe (ἐπίστευσεν) not in signs and wonders, but "in the word [τῷ λόγῳ] of Jesus," and went (ἐπορεύετο). The redundant narration of Jesus' command (πορεύου . . . ἐπορεύετο) affirms the right response of the man to Jesus' challenge and direction.

The final verses of John 4 narrate the consequences of the man's belief in the word of Jesus (vv. 51–54). Even as he is going down to Capernaum, he is met by his slaves, who tell him that his child would

---

74. A number of scholars suggest redactional theories to deal with this "rebuke" of Jesus. For surveys, see Schnackenburg, "Traditionsgeschichte," 62–63; and van Belle, "Jn 4,48 et la Foi."

75. It could indicate a moment of "faith, however imperfect, which springs out of a father's love" (Westcott, *St. John*, 79. See also Moloney, *John*, 161.

76. See also Jesus' directives that follow his mother's response to his covenantal challenge in 2:6–8.

live (v. 51).[77] He then inquires about "the hour" (τὴν ὥραν) of his child's improvement, and, in direct speech, they confirm, "Yesterday at the seventh hour, the fever left him" (v. 52).[78] The precision in their response allows the official, here characterized solely in the familial role that readers now know motivated his own journey, ὁ πατήρ, to come to know (ἔγνω) that this healing correlates directly with the word of Jesus that "Your son will live" (v. 53). An exegetical difficulty arises with the father's response to this realization. The narrator states, "And he himself began to believe along with his whole household." When, therefore, did the father believe? Did he believe in the word of Jesus, or not until the sign was confirmed?[79] Is this an example of authentic faith? The reiteration of the father's process of believing now includes his entire household's process of coming to belief. This seems to be the key to understanding the evangelist's intention here. Even authentic belief is not static, but it is a dynamic journey of coming to knowledge that deepens hand in hand with the missionary aspect of witnessing.[80] It is in sharing his belief in Jesus, however authentic in foundation, that the royal official, who is also fully human and a father, can realize its full consequence for living. The final verse brings this encounter to a close in a manner that once again parallels the first sign at Cana of Galilee (v. 56; see 2:11–12). This now is the second sign that Jesus did here. The journey from Cana to Cana is complete, concluding in many ways like it began.

The Dialogue of Covenant in John 2–4

The Cana-to-Cana narrative recounted in John 2–4 is a catechetical journey that teaches the nature of authentic faith. As we finally arrive at

---

77. There is textual instability here with regard to how the official's child is identified. There is strong external evidence for the reading, παῖς αὐτοῦ. There is also evidence for reading the pronoun in the second person, παῖς σου. The Vulgate and many other Latin witnesses read υἱὸς αὐτοῦ, in line with the words of Jesus in v. 50. This debate has been found in scholarship in Kilpatrick, "John IV:51"; and Freed, "John IV:51." For the purposes of this study, παῖς αὐτοῦ is accepted as original, in line with the humanizing familial progression of the description of the official.

78. For a symbolic reading of the evangelist's detail of "the seventh hour," see Robinson, "Meaning and Significance."

79. The redactional theories mentioned above affect the understanding of the clumsiness here as well; see Schnackenburg, "Traditionsgeschichte," 67–70.

80. See Gnilka, *Johannesevangelium*, 38; Moloney, *John*, 162.

4:54, the ministry of Jesus has come a long way. All those whom he has encountered have been affected by his word and deed: some changed forever (John the Baptist, the Samaritan villagers), others resolutely unchanged ("the Jews"), and still others slowly making the first steps along their own journeys of faith (Nicodemus, the Samaritan woman). Jesus, too, has been affected by these encounters. His interactions with people along the way are marked by his human experience of them and with them. As his renown spreads he is brought into contact with more and more people. Yet, in these ensuing encounters, he pushes harder for those he meets to believe in his word, despite that renown. His disciples, too, are journeying, watching, and remembering (2:11–12, 22; 3:22; 4:27–38). This is a dynamic process of being challenged and gaining deepening belief in the word, based in covenantal relationship (2:1–12; 3:31–36; 4:46–54). Readers, likewise, are making this journey along with them.

The background of this journey is the language and imagery of covenant. The pattern of temporal and spatial markers across 1:19—2:12 manifests the symbolism of the feast of Pentecost as the theological canvas of this narrative portrait. By NT times, the revelation of the glory of God and the foundation of the covenant between God and all Israel at Sinai was linked to the feast of Pentecost.[81] This annual pilgrimage festival of the First Fruits (Exod 34:22; Lev 23:17; Num 28:26; 2 Chr 8:13), also known as the Feast of Weeks (Exod 34:22; Deut 16:10), was in origin a harvest festival of thanksgiving for God's blessings (Exod 23:16).[82] By the mid-second century BC, the *Book of Jubilees* associates the festival with a series of covenants, all of which were made in the third month (*Jub* 6:1, 17–18 [Noah]; 6:19; 14:20; 15:1–4 [Abraham]; 1:1; 6:11, 20–22 [Sinai; see Exod 19:1]).[83] The Qumran literature relates the Feast of Weeks to the creation of a covenantal people founded in response to the word of God.[84] In the rabbinical Judaism that developed after the destruction of the temple (AD 70), the focus of the festival

---

81. Pentecost was the name given this feast in Greek in the later Deuterocanonical books. See Tob 2:1; 2 Macc 12:32. The feast of Pentecost is mentioned by name in the NT at Acts 2:1; 20:16; 1 Cor 16:8.

82. Vander Kam, "Weeks," 6:895–96.

83. Ibid., 6:896.

84. See CD 16.1–5. For a discussion of the Pentecost experience and celebration in the Qumran community and literature, see Potin, *Fête juive*, 124–31. See also Vander Kam, "Weeks," 6:896–97.

experience shifted to the giving of Torah on Sinai as the mark of God's covenantal relationship with Israel.[85]

The celebration of the festival of Pentecost began after seven weeks in relation to the day of the wave offering at the Passover festival (Lev 23:15–16; Deut 16:9–10). The three days (Exod 19:11) were preceded by four days of preparation, and thus "on the third day" the remembrance of God's covenantal gift culminated in the celebration of the revelation of the glory of God.[86] This rich symbolic framework is the foundation upon which the dialogical encounter between Jesus and his mother at the wedding feast at Cana is built. The catechetical journey that follows this revelatory event is one of discovery and ever deepening understanding of the covenantal process of belief in the Word, which empowers all who encounter Jesus to become children of God.

As a result of that initial dialogue, the mother of Jesus unconditionally accepts his covenantal challenge by extending his word to those who can put it into action, using words that recall those of the children of Israel at Sinai: "Whatever he might say to you, do." Through her acceptance of Jesus' challenge through words of covenant, she then becomes the paradigmatic disciple in the time before Jesus' "hour." As Jesus' journey through Jewish territory begins (2:12), readers hold her covenant response in the background of their reading experience as the model against which all further responses to Jesus can be measured. As Jesus goes up to Jerusalem for the Passover festival and, standing amid what he sees to be the locus of commerce in the temple, commands, "Stop making my Father's house a marketplace!" (2:13–16), and then, in the face of the stubbornness of "the Jews" (2:18), challenges, "Destroy this temple and in three days I will raise it up" (2:19), readers recognize their refusal to understand Jesus' symbolic challenge as a rejection of this covenantal relationship (2:20–22). The hope readers find in the disciples is based in the narrator's proleptic assertion of their remembrance and belief (2:22). When Jesus speaks to Nicodemus of the love of God for the world and the spiritual birth necessary to enter into relationship and see the kingdom of God introduced in the prologue (3:1–21; 1:1–18), readers can appreciate Nicodemus's question "How can this be?" (3:9) as an openness to the covenant of belief in the word

---

85. Potin, *Fête juive*, 131–40; Coloe, *Household of God*, 42.

86. See Moloney, *John*, 50. Moloney bases his reading on the *Mekilta on Exodus 19*. See Lauterbach, ed., *Mekilta de-Rabbi Ishmael*.

of Jesus that indicates that his journey is only partially complete. When John, the witness sent from God, appears again (3:22–26), his countercultural response to the increase of Jesus' ministry (3:27–30) based in the covenantal imagery of the love of the true God (3:31–36) assures readers of his full faith and the fulfillment of his mission.

As Jesus leaves Jewish territory and starts back to Galilee by way of Samaria, where he meets a woman at Jacob's well and engages her in dialogue (4:1–30), his covenantal dialogue with the first woman remains as the model. The present dialogue does not progress initially, as the woman's misunderstanding of Jesus' intentions lead her to reject his offer of the living of water of eternal life with a naïve response regarding her daily chore of coming to the well (4:1–15). Jesus then takes a different tactic, questioning her in terms of her husbands, which leads to dialogue about covenantal claims of ancestry, worship, and eventually her knowledge of the Messiah (4:16–25). Her claim opens the door for Jesus' own christological claim, "I am" (ἐγώ εἰμί, 4:26). As Jesus' disciples arrive, she goes to share her discovery but reveals the incomplete nature of her faith journey by her still-questioning words, "Come and see a man [ἄνθρωπον] who told me everything I have done! Could this one be the Messiah?" (μήτι οὗτός ἐστιν ὁ χριστός; 4:29). The Samaritan villagers then provide the full response to Jesus modeled by his mother at Cana, when the narrator remarks, "And many more began to believe because of his word" (καὶ πολλῷ πλείους ἐπίστευσαν διὰ τὸν λόγον αὐτοῦ, 4:41).

When Jesus returns to Cana, his covenantal activity there is brought to the foreground once again (4:46). When he is engaged in dialogue by a royal official (4:47) who is described as a man (4:50) and father (4:53) with a sick boy (4:47), readers are ready for Jesus' challenge to the authenticity of his faith (4:48). The covenantal nature of the royal official's response is revealed in the similarity of this entire scene with that of the first sign at Cana, including the father's belief in the word of Jesus and obedience to his command (4:49–50). Like the first sign at Cana, this sign is confirmed by unwitting witnesses (4:51–53; 2:9–10), and belief in Jesus spreads through the covenant household of faith as the narrator confirms that this journey from Cana to Cana, inaugurated by the unconditional acceptance of the mother of Jesus to his covenantal challenge, has come full circle (4:54; 2:12).

The fullness of this covenant will not be revealed until the very hour of the true glory of God, introduced in the first dialogue in Cana of Galilee (19:16b–37; see 2:1–12). At the foot of the cross of her son, the woman who is also mother appears again, and "when Jesus saw his mother, and the disciple whom he loved standing near, he said to his mother, 'Woman, behold, your son!' Then he said to the disciple, 'Behold, your mother!' And because of that hour the disciple took her to his own home" (19:26–27). Though his own people may have neither known nor received him from the beginning (1:11), Jesus establishes his own anew through the covenant of the believer, which is ultimately manifested through the covenant of family.[87] This, therefore, becomes the essence of church: to live as the Word's own even at the foot of the cross. It is only then that the ministry of Jesus and the glorification of God is perfected (19:28–30) and life in that revelation can begin (John 20–21 and beyond).

But this hour has not yet arrived. Jesus has much yet to testify and teach about himself and his relationship with the Father. His work in Jerusalem has only just begun (2:13–22). His ministry now turns to the rest of the major feasts of Judaism, where God's covenantal relationship with Israel is remembered and experienced as ongoing and present in its daily life (John 5–10). With the temple as his background, Jesus now places himself in dialogue with "the Jews" so that he might render those feasts christological and thereby give himself as the covenantal fulfillment of the presence of God in their midst. Readers, too, must make their way, along with Jesus and his disciples, from this initial catechetical journey of faith through the christological experience of the feasts of Israel.

---

87. See chapter 6 for the analysis of the passion narrative in the Gospel of John.

5

Covenantal Dialogue in John 5–12

IN BIBLICAL LITERATURE, THE FEASTS OF ISRAEL ARE PRESENTED AS cultic celebrations that recall God's saving action in the past and render that action present in the current community.[1] For the Johannine Christians to be expelled from the synagogues (see 9:22; 12:42; 16:2), they were not simply being excluded from these celebrations (a social experience); they may have felt that they were losing contact with the God of creation and God's saving action in history (a religious experience). As believers in the saving action of the Christ event, they were taught that covenantal relationship with God is engendered through the Word of Jesus (see 2:1—4:54). But this presents another problem: what about these feasts and the experience of God's presence they facilitate? Not only does the Fourth Evangelist have to care for the community members pastorally because they are no longer in that world, he also has to show God's fidelity to them and God's continuing presence in their lives as members of the new covenantal community.[2]

This reshaping of the experience of God in the life of the community is the background for the narrator's indications of the feasts of Judaism in John 5–10 (see 5:9b; 6:4; 7:2; 10:22).[3] The evangelist renders christological the feasts of Judaism. It is Jesus the Christ who is the per-

---

1. See Lev 23:1–44 for YHWH's appointment of the feasts through Moses. The celebration of a Jewish feast is a *zikaron*, a "memorial" (Lev 23:24) of God's past active presence in the lives of his chosen people. Celebrating the liturgy of the feast manifests God's presence among the people in the current age (Moloney, *Signs and Shadows*, 1). For more detail, see Chenderlin, "*Do This as My Memorial*," 88–167.

2. This problem of having to rethink the celebrations of God's presence was not exclusive to the Johannine Christians at the end of the first century AD. Postwar Judaism was shifting from temple- to synagogue-centered worship. "The liturgical feasts of the temple and the piety of the people were in a state of transition" (Yee, *Jewish Feast*, 21).

3. Moloney, *Signs and Shadows*, 2.

fection of Jewish liturgy and theology.[4] It is Jesus the Christ who renders God present in the ongoing lives of the community. This process began in John 2–4, in the presentation of the feast of Pentecost as the theological canvas behind the portrait of the wedding feast at Cana, and the ensuing catechetical journey of faith from Cana to Cana. In John 5–10, the evangelist turns to the remaining major feasts of Judaism, Passover, Tabernacles, and the feasts of Sabbath and Dedication. The climactic close of John 10 is the revelation that Jesus and God are one.

The celebration of the feasts of Israel was also intimately connected with the experience of God's covenantal action in and with creation. Although the term "covenant" does not appear, this narrative imagery of covenant forms the backdrop of all that Jesus says and does in this segment of his public life. In this light, the present chapter will examine this second major narrative unit of the Gospel (John 5–10) and focus upon Jesus' dialogues during the Feast of Tabernacles (John 7–8).[5] We will also give attention to the conclusion of the public ministry and the christological move to glory that points to a "lifting up" that will attract all the nations and gather into one the scattered children of God (John 11–12).

The Feasts of Israel (John 5–10)

The dialogues and discourses of John 5–10 are contextualized by the central feasts of the Jewish ritual calendar. A year's time in the narrative passes, marked temporally by the general μετὰ ταῦτα ("after these things," 5:1; 6:1; 7:1) until the culminating temporal designation ἐγένετο τότε ("it happened then," 10:22). The feast of Pentecost was presented symbolically at the inauguration of Jesus' public ministry in Cana (2:1–12). Following his return to Cana (4:46–54), Jesus goes up to Jerusalem to an unnamed "feast of the Jews" (5:1) where he eventually engages in dialogue about the weekly feast of Sabbath (5:10). John 6 focuses on the spring festival of Passover (6:4). John 7 introduces an extended narra-

---

4. Ibid., ix.

5. As presented below, Jesus' verbal exchanges with others in John 7–8 quickly become very heated and angry and culminate in the physical threat of stoning (8:59). Recall that the term "dialogue" is being used in the dramatic sense to indicate that two or more people are speaking to each other in an ongoing verbal interaction where speech often constitutes the primary action of the scene. See Brant, *Dialogue and Drama*, esp. 74–158.

tive section complete with discourse and dialogue, all contextualized by the autumn Feast of Tabernacles (7:2). The final feast that "was taking place" (ἐγένετο) in these chapters is the winter festival of Dedication (10:22). Pervading each festival narrative and discourse is a perfection of the liturgical celebration of God's presence in the context of the fulfillment of God's plan for humankind to live in relationship as children of God through belief in the Word of Jesus.

The Flow of the Narrative

The next major movement in Jesus' public ministry begins in John 5 at an unnamed "feast of the Jews" (5:1). The narrator's designation of this setting introduces themes of the next six chapters: how Jesus relates to the presence of God celebrated in the Jewish feasts, and how the Johannine community is to begin to reshape its liturgical life. Readers learn that the weekly feast of Sabbath is the focus of this first narrative and discourse, as Jesus sees a man lying near the pool by the Sheep Gate in Jerusalem and heals him on the Sabbath (vv. 2–9).[6] As part of the healing command, however, Jesus instructs the man to carry his pallet (v. 8). The man complies, thereby breaking Sabbath law (v. 9).[7] What Jesus claims in these verses about his relationship to God and Sabbath is essential for further understanding who he is and the revelation of God that he brings. Jesus, as the Son of God the Father, transcends human bonds chronologically, historically, and legally (vv. 17, 19–47). "The Jews" reject this claim of transcendence and begin to seek "all the more to kill him" (v. 18).[8] The custom of the day associated sin with death, but

---

6. For the tradition history of this sign, see Witcamp, "Use of Traditions." For a narrative-critical exegesis, see Culpepper, "John 5.1–18."

7. See Exod 20:8–11; Jer 17:19–27. Thomas, "Fourth Gospel and Rabbinic Judaism." Moloney (*Signs and Shadows*, 6) notes that "the incipient faith of the man will surely be put to the test as he has carried his pallet on a Sabbath."

8. Since the dialogue that ensues becomes angry and aggressive, it is important to reiterate that I continue to enclose the term "the Jews" in quotation marks because it does not indicate the Jewish people generally. The evangelist uses the term most often to indicate the opposing side of the christological debate about Jesus. For a further discussion of the dramatic characterization of "the Jews" as the "corporate voice of deliberation" in the ongoing dialogue of the Fourth Gospel, see Brant, *Dialogue and Drama*, 178–87. In addition, the exegesis of this exchange will reflect the Johannine perspective and context, including the extreme tension and conflict inherent in Jewish-Christian relations of the first century AD. This perspective should by no means be extrapolated to contemporary Jewish-Christian dialogue and relations.

Jesus shows an authority as giver of life and judge (vv. 25–30) and hints that he has been granted functions traditionally restricted to God (vv. 39–47).

The healed man begins with full faith in his response (v. 9), becomes fragile as he shifts responsibility (v. 11), then falls away as he turns to stand with "the Jews" and accepts their authority and their categories as well as the application of both of these to his life (vv. 15–16). For his part, Jesus remains constant and in control ("My father is working still, and I work," v. 17). The Sabbath was established for rest because God rested, but the sun keeps rising and babies continue to be born. Therefore, God rests save for two primary functions: giving life and judging. Through the discourse of John 5 that follows his sign, Jesus places himself in the roles of life-giver and judge as well. He claims that he transcends Sabbath law, without destroying or replacing it, by fulfilling the roles the Father has given him (vv. 12–47).

The expression μετὰ ταῦτα ("after these things," 6:1) once again marks a new temporal setting, which allows for a new geographical setting as well. The narrator resumes his practice of setting the scene and gathering the active characters by informing the readers that as the feast of Passover drew near, Jesus and his disciples, followed by a large crowd, went to the other side of the Sea of Galilee (vv. 1–4).[9] This annual spring festival of Judaism will contextualize the events and discourse at hand. The narrator also clarifies the reason for the presence of the crowds: "because they saw the signs he did on those who were sick" (v. 2; see 2:23–25). All this takes place as Jesus positions himself "on a mountain" (v. 3). These introductory remarks bring to mind the covenant-making

---

9. The narration of these verses that set the scene of John 6 "on the other side of the sea" in Galilee while John 5 is set in Jerusalem (5:1) and 7:15–24 "harks back directly to the Sabbath healing that lies far off in chapter 5," is one of several instances that led Bultmann (*John*, 10) to observe, "The thesis has been presented . . . that the original order of the text has been disturbed, through an interchange of leaves or by some other means." He concludes that "it must be presumed that the present order of our Gospel is not derived from the author." Regarding John 5–7, he suggests that "ch. 6 has no connection with ch. 5. On the other hand it would follow ch. 4 very well. Correspondingly 7.1 assumes that Jesus had been staying in Judea (Jerusalem) up till then, and ch. 7 would thus link with ch. 5. So the original order must have been chs. 4, 6, 5, 7" (209). Bultmann builds upon the work of Howard, *Fourth Gospel*; Strathmann, *Johannes*; Wikenhauser, *Johannes*. This concern for geography does not take seriously the temporal marker μετὰ ταῦτα and the time that passes between the feasts that indicate the evangelist's selective narration, nor does it give proper attention to the evangelist's primary concern in these chapters: the christological effect of fulfillment that Jesus has upon the feasts of Israel.

event at Sinai (Exod 19–24) and lead into the miraculous feeding of five thousand people with a boy's provision of five barley loaves and two fish (vv. 5–15). The crowds clamor to make Jesus king by force, leading him to withdraw (v. 15). He later comes to his disciples by night across the sea during the storm (vv. 16–21).[10]

The narrator regathers the characters and details the scene once again (vv. 22–24) to prepare for the so-called Bread of Life discourse (vv. 25–59; see vv. 35, 48). In these verses Jesus establishes himself as the true bread from heaven that will give life so that those who eat of it will neither hunger nor thirst.[11] When "the Jews" murmur about his origin and ability to speak in this way (vv. 41–42), Jesus responds with further claims of his heavenly origin. He speaks of his flesh as the living bread, the perfection of God's wilderness gift of manna at Sinai (vv. 43–51). The questioning of "the Jews" (v. 52) only prompts Jesus to press further, establishing the Son of Man, sent from the Father, whose flesh and blood sustains life, as the one in whom they can abide forever (vv. 53–59).[12]

With these provocative words, Jesus verbally challenges the crowds further than he has thus far in his public ministry, to the very limits of their religious worldview. "The Jews" and many disciples are unable to go any further in their response to Jesus as the ongoing revelation of God, for in their worldview, "Moses, the manna, and the Law exhaust all possibilities," and they choose to "remain with Moses," thus choosing "to stay with the former gift, denying the fullness of the gift of the truth" (see 1:16–17).[13] As a result, "When many of his disciples heard it, they said, 'This is a hard saying [Σκληρός ἐστιν ὁ λόγος οὗτος], who can listen

---

10. For a survey of the scholarship on the structure of John 6, see Roberge, "Discours sur le pain de vie."

11. For the suggestion that this "discourse" is a homiletic midrash on the text, "He gave them bread from heaven to eat" (6:31), see Borgen, *Bread from Heaven*, esp. 40–42. Dramatic aspects of John 6 as "a dialogue in action" are the focus of Brant, *Dialogue and Drama*, 149–58.

12. For the life-giving nature of the encounter between the flesh and blood of Jesus and the believer who is called to make a decision for or against the revelation of God, see Hoskyns, *Fourth Gospel*, 297; Lee, *Symbolic Narratives*, 148–53; Moloney, "John 6," 243–51; Moloney, *Signs and Shadows*, 59.

13. Moloney, *Signs and Shadows*, 64. See my exegesis of the prologue (1:1–18) in chapter 3 for the presentation that both the gift of the Law offered through Moses and the gift of the truth offered in and through Jesus signify God's covenantal action in history.

to it?'"(v. 60). Jesus acknowledges their limits of belief, and for the first time in the narrative "many of his disciples turned back and no longer went about with him" (v. 66). The crisis created by the word of Jesus begins to take its toll. Jesus turns to "the Twelve" and puts the decision to them, "Do you also wish to go away?" On behalf of the disciples, Simon Peter makes his confession: "Lord, to whom shall we go? You have the words of eternal life. We have come to believe and to know that you are the Holy One of God" (vv. 68–69).[14] The narrator advises, however, that the disciples are only beginning to understand the full ramifications of such belief in the origins and destiny of Jesus, as he introduces readers to Judas Iscariot, "who was going to betray him" (v. 71). The discourse and dialogue of John 6 leads to a turning point in the narrative, as readers participate not only in the mass exodus of the crowds and some of Jesus' disciples from uncritical following of and belief in Jesus, but also in the proleptic revelation of the beginning of the end of the Son of Man's earthly mission.[15]

The narrative tempo and tone shifts once again, with the marker μετὰ ταῦτα ("after these things") and the information that "Jesus went about in Galilee," for in Judea "the Jews were seeking to kill him" (7:1). This temporal expression designates that the entirety of John 7:1—10:21 takes place in the context of the Jewish Festival of Tabernacles (v. 2).[16] Detail of this narrative section is the focus of the analysis below. For the present study of the flow of the narrative, it is notable that this lengthy section falls in two major sections once Jesus goes up to Jerusalem (see 7:3-13). The first section is primarily dialogue, as Jesus uses the backdrop of the Feast of Tabernacles as the canvas for his teaching of himself as the living water and light of the world that brings about the integration and fulfillment of their scriptural history (7:14—8:59). The second

14. Several scholars argue that with this title Peter acknowledges that Jesus is the "agent of God." See Domeris, "Confession of Peter"; Borgen, "John 6," 286-87; Joubert, "Holy One of God."

15. Moloney (*Signs and Shadows*, 63) states, "If there is a betrayer, then there will be a betrayal. The shadow of a violent death, which has been across much of this celebration of the Passover (see vv. 12–13, 15, 27, 51, 53–54), emerges as the account of Jesus' activity on the occasion of the feast comes to a close (vv. 70–71). The author is working at several levels, telling the reader that not even correct confessions of faith will make the perfect disciple; there is also a message of a future betrayal and death that will test the disciples further."

16. La Potterie, *Verité*, 816–19; Lincoln, *Saint John*, 241; Moloney, *Signs and Shadows*, 65–66; Schenke, "Joh 7–10."

section focuses on Jesus' healing of a man born blind. This sign provides for an extended discussion of Jesus' identity by others, as well as Jesus own self-identification as the Good Shepherd who will lay down his life for his own (9:1—10:21).

The final temporal and festal marker of this section is found at John 10:22, when the narrator indicates that "at that time the festival of Dedication occurred [ἐγένετο] in Jerusalem." This relatively brief scene (21 verses) closes the feasts section by focusing on Jesus' teaching (vv. 25–39) framed by minimal narrative: a brief introduction (vv. 22–23) and a final confrontation by "the Jews" (v. 24) opens the scene, while Jesus' exit and the speculation it produces closes the episode (vv. 40–42).[17] These few verses, however, are important for understanding the conclusion to this larger section that moves through the annual feasts of Judaism. The narrator designates that it is now winter and Jesus is walking in the Portico of Solomon during the festival of Dedication (the month of Kislev; November–December). The celebration of this festival relives the experience of rededicating the temple after the Hellenizing "desolating sacrilege" of Antiochus IV Epiphanes was destroyed and the altar was cleansed following the successful Maccabean revolt of 167–164 BC (see 1 Macc 1–4).[18] Solomon's Portico, the oldest colonnade on the eastern face of the temple, is a fitting backdrop for this final confrontation that occurs during the festival commemorating Judaism's resistance to blasphemy, idolatry, and apostasy. Speculation about the messiahship of Jesus has been in the air for some time, and "the Jews" seek to put an end to it: "If you are the Messiah, tell us plainly" (v. 24).

Jesus takes up the shepherding imagery of his previous discourse to place himself once again in the role of shepherd (vv. 25–30; see 10:1-18). He presses far beyond his interrogators' messianic imagery by presenting his oneness with God: ἐγὼ καὶ ὁ πατὴρ ἕν ἐσμεν ("I and the Father are one," v. 30).[19] Even as "the Jews" take up stones against him for his perceived blasphemy (v. 31), Jesus responds verbally to their unspoken accusation (vv. 32–38) by appealing to Torah specifically (v. 34), Scripture generally (v. 35), and his own divine works (vv. 37–38). But his final declaration, "that you may know and understand that the

---

17. Brown, *John* 1:411.

18. For more on the history and tradition of the Feast of Dedication, see Rankin, *Origins of the Festival*; Yee, *Jewish Feasts*, 83–86.

19. Moloney, *Signs and Shadows*, 145–48.

Father is in me and I am in the Father," falls on uncomprehending ears as "the Jews" attempt to arrest him. His hour, however closer, has not yet come, and Jesus once again escapes from their hands (v. 39).

This narrative section comes to a close with Jesus returning across the Jordan, where "many began to believe in him" (10:41–42). This lengthy portion of Jesus' public ministry, which explores and perfects Israel's remembrance and celebration of the presence of God in and through Jesus as Christ and Son of God, draws to a close in belief rather than condemnation. The extended dialogical encounters that take place during the Feast of Tabernacles form a crucial component of that narration. We turn to an examination of these dialogues and the symbolic rhetoric of Jesus' covenantal challenge they contain.

The Covenantal Dialogue at the Feast of Tabernacles (John 7–8)

As a literary piece, John 7–8 is one of the most difficult movements in all of the Gospel narratives. When the dialogue between Jesus and the Jewish leaders and the crowds in the temple during the Feast of Tabernacles reaches its climax (8:31–59), it is the most passionate, and even vitriolic, conflict narrated in the Gospels. Both sides of this encounter are very heated: "the Jews" accuse Jesus of having a demon (v. 48), and Jesus calls them children of the devil, the father of lies (vv. 42–47). The entire encounter brings the people (and the readers) to a crisis, to a point where they are forced to begin to make decisions about where they stand in the mounting christological conflict between Jesus and the Jewish authorities.

All of John 7:1—10:21 takes place in the context of the Feast of Tabernacles. In John 9, the focus shifts to Jesus' healing action through his encounter with the man born blind. John 7–8 forms a unified whole in terms of Jesus' teaching and his very being viewed through the lens of the Feast of Tabernacles.[20] John 9:1—10:21 narrates how Jesus is what he teaches about himself in 7:14—8:59: he is the living water that gives

---

20. Lincoln (*Saint John*, 241) observes that "smaller units" of Jesus' teaching are here "given a certain cohesiveness through their present setting in relation to the festival and through the sense of mounting conflict which they convey, including the note of increasing threat to Jesus' life (cf. 7.1, 19, 25, 30, 32, 44; 8:37, 40, 59)."

light to the world and sight to the blind through the waters that come from within him.

Readers of 7:14—8:59 follow events that take place in the temple during the Feast of Tabernacles. Tabernacles was regarded as the most popular of the three pilgrimage feasts, known as the "feast of YHWH" (Lev 23:39; Num 29:12; Judg 21:19) or simply "the feast" (1 Kgs 8:2; Ezek 45:25; Neh 8:14).[21] The Jewish historian Josephus describes Tabernacles as "especially sacred and important to the Hebrews" (*A.J.* 8 §101). This feast, designated the Feast of Ingathering in the earliest liturgical calendars (Exod 23:16; 34:22) and the Feast of Booths or Tabernacles (*sukkôt*) in the later calendars (Deut 16:13, 16; Lev 23:34), was originally an autumn celebration of the grape and olive harvest that was later historicized and associated with the Sinai covenant and God's care and guidance during the wilderness experience. By the later prophetic age and into NT times, the Feast of Tabernacles had also been eschatologized, and the celebration included explicit hopes for the coming of the Messiah and messianic age (see Zech 14).[22]

Ancient sources for ritual practice and celebration of the feasts of Israel are found in rabbinic literature, dated well after NT times and the existence of the temple. The description that follows is therefore necessarily speculative in nature.[23] In the Mishnah, the laws regarding Tabernacles are found in the tractate *Sukkah* in the second division *Moed*. The feast was to begin on the fifteenth day of the seventh month, Tishri (September–October). It is highlighted by the building of tabernacles, or shelters, representing the tent experience of the Israelites in the wilderness, who were cared for by God with whom they were now in covenant. For seven days the men celebrating the festival ritual sleep and eat in their shelters. After the initial seven days there is an

---

21. The summary presentation that follows is culled from information found in the following sources: Danby, *Mishnah*, 172–81; Bienaimé, *Moïse et le Don de l'Eau*; Goodman, *Sukkot and Simkah*; MacRae, "Meaning and Evolution"; Moloney, *Signs and Shadows*, 65–116; Yee, *Jewish Feasts*, 70–77.

22. Lincoln, *Saint John*, 242; Moloney, *Signs and Shadows*, 66. For more detail on the eschatological component of the celebration, see Bienaimé, *Moïse et le Don de l'Eau*, 200–29.

23. On the value of using this material for contextualization and insight into John 7–10, see Manns, *Jean*, 185–94; Moloney, *Signs and Shadows*, 66–67; Vermes, "Jewish Literature."

additional eighth day that specifically recalls YHWH's protection in the wilderness.

Three major elements form the festival ritual. The festival begins with the Water Libation Ceremony (*m. Suk.* 4.9–10). At the dawn of each day a procession accompanied by blasts of the shofar moves down to the pool of Siloam to gather water in a golden container before returning through the Water Gate. According to the rabbis, this gate marked the source from which the waters of life, issuing from the temple, would flow in the messianic age (*t. Suk.* 3.2; *Gen. Rab.* 28.18; *m. Sheq.* 6.3; *m. Mid.* 2.6). Singing psalms (the Hallel, Pss. 113–118), the procession arrives at the altar where the water is mixed with wine and allowed to flow out onto the altar (repeated seven times on the seventh day of the feast; *m. Suk.* 4.5, 9). This ritual was linked with the giving of rain in the wilderness but also with current messianic expectations. The rabbis looked to a time of the final giving of the water. This expectation linked the Messiah with a Moses-like teacher and the definitive gift of water from the well of Torah, the ultimate perfection of the Law (*m. Suk.* 3.3–9; *Eccl. Rab.* 1.8).

The second component of the ritual is the Ceremony of Light (*m. Suk.* 5.1–4). Four menorahs are placed at the center of the court of the women. To the sounds of Psalms 120–134, celebrations under these lights last most of the night each of the seven days of the feast. The temple then also becomes the beacon that looks back at God's guidance in the wilderness through the pillar of fire and forward to the pillar's expected return in the age of the Messiah (Exod 13:21; Isa 4:5; Bar 5:8–9; *Song Rab.* 1.7).

The daily celebration culminates with the Rite of Facing the Temple (*m. Suk.* 5.4). At cockcrow of each of the seven days of the feast the men proceed to the east gate of the temple and face toward the east, away from the temple. At sunrise they turn and face the temple and recite, "Our fathers when they were in this place turned with their backs to the temple of the Lord and their faces to the east, but for us, our eyes were turned toward the Lord." This ritual greeting the light of the new day affirmed that YHWH is the one true God to whom all honor, glory, and obedience is due.

Although it is difficult to date the time frames rabbinical sources reflect, one can reasonably conclude that what marked a first-century Tabernacles celebration was increased messianic expectation coupled with profound symbolism of God's covenantal action in Israel, manifested in daily water libation rituals and the lighting of great candelabra.[24] This tenor in the air provides the sensory backdrop of Jesus' encounters in the temple area during the Feast of Tabernacles recounted in John 7–8.

STRUCTURE OF THE PASSAGE

The narrator opens John 7 with a word about the threat rising in Judea against Jesus as the Jewish Festival of Tabernacles drew near (vv. 1–2). After a conflict between Jesus and his brothers about how he should manifest himself "to the world" (vv. 3–9), Jesus goes up in secret to Jerusalem.[25] His absence to this point caused division among "the crowds," though fear of "the Jews" had kept such speculation private (vv. 10–13).[26] The dialogical encounters that ensue between Jesus and "the Jews" and "the crowds" unfold in two major sections: the dialogue that occurs "about the middle of the festival" (7:14–36), and the dialogue that is engaged "on the last day of the festival" (7:37—8:59).[27]

The initial encounter that takes place about the middle of the festival (7:14–36) is marked by two dialogical exchanges (vv. 14–24; vv. 32–36) centered around a narration of the division among the people that Jesus' teaching in the temple area causes (vv. 25–31).[28] Mosaic imagery dominates as Jesus brings the historical backdrop of the festival to bear on his teaching about himself. The messianic questions regarding his origin and destiny create conflict for the people.

The dialogical encounters at the Festival of Tabernacles begin to reach their climax in the second major section (7:37—8:59) when Jesus

---

24. Moloney, *Signs and Shadows*, 70.

25. For an argument that Jesus' intention in these verses to go up separately to Jerusalem reflects his unwillingness to actually participate in the festival ritual, see Bowen, "Notes on the Fourth Gospel," 26–27.

26. These verses offer further evidence that the evangelist does not indicate the Jewish people in general by the term "the Jews" but more particularly those who form one side of the christological debate about Jesus, for both "the crowds" (v. 12) and "the Jews" (v. 13) referred to here are ethnically Jewish. See Ashton, *Understanding the Fourth Gospel*, 131–59; Moloney, *Signs and Shadows*, 74 n. 33.

27. For more detail on the full Tabernacles scene, see Cory, "Wisdom's Rescue."

28. For more on the structure of John 7, see Schneider, "Zur Komposition von Joh 7"; and Bammel, "Joh 7:35."

reveals that he personifies the water rite of the feast (7:37–39). This claim to be the embodiment of the living waters in fulfillment of Torah creates a crisis of judgment and a schism among the people, particularly as to whether Jesus is the expected Messiah (7:40–52). When the discourse resumes at 8:12, it flows in two further sections.[29] In 8:12–30 Jesus reveals himself as the giver of the light of life. He continues the teaching he began at 7:37–39 and claims to be the fulfillment of the remaining symbolism and purpose of this Jewish feast: "I am the light of the world" (8:12). Verses 12–20 mark the first stage of this dialogue, presenting the fundamental divide between Jesus and his opponents. In vv. 21–30, the characters openly debate the issue simmering under the surface in the first section: Jesus' origins and destiny. Jesus and his opponents come closest to a meeting of hearts here (v. 30). However, this leads to a conflict concerning the identity of the true children of God based on the progeny of Abraham (vv. 31–58). The dialogue draws to a close at an impasse at v. 59. It becomes apparent just how wide the gulf is between them as Jesus challenges his opponents beyond their categorical expectations and the worldview of Judaism to understand his being as the incarnate Son of the one Father.[30] Father and child imagery pervades this portion of the dialogue, and Jesus eventually resorts to characterizing his opponents as children of the devil (v. 44). Jesus, by contrast, is the Son who is the ἐγώ εἰμι, the "I am": the incarnation of covenant fulfillment and messianic expectation (v. 58).[31]

The flow of the dialogues of John 7–8 can thus be structured as follows:

---

29. John 7:53—8:11, the passage often referred to as the woman taken in adultery, has a lengthy textual history and, although it has found a place here, was not originally part of this encounter set in the context of Tabernacles. Therefore, it is not structured as part of this dialogue. For concurrence, see Barrett, *St. John*, 589; Brown, *John*, 1:332–38; Lincoln, *Saint John*, 242; Moloney, *John*, 259; Pickering, "John 7:53—8:11." For a detailed textual analysis, see Metzger, *Textual Commentary*, 187–89. For a recent text-critical study of the transmission history of the pericope, see Rius-Camps, "Pericope of the Adulteress."

30. For detailed analyses of the christological imagery and assertions in this portion of the dialogue, see, e.g., Freed, "Ego Eimi in John 8:24"; and Miller, "Christology of John 8:25."

31. For detail on the tradition incorporated in the claim of 8:58, see Freed, "Who or What."

7:14–36		The Dialogue at the Middle of the Feast
	7:14–24	Jesus teaches "from God," appealing to Moses and right judgment
	7:25–31	People are divided about Jesus and the question of his messiahship
	7:32–36	Facing the threat of arrest, Jesus teaches about his destiny
7:37—8:59		The Dialogue on the Last Day of the Feast
	7:37–52	Jesus' self-revelation as the living water and the division it causes
	8:12–30	Jesus dialogues about his self-revelation as the Light of the World
	8:31–59	Jesus dialogues with "the Jews" about the true children of God

A close exegetical analysis of the entirety of this encounter is beyond the scope of the present study. For our purposes of examining the dialogue of covenant in the Gospel of John, the portion of this extended dialogue that will be the focus of analysis is the final movement of the conflict that leads to a dialogical impasse and the ultimate rejection of the word and person of Jesus in vv. 31–59. The literary unity of this movement is effected by the increasing hostility between Jesus and his interlocutors, "the Jews." Initially, it can be subdivided into two sections: vv. 31–47 and vv. 48–59.[32] As noted above, the previous section closes with Jesus and his dialogue partners at the nearest point to a meeting of hearts and minds: "As he was saying these things, many believed in him" (v. 30). The new section opens with Jesus characteristically challenging those who profess belief in him further, beyond their earthly categories. Thus the narrator recounts, "Then Jesus said to the Jews who believed in him" (v. 31). This portion of the dialogue continues through v. 47, when the tension has increased such that Jesus pronounces that they "are not from God" (ἐκ τοῦ θεοῦ οὐκ ἐστέ). The second subdivision of this final movement thus begins, "The Jews answered him" (v. 48). Jesus' interlocutors have retreated to their former position and can no longer be understood as holding even a partial belief in Jesus. This last section includes the rest of the chapter (vv. 48–59).

To construct a more detailed roadmap for analyzing these verses, we must examine the nature of this dialogical interaction. Scholars

---

32. Lincoln, *Saint John*, 263–64.

have noted the forensic nature of this encounter between Jesus and "the Jews," and gleaning the trial motif that pervades all of 8:12–59 can be elucidating.[33] The use of a trial structure or tone allows for a dual function on the part of the evangelist: organization of both the plot and the experience of the reader who is called to decision.[34] The forensic trial motif is highlighted by the rhetoric of dialogue and drama as it resonates the OT prophetic pattern of a covenant lawsuit.[35] In this vein, Andrew Lincoln ties the "I am" sayings across the Gospel and here in the culminating statement of v. 58 with the covenantal lawsuit of Isaiah 44:6–8 in which Israel puts God on trial and God testifies on his own behalf.[36] In Isaiah, the purpose of the lawsuit is to demonstrate that although God's sovereignty has been called into question by the Babylonian conquest and exile, God is in full control. In the Gospel of John, the crucifixion and death of Jesus likewise put this sovereignty into question, requiring that God's agent, Jesus, take the stand.[37] More specifically, in the two major sections of the dialogues of vv. 12–59, the first (vv. 12–30) corresponds to this covenantal lawsuit of Isaiah. The Pharisees appear as plaintiffs and Jesus takes the role of defendant by responding to them and then lodging a countercomplaint.[38] In the second (vv. 31–59, the passage considered here), "Jesus is the plaintiff and directs his charges to the Jews who had believed in him (vv. 31–47), the defendant's speech is reduced to a countercharge (v. 48), and Jesus then defends his position as plaintiff against the Jews (vv. 49–59)."[39] Jesus speaks in the role of the plaintiff who eventually charges his interlocutors with breach of covenant by challenging "the Jews'" claim to know God and be free by virtue of their status as descendants of Abraham. As is common in the OT Prophets, in an effort to establish his case for what it means to live

---

33. Neyrey, "Jesus the Judge"; idem, "Trials (Forensic) and Tribulations"; Lincoln, *Truth on Trial*, esp. 82–96. The groundbreaking study on the trial motif in the Gospel of John in general remains Harvey, *Jesus on Trial*.

34. Brant, *Dialogue and Drama*, 141.

35. Lincoln (*Truth on Trial*, 90–96) points particularly to Isa 41:8–14, 26; 42:3, 8, 18–20; 43:9–14, 23–27; 44:9, 18, 22–25; 45:13–20, 25; 47:4, 12–13; 48:1, 8–11, 17, 20; 49:3–6, 25; 50:1; 51:1–14; 52:3; 53:4–6; 55:5–9; 59:1–20; 65:11; Hos 1:2; 2:4. For more on this discussion, see Brant *Dialogue and Drama*, 140.

36. Lincoln, *Truth on Trial*, 43–50.

37. Brant, *Dialogue and Drama*, 140.

38. Ibid., 143.

39. Ibid.; for the full discussion, see 143–49.

in covenant as well as what it means to breach covenant with God, Jesus speaks not specifically of "covenant" but of what both he and his opponents "know" and whether they "know" God (see vv. 32, 43, 55 for forms of the verb γινώσκω, vv. 37, 55 [3 times] for forms of the verb οἶδα).[40] Jesus also takes the role of witness in these verses by supporting his own testimony as the Son of God who offers the gift of truth and the power to become true children of God (vv. 31–32, 39–40, 44–45).[41]

In terms of dramatic technique, the rhythm of the dialogue proceeds as a flyting contest, with Jesus' longer speeches resembling the sustained arguments of a formal debate (ἀγνών).[42] In the first part of the dialogue (vv. 31–47) Jesus initiates and concludes the movement as he challenges "the Jews" who begin to believe in him to accept his claims for his origin and destiny with God and thereby receive his gift of truth.[43] Three segments to this movement emerge: the first in three

---

40. The verb γινώσκω also appears in 8:52 as part of "the Jews'" self-defense. In the Tabernacles dialogues of John 7–8, see 7:17, 26, 27, 49, 51; 8:27, 28; 10:6, 14 (2), 15 (2) for forms of this verb; 7:15, 27, 28 (3), 29; 8:14 (2), 19 (3); 9:12, 20, 21 (2), 24, 25 (2), 29 (2), 30, 31; 10:4, 5 for forms of the verb οἶδα. On the covenantal aspect of "knowing God," see Huffmon, "Treaty Background"; idem, "Further Note"; Hillers, *Covenant*, 120–42. For more on the covenant lawsuit in the Prophets, see Huffmon, "Covenant Lawsuit"; McCarthy, *Old Testament Covenant*, 35–40. Examples of prophetic texts that identify knowledge of God with God's covenantal action and relationship with Israel include Amos 3:1–2; Hos 4:1–11; 13:4–5; 14:4–9; Isa 5:13; Mic 6:1–8; Jer 2:4–13; 24:7; 31:31–34; Ezek 12:15–16; 34:15–31.

41. See chapter 2 for the establishment of "truth" and the language of "family" as covenantal language, and my exegesis of the prologue (1:1–18) in chapter 3 for the contention that the power to become children of God is the covenantal gift of truth that Jesus (the incarnation of this gift) reveals.

42. The discussion of speech as action presented in chapter 1 of this study stated that the "formal debate" is identified by language in literary scenes forensic in nature that resonate a trial structure and include testimonies, accusations of legal infractions, and rendering of judgment by characters in the story, whereby readers are urged to render a judgment of their own. "Flyting" is a dialogical technique that is often used to demonstrate prowess in the verbal exchange of the formal debate. Flyting consists of language that exploits the different meanings of words for subtlety and cleverness, and includes insults, curses, boasts, riddles, miniature stories, and especially irony. See Brant, *Dialogue and Drama*, 130, 123–49, who further accepts the incorporation of the covenant lawsuit language in the pattern of the formal debate.

43. Jesus thus initiates the flyting with the challenge of a contract that would establish peace by having his opponents accept his word, in return for which he will grant them the gift of truth. Brant (*Dialogue and Drama*, 130) notes that the conflict of a flyting contest often ends with the giving of gifts. In terms of the covenantal lawsuit, the acceptance of this word and the receipt of the gift of truth would be the grounds

parts initiated and concluded by Jesus (vv. 31–32, 34–38), the second and third in two parts each initiated by "the Jews" (v. 39a, v. 41b) and rejoined by Jesus (vv. 39b–41a, vv. 42–47). In the second part of the dialogue (vv. 48–59) "the Jews" fully reject Jesus and all that he claims and offers. This movement also falls into three segments: the first and second in two parts each still initiated by "the Jews" (v. 48, vv. 52–53) and rejoined by Jesus (vv. 49–51, vv. 54–56), and the third in three parts initiated verbally by "the Jews" (v. 57), answered by Jesus (v. 58), and concluded physically by "the Jews" (v. 59).[44] The evangelist seems to have borrowed from the contents of the covenantal lawsuit and the formal debate without making use of their entire form and blended them into the design for the larger contest.[45] Therefore, the exegetical analysis to come will follow the rhythmic flyting pattern of a formal debate. The structure can thus be mapped as follows:

8:31–47		Jesus Further Challenges "the Jews" Who Had Begun to Believe in Him
	8:31–38	Jesus (vv. 31–32, 34–38) and "the Jews" (v. 33): Truth & Freedom
	8:39–41a	"The Jews" (v. 39a) and Jesus (vv. 39b–41a): Children of Abraham
	vv. 41b–47	"The Jews" (v. 41b) and Jesus (vv. 42–47): Children of the Devil
8:48–59		"The Jews" Reject Jesus' Challenge to Become Children of God
	8:48–51	"The Jews" (v. 48) and Jesus (vv. 49–51): Glory of the Father
	8:52–56	"The Jews" (vv. 52–53) and Jesus (vv. 54–56): Death and Life
	8:57–59	"The Jews" (vv. 57, 59) and Jesus (v. 58): Rejection of the "I AM"

---

for settling the dispute and establishing covenant between the parties. This does not happen here, and the debate rages forward.

44. In terms of the dialogue of drama, the flyting contest shaped by the formal debate thus "ends with a gesture on the part of the Jews that defines the terms of the physical conflict" (Brant, *Dialogue and Drama*, 130).

45. Ibid., 142.

The exegesis of the final dialogue between Jesus and "the Jews" during the Feast of Tabernacles will follow this dialogical pattern of the debate.

Exegetical Analysis

The whole of John 8 presents the most extended verbal interaction between Jesus and any interlocutors in the Gospel. Although Jesus retains center stage throughout this dialogue, his conversation partners are also very involved, with considerable opportunity for questions and responses of their own. Nonetheless, Jesus continues to lead the discussion with teaching about himself and the re-presentation of the experience of God in the Feast of Tabernacles through what God the Father has done and is doing through the Son. By v. 30, Jesus' testimony has led many to believe in him. Readers have learned, however, that these early stages of belief that remain in preconceived religious categories are not rooted in the abiding word necessary for full faith. Therefore, it is not surprising that at v. 31 Jesus begins to challenge those "who had believed in him" to let go of those categories and take root in his word.

Jesus Further Challenges "the Jews" Who Began to Believe in Him

Verses 31–47 of John 8 form the decisive segment of the Tabernacles dialogue between Jesus and "the Jews." With the temple as his backdrop, Jesus challenges them to abide in the truth and see the presence of the Father in him, the Son.

Jesus and "the Jews": Truth and Freedom (vv. 31–38) Jesus then turns specifically to "the Jews" who had expressed belief in him and transitions his teaching imperative to the covenantal demand of abiding in truth.[46] The transitional conjunction οὖν here carries an inferential force as it so often does in John's narrative.[47] Jesus presents them with the condition of authentic discipleship. Rather than asking simply for an expression of belief, Jesus calls them to abide (μείνητε) in his word

---

46. On the covenantal aspect of the term "abide" in the Johannine literature, see Malatesta, *Interiority and Covenant*.

47. Wallace, *Greek Grammar*, 674. See also John 1:22; 2:18, 20; 3:25; 4:33, 46; 5:19; 6:60, 67; 7:25, 28, 33, 35, 40; 8:13, 21, 22, 25, 57; 9:10, 16. Note how the conjunction with the dual force has moved the Tabernacles dialogues of John 7–8 forward.

(τῷ λόγῳ τῷ ἐμῷ) to establish the existential state (ἐστέ) of true discipleship: "if you abide in my word, you are truly [ἀληθῶς] my disciples" (v. 31).[48] Abiding in the word of Jesus allows those who are his disciples to come to know the truth (γνώσεσθε τὴν αλήθειαν), which will in turn set them free (ἡ ἀλήθεια ἐλευθερώσει ὑμᾶς, v. 32). Jesus verbalizes the role and mission with which he was characterized in the prologue: the covenantal gift which is truth comes through Jesus Christ and can be received by all through his fullness (1:14, 16–17).[49] Here in dialogue with "the Jews" who have expressed a belief in him, however partial, Jesus explains how this happens. Active abiding in his word will bring about recognition of the truth that is in him and in his gift, and this knowledge gives freedom from the bonds of this world which in turn perfects the gift of the Law.[50] Belief and knowledge of the truth is therefore neither "blind acceptance of dogma" nor "esoteric knowledge in mystagogical teaching" because "faith always remains bound to the Word."[51] Rather, faith is an attitude that surrenders the previous self-understanding of knowledge to an openness to God and God's revealer.[52] Rhetorically, the flyting challenge that Jesus extends plays on the subtleties and nuances of the existential language he uses.[53] The formal debate between Jesus and "the Jews who had believed in him" has begun, and the initial issue at hand is freedom.[54]

---

48. Moloney (*John*, 227) notes the particle ἐαν followed by the aorist subjunctive indicates Jesus' desire that an action already begun come to fruition. See BDF §373.

49. For the connection of these verses to the "truth" of the "eternal existence and saving mission of Jesus" established in the prologue, see Barrett, *St. John*, 344.

50. Brown notes in early rabbinic writing the idea that the study of the Law liberates one from worldly care. "Thus, we *may* once again have an implicit contrast between the power of Jesus' revelation and that of the Law" (Brown, *John*, 1:355).

51. Bultmann, *John*, 435.

52. Ibid. He prefaces these observations with the statement that the "promise of knowledge of the ἀλήθεια therefore is actually identical with the promise of ζωή," (434).

53. Regarding the existential nuances of the language, Bultmann (*John*, 436–37) observes that in "John ἐλευθερία cannot be described as the substance of the knowledge that reveals the being of man." Rather "in so far as faith can never cease, in so far therefore as this becoming free has to continue [as "abiding in the word"] and therefore has constantly to be achieved anew, a man experiences this condition of *being* free only as a perpetual *becoming* free."

54. For more on the concept of freedom in these verses, see Lategan, "Truth That Sets Man Free."

For their part, "the Jews" verbalize their misunderstanding of the existential component of the freedom Jesus offers in the truth of the gift of himself. They respond in terms of slavery. Although they are standing in the temple on the culminating day of the Feast of Tabernacles and celebrating the experience of the covenantal care of God in the Sinai wilderness following the Exodus from Egyptian slavery, "the Jews" reach back beyond Moses to Abraham and bring in progeny as the link to their freedom. They assert themselves not to be Jesus' disciples (see v. 31) but to be "descendants of Abraham" (σπέρμα Ἀβραάμ ἐσμεν, v. 33). Their emphatic claim is that by virtue of being the seed of Abraham they have never been enslaved by anyone. By their self-designation as the descendants of Abraham, they do, however, enter into the dialogue of covenant with Jesus.[55] Rhetorically, by contrast, the reality that they are not on the same conversational playing field is affirmed when they misquote him in their sarcastic reflection of his claim.[56] The deictic personal pronoun underscores the distancing of themselves from his words: "How can you [σύ] say" (v. 33b). They then quote his promise of freedom in terms of indeterminate "becoming" (ἐλεύθεροι γενήσεσθε) instead of the dynamic freedom determined by the activating power of truth that Jesus asserted (v. 32). However synonymous the statements may be, the rhetorical distinction reflects the different levels of understanding from which the two dialogue partners are working.[57] "The Jews" want to speak of physical enslavement, whether political or religious, and thus their status as descendants of Abraham (σπέρμα Ἀβραάμ), whereas Jesus is speaking of the freedom to receive his gift of empowerment to become children of God (τέκνα θεοῦ, see 1:12).

Jesus then takes their terminology of slavery and applies it to the relationship with God that he wants to bring to issue. Introducing his

---

55. Lincoln (*Truth on Trial*, 90–91) further notes the irony on the political level that they make such a claim while under Roman occupation. The positive expression would be of their internal religious freedom "on the basis of their relation to God through the covenant with Abraham." Bringing Abraham and his progeny into the dialogue also brings that covenantal relationship to bear upon the current situation.

56. Their "incomprehension" (Lincoln, *Truth on Trial*, 90) is compounded by their "sarcasm" (Kelly and Moloney, *Experiencing God*, 192).

57. This is the countering force of the speech-action index of redundant narration. The discrepancy in their reiteration, instead of the veracity and integrity of their understanding, confirms its disconnect. For detail on redundant narration, see Brant, *Dialogue and Drama*, 109–10.

teaching with his characteristic double-amen formula, Jesus speaks of sin and the "doer" of sin as its slave (v. 34).[58] Thus belief must produce action, and the resulting conduct determines freedom.[59] He integrates the slavery issue with the operative action of "abiding" he introduced in v. 31, then brings in the familial language of covenant that will be at stake in this dialogue: "Now a slave does not abide [οὐ μένει] in a household forever, the son abides [ὁ υἱὸς μένει] forever" (v. 35). By using the familial metaphor of the abiding son in contrast to the slave, Jesus uses covenantal language to describe the relationship between God and those who are empowered to become children of God, a state not achieved by being "descendants of Abraham" (σπέρμα Ἀβραάμ) alone.[60]

Jesus begins to speak of the character and role of the son in this dialogue without initially applying that image to himself. In this way, he allows the depth of the image to have its effect before he identifies himself with it. He returns to the existential language of being and freedom he used in vv. 31–32 and identifies the son of the household of God with the truth. Just as with his promise of the action of truth (v. 32), he now reveals the Son as the agent of freedom that abides in the household of God ("So if the son sets you free, you will be free indeed," v. 36).[61]

Jesus acknowledges their physical descent in the covenantal line of Abraham (σπέρμα Ἀβραάμ ἐστε, v. 37), but then begins to distinguish this physical descent (σπέρμα Ἀβραάμ) from an authentic familial relationship in covenant based in his word (ὁ λόγος ὁ ἐμός), which is not holding in their hearts (οὐ χωρεῖ ἐν ὑμῖν), emphasizing his personal agency in this process. He then reiterates this point with the deictic first-person pronoun emphasizing what he has seen (ἐγὼ ἑώρακα) in the presence of the Father (παρὰ τῷ πατρί) and the action that results: he speaks (λαλῶ). The use of the perfect tense highlights the ongoing

---

58. For occurrences of the double Amen introductory formula to significant sayings, see 1:51; 3:3, 5, 11; 5:19, 24, 25; 6:26, 32, 47, 53; 8:51, 58; 10:1, 7; 12:24; 13:16, 20, 21, 38; 14:12; 16:20, 23; 21:18.

59. Carson notes that not only does the practice of sin "prove that one is a slave to sin, but the practice of sin actively enslaves. For Jesus, then, the ultimate bondage is not enslavement to a political or economic system, but vicious slavery to moral failure, to rebellion against God who has made us" (*John*, 350).

60. See chapter 2 for the establishment of the intrinsic link between the language of family and the language of covenant.

61. For more on roles of the slave and the son, see Lindars, "Slave and Son."

unmediated relationship he has with the Father.[62] This reference to the Father (v. 38) coupled with his designation as the Son (v. 36) reflects the prologue's declaration that in God's new covenantal in-breaking into the world it is Jesus the Son who makes God the Father known (1:16–18). Jesus does not stop here but goes on to acknowledge that their relationship also leads to action: "You also then, do what you heard from the father" (v. 38). He is beginning to make a distinction, not only between progeny and childhood, but now also between the Father who activates his being and mission and the father to whom they listen and who guides their actions.

"The Jews" and Jesus: Children of Abraham (vv. 39–41a) The first exchange of this portion of the Tabernacles dialogue, vv. 31–38, establishes the initial criterion for identifying the disciples of Jesus: they have Jesus' word. The next two exchanges establish the criterion for identifying authentic children of God in the line of Abraham's covenantal response: conduct.[63] In v. 39a "the Jews" in dialogue with Jesus respond to his distinction between his Father and their father (v. 38) by identifying their father as Abraham. This is a stronger statement than their claim to be descendants of Abraham (σπέρμα Ἀβραάμ ἐσμεν, v. 33). Jesus accepted their assertion of physical descent (v. 37), but this claim of Abraham as their father (ὁ πατὴρ ἡμῶν Ἀβραάμ ἐστιν; v. 39a) is unacceptable. Claiming a father indicates a self-identification as children, and Jesus does not accept their implication to be "children of Abraham" (τέκνα τοῦ Ἀβραάμ) in terms of covenantal obedience. He therefore demands that if they had this claim they would be behaving accordingly and "be doing the works of Abraham" (τὰ ἔργα τοῦ Ἀβραάμ ἐποιεῖτε, v. 39b).[64] Conduct, specifically one's response to the word of God, is the criterion

---

62. Contrast this perfect tense with the aorist tense he uses of "the Jews." For more on this distinction, see Brown, *John*, 1:356.

63. Culpepper, "Pivot," 28. See chapter 2 for the analysis of Gen 12–22 and the relationship between God and Abraham, particularly how Abraham accepts God's offer of covenant through his conduct (Gen 12:1–4; 15:1–6; 17:1–27).

64. Coloe observes, "Although physically descended from Abraham, 'the Jews' are not true children for they do not *do* what Abraham did. There is a principle working here that has already been established in the Gospel, that is, sons do what their fathers do. In chapter 5 Jesus had claimed to be a true son of the Father, 'for whatever he does, that the Son does likewise' (5:19)" ("Like Father, Like Son," 5).

for identifying paternity and thereby authentic childhood, as opposed to physical descent alone.[65]

For the second time in these verses Jesus acknowledges what they are doing: "You are seeking to kill me" (ζητεῖτε με ἀποκτεῖναι, vv. 37, 40). As one fulfilling his earthly mission of revealing the gift of truth that comes from God (ἀλήθειαν ... παρὰ τοῦ θεοῦ), he is doing what Abraham did. By seeking to kill him, and thereby to silence the truth, they are doing what Abraham did not do (τοῦτο Ἀβραὰμ οὐκ ἐποίησεν). The demonstrative pronoun rhetorically underscores their action: they are behaving like murderers. Falling back on their religious system, they plan "to kill the Son of God, who could set them free, because of a physical line that has generated" this closed system.[66] Therefore, their father cannot be Abraham, whose openness to the word of God characterized his life and journey of faith (Gen 12–22), but someone else whose works they are emulating. Jesus states, "You are doing the works of your father" (v. 41a).

"The Jews" and Jesus: Children of the Devil (vv. 41b–47) Inferring his implication that their authentic father cannot be Abraham, Jesus' interlocutors take a defensive position that has the rhetorical effect of a further retreat into their historical religious system. With reference to Levitical law (see Lev 18), they assert their legitimacy in birth, and God as their sole father (v. 41b). Their use of the first-person pronoun ἡμεῖς points verbally to their own subjectivity in distinction from Jesus. The implication is an additional offensive innuendo of illegitimacy to Jesus' birth.[67] Further, their positive claim of God as their one Father resonates the affirmation of faith reiterated by the priests at the dawn of each new day during the Feast of Tabernacles, the setting to this very

---

65. Although not characterized in terms of fatherhood and childhood, this is the same principle that was operative in the positive response of the mother of Jesus to his covenantal challenge as well as in the resulting obedient "doing" of servants in Cana (2:1–12). See chapter 4 for the analysis of that dialogue.

66. Moloney, "Narrative and Discourse," 208–9. They do not match the deeds of Abraham, who rejoiced "for he knew and he perceived that from him there would be a righteous planting for eternal generations and a holy seed from him" (*Jub.* 16:26). Moloney observes, "Unlike Abraham, whom they claim as Father, 'the Jews' response to Jesus, the 'holy seed,' is hatred and murder rather than joy" (ibid.).

67. Brown, *John*, 1:357.

conversation.⁶⁸ The irony of this claim lies in their active rejection of the one who can make the truth of God known to them and perfect the experience of God that the festival celebrates while they are standing in the midst of the feast's culminating moments (see 7:37).

Jesus' response in this flyting segment ends the first part of this section of the dialogue (vv. 42–47). He takes the offensive with the most aggressive onslaught of his entire ministry. The hypocrisy, or at best ignorant rejection, he perceives in their monotheistic claim leads him to articulate their paternity of "lies" that is of "the devil," not of God (vv. 43–44). He introduces the nature of the proper response if they were children of God as love, and specifically love of him: εἰ ὁ θεὸς πατὴρ ὑμῶν ἦν ἠγαπᾶτε ἂν ἐμέ, (v. 42).⁶⁹ Emphasizing his own agency with the first-person pronoun, Jesus then restates his sonship as being the one who proceeded from God and has come not for his own purposes but to fulfill the mission of God who sent him (ἀλλ᾽ ἐκεῖνός με ἀπέστειλεν, v. 42).⁷⁰ The present ἥκω highlights the results of God's past action of sending him forth through Jesus' current presence in their midst.⁷¹ This is their opportunity to respond positively to God's covenantal action of sending his Son by embracing and abiding in the word of Jesus. But they are rejecting it. By rejecting Jesus, they are rejecting the spiritual fatherhood of the very God (ἐκεῖνος) they claim as their own (v. 42).

Jesus asks why they are not understanding him (v. 43) and thereby coming to know the truth (γνώσεσθε τὴν ἀλήθειαν, v. 31; see v. 45). He immediately answers his own rhetorical question: it is his word (τὸν λόγον τὸν ἐμοῦ), which is the word of his Father, God (v. 40), that they are unable to hear. But they are hearing the words of their spiritual father and doing what that father desires. Jesus then inundates them with a description of the identity of this father of theirs.

With his verbal index finger, Jesus points to his interlocutors, "You," (ὑμεῖς) and pushes beyond obedience in conduct to willfulness and their "desires" (τὰς ἐπιθυμίας), which reflect from whom they come: their "father the devil" (ἐκ τοῦ πατρὸς τοῦ διαβόλου, v. 44).⁷² As authentic

---

68. Moloney, "Narrative and Discourse," 209.

69. Carson, *John*, 352.

70. Barrett (*St. John*, 348) observes how "ἐξῆλθον denotes the departure of Jesus ἐκ τοῦ θεοῦ, ἥκω his arrival in the world."

71. Wallace, *Greek Grammar*, 532–33.

72. Note the double definite article–noun occurrence that forms a hendiadys of

children of that father, they are seeking to kill Jesus (vv. 37, 40). "That one [ἐκεῖνος] was a murderer from the beginning" (ἀνθρωποκτόνος ἦν ἀπ' ἀρχῆς), in contrast to Jesus, who was turned toward God in the beginning (οὗτος ἦν ἐν ἀρχῇ πρὸς τὸν θεόν, 1:2). That one "has not stood in the truth" (ἐν τῇ ἀληθείᾳ οὐκ ἔστηκεν), in contrast to Jesus, who brings about "the gift which is truth" (ἡ χάρις καὶ ἡ ἀλήθεια διὰ Ἰησοῦ Χριστοῦ ἐγένετο, 1:17). They cannot abide in the truth of Jesus because there is no truth in their father. The essence of their father the devil is lies, and therefore "he is a liar and the father of the lie." This is the reason that they do not believe him, precisely because he speaks the truth. Jesus turns the index back to himself (ἐγώ) as the one whose essence is truth (τὴν ἀλήθειαν λέγω, v. 45).

Jesus then asks which of them can convict him of sin (v. 46). The two issues at stake here are hearing the word of God and the action that results from abiding in that word. Truth and freedom, the concepts with which Jesus opened these verses (vv. 31–32) are found, somewhat paradoxically, in openness and obedience to the dynamic word of God. Obedience, in turn, is lived in active response to that word, as modeled by Abraham (vv. 39–40). This is the process of faith in action: "believing" (πιστεύετε). Jesus now speaks of sin, in the singular (ἁμαρτία), as the opposite action: hearing the truth and not believing. Since he has established that he hears and speaks the word of his Father, he asks, "If I speak the truth, why do you not believe me?" He then specifies the answer, clarifying for them their own rejection of him: "The one who is from God [ὁ ὢν ἐκ τοῦ θεοῦ] hears the words of God. For this reason you [ὑμεῖς] do not hear, because you are not from God" (ἐκ τοῦ θεοῦ οὐκ ἐστέ, v. 47). Jesus concludes by pointing with finality to the crucial nature of origins in terms of the covenantal bonds of the ongoing father-son relationship.[73]

Even as he asks them how he can be convicted of sin, Jesus convicts them of the same sin. They have listened to his words and yet not heard in them the word of God. It is not enough for them to profess belief in him insofar as his mission appeals to their needs and aligns with their closed religious system (v. 30). They must abide in him, and this neces-

---

demonic paternity. Brown prefers to translate the phrase as "the devil is the father" (*John*, 1:357–58).

73. Lindars claims this to be "central to the whole argument" (*John*, 330). See also Moloney, *John*, 282.

sitates openness. They must be open to the movement of God in history *now*. The freedom found in Jesus' gift of truth, the power to become children of God (1:12), can be realized only by hearing the word of God when they hear the word of Jesus, by seeing God when they see Jesus. This is the believing that abides. All else is rejection, all else is sin. And this they cannot do. This refusal to see, hear, and know Jesus is tantamount to a breach of covenant and rejection of Jesus' challenge of covenant with God through his word.

8:48–59: "The Jews" Reject Jesus' Challenge to Become Children of God

Verses 48–59 form the consequential segment of the Tabernacles dialogue between Jesus and "the Jews."[74] Rejecting Jesus as the true Son of God the Father, their decision is determinative of the future presence of God in their lives and in their temple. The physical reaction of "the Jews" to their verbal encounter leads Jesus, who would reveal God's presence in himself, to hide himself and leave their midst.

"THE JEWS" AND JESUS: GLORY OF THE FATHER (VV. 48–51) Jesus' interlocutors are identified again for the first time since v. 31, but now the narrator indicates that none remain who believe in Jesus. Identified simply as "the Jews," they verbalize their fierce rejection of Jesus through their certainty that he is insane (σὺ καὶ δαιμόνιον ἔχεις; v. 48). They accuse Jesus of being both one of the mixed, apostate Samaritan people and possessed by a demon.[75] The deictic techniques of both sides in distinguishing themselves from the other by using the personal pronouns continues through this final section (ἡμεῖς . . . σύ, v. 48; ἐγώ. . . . ὑμεῖς, v. 49). The dialogue partners are careful to separate themselves aggressively even as they continue to seek to be understood and correctly characterized by the other.

---

74. Moloney (*John*, 283) notes that this section is "a genuine dialogue" in the sense of an in-depth interaction in which two points of view clash. "The Jews" interrogate (vv. 48, 53, 57), affirm their point of view (v. 52), and react (v. 59a). Jesus answers their questions (vv. 49, 54–55), affirms his point of view (vv. 50–51, 56, 58), and reacts (v. 59b).

75. It is difficult to determine the relationship between the charge of being a Samaritan and the charge of demon possession. It could be that they are an equivalent accusation of madness (as indicated by Jesus' single response in v. 49). See Barrett, *St. John*, 350.

Jesus responds by renouncing their accusations directly (ἐγὼ δαιμόνιον οὐκ ἔχω) and returning the focus to the issue of fatherhood and the right conduct of children in the same familial relationship (vv. 49–50). He introduces the concept of honor and dishonor (τιμῶ . . . ἀτιμάετε) and asserts his right action in relation to the Father as it correlates to the false action of "the Jews" in rejecting him as insane (v. 49). The concept of honor leads to the notion of glory (δόξα). Jesus does not seek his own glory but points to the Father as the one who seeks and judges (v. 50). He implies that it is God the Father who seeks the glory of Jesus the Son.[76]

Jesus concludes this flyting exchange with the pronouncement that will set him apart further from his interlocutors. The double-amen formula introduces the saying and prepares his audience for his teaching. He astounds them by asserting, "Whoever keeps my word [τὸν ἐμὸν λόγον] shall not see death" (v. 51). Using the emphatic negation (θάνατον οὐ μὴ θεωρήσῃ), Jesus rules out the idea as being a possibility.[77] Returning to the directive with which he began this challenge, now in terms of "keeping" (τηρήσῃ), Jesus affirms that it is ongoing life in his word that is itself life-giving. Eternal life flows from the word of Jesus. His response to their "rejection of his person (v. 48) is to reaffirm the central function of the revelation of God that takes place in him, leading to either life or death (vv. 49–51)."[78] As the Father seeks the glory of the Son, the Son overcomes death and gives life to all who receive his word and become children of God.

"The Jews" and Jesus: Death and Life (vv. 52–56) "The Jews," once again identified without qualification, react to Jesus' new turn in the dialogue toward giving life with further certainty of their rejection of all he has to offer. They say, "Now we know [ἐγνώκαμεν] that you have a demon." Jesus' desire for them was that by abiding in his word, they

---

76. Brown, *John*, 1:359. Brown goes on to suggest an echo here of Isa 16:5: A throne shall be set up in covenant love, and on it shall sit in truth one who passes judgment and seeks justice.

77. In Greek, οὐ μή plus the aorist subjunctive "is the most decisive way" of negating something in the future (BDAG, s.v. μή). It is found primarily in the mouth of Jesus. Wallace notes that "a *soteriological* theme is frequently found in such statements, especially in John: what is negatived is the possibility of the loss of salvation" (*Greek Grammar*, 468–69).

78. Moloney, *John*, 283.

"will come to know the truth" (γνώσεσθε τὴν ἀλήθειαν, vv. 31–32).[79] By contrast, they have rejected his word and "have come to know" a lie (see v. 49 where Jesus has already asserted his sanity: "I do not have a demon").[80] They once again reach back to Abraham and the Prophets for their authority, without regard for the openness to God's continuing word found in Abraham and the Prophets that Jesus has been trying to impress upon them. In their repetition of Jesus' claim (καὶ σὺ λέγεις) they once again misquote him. As in v. 33, the idiom they employ for dying (οὐ μὴ γεύσηται θανάτου) could be argued to be synonymous with Jesus' construction (θάνατον οὐ μὴ θεωρήσῃ), but the rhetorical effect of the grammatical difference between the two statements reinforces the growing disconnection between the dialogue partners.[81] As Jesus speaks of life from above, "the Jews" conceive of merely physical death in the world below.[82] The spiritual separation between the two parties is confirmed in "the Jews'" follow-up questions for Jesus. They continue to claim Abraham as their father and ask Jesus, "Are you greater than our father Abraham, who died?" (v. 53a).[83] Their construction (μὴ σὺ μείζων εἶ) assumes the answer no. The irony in their misunderstanding is unmistakable to the reader, who has read the prologue and therefore knows the answer to be a yes that is clearly beyond the ken of these interrogators. They follow with τίνα σεαυτὸν ποιεῖς; (v. 53b). This question might be rendered in idiomatic English, "Who do you think you are?" But the Greek construction using the verb ποιέω deepens the irony of

79. Bultmann's observation regarding vv. 31–32 is once again pertinent here: "The promise of knowledge of the ἀλήθεια therefore is actually identical with the promise of ζωή," (*John*, 434).

80. In terms of the covenant lawsuit motif of this passage, this exchange of what each party knows is particularly powerful. "The Jews" are making it clear that they do not "know" Jesus' true identity. In the Johannine context, failure to know Jesus is failure to know God. In the language of the Prophets this is a breach of covenant.

81. Again, see Brant, *Dialogue and Drama*, 112, for the dialogical technique of redundant narration. For the custom in biblical literature of verbatim repetition to indicate understanding and integrity, see Alter, *Art of Biblical Narrative*, 182.

82. Brown, *John*, 1:366. He suggests the "word of Jesus is the antidote to the sin and death which the devil brought in to the world in the Garden of Eden. It is not at all unlikely that we should interpret the promise of immortality in v. 51 in light of the murdering proclivities of the devil mentioned in 44."

83. Note the similarity of their query to that of the uncomprehending Samaritan woman who questioned how Jesus could be "greater than our father Jacob" (4:12). She eventually opens to the word of Jesus. At this point in the dialogue, these "Jews" are by contrast confirming their rejection of Jesus and his word.

their rejection, as Jesus has been pointing to precisely what he "does" in the name of God the Father and "does not" do of himself throughout this Tabernacles dialogue. Those with whom he is in dialogue have proven themselves unable to "hear" the answers he gives.

In vv. 54–56, Jesus begins to answer who he is once again using their terms of what he does. However, he continues to refer to what he does back to his Father (ὁ πατήρ μου) and reiterates his position on glory from v. 50 that he first asserted at the beginning of this Tabernacles scene at 7:18 (ἡ δόξα, v. 54). He then takes the additional step of claiming what God does for the Son: "My Father is the one who glorifies me." He grounds his claim for the Father in their own claims for God, "of whom you say, 'He is our God'" (see v. 41). But despite their claims, Jesus reasserts their ignorance—"You do not know him" (οὐκ ἐγνώκατε αὐτόν, v. 55; see v. 43)—as well as his own intimate relationship with the Father: "but I know him (οἶδα αὐτόν) and I keep his word" (τὸν λόγον αὐτοῦ v. 55; see v. 51). With the deictic personal pronoun ἐγώ, pointing to himself, Jesus distinguishes his knowledge of God from their failure to know God and recognize God in him.

This failure, coupled with "the Jews'" explicit rejection of Jesus (vv. 48, 52), renders them "liars" (v. 55; see v. 44). The knowing and keeping that Jesus claims for himself, by contrast, is the covenantal language of the Prophets.[84] Jesus asserts that he is standing in covenantal relationship with God, his Father. Should he disavow this relationship, he would be a liar just as they are. With this language of the covenant lawsuit ("You do not know him," see Amos 3:1–2; Hos 4:1–11; Isa 5:13), Jesus pronounces his accusation (and even judgment) of their breach of covenant with God when they fail to know the Father and the Son.[85] To underscore his point, Jesus refers once again to Abraham, their covenantal paradigm *par excellence* from Scripture. Abraham, who they have rightly claimed to be their genetic father, knew God and believed God, and it was credited to him as righteousness (Gen 15:6). Abraham "rejoiced that he might see my day, and he saw it and was glad" (v. 56). Jewish tradition held that in response to Abraham's faith, God had given

---

84. See chapter 2 for my detailed discussion of the covenant metaphor in the Prophets, specifically the language of knowledge for accepting and keeping the covenant, e.g., Jer 31:31–34.

85. See nn. 35, 40 above for further references from the Prophets. See also Lincoln, *Truth on Trial*, 92–96.

him the revelation of the secrets of the ages to come.[86] Jesus here reveals that he and his mission in the world are the content of those secrets. Abraham, in his privileged status as a covenantal father and in striking contrast to "the Jews" standing in dialogue with Jesus, saw the day of Jesus and "rejoiced."

"THE JEWS" AND JESUS: REJECTION OF THE "I AM" (vv. 57–59) The final exchange of the lengthy Tabernacles dialogue is framed by the response of "the Jews" to Jesus' covenantal claims for himself and disclaims for them. The first is verbal (v. 57) and the last is physical (v. 59). For his part, Jesus voices the teaching that culminates all that he has put forth to "the Jews" in this dialogue (v. 58).

Again confirming their complete disconnection from who Jesus is and what he has been teaching and trying to do for them, "the Jews" respond to his claims "from above" through the purely physical perspective of the world "below." Again they misrepresent what he has said about himself. They ask, "You are not yet fifty years old and you have seen Abraham?" Jesus' physical age is of course irrelevant, and he did not claim to have seen Abraham (καὶ Ἀβραάμ ἑώρακας; v. 57), but rather that Abraham saw his day (ἴδῃ τὴν ἡμέραν τὴν ἐμήν, v. 56).

With regard to the covenantal underpinnings of this dialogue of accepting or rejecting Jesus as the Son who gives the word of God, Jesus throws down the verbal gauntlet and proclaims, "Amen, amen, I say to you, before Abraham came to be [γενέσθαι], I am" (ἐγώ εἰμί, v. 58). Jesus' words reflect the first words of the prologue (1:1–2) and give voice to his preexistence as the Word of God. He further points to himself as the incarnation of that word of God to Abraham, now offered to all who would receive him in his day and beyond. The entirety of the Tabernacles encounters to this point is encapsulated in this one proclamation of existence beyond this world "below" with the Father "above." Jesus has spoken of himself in terms of ἐγώ εἰμί three times in this dialogue (8:24, 28, 58). On the lips of Jesus, these words reveal aspects of his mission as the Messiah with increasing effectiveness.[87] In

---

86. *Targum Onkelos* on Gen 17:16–17; *Gen. Rab.* 44.22, 28; *4 Ezra* 3:14; *T. Levi* 18:14; *2 Bar* 4:4; *Apoc. Abr.* 31.1–3; *Tan. Ber.* 6.20; *b. Sanh.* 108b). See Brown, *John*, 1:359–60; Moloney, *John*, 284.

87. Freed, "Who or What," 57. Lindars (*John*, 336) further notes the unifying use of ἐγώ εἰμι across the dialogue of John 8. Lincoln (*Truth on Trial*, 43–50) ties these statements to the covenant lawsuit as Jesus identifies himself with the role of God in these lawsuits.

this emotional climax of self-revelation that takes on the divine name without qualification, Jesus gives full voice to the messianic implications of his person and the gift of truth that he offers through his word: a perfected life-giving covenantal relationship with God the Father that transcends the temporal and spatial boundaries of this world.

The Jews "stand outside the world of the prologue," and this word of Jesus leads not to reconciliation and salvation for them but to the shock and dismay of blasphemy.[88] Apparently reacting based on the prescribed punishment for blasphemy (Lev 24:16), "the Jews took up stones that they might throw at him" (v. 59). They have no words left for Jesus; their response to him now is purely physical. They seek to stone him in defense of a closed religious system, fully rejecting Jesus' self-revelation and covenantal challenge. They choose to abide as descendants of this world (σπέρμα Ἀβραάμ, vv. 33, 37) and thus choose to reject the gift that Jesus gives to become children of God (τέκνα τοῦ Ἀβραάμ, v. 39; and thereby τέκνα θεοῦ, 1:12).[89]

Jesus, too, must respond physically. The one who has taken such pains to reveal his true self to his dialogue partners at the Feast of Tabernacles must now hide himself from their midst. Jesus leaves the temple precincts and thus leaves their presence so that God's plan for the Son, the hour of his lifting up in true glory, may be fulfilled.

Conclusion: The Fulfillment of the Feast of Tabernacles in Jesus

The gulf separating Jesus and "the Jews" he encounters at the Feast of Tabernacles is a profound *closedness*. Readers of John 7–8 have the prologue resonating in their ears as they listen to Jesus' teaching in this most heated segment of his public ministry. They have been given information about Jesus and the glory of God's action in and for the sake of the world through the covenantal gift of truth manifest in Jesus. Thus, when readers experience Jesus verbalizing what God is doing through him in the tenor of his own voice, there is room for his word. "The Jews," who stand outside the world of the prologue, are ultimately not open to hearing and seeing God the Father in the voice and person of Jesus

---

88. Moloney, *John*, 285.
89. See Culpepper, "Pivot," 28–31.

the Son.[90] Although many can come to a partial faith in the messianic mission of Jesus when it rings familiar to their long-standing religious system, they cannot take root and abide in his word when he reveals the full implications of the life-giving truth of his messiahship. They cannot appreciate nor participate in the openness of the very figures of their religious history to which they appeal. Thus, even as authentic progeny, they choose to remain outside the covenantal realm of the children of God, for children hear the word of their father and do as their father does, as manifested in the Son that God the Father gives to them. The covenantal challenge given by Jesus to "the Jews" in the setting of the Feast of Tabernacles is initially taken up in part by "many of the Jews" (v. 30). However, when the full messianic implication of abiding in the word of Jesus is revealed, they ultimately reject the covenantal gift to become children of God.

For his part, Jesus stands in the temple area in the midst of the Feast of Tabernacles, which celebrates the experience of God's care for the children of Israel in the wilderness at Sinai, and presents himself as the covenantal mediation of the experience of God's life-giving care now and forever. As the participants in the Tabernacles celebration relive their ancestors' experience of God through rituals of water and light, Jesus shows himself to be the living water and true light that reveals God to all who would open themselves to him and take root in his word, thus empowering them to become the covenantal children of God. In the dialogue of Tabernacles, Jesus reveals that all that is accomplished in that annual feast is perfected in him through the covenantal love between the true Son and the living Father, now and forever.

The formal debate that manifests through these dialogues is forensic in nature, manifesting the tone of a trial scene in the tradition of the covenantal lawsuit of the Prophets. Jesus acts as both witness and prosecutor in the name of God the Father.[91] He extends the covenantal challenge to abide in his word, claiming himself to be the incarnation of God's covenant love for the world and putting "the Jews" on trial, including those who have made the partial move of belief. Even these are not open to God's new covenantal action in Jesus and thus do not know the Father and cannot accept the fullness of Jesus' covenantal challenge.

---

90. Moloney, *John*, 285. They necessarily judge him a blasphemer and take up stones against him.

91. Lincoln, *Truth on Trial*, 82–96; Neyrey, "Jesus the Judge."

Jesus pronounces them guilty, depicting them as children not of the covenant of God but of the lies of the devil. In this regard, Andrew Lincoln notes the following:

> The refusal to recognize the claims of Jesus is shown ... to have profound repercussions. It casts doubt on any claim to be a free descendant of Abraham and to know the one true God of the covenant. For this Gospel, such claims are now to be judged in terms of whether or not they facilitate belief in the one who is presented as so identified with the divine sphere that he is able to take upon his own lips the 'I Am' formulation that had functioned in the Jewish Scriptures as Yahweh's self-designation.[92]

In turn, "the Jews" attempt to put Jesus on trial, but his dialogical prowess in the truth of God's work through the Son eventually renders them speechless. They attempt to condemn him of blasphemy in their spontaneous physical response of taking up stones against him. But the true verdict of God in this covenantal lawsuit is presented in Jesus' successful evasion of their action. The hour of the glory of the Son of God will come on God's time, when God's covenant with the world can be perfected.

Moving to Glory (John 11–12)

The narrative section that explores and christologically perfects the feasts of Judaism comes to a close at 10:40–42 with Jesus moving back across the Jordan and abiding there. A final reference to the truthful witness of John allows the narrator to provide a moment of reflection for the reader. The words of the prologue resonate as the testimony of Jesus and about Jesus reconstitutes "his own" not as the ethnic Judaism of the past but as those who "receive him," that is, believe in him (10:42; see 1:11–12). With these suggestions in mind, readers move with Jesus to glory.

Chapters 11–12 of the Fourth Gospel are crucial to the theological flow of this good news because they move the narrative from the ministry to the cross. In the words and actions of Jesus, the evangelist culminates the themes of life and light that have permeated his Gospel from their introduction in the prologue (1:3–5). The entrance into a new segment in the story is indicated by the introduction of a new setting (Bethany, 11:1) and new characters (the siblings Mary, Martha, and

---

92. Lincoln, *Saint John*, 277.

Lazarus, whom Jesus loves, 11:5). These first verses also reveal that Jesus' role as the life-giver who sheds light on those who walk with him will be perfected (11:7–15). At the same time, the narrator's proleptic aside that Mary is the one who anointed Jesus raises a note of tension about the events to come and the death that is impending (11:2; see 12:1–8). Although it is Lazarus whose physical life is at stake (11:1), the intricately constructed narrative that unfolds across 11:1–54 emphasizes the faith journeys of Jesus' friends Mary and Martha as he challenges them to see in him not the culmination of a historical religious system but the perfection of life in the spirit through the covenantal relationship of believing in God. He asserts, "I am the resurrection and the life. Whoever believes in me, even though he dies, will live, and everyone who lives and believes in me will never die" (vv. 25–26).[93] Although Jesus does give life to Lazarus, and "many of the Jews therefore, who had come with Mary and had seen what Jesus did, began to believe in him" (v. 45), his gift of life serves to render his own death all the more imminent. At the pinnacle of irony, the high priest Caiaphas prophesies that this "one man" would "die instead of the people" (v. 50). The narrator steps in and clarifies the prophetic word so that readers can grasp that Jesus was about to die, "not for the nation only, but to gather into one the dispersed children of God" (τὰ τέκνα τοῦ θεοῦ, v. 52), such that even in the face of death (vv. 53–54) Jesus gives the gift of life in covenantal relationship as a child of God to all who call on his name (see 1:12). Indeed, Jesus' death will effect the restoration and union of the covenant people of God, a reconstituted Israel, as the true children of God.[94]

The arrival of the final festival of the Jews in this story is announced at 11:55. The Passover is at hand and the many who have arrived in Jerusalem are abuzz with what might occur. The tension is high and the crisis is at hand (11:56–57). This is confirmed for readers as John 12 begins and Mary's foretold anointing of Jesus with perfumed oil comes to pass and, defending her actions, Jesus confirms its purpose: "so that she might keep it for the day of my burial. . . . You will not always

---

93. For further detail on this reading of John 11, see Moloney, "Can Everyone Be Wrong?" See also Schneiders, "Death in the Community"; Stibbe, "Tomb with a View"; Wuellner, "Putting Life Back."

94. Dennis, *Jesus' Death*, 292. Dennis shows that the concept "children of God" is "a clear reference to the covenant people of God" through a survey of OT/Jewish literature, esp. Exod 4:22; Deut 14:1; 32:5–6, 18–19; Jer 3:19; 31:9; Isa 63:16; 64:8; Hos 11:1, 10. For the full discussion, see ibid., 247–92. See also Culpepper, "Pivot," 18–19.

have me" (vv. 7–8). It is this intimate scene of burial preparation that lies behind Jesus' heralded entry into Jerusalem (vv. 12–15). This event confounds Jesus' disciples, but remains with them and in their memory when Jesus is glorified (v. 16). The narrator steps in again, however, to warn the reader of the superficial sign-oriented nature of the faith of the people, which may not abide (v. 17–18). The triumph of Jesus' entry into Jerusalem for the Passover may also prove fleeting.

The hour that will bring about the crisis of these faith journeys in the glorification of Jesus is foreshadowed with the exclamation of the Pharisees that "the world has gone after him" (v. 19) and precipitated by the arrival of the Greeks who seek to see Jesus (vv. 20–22). Upon hearing this, Jesus announces that his long-forecast hour has finally come: "The hour has come for the Son of Man to be glorified" (v. 23). He speaks of love, service, and honor, in relationship with the Father, but his soul is troubled (vv. 24–27). The hour of his glorification is also an hour of distress for Jesus, who, despite his foreknowledge, is no less affected by his mission as the Son of Man in the world.[95] He confirms his mission through a prayer of determination ("Father, glorify your name") and is acknowledged and affirmed by the voice from heaven (v. 28). The discussion among the people that results from this voice leads Jesus to affirm his role as the Son of Man and his desire to "draw all people" to himself. In the covenantal language of the family of the children of God, he urges, "While you have the light, believe in the light, so that you may become children of the light" (vv. 30–36a).[96] However, in fulfillment of the word of Isaiah, who saw his glory, Jesus departs from the people, who are then left to their own crises: the glory of God or the fear of being put out of the synagogue and the world they know (vv. 36b–43). Those who choose the former accept Jesus' covenantal challenge and are empowered to become children of God. Those who choose the latter reject Jesus' covenantal challenge and remain the progeny of the world.

Jesus then cries out his final words in the public sphere, giving a climactic voice to the themes of mission and light first introduced in the prologue (vv. 44–50; see 1:1–18). With these words, he summarizes

---

95. For more on the hour of Jesus in John as an hour of distress, see Morrison, "Hour of Distress." For the counterargument that Jesus was not affected by distress in this "hour," see O'Day, *John*, 712.

96. For detailed discussion of this final interaction between Jesus and the people, particularly their OT expectations of the Messiah, see van Unnik, "Quotation from the Old Testament"; and Bampfylde, "More Light on John 12:34."

the revelatory discourse of his entire public ministry.[97] Jesus defers all honor and impetus for his life and mission to the Father who sent him. His word is the word of the Father, and his mission is to give eternal life (vv. 49–50). These verses resonate with the covenantal themes of Deuteronomy. The words of God are now uttered by the prophet-like-Moses incarnate in Jesus the Son of God (v. 49; Deut 18:15, 18–19), and these commandments set the pattern of daily life for the people (vv. 47–48; Deut 8:3), and breathe the life of Israel (v. 50; Deut 32:45–47).[98] It is the word of God "spoken through Jesus that now sums up the covenant obligations of the believer."[99] With the intricacy and intimacy of the relationship between God the Father and Jesus the Son, as well as their shared desire to extend this covenantal relationship of family to all who would become children of God, we move to the glory of the hour of Jesus.

The Dialogue of Covenant in John 5–12

As in the first part of Jesus' public ministry, John 2–4, the language and imagery of covenant provide the background for the remaining segments of his mission to the world, John 5–10 and 11–12. The symbolic rhetoric of Jesus' dialogues throughout these chapters flows from the well of the OT covenant metaphor, as over and again Jesus issues the challenge to embark upon a journey of faith that will bring everyone he encounters into covenant relationship with him. The action his speech evokes in his dialogue partners is a movement toward him or a turning away from him in acceptance or rejection of his challenge of covenant relationship in the family of God. Throughout, he verbally points to himself as the revelation of the Word of God who gives this gift of truth to those who would become children of God.

The narrative imagery of the feasts of Israel, all of which are intimately connected to the experience of God's covenantal action in and with creation, forms the backdrop of all that Jesus says and does in this major segment of his public life. The identity of Jesus is revealed in his relationship to God, the one who is celebrated through these festivals.

---

97. Schnackenburg, *St. John*, 3:1.

98. See Chennattu, *Johannine Discipleship*, 79; Beasley-Murray, *John*, 218; Schnackenburg, *St. John*, 3:424–25.

99. Brown, *John*, 1:493.

He reveals a unique Father-Son relationship, a relationship of family, that itself emanates the imagery of covenant. Further, the Father has sent the Son for the purpose of summoning all the children of God to himself. These children know the voice of the Son and respond as sheep to a shepherd, gathering and abiding in the light of life that he gives. As Jesus moves through the feasts of Israel, he voices a continual clarion call of this invitational challenge to covenant, heard by the disciples, the crowds, "the Jews," and the reader. The ever-increasing intensity of both his covenantal rhetoric and the potential consequences imposed by those who reject his self-revelatory challenge marks the progress of the Gospel story.

In John 5, within the literary context of the feast of Sabbath, Jesus heals a man who is crippled and instructs him to carry his pallet, thereby having them both break Sabbath law (5:1–18). In the conflict with "the Jews" that follows, Jesus reveals his oneness with the Father that transcends the Law, allowing him to continue God's good works. The healed man, who initially responds with obedience to the word of Jesus (v. 9), ends by pointing out Jesus to "the Jews" who "were seeking all the more to kill him" (v. 18). In his discourse, Jesus refers to the witness of the Scriptures and John the Baptist, his own works, and the Father in a "juridical controversy" of persuasion for his christological claims (vv. 30–47).[100] The scene comes to an end with no resolution. Jesus' accusers make no response to his challenge.[101] The healed man does not seem to have even understood that a challenge was at stake. The entire chapter serves to introduce this series of christological perfections of the Jewish feasts within their covenantal contexts.

In the extended narrative and dialogue of John 6, Jesus stands in the countryside of Galilee during the time of Passover and reveals himself to be the true bread from heaven. He is the perfection of the gift of God to Israel in the Sinai wilderness that gives life to all who partake of his offer of himself (6:25–40). In response to the murmuring of the crowd regarding his identity, Jesus claims, "I am the bread of life" (v. 48). He goes on to reveal that the gift of God celebrated at Passover "was but a sign and shadow of the perfection of the gift of God in the person Jesus Christ, the true bread from heaven, who brings eternal life

---

100. Asiedu-Peprah, *Johannine Sabbath Conflicts*, 16; see 52–116 for the full discussion.

101. Ibid., 25.

to all who would believe in him."[102] Using the ceremonial imagery of eating and drinking the covenant meal—and offering himself as that meal—Jesus challenges the characters in the story, both the crowds and those who claim to be his disciples, to open themselves to the ongoing revelation of God in himself and into eternal relationship with him (vv. 52–59).[103]

The enormity of the progression of Jesus' public challenge in these verses is borne out by the varying responses to it narrated in vv. 60–71. Curiously, only responses of the disciples are recounted here. "The Jews" mentioned in vv. 41 and 52 as those facilitating Jesus' discourse by murmuring and disputes do not yet respond, as in John 5. As for the disciples, many find Jesus' teaching hard to bear: "This is a hard saying [Σκληρός ἐστιν ὁ λόγος οὗτος]; who can listen to it?" (v. 60). Their response is to reject Jesus by no longer following him (v. 66). Jesus understands this (vv. 61–65), and in this context challenges the Twelve directly: "Do you also wish to go away?" (v. 67).[104] Simon Peter, for the first time in the story, takes a leadership position and responds on behalf of the disciples by making a public confession of their growing belief in Jesus as well as their determination to follow him. He professes, "You have the words of eternal life; we have come to believe and we have come to know, that you are the Holy One of God" (vv. 68–69). These sincere words of acceptance, however, are marked with the foreboding of trial and betrayal, as in the final words of this episode Jesus reveals that intrinsic in the choice of his own is the path to the hour of his suffering and glory (v. 71).

In the dialogues of the Feast of Tabernacles (John 7:1—8:59) Jesus stands in the temple area and reveals his messianic origins and destiny in the context of the light of God's gift of Torah to the faithful. The results of this stand have been detailed above. What must be noted here is that these extended scenes of dialogue and narrative in the context of the celebration of God's covenantal gift of Torah that escalate to violent controversy are the point in this feasts section where "the Jews" begin

102. Moloney, *Signs and Shadows*, 64.
103. Chennattu, *Johannine Discipleship*, 75.

104. This is the first time in the story that Jesus' inner circle of the Twelve is identified, and their number is mentioned three times in this passage (vv. 67, 70, 71), both in the context of acceptance and the ultimate rejection by Judas (v. 71). The only other time in the Gospel of John that Jesus' inner circle is identified as the Twelve is at the first resurrection appearance to the disciples (20:24).

to come to decision about Jesus. The evangelist narrates their ultimate response of rejection to his challenge of abiding in his word as they attempt to stone the Son of Man for blasphemy (8:59). The controversy continues as Jesus heals a man born blind, and the evangelist gives a glimpse into the conflict of his own time as the threat of expulsion from the synagogue to those who follow Jesus is articulated (9:22, 34). Jesus affirms that acceptance and belief have their own rewards, for he is the Good Shepherd who lays down his life for his sheep (9:35—10:18, esp. 10:11).[105] Jesus' extended use of the shepherd imagery to describe himself resonates with YHWH's self-characterization in the words of the prophet Ezekiel. There Israel's failure to "know" YHWH resulted in it being convicted of breach of covenant, the punishment for which was exile (see, e.g., Ezek 12:15-16). Once YHWH begins to speak of establishing a covenant with Israel anew, he calls himself the "shepherd" who will seek out and care for his sheep (Ezek 34:15-16) and "make with them a covenant of peace" so that "they will know that I am YHWH" (Ezek 34:25-31). By employing the shepherd imagery here at the conclusion of the events in the context of the Feast of Tabernacles, Jesus reverberates the covenantal declarations of God in Ezekiel. He identifies himself first as the Gate (ἐγώ εἰμι ἡ θύρα, v. 9) through which anyone can enter the fold of the sheep of God, then as the Good Shepherd (ἐγώ εἰμι ὁ ποιμήν ὁ καλός, vv. 11, 14) who is known by his own and God the Father (vv. 14b-15a).[106] At this point in the Gospel according to John, the schism among "the Jews" over Jesus' identity and implicit covenant offering continues (vv. 19-21).[107]

In the brief encounter during the Feast of Dedication that closes the feasts section (10:22-42), Jesus challenges all those in doubt and discussion about him to accept his word and works in the name of the Father who sent him. He concludes, "I and the Father are one" (v. 30). The general schism seems to have come to an end as "the Jews" once again take up stones against Jesus for blasphemy (v. 31). Jesus denounces their accusation and acknowledges that their rejection of him is rejection of God the Father (vv. 32-39). He escapes their renewed attempt to

---

105. For more on this, see Chennattu, "Good Shepherd."

106. See chapter 2 for the establishment of "knowledge of God" as covenantal language.

107. For more on the connections between John 9 and 10, see Du Rand, "Syntactical and Narratological Reading."

arrest him (v. 39) and continues unhindered to find acceptance in new believers (vv. 40–42).

The narratives and dialogues that close Jesus' public ministry bring the themes of life and light to their peaks, as Jesus places himself in the midst of the Jewish people and reveals himself to be the resurrection and the life on the eve of the hour of his glorification (11:1—12:50). In the aftermath of the sign that Jesus performs in the raising of Lazarus, the Jewish authorities are prompted to make the final decision that Jesus must die (11:45–57). The evangelist continues to distinguish between superficial belief and the abiding in the word of Jesus that reflects authentic faith of true children of God. Mary, Martha, and the disciples continue on their journeys of faith, while the persistent unbelief of the crowds is finally confirmed (12:37). The fear of many among the authorities who began to believe (ἐπίστευσαν) to confess Jesus as the Messiah lest they be expelled from the synagogue (ἵνα μὴ ἀποσυνάγωγοι γένωνται) is condemned by the narrator as the failing of human will (12:42–43). Readers of this Gospel find themselves in the midst of these journeys of faith. They, too, are being brought to a crisis and must determine with whom to identify as they decide the direction their own journey will take.

Jesus himself then sums up his revelatory discourse through the word of God in terms of the covenantal obligations of the believer (12:44–50).[108] In stark contrast to those who love human praise more than the praise of God (v. 43), Jesus and those who accept him, whom he has empowered to be the true children of God, speak out the words the Father has commanded, regardless of the earthly consequences. Those who reject him do not, and God will be their judge (v. 48). Jesus has been sent to save the world (v. 47) and those who receive him receive the commandment of God, which is eternal life (v. 50). As Jesus' public ministry comes to an end, he turns toward his own and the hour of his glorification, when the mission of his covenantal gift to the world will be fulfilled.

---

108. Brown, *John*, 1:491; Schnackenburg, *St. John*, 3:1.

6

Covenantal Dialogue in John 13–20

THE BOOK OF SIGNS (1:19—12:50) DEPICTS THE PUBLIC MINISTRY OF Jesus. His words and deeds address a wide audience and provoke a crisis of faith wherein some believe and some refuse to believe. The Book of Glory (13:1—20:31) can be characterized as the result of that crisis. It is addressed to the restricted audience of those who believe. If the Book of Signs anticipated what Jesus would do for humankind once glorified, the Book of Glory describes that glorification. This, finally, is "the hour" of his passion, crucifixion, and resurrection. These distinctions are made apparent in the first verse of this portion of the narrative (13:1).[1] Literarily, the Book of Glory reverses the narrative action of the Book of Signs. In that first part of the body of the Gospel, Jesus' dialogues and discourses followed and served to interpret the signs. In this second part, the last supper and discourse (13:1—17:26) precede the action of glorification and serve to foretell and interpret that action.

The present chapter focuses on this second half of the Gospel according to John. In the study that follows, the covenantal discourse of John 13–17 will serve as the starting point for an analysis of the passion narrative, specifically the dialogue on kingship and truth between Jesus and Pilate (18:28—19:16a) as well as the consequences of that truth particularly for the mother of Jesus and the Beloved Disciple at the cross (19:16b–37). We will conclude with a look at the resurrection of the Word (John 20) and the dialogue of covenant across this portion of the Johannine story.

---

1. See Grossouw, "Note on John"; Brown, *John*, 2:540; Moloney, *John*, 370–72.

The Last Discourse (John 13–17)

The form and content of the last discourse has lent itself to considerable scholarly discussion regarding its structure and integrity. Repetitions and discrepancies in sequence and content in these chapters have resulted in various approaches to interpreting the extended scenes narrated within them.[2] Despite these difficulties, there is an increasing consensus that John 13–17 presents a coherent narrative unit.[3] For the purposes of the present study, the recent work of Rekha Chennattu on covenant and Johannine discipleship provides a guide for understanding these crucial scenes between Jesus and "his own." Chennattu presents a comparison of these chapters to the covenant renewal ceremony of Joshua 24 and argues that this narrative unit relates a renewal and sealing of the covenant relationship between Jesus and his disciples in the context of his farewell speech.[4] The narrative of Joshua 24 "shows how to establish a covenant partnership with God and a community seeking to become God's covenant people," and is analogous in function to John 13–17.[5] She is quick to note the differences in the patterns found in Joshua 24 and John 13–17, but identifies "the essential elements of the OT covenant traditions appearing in John 13–17," and thus indicates that the paradigms "of the OT covenant relationship are significant for the interpretation of discipleship in John 13–17."[6] The overview of John

---

2. For a survey and analysis of these solutions, see Segovia, *Farewell of the Word*, 2–58.

3. See, e.g., O'Day, "'I Have Overcome.'" O'Day argues that John 13–17 is framed by the metaphor of "the hour" and focuses on the consummation of that hour. Likewise, Moloney ("Structure and Message"; *Glory Not Dishonor*, 1–7; "Function of John 13–17") has presented a chiastic structure that respects the unity of the final form of these chapters and turns on Jesus' command to his disciples to love one another and abide in a relationship of love formed in union with the Father and the Son (15:12–17).

4. Chennattu, *Johannine Discipleship*, 81–139.

5. Ibid., 68. For a consideration of Josh 24 as a "report of covenant making," see McCarthy, *Treaty and Covenant*, 241. For the argument that this passage reflects a covenant renewal form that is repeatedly used within Israelite traditions, see Muilenburg, "Form and Structure." See chapter 2 for an analysis of the text.

6. Ibid., 69–70. For a detailed analysis of the farewell discourse, also with covenant-making conclusions, but noting the similarities of these chapters with the Moses traditions in Deuteronomy, see Lacomara, "Deuteronomy and the Farewell Discourse." He concludes that by incorporating various elements from Deuteronomy, the evangelist has included in the last discourse "the basic elements of traditional covenant-form. Thus, on the part of God who is identified as the source, Christ, a uniquely qualified mediator, presents a new commandment" (83).

13–17 that follows thus highlights the covenant motif as it manifests in this evangelist's story of Jesus' last meal and discourse with his disciples before his crucifixion.

The Covenant between Jesus and the Disciples

Jesus began to gather disciples in the first days of his public ministry (1:35–51). Covenant themes of chosenness, knowledge of God, and abiding relationship with God suggest that these early scenes represent the initiation of these disciples into a covenant relationship with God through Jesus.[7] Throughout the narrative of Jesus' public ministry in John 2–12, the disciples witness and participate in the signs and mission of Jesus that call them to a decision about Jesus and about their role in his ministry. By 6:67–71, Jesus has singled out the Twelve for special status as "his own" inner circle. When he puts the question to them of whether they too will go away like so many others or remain with him, Peter answers on behalf of the Twelve that they have come to "know" and "believe" that Jesus, the Holy One of God, has the words of eternal life (6:68–69). From this point through John, Jesus' challenges to relationship with him become all the more potent and provocative. By John 11–12, the disciples consciously choose to accompany Jesus to Judea and eventually to Jerusalem, even under the threat of death (see 11:16). With regard to the disciples, then, the narrative thus far has functioned "as a hortatory preparation for the covenant renewal in 13–17" that culminates in the prayer that "seals the new covenant instituted by Jesus" and perfects "all former covenant traditions."[8] This process begins with a gathering of Jesus and "his own" for a farewell meal and discourse.

JESUS AND THE DISCIPLES GATHERED TOGETHER FOR THE FAREWELL MEAL (13:1–38)

John 13 is a literary unit that introduces the themes of the entire last discourse (John 13–17) and serves as a foundational element of the

---

7. Chennattu, *Johannine Discipleship*, 88; for detailed analysis see 22–49. See chapter 2 for a survey of OT covenant texts and the establishment of chosenness, knowledge of God, and abiding relationship with God as the language and themes of covenant and the OT covenant metaphor.

8. Ibid., 88.

covenant metaphor that unfolds across these chapters.⁹ The first verses provide a solemn introduction that is "the most significant transition in the Gospel, introducing not only the scene of the footwashing but the entire second half of the Gospel."¹⁰ Beginning with the characterization of the disciples as Jesus' own (τοὺς ἰδίους), vv. 1–3 set the scene of a covenant meal in which Jesus participates with "his own" whom he loves "to the end." Just as the OT covenant meals signify both YHWH's choice of covenant partners and the acceptance of the covenant by those partners (see Gen 26:26–30; 31:43–54; Exod 24:5–11; Deut 27:6–7), Jesus' final meal with his disciples signifies the covenantal nature of their relationship: an intimate bond of friendship, shared knowledge, and acceptance that binds them as the new family of God.¹¹ The action of the footwashing symbolizes Jesus' self-sacrificing, perfecting love in relationship with the disciples (vv. 4–20).¹² The OT narrates footwashing as a gesture of hospitality (Gen 18:4; 19:2; 24:32; 43:32; Judg 19:21; 1 Sam 25:41) and as preparation for meeting God (Exod 30:17–21), and washing in general is associated with ushering in the promise of the new covenant (Ezek 36:25–28).¹³ By washing the feet of his disciples, Jesus thus allows them to have a share in his mission and destiny in relationship with God (v. 8).

---

9. On the literary unity of John 13, see Lombard and Oliver, "Working Supper in Jerusalem." For detailed analysis of the thematic unity of 13:1–38, see Culpepper, "Johannine *Hypodeigma*"; Moloney, "Structure and Message"; Niccaci, "L'unita letteraria." For an argument that 13:31–38 must be distinguished as a bridge into the coming discourse, see Mlakuzhyil, *Christocentric Literary Structure*, 221–23. For the inclusion of 13:31–38 with 14:1–31 as the first discourse of this section, see Segovia, *Farewell of the Word*, 21–24; Du Rand, "Story and a Community"; Tolmie, *Jesu' Farewell*, 29–30; Woll, "Departure of 'The Way'"; Segovia, "Structure, *Tendenz*." On the unfolding covenant metaphor across John 13–17, see Chennattu, *Johannine Discipleship*, 82; and Simoens, *Gloire d'aimer*, 52–80.

10. Culpepper, "Johannine *Hypodeigma*," 135.

11. See Chennattu, *Johannine Discipleship*, 89–91. She points to the OT evidence for the conclusion of a covenant ceremony with a communal meal shared by the covenant partners. See chapter 2 for the establishment of the language of love, chosenness, and family as OT covenantal language.

12. Ibid., 91–96. For a proposal that the footwashing of Jesus could be a symbolic act of love that facilitates communion based on reference to the Jewish work *Joseph and Aseneth* (composed between 100 BC and AD 200), see Schwank, "Exemplum dedi vobis." In the same vein, see also Brown, *John*, 2:558, 564–65.

13. Chennattu, *Johannine Discipleship*, 94–95.

The narrative that ensues from this communal meal and symbolic action (vv. 21–30) provides the impetus for a new covenant commandment based in mutual love, as modeled by Jesus' own humble self-sacrificing mission that will ultimately lead to glorification (vv. 31–35).[14] The remainder of the chapter narrates three possible responses to this covenantal challenge, represented in the figures and actions of Judas (vv. 2, 11, 18–31), Peter (vv. 6–9, 36–38), and the Beloved Disciple (vv. 21–30). These responses correlate with the reactions to Jesus and his word by those he encountered throughout his public ministry.[15] The Beloved Disciple comes forward in the narrative as the one who shares intimate relationship with Jesus and the only disciple who seems to travel in lockstep with Jesus on his journey through the hour of his glorification. He begins to emerge as the disciple who is the model witness to Jesus' true destiny and meaning for the world. As the final meal between Jesus and his own comes to a close and night falls (see v. 30), Jesus begins to speak in earnest of the promises this covenantal relationship offers.

The Promise of God's Indwelling Presence and Guidance (14:1–31)

The movement of the last discourse shifts at 14:1 as the scene moves from the dialogue between Jesus and Peter (13:36–38) to a dialogue between Jesus and the disciples as a group, marked by his double use of the second person plural imperative πιστεύετε ("believe," v. 1bc). A framework that is both verbal and thematic unifies 14:1–31 as, alongside this belief (v. 1; v. 29), Jesus encourages the disciples through his command, "Let not your hearts be troubled" (vv. 1a, 27).[16] The primary focus of this section of Jesus' discourse is the content of the promises

---

14. Ibid., 97–98.

15. Ibid., 98–101. The character and action of Judas present a model of complete rejection of Jesus and the relationship he offers (see v. 30). The character, words, and actions of Peter represent a partial acceptance of Jesus (or "partial failure" to heed the call to covenant relationship based in misunderstanding; see vv. 36–38). The character, words, and action of the Beloved Disciple represent total faithfulness or complete acceptance of Jesus' call to covenantal relationship (see vv. 23).

16. For this framing theme of encouragement, see all of vv. 1–3 and vv. 27–31. Chennattu, *Johannine Discipleship*, 83–84. For detailed discussion of the internal unity and structure of 14:1–31, see Moloney, *Glory Not Dishonor*, 29–54; Niccaci, "Esame letterario di Gv 14"; Segovia, *Farewell of the Word*, 64–65.

he offers to his disciples who have entered into relationship with him. Chennattu points out that these promises correlate thematically with the covenantal promises of a renewal ceremony and fall into three types: the indwelling presence of the divine (vv. 3, 12-21, 23, 28; see Exod 25:8), the knowledge of the divine (vv. 7, 17, 20-21, 26; see Exod 29:45-46; Lev 26:11-12), and the gift of peace (v. 27; see Isa 9:6-7; 52:7; 57:19; Ezek 34:25; 37:26; Hag 2:9).[17] Interspersed throughout this portion of Jesus' last discourse that focuses on the promises he offers to his disciples who are in covenant relationship with him is a call to believe and keep the commandments of his word. All Jesus' words are encapsulated in two commandments: to believe in him (vv. 1, 10-12) and to love God (vv. 15, 21, 23-24). The entire covenantal obligation of disciples in this relationship that invokes Jesus' promises comes down to keeping these commandments. In John 15, Jesus then turns to a more detailed exposition of this call.

A Call to Abide and Keep the Commandments (15:1-17)

The next section of Jesus' last discourse with his disciples is united by the overarching theme of the obligations of discipleship in this covenant relationship. John 15:1-17 provides the metaphor of vine and branches that symbolically describes "the covenant relationship between God/Jesus and his disciples," as well as the command to abide in Jesus and to love one another. Chennattu claims:

> In the OT prophetic traditions, YHWH is the gardener and Israel is God's fruitful vine (Ezek 19:10), a choice vine (Jer 2:21), and God's vineyard (Isa 5:1-7; 27: 2-6). Both the prophetic texts and the OT covenant texts articulate the need to obey God's voice and keep God's covenant commandments in order to be God's vine (Jer 2:21; 3:13) and God's treasured possession (Exod 19:5; Josh 7:11; 24:25). The metaphor of the vine and the command to love of John 15 likewise describe the status and obligations of the covenant partners.[18]

17. Chennattu, *Johannine Discipleship*, 101-11.
18. Ibid., 84-85. For detailed analysis, see 111-18, where she presents this section as "an evocative and powerful *mashal* . . . about discipleship in terms of an abiding covenant relationship" (111). For more on the structure and genre of the early verses of John 15, especially in terms of a *mashal*, identified in Jewish tradition as all types of figurative illustrations and discourses (111n90), see Brown, *John*, 1:390-91, 2:668-69; Hermaniuk, *Parabole évangélique*; Wead, *Literary Devices*, 74-82, 92-94.

After his initial call for departure in 14:31, Jesus uses the metaphor of the vine to describe himself, with God the Father as the vine grower (15:1). The journey of the disciples with Jesus thus far has been one of pruning and cleansing as the branches of the vine (vv. 2–3). The challenge for the disciples from this point is one of abiding in that integral relationship of the vine and vine grower. As he continues, Jesus identifies himself and his actions with the love of the Father, and therefore expands his call for the disciples to abide in his love (μείνατε ἐν τῇ ἀγάπῃ τῇ ἐμῇ, vv. 9–11).[19] Jesus' explicit covenant command follows as he exhorts the disciples whom he has chosen (v. 16) to love one another as he has loved them (vv. 12–17). Both the description of the covenant partners as specifically "chosen" and this sort of exhortation to keep God's commandments are integral parts of speeches that precede OT covenant-making and renewing processes (see Deut 30:16; Exod 34:11; Josh 24:14–15).[20]

In these final verses of this section, as Jesus is imparting the command to love to his chosen disciples, he also begins to speak in terms of friendship, and integrates friendship with that love to which he is calling them. Sharon Ringe notes that OT narratives of friendship may underlie the perspective of these verses, as they "would certainly have been familiar and precious" to the community of the Fourth Gospel.[21] Her analysis of these OT narratives explores "how 'friendship' does not depend on the traditional or legal bonds of kinship, but rather should manifest the same חסד ('covenant faithfulness') that defines God's relationship to Israel."[22] The love and fidelity the friends in these stories show to one another mirror "God's own covenant faithfulness" and, as part of the scriptural heritage of the Johannine community, informs the

---

19. Edward Malatesta (*Interiority and Covenant*, 60) has shown that constructions of μείνειν ἐν are associated with covenant theology in 1 John. More recently, John Pryor ("Covenant and Community") has argued that this same usage is applicable to John 15. For more on discipleship as an abiding relationship, see Lee, *Flesh and Glory*, 90–91; Winbery, "Abiding in Christ."

20. Chennattu, *Johannine Discipleship*, 85. Brown (*John*, 2:557) also argues for an implicit covenant theme in 15:12 and 15:17 (as well as in 13:34). See also O'Connell, "Concept of Commandment."

21. Ringe, *Wisdom's Friends*, 72. She notes in particular the story of David and Jonathan told in 1 and 2 Samuel and the story of Ruth and Naomi that fills the book of Ruth as "a part of Israel's scriptural heritage."

22. Ibid.; see 72–74 for detail.

language of abiding friendship and commandment to love in John 15.[23] Jesus then turns to the ramifications of the abiding relationship of love and friendship to which he calls his disciples.

Jesus' Warning of the Consequences of Discipleship (15:18—16:24)

Jesus then shifts the focus of his discourse from the covenantal community of disciples itself to the consequences this relationship will bring as the disciples face the larger world.[24] Jesus first warns the disciples of the suffering and persecution they will encounter but follows his warnings with both the reasons behind the tribulation and the rewards for their perseverance. Despite the hatred and alienation the members of the community of disciples may experience (15:18–20; 16:2), they must not falter (16:1). Although the community will be accused of apostasy, it is the opponents of Jesus and his community who have not remained faithful to the covenant relationship with God for they do not know the Father (15:21–25; 16:3; see Exod 29:45–46; Jer 9:24; Isa 1:2).[25] The reward and consolation that Jesus gives to his community for standing fast in the midst of this tribulation is the gift of the Paraclete (15:26–27; 16:4–24).

Jesus indicates that the purpose of these consequences to abiding in relationship with him is for them to be strengthened so that they might be prevented from falling away on their journey (16:1). The ultimate reward for their perseverance is the gift of the Paraclete (16:4–24), who is judge of the world (vv. 4–11), and who will guide the disciples into the truth the covenant relationship manifests (vv. 12–15; see Pss 25:5, 9; 143:10). In the end, their hearts will rejoice and their joy will be complete (vv. 16–24). With these words of challenge and consolation, Jesus now turns to his disciples for their response.

---

23. Ibid., 73. See also Birch, *1 and 2 Samuel*, 2:1133. For more on *hesed*, friendship, and covenant, see Sakenfeld, *Faithfulness in Action*, 1–15; idem, *Meaning of Hesed*, 233–34.

24. For detail on the use of the term ὁ κόσμος ("the world") in John (here, and esp. 15:18–25), see Cassem, "Grammatical and Contextual Inventory."

25. Chennattu, *Johannine Discipleship*, 121. For the structure and analysis of 15:18—16:24 see 119–28. See chapter 2 for more detail on knowledge of God as constitutive of covenant faithfulness in the Prophets.

The Disciples' Profession of Faith (16:25–33)

This section of Jesus' last discourse and dialogue with the disciples articulates their acceptance of the relationship, including all its promises, obligations, and consequences, through their profession of belief in Jesus and his word. Despite its brevity, this section is a climactic moment in both the larger discourse of John 13–17 and in Jesus' ongoing relationship with his disciples. Both the disciples in the story and the readers of the story are challenged by Jesus to decide definitively either for or against him in terms of the belief and love that have been the primary concerns of his discourse thus far.[26] The first part of this section concerns the ultimate self-revelation of Jesus to his disciples (vv. 25–28), while the second part provides the disciples response to him: their profession of faith as a group (vv. 29–33).

The section is introduced and concluded by Jesus with reference to his coming hour (vv. 25–26a, 32–33) in which the disciples will face the consequences of their relationship with Jesus and yet also come into their own as children of God. In vv. 26b–28, Jesus reaffirms his origins and destiny with the Father, an intimacy that will also be shared with the disciples who love and believe in Jesus. For the first time in the narrative the disciples respond as a group (μαθηταὶ αὐτου, v. 29) to Jesus' challenge of relationship. Their emphasis on "now" (νῦν), what they "know" (οἴδαμεν), and what they "believe" (πιστεύομεν) about Jesus and his origins affirms in covenantal overtones that they are responding to the commandments with which Jesus has challenged them (v. 30). Although the disciples may not yet fully understand the mission of Jesus and his pending return to the Father, this acknowledgement of a commitment to God is integral to the covenant ceremonies of the OT (see Exod. 24:3, 7; Josh 24:21, 24), and is followed by a covenant-making ritual.[27] Jesus' concluding words here (vv. 31–33) emphasize his power over the world and his ability to grant peace in the face of persecution.[28] His turn to God in prayer on behalf of the disciples that follows (17:1–

---

26. Ibid., 86. For a more detailed analysis of this section of the discourse, see 128–30.

27. Ibid., 86. Again, see also chapter 2 for the prophetic traditions that correspond knowledge of God with covenant faithfulness.

28. For more on this, see O'Day, "I Have Overcome."

26) indicates his intention to bring them into the covenant relationship that he has promised as authentic children of God.

A Prayer Consecrating the Covenant Community of the Disciples (17:1–26)

Jesus' last discourse concludes with a prayer (17:1–26) through which Jesus consecrates the disciples as the first fruits of his covenantal community. The narrator steps in briefly to shift the focus and indicate that Jesus takes up a formal position of prayer (v. 1).[29] This theological climax is the "crown of the process of initiation" for the disciples into the light of new life.[30] Jesus begins by entreating the Father to bring about the glorification of the Son (vv. 1–5). He then affirms that the disciples have believed in God's self-revelation in Jesus the Son (vv. 6–8). From this point Jesus prays to the Father on behalf of these and all future disciples (v. 9).

Jesus' entreaties include the keeping of the disciples in the name of the Father (vv.11–16) and the consecration of the disciples in the truth (vv. 17–19). The covenant theology of the OT associates knowing God's name with the eschatological realization of God's covenant relationship with Israel in the age to come (Isa 52:6).[31] The prologue of the Gospel of John associated the "children of God" with those who receive Jesus, who is full of the gift of truth, and believe in his name (1:12). Here in this final prayer on behalf of his disciples, Jesus acknowledges that they have received his gift of truth and consecrates them in the name of the Father. They are the first fruits of the community of the children of God. In v. 20, Jesus moves beyond the disciples at the table with him to all who do or will believe through their word. He therefore closes the prayer with his "vision for the new covenant community" based in unity through the supplication that all the disciples may be one (v. 21; see vv. 21–26). Chennattu concludes that "what is implied in the oneness that is expected from the disciples is the mutual abiding in God's love, the covenant relationship with God, which unites and empowers them to become the visible presence of God in the world."[32]

29. Moloney, *Glory Not Dishonor*, 102.
30. Dodd, *Interpretation*, 420.
31. Chennattu, *Johannine Discipleship*, 132.
32. Ibid., 135; for the full discussion see 130–37.

Jesus' prayer concludes the lengthy section of Jesus' last meal and discourse with his disciples before his death. His time for teaching and building a covenant relationship with his own in this world must end so that the fullness of his hour of glorification may arrive. Chennattu claims that in John 13–17, "The evangelist rereads and interprets the OT covenant motif springing from different OT traditions and uses them to redefine and establish the identity of his community as the children of God (1:12) or the treasured people of God (cf. John 13:1; Deut 26:16–19)."[33] For this evangelist, only now can Jesus turn toward the hour of his passion and his glorification.

The Passion: The Covenantal Dialogue of the Cross (John 18–19)

The preservation and telling of the passion story must have had its beginnings in the earliest development of the church. In the Jewish tradition from which the Gospel arose, messiahs do not get crucified. Thus, the earliest church had to handle this historical fact both for its own identity and for its missionary purposes.[34] Each evangelist gives his own perspective to illustrate his particular theology, but they all tell the same story with the same plotlines: the arrest, a Jewish trial process, a Roman trial process, the crucifixion, burial, and an empty tomb (see Matt 26–27, Mark 14–15, Luke 22–23).[35] In the passion narrative of the Gospel of John (chs. 18–19), we must note that Jesus is always in control of his destiny. In addition, an acute focus on the disciples continues from the last discourse (John 13–17).

The cross is presented in John as the highest human experience (contrary to typical Christian understanding). God exalts Jesus (ὑψόω, 3:14, 8:28, 14:32) in this "lifting up" on the cross. This same phenomenon of circumventing human understanding and expectation appears in the evangelist's use of the term "glory" (δόξα, 1:14; 2:11; 5:41, 44; 7:18; 8:50, 54; 9:24; 11:4, 40; 12:41, 43; 17:5, 22, 24). The glory of God and the

---

33. Ibid., 87.

34. See, e.g., Paul's statement in 1 Cor 1:23: "Here we are preaching Christ crucified, a stumbling block to Jews and foolishness to Gentiles."

35. This correspondence leads many scholars to posit a pre-Markan passion narrative. For more on this scholarship, see Moloney, *Gospel of Mark*, 276 n. 2; Brown, *Death of the Messiah*, 2:1492–524.

means by which Jesus is glorified (through his crucifixion) flows from the evangelist's understanding of revelation. For the Fourth Evangelist, God so loved the world that he handed over his only Son (3:16). This handing over is an incredible act of love. Further articulation of this self-gift in love was presented in the last discourse (John 13–17) as the revelation of God that Jesus brings and the power to become children of God that he offers. Jesus the Son given to the world loved his own to the end (13:1). The glory of God and God's glorification of Jesus lies in this gift of the Son that begins with the incarnation (1:1–18) but is not complete until he is lifted up on the cross (John 18–19; see Jesus' final word on the cross, τετέλεσται, "It is finished").[36]

What follows first discusses the flow of the Johannine passion narrative as a whole, noting the steps in this process of Jesus' glorification as they unfold through five geographical locations. In the third of these five scenes, Jesus faces Pilate, the Roman governor, with whom he has a dialogue on kingship and truth as his earthly destiny is determined (18:28—19:16a). This dialogue will be the focus of exegetical analysis, as Jesus challenges Pilate with the nature of truth that is his gift to the world (19:37; see 1:14). Jesus has renewed his covenantal relationship with his disciples in preparation for his passion and glorification. The question now explored is how the role of Pilate plays into the destiny and covenantal claims of Jesus the Son of Man.

The Shape of the Johannine Passion Narrative

Across John 18–19 the narrative of the passion of Jesus moves through five distinct geographical locations: the garden across the Kidron wadi (18:1–11); the house of Annas, the father-in-law of the high priest (18:12–27); the Roman praetorium (18:28—19:16a); Golgotha, the place of the skill (19:16b–37); and the new garden of Jesus' burial (19:38–42). As Jesus moves to each new location, the narrator describes the place as well as the characters and activity that will be involved there. This action on the part of the evangelist has become his typical pattern of

---

36. See Moloney, *Glory Not Dishonor*, 127–52. For varying studies on the Johannine perspective of the passion narrative see, e.g., Brown, "Passion according to John"; Garland, "John 18–19"; Haenchen, "History and Interpretation"; Koester, "Texts in Context"; Neyrey, "Despising the Shame"; Pfitzner, "Coronation of the King."

distinguishing new acts in the story.[37] Therefore, the Johannine passion narrative can be divided in five acts through these changes in location.[38] In addition, the narrative acts begin and end in a garden, first as Jesus is confronted by his enemies and finally as he is buried by his friends. Similarly, the interrogation process of Jesus before his enemies in the second act is countered by the further formation of his own community in the fourth act. All of this action turns on the central encounter at the Roman praetorium between Jesus and Pilate, which concludes with Pilate handing Jesus over to be crucified. The passion narrative in the Gospel according to John is thus presented in a chiastic pattern, unfolding along the following structure:

A   18:1–11   Jesus Is Arrested by His Enemies in a Garden

    B   18:12–27   Jesus Is Interrogated by "the Jews": Condemnation

        C   18:28—19:16a   Jesus before Pilate: The Challenge of Truth

    B′   19:16b–37   Jesus Is Crucified before the Jews: Completion

A′   19:38–42   Jesus Is Buried by His Friends in a Garden

This outline will provide the guide for exploring the flow of the passion narrative in the Gospel according to John and establishing the crucial dialogue between Jesus and Pilate on the nature kingship and of God's gift of truth through Jesus at its crux.

A   Jesus Is Arrested by His Enemies in a Garden (18:1–11)

The passion narrative in the Fourth Gospel begins with Jesus in a garden (18:1) surrounded quickly by enemies who appear by dark (vv. 2–3), an odd collusion between Rome and "the Jews" that continues through this process. Judas, the betrayer (ὁ παραδιδούς, v. 2), leads the arresting party, which is equipped with lanterns, torches, and weapons. Raymond Brown notes the irony of this scene: "Judas has preferred darkness rather than the light which has come into the world (3:19); when he left Jesus it was truly night (13:30), and now he needs artificial light."[39] Jesus, "knowing

---

37. See, e.g., 2:1–2, 13–14; 3:1–2; 4:1–7; 5:1–5; 6:1–4; 7:1–14; 9:1–5; 11:1–4.

38. Moloney, *John*, 482; idem, *Glory Not Dishonor*, 128–29; Giblin, "Confrontations."

39. Brown, "Passion," 127. See also Culpepper, *Anatomy of the Fourth Gospel*, 192; Giblin, "Confrontations," 216–17; Heil, *Blood and Water*, 19–20; Moloney, *John*, 483.

everything" (εἰδὼς πάντα, v. 4), assumes the lead in the interrogation. In terms that resonate his first words to his disciples, Jesus asks the arresting party, "Whom are you seeking?" (τίνα ζητεῖτε, vv. 4, 7).[40] What results from their response of "Jesus the Nazorean" (vv. 5, 7) is the "I am"—the self-revelation of Jesus in the face of the collusion of his enemies in the world (ἐγώ εἰμι, vv. 6, 8).

This narrative is ecclesial from its inception as Jesus commands the arresting party to "let these go" (v. 8, a reference to his disciples who are to go forth; see the prayer of John 17).[41] Likewise, the narrative is oriented toward the fulfillment of the word from its beginning, as the word of Jesus begins to come to completion even in this first act (v. 9). For his part, however, Peter merely begins his journey through the passion of Jesus as he tries to fulfill his own promise to Jesus (v. 10; see 13:36–38) but is thwarted by Jesus himself who speaks to him once again in terms of his destiny: "Shall I not drink the cup which the Father has given me?" (v. 11). Although Peter's response to Jesus' question is not recorded, his behavior in the acts to come shows that his self-understanding has been thrown such that he must continue on his own journey of faith through Jesus' passion and resurrection before he can fully regain his composure and sense of mission in the community of disciples.

B Jesus Is Interrogated by "the Jews": Condemnation (18:12–27)

Following introductory verses that describe the change of place and introduce new characters (vv. 12–14), the narrative of the Jewish hearing process is framed by the continuation of the journey of Peter, who models the struggle of the early Christians in finding and asserting identity in Jesus (vv. 15–18, vv. 25–27).[42] Within the frame of Peter's denial, Jesus claims that he has spoken openly but that his teaching to "the Jews" is over. Yet there are those who know, claims Jesus—ask them (vv. 19–24).

---

40. See 1:38: "What are you seeking?" Here Jesus' question is explicitly self-referencing. The question of his identity has been asked and answered repeatedly over the course of his public ministry. His disciples indicate that they are satisfied with his response at the end of his last discourse (16:29–30). "The Jews," by contrast, have either misunderstood or explicitly rejected his responses. "Knowing all," it is with a certain irony that Jesus asks his arresting party this question now.

41. Moloney, *John*, 481–82.

42. Moloney, "John 18:15–27"; and Rensberger, "Politics of John," 400.

These scenes exemplify the frailty of the church and its propensity to fail even as it struggles to find its way and identity in a hostile world.

The collusion of Jesus' enemies that bands together and arrests him now binds and leads him to Annas, the father-in-law of the high priest Caiaphas, for interrogation.[43] This process, the narrator implicitly reminds the reader, is bringing to fulfillment the prophecy of Caiaphas that "one man should die for the people" (v. 14; see 11:49–51). The action that this scene narrates has the "other disciple" give Peter access to the court of the high priest (vv. 15–16). Yet Peter, apparently disturbed by the gatekeeper's query as to whether he is a disciple of the accused, responds, "I am not" (οὐκ εἰμί), and warms himself by the charcoal fire (ἀνθρακιά) with Jesus' enemies (vv. 17–18). Peter's encounter thus sets the scene for the interrogation of Jesus about "his disciples and his teaching" (v. 19). Jesus speaks boldly in defense of his teaching openly (παρρησίᾳ, vv. 20–21) and rightly (καλῶς, vv. 23–24) and is beaten and bound as a result (vv. 22, 25). The focus returns to Peter as the narrator indicates that at the same time Jesus is condemned for his open integrity Peter, the disciple who has claimed so much from Jesus' teaching is preserving himself with obfuscating denials (vv. 25–27).

The act closes with the cockcrow. The word of Jesus continues to be fulfilled as the narrative of his passion hurtles toward its inevitable climax (18:27; see 13:38).

C Jesus Stands before Pilate: The Challenge of Truth (18:28—19:16a)

There is a gap in the narrative of Jesus' trial process from the time he was bound and sent to Caiaphas (18:24) until he is led from the house of Caiaphas to the praetorium to stand trial before Pilate (18:28). The act of Jesus' Roman trial unfolds in seven scenes (18:29—19:15) as Pilate moves outside and inside of the praetorium to speak with "the Jews" who refuse to come inside for fear of defilement, and to speak with Jesus

---

43. The roles of Annas and Caiaphas in this narrative are complex. Annas was high priest from AD 6–15. Caiaphas was high priest during the historical period of the passion narrative (AD 18–36). Although this evangelist narrates only an interrogation before Annas, he is careful to note the prophecy of Caiaphas being fulfilled in the current narrative action (vv. 13–14; see 11:49–51). For a survey of the scholarship on the Jewish trial process in the Fourth Gospel as well as his own presentation of the Markan source background of the Johannine passion narrative, see Matera, "Jesus before Annas."

who has been handed over to him for crimes against the state.⁴⁴ The surreal scenes of the Roman governor flitting back and forth between the accusers and the accused, seemingly trying to assuage both parties, emulates physically the wavering Pilate's own position on the charge of "the Jews" and the challenge of the person of Jesus, who stands before him discussing kingship and truth.

The truth of Jesus as King is mitigated neither by Pilate's questioning and scourging nor by "the Jews'" manipulative accusing and mocking, as only in the Johannine narrative does Jesus go to the cross dressed as a king.⁴⁵ The narrative of Jesus' passion turns on Pilate's inexorable decision: "Then he handed him over to them to be crucified" (19:16a).

B′   THE CRUCIFIXION OF JESUS BEFORE THE JEWS: COMPLETION (19:16B–37)

The act of the crucifixion of Jesus is presented in five scenes, framed by typical introductory verses of character and setting (19:16b–18) and concluding verses of reflection upon the consequences of the action (19:35–37). The central scenes narrate the inscription (vv. 19–22), the seamless tunic (vv. 23–24), Jesus' interaction with his mother and the Beloved Disciple (vv. 25–27), Jesus' last words (vv. 28–30), and the piercing of Jesus' side (vv. 31–37).⁴⁶

In a moment of profound dramatic irony, Jesus' last breaths on the cross establish the church, as symbolized by the garment that cannot be torn apart. The Beloved Disciple and the mother come together (εἰς τὰ ἴδια) "because of that hour" (ἀπ' ἐκείνης τῆς ὥρας, v. 27).⁴⁷ The first to believe and the beloved model disciple are given to each other to establish a new community in faith and love.⁴⁸ The earthly life and

---

44. Giblin, "John's Narration"; Rensberger, "Politics of John," 401–11. See below for detail.

45. Moloney, *John*, 495–97.

46. This structure adapts the structures of Culpepper and Moloney. See Culpepper, "Theology of the Johannine Passion Narrative"; idem, "Death of Jesus"; Moloney, *John*, 502–6.

47. Moloney, *John*, 503.

48. Moloney, *Glory Not Dishonor*, 142–49; and Neirynck, "Short Note on John." For a selection of scholars who understand vv. 25–27 as the foundation of the Christian community by the crucified King, see Boguslazwski, "Jesus' Mother"; Heil, *Blood and Water*, 94–98; Hoskyns, *Fourth Gospel*, 530; Koester, *Symbolism in the Fourth Gospel*, 214–19; Moloney, *John*, 508.

ministry of the Son of Man ends in τετέλεσται—the affirmation that all has been brought to perfection (vv. 28–30). Only after the acknowledgment of his glorification and the completion of his mission can he go. Jesus finally bowed his head and "handed over the spirit" (παρέδωκεν τὸ πνεῦμα, v. 30).[49] Jesus' side is pierced to confirm his death on the Day of Preparation, the day of the sacrifice of the Passover Lamb (vv. 31–34; see 19:14), and a flow of mingled blood and water is witnessed from his side.[50] The intensifying fulfillment language across the passion narrative comes to its climax here as the Beloved Disciple, now given into the family of the new community of God, affirms the truth of his testimony so that all future readers may believe (v. 35) that these things took place so that the Scripture might be fulfilled (ἵνα γραφὴ πληρωθῇ, v. 36). The new community of the children of God (see 1:12) immediately begins its own mission of faith and witness through the testimony of the Beloved Disciple, who is joined in the community of family with the mother of Jesus.[51]

A′ Jesus Is Buried by His Friends in a Garden (19:38–42)

The passion narrative is brought full circle as Jesus comes once again into a garden, this time brought to rest in a new tomb by friends (vv. 40–42). Nicodemus finally finishes his journey as he comes forward with spices to anoint Jesus for his burial (v. 39).[52] Joseph of Arimathea, otherwise unknown in the Johannine narrative, fulfills his role of providing the burial place (v. 39). The scene is set for what was destroyed in a garden (18:1; see also Gen 1–3) to be restored in a garden (John 20).[53]

---

49. For this interpretation of Jesus' final act in his mission, see Bampfylde, "John xix 28"; Beasley-Murray, *John* 353; La Potterie, *Hour of Jesus*, 163–65; Hoskyns, *Fourth Gospel*, 532; Moloney, *John*, 508–9.

50. See Ford, "Mingled Blood"; and Culpepper, "Death of Jesus."

51. More will be said on this following the exegetical analysis below. See chapter 3 for the establishment of the "children of God" as those who believe in Jesus and accept his covenantal gift of truth.

52. See Sylva, "Nicodemus and His Spices."

53. For a brief discussion of the garden symbolism in John 19:38–42 and its history in tradition and scholarship, see Brown, *Death of the Messiah*, 2:1268-70.

The Covenantal Dialogue of Truth (18:28—19:16a)

Now that we have established the flow of the passion narrative in the Gospel according to John over five acts falling in a chiastic pattern, we turn to a detailed analysis of the central act upon which the entire narrative turns: the Roman trial (18:28—19:16a). This act further provides for a distinctive dialogue between Jesus, Pilate, and "the Jews" that focuses on kingship and truth. As Pilate investigates the crime set before him and wavers between the accusers and accused, he is stopped momentarily by his own question on the nature of truth. We turn to this dialogue to explore how it affects the underlying covenantal metaphor of the Gospel.

STRUCTURE OF THE PASSAGE

The structure of the dialogue between Pilate, Jesus, and "the Jews" unfolds, after an introduction (18:28), in seven scenes as Pilate moves outside and inside of the praetorium in order to speak with both "the Jews" and Jesus.[54] The final verse concludes this act as Pilate makes the ultimate decision to hand Jesus over to be crucified (19:16a). The passage is thus structured as follows:[55]

18:28		Introduction: Gathering at the Praetorium for the Roman Trial
	18:29–32	Scene 1: Pilate and the Jews, Outside
	18:33–38a	Scene 2: Pilate and Jesus, Inside
	18:38b–40	Scene 3: Pilate and the Jews, Outside
	19:1–3	Scene 4: Pilate and Jesus, Inside
	19:4–8	Scene 5: Pilate, Jesus and the Jews, Outside
	19:9–11	Scene 6: Pilate and Jesus, Inside
	19:12–15	Scene 7: Pilate, Jesus and the Jews, Outside
19:16a		Conclusion: Handing Over for Crucifixion

54. Giblin, "John's Narration," 221.

55. For the basics of this structuring pattern, see Moloney, *John*, 492–97; and Brown, *John*, 2:857–59. It is widely recognized by scholars that the Roman trial progresses in seven brief scenes. See also, e.g., Baum-Bodenbender, *Hoheit in Niedrigkeit*, 28–29; Brown, *Death of the Messiah*, 1:743; Ehrman, "Jesus' Trial," 126–27; Giblin, "John's Narration," 221–24; Howard-Brook, *Becoming Children of God*, 391; Moloney, *Glory Not Dishonor*, 137; Westcott, *Saint John*, 258; Schnackenburg, *St. John*, 3:242.

Pilate's physical movement inside to Jesus and outside to "the Jews" illustrates his own ambivalence about Jesus as he tries to discern who Jesus is and what threat he might pose to Pilate himself and to the larger societal structure. Pilate's response to the challenge extended by Jesus comes in the midst this movement in which he raises the question of the nature of truth. It is to this dialogue that we now turn.

Exegetical Analysis

The narrative of the Roman trial in the Fourth Gospel is marked by verbs of motion to show that Pilate and/or Jesus comes out of or goes into the praetorium. These verbs of motion, coupled with the change of place and dialogue partners they produce, facilitate the distinction of the seven scenes that make up this pericope (18:28—19:16a). After they brought (ἄγουσιν) Jesus into the praetorium in the introductory verse, Pilate went outside (ἐξῆλθεν) to speak with "the Jews" twice (18:29, 38b). In addition, Jesus went outside (ἐξῆλθεν οὖν ὁ Ἰησοῦς ἔξω) after Pilate to be presented to his accusers (19:5). Pilate also entered (εἰσῆλθεν) the praetorium to speak with Jesus on two occasions (18:33; 19:9) before he brought Jesus outside (ἤγαγεν ἔξω τὸν Ἰησοῦν) to face his accusers one last time (19:13). In the concluding moment of the Roman trial Pilate handed Jesus over (παρέδωκεν αὐτόν) to be crucified (19:16a). Of these seven core scenes and their narrative frame, only one scene, 19:1-3, contains no verb of motion and no dialogue. "In that scene, which takes place inside the praetorium, Jesus is crowned, dressed as a king, and ironically proclaimed: 'Hail, the King of the Jews' (v. 3)."[56] This narration and ironic proclamation of the kingship of Jesus that stands at the center of the passage becomes the scene around which the entire Roman trial narrative turns.[57] The truth of the kingship of Jesus and how this affects and is affected by Pilate, "the Jews," and Jesus' own life and mission are all at stake in this narrative.

The dramatic techniques of the Fourth Evangelist that we have noted throughout the Gospel reach their peak in the Johannine account of the Roman trial. This act has been called "one of the master dramatic

---

56. Moloney, *Glory Not Dishonor*, 137.

57. This leads Brown (*John*, 2:857–59) to render the structure of the Roman trial as a chiasm. For a chiastic rendering of the Roman trial, see also Howard-Brook, *Becoming Children of God*, 391–93.

constructions of this Gospel."[58] The deictic language of this passage is pronounced, as the characters not only describe their own actions; their words further articulate the actions of other characters.[59] The effect of the refusal of "the Jews" to enter the praetorium at the onset of the trial is to send Pilate shuttling back and forth between Jesus and his accusers, acting on two stages as it were, a front stage and a rear stage.[60] This staging "enhances the drama of the narrative" by ensuring that "the Jews" "do not hear Jesus' self-disclosing claims before Pilate."[61] At the same time, it "portrays the human predicament in which one must choose between Jesus and the world."[62] The two stages also ensure that Pilate is the only figure who appears in every scene. Nonetheless "it is Jesus himself, and the nature of his kingdom, that occupy center stage."[63] The "Jesus who comes at last to his hour . . . is a different dramatic character from the Jesus of the synoptic passion narratives," for he knows all and controls even the dialogue of the trial. So "eloquent and self-assured" is Jesus that "it is Pilate who is put on trial to see whether he is of the truth."[64] This is the covenantal aspect of the unfolding drama of the passion narrative in the Fourth Gospel. Jesus, the bearer of the gift of truth that fulfills the gift of the Law (1:14, 17), in the hour of his glorification places himself before Pilate to bear witness one last time to the truth (18:37).[65] Pilate's response determines where he stands in the new covenant community.[66] The dialogue begins outside the praetorium.

---

58. Brown, *Death of the Messiah*, 1:743. Affirming this dramatic nature, Craig Koester ("Passion and Resurrection," 87) calls this text "a literary masterpiece that demands to be read and heard." Likewise Schnackenburg (*St. John*, 3:242) asserts that the "whole episode is a well-considered and dramatically-developed play."

59. Brant, *Dialogue and Drama*, 87. See chapter 1 for a brief discussion of deixis in the Fourth Gospel. In this passage the deictic language is particularly pronounced in 19:4–6, 14–15 as the trial reaches its climax. The language will be specified in the exegesis below.

60. Dodd, *Historical Tradition*, 96. See also Garland, "John 18–19," 488.

61. Carson, *John*, 589.

62. Duke, *Irony in the Fourth Gospel*, 126.

63. Carson, *John*, 287. See also Giblin, "John's Narration."

64. Brown, "Passion," 126–27, 129.

65. See chapter 2 for the establishment of "truth" as the language of covenant, and chapter 3 for the exegesis of the prologue (1:1–18) and the gift of truth that fulfills the gift of the Law of the Sinai covenant.

66. In this vein, Brown ("Passion," 130) notes that the "real question is not what will happen to Jesus who controls his own destiny, but whether Pilate will betray himself by bowing to the outcry of the very people he is supposed to govern (19:12). The

Introduction: Gathering at the Praetorium for the Roman Trial (18:28)

The introductory verse (18:28) serves as an "exposition" of the drama of the Roman trial by "setting up the staging for the subsequent action and establishing the highly charged irony of the entire proceeding."[67] The narrator presents the scene vividly and "without circumlocution," using the historical present: "Then they led Jesus from Caiaphas to the praetorium" (v. 28a).[68] This succinct summation creates a narrative gap in the Jewish trial process, as Jesus was last sent bound to Caiaphas in v. 4. Now in v. 28 an unnamed group lead Jesus to the praetorium for the next stage in the trial, apparently already convicted by those to whom he came as "his own" (1:11).[69] The gap creates tension as the narrative suddenly moves to the final stage of the trial of Jesus. The narrator's temporal designation, ἦν δὲ πρωΐ, indicates, however, that the darkness of the night is coming to an end and Jesus is on the verge of his promised glorification.[70]

Those who have delivered Jesus to the praetorium refuse to enter lest they be defiled and thus prevented from eating the Passover. The evangelist does not articulate how entry into the praetorium would render Jesus' accusers unclean, but Numbers 9:6–12 specifies that those who contract impurity and cannot not eat the Passover meal at the appointed time have to postpone the celebration for one month.[71] The

---

price he exacts from them by way of an insincere allegiance to Caesar (19:15) is a face-saving device for a man who knows the truth about Jesus but failed to bear witness to it (18:36–37)."

67. Ehrman, "Jesus' Trial," 126.

68. Schnackenburg, *St. John*, 3:243.

69. Jesus has already been convicted by "the Jews" throughout his public ministry. See esp. John 7–8, 10. Schnackenburg (*St. John*, 3:243) notes the group must be "the Jews" of 18:31.

70. Brown, *John*, 2:866; and Bultmann, *John*, 651. It should also be noted that *prōï* is the last of the four Roman divisions of the day, placing the trial in the Roman context just before dawn (Howard-Brook, *Becoming Children of God*, 394). The dawning of the new day also places the trial on the 14th of Nisan, the day of preparation for the Passover (Lincoln, *Saint John*, 460).

71. For detail see Brown, *Death of the Messiah*, 1:745–47. General exposure to Gentiles would have been a danger only to priests on temple duty. Others could remove the impurity by a ritual bath at sunset. Contact with a corpse would render someone contaminated for a seven-day period (Num 9:11). The perceived Gentile practice of burying the dead in building foundations could be the practical issue at stake here. See also Carson, *John*, 587–89.

irony of the scene is striking, as Jesus, the Lamb of God (1:29), is handed over for trial by those who desire to maintain ritual purity in order to partake of the Passover lamb that very day.[72] The primary function of the comment is therefore rhetorical, serving to heighten the irony of the trial and structure the scenes that follow.[73]

Scene 1: Pilate and the Jews, Outside (18:29–32)

Pilate is introduced to the scene in v. 29 without qualification.[74] Apparently a known personage who needs no further introduction, Pilate goes outside to those who have delivered Jesus to him and asks for the charge (κατηγορίαν) brought against "this man" (τοῦ ἀνθρώπου τούτου). The demonstrative pronoun articulating Jesus as "this man" serves as a speech gesture that allows readers to visualize Pilate gesturing toward Jesus, who is inside, as he stands outside before the accusers. Pilate's question formally opens the proceedings.

The accusers respond with a contrary-to-fact conditional clause that does not so much answer Pilate's question as offer a defense of their own action (v. 30). By using the demonstrative pronoun themselves (οὗτος) they affirm that the man in custody, Jesus, is indeed worthy of the arrest. They call his actions evil and refer to their own action as "handing him over" (παραδίδωμι). Prior to this point only Judas has been cast in the role of ὁ παραδιδούς (6:64; see also 6:71; 12:4; 13:2, 11, 21; 18:2, 5). Now Jesus' accusers place themselves in this same role. Doing evil is not a formal charge, but it does reflect Jesus' defiant response in the Jewish trial process ("If I have spoken badly [κακῶς ἐλάλησα], give testimony to what is bad [μαρτύρσαν περὶ τοῦ κακοῦ]," 18:23). The irony here in Johannine terms is that it is the accusers who are guilty of this very accusation. The "uncooperativeness that greets Pilate's question is part of the Johannine dialogue technique: It creates a tension that will

---

72. Brown, *Death of the Messiah*, 1:746; Bultmann, *John*, 652; Moloney, *John*, 494.

73. Bultmann, *John*, 652. Brown (*Death of the Messiah*, 1:744–45) calls this a "theological irony," in that "the forces of darkness and light" are thus initially separated so that readers are called to judge for one or the other. Giblin ("John's Narration," 224) suggests that both this transition and the first scene distance the Jews from Pilate.

74. Brown, *Death of the Messiah*, 1:746; and Schnackenburg, *St. John*, 3:244. Pontius Pilate received his appointment as governor of Judea from the Emperor Tiberius in AD 26 and held the post until AD 37.

be used to uncover what lies beneath the surface."[75] Pilate responds to them in kind.

Pilate dismisses the "unreal accusation" and reassigns responsibility to "the Jews."[76] Using the second person pronoun for emphasis, Pilate commands, "Take him yourselves [λάβατε αὐτὸν ὑμεῖς] and judge him according to your Law" (τὸν νόμον ὑμῶν, v. 31).[77] Pilate's dismissive reference to the Law ironically articulates the true nature of these proceedings in Jesus' mission. Severino Pancaro understands the Roman trial to represent "the climax of the whole drama" and thus the "fact that the word νόμος is found only twice during the trial should not mislead us. The Law is everywhere present and the trial shows, more clearly than ever, that John wishes to present Jesus not as one who is opposed to the Law, but as the one who comes to fulfill the Law."[78]

Jesus' accusers, now identified as "the Jews" (v. 31b), are forced to acknowledge the limits of their jurisdiction. They also reveal their objective in bringing Jesus to Pilate: capital punishment.[79] They assert, "It is not permitted for us to put anyone to death" (v. 31b). The accuracy of this claim for "the Jews" who are under Roman rule is debated by scholars, especially since they attempted to stone Jesus twice already (8:59; 10:31).[80] The evangelist's unfolding drama is serving his theological interest rather than historical accuracy.

The narrator interrupts the direct speech of the scene to confirm that God's plan and Jesus' prescience in the fulfillment of his role continue to control the process despite external evidence to the contrary. Jesus was brought before the Roman governor so that he might be convicted and put to death by the Roman method of execution, crucifixion, "so that the word of Jesus [ὁ λόγος τοῦ Ἰησοῦ] that he spoke might be fulfilled [πληρωθῇ], signifying by what kind of death he was going to die" (v. 32). The word of Jesus at the close of his public ministry is com-

---

75. Brown, *Death of the Messiah*, 1:746.

76. Bultmann, *John*, 652.

77. The αὐτον following κρίνατε is absent from several MSS, but the majority attests to its presence.

78. Pancaro, *Law in the Fourth Gospel*, 307; for the full discussion, see 307–15. He further claims that the two guiding principles in the Johannine presentation of the trial before Pilate are theological and dramatic.

79. Bultmann, *John*, 653.

80. Moloney, *John*, 498. For detail, see Brown, *Death of the Messiah*, 1:747–49; and Carson, *John*, 590–92.

ing to fulfillment now that his hour has arrived and his glorification is in process (see 12:31–33).[81] The divine teleology thus continues to direct the action.[82] In the Johannine account of the passion narrative both "Jewish accusers and Roman judge are actors in a drama scripted by a divine planner."[83] The narrator's affirmation of the divine plan closes the first scene. "The Jews'" acknowledgement that it is capital punishment they seek sends Pilate back inside to Jesus.

Scene 2: Pilate and Jesus, Inside (18:33–38a)

Pilate entered the praetorium again and began to interrogate Jesus on the charge that is at stake for the Roman state, the claim of kingship, which would indicate sedition (v. 33). The "inside" interaction between Jesus and Pilate forms the heart of the Roman trial. Their relatively lengthy dialogues provide powerful integration and articulation of the God-sent mission of Jesus, the Son of Man, and its manifestation among Jesus' own in the world.[84] The fundamental questions at stake are what it means to be king and what it means to be of the truth.[85]

Pilate interrogates Jesus, "Are you the king of the Jews?" There is no lead-in to this line of questioning in the immediate context, but the larger narrative has already recounted the crowds seeking to proclaim Jesus king (6:14–15). This sort of pretension to kingship in the political sense is Pilate's only concern.[86] Jesus' initial riposte is to answer the question with a question of his own, a parry that asserts his own agency as a participant in the dialogue and provides for the extended interaction on the nature of Jesus' kingship.[87] Jesus asks whether Pilate is speaking on his own or on hearsay (v. 34). The repetitive use of pronouns point

---

81. The same phrase occurs in both 12:33 and 18:32. Brown (*Death of the Messiah*, 749) argues, "Ironically, 'the Jews' want to force the Roman to contribute to the glorification of Jesus."

82. Bultmann, *John*, 653.

83. Brown, *Death of the Messiah*, 748.

84. Brown (ibid., 757) notes that the Johannine account of the Roman trial is three times the length of the Markan version. Haenchen (*History and Interpretation*, 209) remarks that this initial "inside" dialogue "is exceedingly important" in the progression of the Johannine passion drama.

85. Garland, "John 18–19," 488.

86. Bultmann, *John*, 653.

87. Neyrey, "Despising the Shame," 123.

emphatically to the parties involved in this trial (ἀπὸ σεαυτοῦ σύ . . . ἄλλοι . . . σοι περὶ ἐμοῦ) as Jesus places testimony to the truth itself on trial. These first words of Jesus serve to put Pilate on the defensive. As Andrew Lincoln observes, "They belong to a pattern by now familiar whereby Jesus, the accused, becomes the accuser, and the one on trial can be seen as the judge."[88]

With the quick response that follows, Pilate attempts to distance himself from any personal stake in Jewish matters of kingship and nationalism (v. 35). The use of the personal pronoun is once again emphatic, and the grammatical construction (μήτι ἐγω Ἰουδαῖός εἰμι) expects a negative answer: "I am not a Jew, am I?" He confirms that Jesus' own people and its religious leaders have handed him over (παρέδωκεν σε ἐμοί). He puts the onus for the proceedings back onto Jesus as he asks specifically, "What did you do?" (τί ἐποίησας). It is only what Jesus has done that is decisive for Pilate, and he gives Jesus the opportunity to defend himself against his accusers. Jerome Neyrey suggests this "initial exchange sparkles with honor challenges" as Jesus spars with Pilate, ultimately "giving a solemn riposte to the challenge to his identity and authority" and further challenging Pilate to take a stand on truth.[89]

In response, Jesus speaks not of himself but of his kingdom (v. 36).[90] He affirms that his kingship is not part of the political system of which Pilate is concerned. It is not "of the world."[91] Nonetheless, it can be witnessed in the world. The term "kingdom" (ἡ βασιλεία) has only been at issue once in this narrative prior to the Roman trial. In 3:3–5, Jesus taught Nicodemus of the need to be born from above (γεννηθῇ ἄνωθεν) by water and the Spirit in order to see and enter the kingdom. The concept of ἡ βασιλεία must thus be given the full weight of its physical and spatial nature. "The kingdom is a 'place' where God reigns, a community, and those who are of God, of the truth, respond to the voice of Jesus and 'see' (ἰδεῖν) and 'enter into' (εἰσελθεῖν εἰς) that kingdom."[92]

88. Lincoln, *Saint John*, 461.
89. Neyrey, "Despising the Shame," 123–24.
90. Bultmann, *John*, 654; Moloney, *John*, 494.
91. Brown (*Death of the Messiah*, 1:750) claims that the "most important aspect of 18:36 is Jesus' three-time-reiterated affirmation that his kingdom is not of this world, not from here—the affirmation of an incarnate Word who as come into this world from above." Jesus' gifts are not of this world; "what makes them true or real (ἀληθινός) is that they are of God" (1:751).
92. Moloney, *John*, 494, 498. See the full discussion in Moloney, *Belief in the Word*, 109–14.

Although Jesus has spoken of what his kingship is not, he has indeed spoken of his kingdom. Therefore Pilate pursues the question, "So you are a king?" (v. 37a). Despite the nuances Jesus has already put forth, Pilate's base understanding of kingship allows Jesus to assert his identity as king positively.[93] Jesus responds, "You say that I am a king" (σὺ λέγεις ὅτι βασιλεύς εἰμι, v. 37b). The response is not a simple affirmative, nor is it a negative, and indeed Pilate will "say" that Jesus is "king" several times in the coming scenes (18:39; 19:14, 15, 19). Jesus modifies the title "King of the Jews" and presents his own phraseology to clarify who he is and what he offers.[94] He then affirms the purpose of his mission: "For this ... I have come into the world, so that I may testify to the truth" (ἵνα μαρτυρήσω τῇ ἀληθείᾳ). Jesus can testify to the truth because he is the truth (14:6).[95] He makes God known and bears God's gift of truth for all who hear his voice and receive it (v. 37; see 1:12, 14–18).[96] Jesus' final statement in this exchange presents a "gratuitous offer of truth" that actually lays bare the real issue at stake in this trial: "Everyone who is of the truth [ἐκ τῆς ἀληθείας] hears my voice." Jesus' statement serves as a covenant formula that returns to the first page of the narrative with a sharp reminder to the reader that Jesus is the gift which is truth (ἡ χάρις καὶ ἡ ἀλήθεια, 1:14, 17) that follows and brings to fulfillment the gift of the law of the covenant of Moses (1:17).[97] Those outside the praetorium are not of the truth, for in handing Jesus over they have refused his gift of truth. Their accusations against him all come down to this. For his part, however, Jesus continues to fulfill his mission. He bears witness to the truth even on trial. Implicit in this final statement is also a challenge

---

93. Brown, *Death of the Messiah*, 1:750; Bultmann, *John*, 654; Giblin, "John's Narration," 226; Lincoln, *Saint John*, 462–63; Schnackenburg, *St. John*, 3:249.

94. Brown, *Death of the Messiah*, 1:751; and Bultmann, *John*, 654.

95. Brown, *Death of the Messiah*, 1:752.

96. Moloney, *John*, 498. For the claim that "bearing witness to the truth" asserts the fundamental purpose of Jesus' mission to make God known, see La Potterie, *Verité dans Saint Jean*, 1:100–116. On hearing the voice of Jesus and the response of the sheep to the Good Shepherd (10:3–4, 8, 16), see Meeks, *Prophet-King*, 66–67.

97. See chapter 3 for the analysis of the prologue as the presentation of Jesus as the covenantal gift of truth. See also de la Potterie, *Verité dans Saint Jean*, 117–241. He concludes this lengthy section on John 1:14–18 with the following: "Qu'est-ce donc que la vérité de Jésus Christ? D'après Jn 1,17, elle constitue l'événement fondamental de l'économie de la révélation. Remplaçant et complétant la Loi de Moïse, la vérité donnée en Jésus Christ est la révélation définitive de l'époque messianique, celle qui ouvre les temps eschatologiques et inaugure la nouvelle Alliance"(240).

to Pilate. Jesus has positively asserted his identity, his purpose, and the nature of the community he offers. Pilate's response will determine his position before Jesus.[98]

This initial "inside" exchange ends as abruptly as it began, as Pilate cuts off his dialogue with Jesus with his brusque reply in the form of a rhetorical question, "What is truth?" (τί ἐστιν ἀλήθεια; v. 38a). With this timeless question coupled with his immediate exit, rather than engaging Jesus further on the gift of truth, Pilate refuses Jesus' offer by shutting himself off from its voice. The irony lies in Pilate's dismissal of the possibility of knowledge of the truth while standing face to face with the embodiment of truth.[99] The criterion for authentic belief in Jesus is openness to his word as the revelation of God. Like many in the story before him, particularly "the Jews" who now stand outside as Jesus' formal accusers (see esp. John 8:31–59), Pilate is closed to that revelation and dismisses the word of Jesus.[100] This is Jesus' final covenantal challenge in his earthly ministry, and Pilate, his partner in dialogue, does not recognize the gift that is standing before him.[101] Pilate rejects the possibility of truth and refuses to recognize the revelation of God in Jesus, but nonetheless seeks to hold a position of neutrality. "The word of Jesus unmasks the world as a world of sin, and it challenges it."[102] Pilate tries to act as if the challenge of Jesus has nothing to do with him. Ironically, this becomes his self-condemnation. Raymond Brown observes, Pilate's "failure to recognize truth and hear Jesus' voice shows that he does not belong to God. This is the last time in John that Jesus shall speak of truth, and his voice has not been heard." Pilate cannot comprehend a kingdom and community not established by human endeavor but by God, and this failure stems "not primarily from the fact

---

98. Bultmann (*John*, 655) observes that with Jesus' final statement, "the question about the *law* becomes a question about *faith*. For without doubt Pilate himself is put on the spot through this statement; he is asked whether he is willing to listen to the voice of the Revealer, and he must show whether he 'is of the truth.'"

99. Later speculation recounted in a Middle Persian Manichaean fragment has Jesus answer Pilate's question "What is truth?" with "I am the truth." See Brown, *Death of the Messiah* 1:752; and Tolman, "Possible Restoration."

100. Moloney, *John*, 498. See chapter 5 for a detailed analysis of John 7–8. For more on the criterion for authentic belief, see Moloney, *Belief in the Word*, 192–99.

101. See chapter 2 for the language of knowledge and truth as covenantal language.

102. Bultmann, *John*, 657.

that he is a representative of earthly dominion but also and primarily because he is not of the truth."¹⁰³ Can this attempt at neutrality stand? Pilate goes outside to state his position to the accusers.

Scene 3: Pilate and the Jews, Outside (18:38b–40)

Pilate went out again to "the Jews" and made his initial ruling: "I find no guilt in him" (v. 38b). He emphasizes his own judicial authority over his audience by using the first-person pronoun. He shows he knows something of the truth, but is not open to the hearing the truth demands. But he is also unwilling to give in to the demands of Jesus' accusers.¹⁰⁴ Jesus is not a political threat to Rome; therefore, Pilate finds no case against him. Pilate will use the term αἰτία three times in this trial process to press his attempts to forgo legal action (18:38b; 19:4, 6).¹⁰⁵ In this second "outside" exchange of dialogue, Pilate uses the phraseology as a basis for his next move: an attempt to release Jesus.

Pilate introduces a "custom" (συνήθεια) of theirs at Passover: "that I release one to you" (v. 39a). Through this custom he tries to release Jesus, but in presenting his offer he uses the title of the very charge the accusers brought before him: "Do you want me to release to you the king of the Jews?" (v. 39b). It is difficult to find unambiguous extrabiblical evidence for such a custom, but it appears in all four Gospels and seems to be part of the earliest passion narrative tradition.¹⁰⁶ The mockery inherent in Pilate's title for Jesus, whom he has just determined is no pretender to the throne in any political sense, serves to further the intensifying Johannine irony interweaving this entire passage.¹⁰⁷ Any hope that Pilate might have that "the Jews" will accept his proposition

---

103. Brown, *Death of the Messiah*, 1:752–53.

104. Koester, "Passion and Resurrection," 88; and Brown, *Death of the Messiah*, 1:793.

105. BDAG, s.v. αἰτία. This term has several connotations but is used in the PNs as a basis for legal action, i.e., a "charge," or "ground for complaint" (see also Mark 15:26; Matt 27:37; Luke 23:14).

106. Some scholars point to *m. Pes.* 8.6 and *b. Pes.* 91a as evidence of such a custom. For a comprehensive discussion of the evidence that is nonetheless inconclusive, see Brown, *Death of the Messiah*, 1:814–20. See also Carson, *John*, 596; and Moloney, *John*, 499.

107. For more discussion on how the evangelist intensifies the irony as the Roman trial progresses, see Ehrman, "Jesus' Trial," 128–31; Meeks, *Prophet-King*, 62–81.

and "that he will then be quit of the affair is disappointed."[108] They ask instead, now shouting (ἐκραύγασαν), for Barabbas (v. 40).[109]

Jesus' accusers shout, "Not this one, but Barabbas." The demonstrative pronoun (τοῦτον) is deictic in nature, signifying the aggressive gesturing in the direction of Jesus inside the quarters that would accompany such shouting. Barabbas, whose pardon they prefer, is otherwise unknown in the Johannine narrative and thus is qualified here by the narrator as a λῃστής ("an insurgent," v. 40).[110] In 10:1–18, Jesus taught that he was the Good Shepherd whose sheep hear his voice. These same sheep, however, have been plundered by the λῃσταί (10:1, 8). The true sheep nonetheless wait for the Good Shepherd and heed his voice. At the Roman trial when Jesus' accusers are given the option of having the "King of the Jews" released to them, they choose not the Good Shepherd but the λῃστής, the revolutionary who would indeed make himself a political king.[111] On the edge of the "slippery slope" he himself introduced, Pilate must once again deal with Jesus and matters inside the praetorium.[112]

Scene 4: Pilate and Jesus, Inside (19:1–3)

Although there is no verb of motion for Pilate in this scene, the narrator does recount that Pilate "took Jesus and had him flogged" (ἐμαστίγωσεν, 19:1). This scene is introduced by the coordinating conjunction and adverb τότε οὖν, indicating that the flogging followed from "the Jews" refusal of his offer to release Jesus in favor of Barabbas.[113] Pilate's at-

---

108. Bultmann, *John*, 657.

109. The verb κραυγάζω signifies the utterance of a loud, generally harsh, sound (BDAG, s.v. κραυγάζω).

110. The term can be used of a robber or bandit, but also, as in this context, for someone standing against the state: a "revolutionary," or "guerilla," or, in more contemporary parlance, a "terrorist" (BDAG, s.v. λῃστής). See also Carson, *John*, 596; Giblin, "John's Narration," 228. Moloney (*John*, 499) notes that Josephus used the term of the Zealots, "whose false messianic pretensions" led to the destruction of the city." For detail, see Brown, *Death of the Messiah*, 1:796–800.

111. On "the Jews" indeed choosing someone who would be king in Pilate's sense just not "this one," see Giblin, "John's Narration," 228. On the link to John 10, see Lincoln, *Saint John*, 464; and Moloney, *John*, 499.

112. Bultmann, *John*, 658.

113. Giblin, ("John's Narration," 229) observes that "John alone among the Evangelists says nothing about the release of Barabbas. John alone relates the scourging of Jesus directly to the Jews' preference for Barabbas."

tempt to release Jesus backfired; now he tries an intermediate punishment by way of the Roman practice of flogging a criminal with a barbed whip called a mastix.[114] Although the flogging immediately precedes the crucifixion in the Synoptic tradition, the Fourth Evangelist presents it as the midpoint of the Roman trial. In the "artistry of the evangelist," this makes the flogging and the mockery to come a prelude to "the climactic moment of having Jesus brought from inside the praetorium to encounter the crowd outside" dressed as a king—"the mid-moment of the trial, breaking Pilate's shuttle, where all three parties meet in center stage."[115] Pilate thus continues the intensifying process of ironically glorifying Jesus.[116]

The next verses (19:2–3) detail the mockery of Jesus. The soldiers' derision includes the coronation of Jesus with a crown of thorns, clothing him in a purple cloak of royalty, and ironically proclaiming of the truth of Jesus as the King of the Jews (ὁ βασιλεύς τῶν Ἰουδαίων).[117] The soldiers' interaction with Jesus is recounted in the imperfect, articulating the ongoing action that heightens the mockery.[118] They kept coming to him and saying their insults, however ironically true. Then the abuse turns physical as the soldiers repeatedly "gave him slaps" (ἐδίδοσαν αὐτῷ ῥαπίσματα).[119] This interlude between the offer of the Passover amnesty and Jesus' presentation to "the Jews" is Pilate's second attempt to act in a politically clever manner to save himself from the necessity of leaving his position of neutrality.[120] However, the effect of his decision is all the more active and powerful as he sends Jesus forward to meet his accusers dressed as a king. This action colors the rest of the proceedings.[121]

---

114. "Flogging" or "scourging" is also mentioned in the OT (e.g., Exod 5:14 by Pharaoh; Deut 25:2–3); see Howard-Brook, *Becoming Children of God*, 403. For detail on the nature of the flogging, see Carson, *John*, 596–98.

115. Brown, "Passion," 130.

116. Howard-Brook, *Becoming Children of God*, 403.

117. For detail on the botanic origin of the thorns in the crown, see Brown, *Death of the Messiah*, 1:866–68. For the irony of this scene, see Duke, *Irony in the Fourth Gospel*, 131–32; La Potterie, *Hour of Jesus*, 101–3.

118. Brown, *Death of the Messiah*, 1:868.

119. This is likely a reference to Isaiah 50:6: "I gave ... my cheeks to slaps" (see ibid., 1:869).

120. Bultmann, *John*, 658; and Schnackenburg, *St. John*, 3:253.

121. Lincoln, *Saint John*, 465.

Scene 5: Pilate, Jesus and the Jews, Outside (19:4–8)

Pilate went outside again (v. 4) to confront Jesus' accusers with the flogged king. He calls their attention (ἴδε) and with the deictic language of drama describes his actions: "I am bringing him outside to you" (ἄγω ὑμῖν αὐτὸν ἔξω).[122] Pilate then explains why: he does so for their knowledge (ἵνα γνῶτε). He then asserts for the second time his judgment of the threat Jesus poses: "I find no guilt in him" (v. 4; see 18:38). Pilate remains intent on not deciding against Jesus, even as he has refused to decide for the truth of Jesus' identity.

Jesus then makes his own entrance, not led out as Pilate claimed, but exiting by his own volition (ἐξῆλθεν οὖν ὁ Ἰησοῦς ἔξω, v. 5).[123] Thus the three parties come together at center stage, each brought to this place by their own choices of roles in God's plan. As a result of Pilate's attempt to ridicule the charge that he is "King of the Jews," Jesus faces his accusers wearing the crown of thorns and the purple cloak of royalty.[124] He is once again characterized with an active, transitive verb. Jesus is not "clothed" by his captors, but "bears" the insignia of a king upon himself.[125]

Pilate nonetheless takes his position of authority and presents Jesus to his accusers with his now famous proclamation, "Behold, the man" (ἰδοὺ ὁ ἄνθρωπος). The meaning of this acclamation has been the subject of much debate among scholars.[126] Some suggest it is simply Pilate's attempt to ridicule the idea that this "man" is a royal claimant.[127] Others give it a particularly christological meaning as a first step toward faith.[128] Some understand the term to be eschatological with reference to Zechariah 6:12 and Numbers 24:17.[129] The more common position is that Pilate is, in his way, presenting Jesus as the Son of Man whom Jesus

---

122. Brant, *Dialogue and Drama*, 87.

123. Duke, *Irony in the Fourth Gospel*, 132; Moloney, *Johannine Son of Man*, 205.

124. Brown, *Death of the Messiah*, 1:827.

125. Moloney, *John*, 499.

126. For a discussion of the history of interpretation of Pilate's presentation, see Brown, *Death of the Messiah*, 1:827–28. On the irony of Pilate's statement, see Duke, *Irony in the Fourth Gospel*, 106–7.

127. See, e.g., Bultmann, *John*, 659; and Flusser, "What Was the Original Meaning."

128. See, e.g., Suggit, "John 19:5"; and Barrett, *St. John*, 540.

129. See, e.g., Meeks, *Prophet-King*, 70–72; and Lindars, *John* 565.

himself predicted would be lifted up (3:14; 8:28; 12:32–34).[130] Along this line, but distinctive in his foundation, Anthony Hanson believes Pilate is unwittingly presenting Jesus as the suffering servant of the Lord "whose suffering and death is to bring redemption to the world," based on Isaiah 53:3.[131] It is difficult to assess the full implication of such a simple though pregnant acclamation. In terms of the drama of the Roman trial proceedings, Pilate seems to be demonstrating Jesus to be no threat to Rome as a royal claimant of "the Jews."[132] Readers of the Gospel thus far, however, may surmise that he points beyond his own ken to Jesus as the Son of Man who will be lifted up and glorified by God the Father despite any and all human machinations.

When Jesus' accusers, now further identified as "the chief priests and the guards," saw him (εἶδον αὐτόν) flogged and dressed in this way, they began to shout once again (ἐκραύγασαν, v. 6a; see 18:40), this time admitting in their fury what it is they demand from these proceedings: "Crucify him, crucify him!" (σταύρωσον σταύρωσον).[133] Pilate, however, will not be pressed into their service by simple rage. He counters with an imperative of his own that must be taken as mockery of their position, for he challenges them, "Take him yourselves and crucify him [λάβετε αὐτὸν ὑμεῖς καὶ σταυρώσατε]."[134] He attempts to conclude his riposte with the third qualification of his position, "I find no guilt in him" (v. 6b). Pilate's presentation of "the man" (v. 5) is thus framed by declarations of Jesus' innocence (vv. 4, 6). The narrative continues to affirm that what Pilate is saying is true: Jesus will die an innocent man.[135]

Jesus' accusers, now identified once again with the more common "the Jews" (v. 7; see 18:38), have a response of their own to Pilate's challenge. This is the second time that Pilate has attempted to shift responsibility to "the Jews" by demanding, "Take him yourselves" (λάβετε αὐτόν ὑμεῖς, v. 6b; see 18:31a). Their response to that initial challenge

130. See, e.g., de la Potterie, *Hour of Jesus*, 78–80; Dodd, *Interpretation*, 436–37; Duke, *Irony in the Fourth Gospel*, 132; Giblin, "John's Narration," 230; Heil, *Blood and Water*, 64–65; Moloney, *Johannine Son of Man*, 202–7.

131. Hanson, *Prophetic Gospel*, 204–5.

132. Brown, *Death of the Messiah*, 1:828.

133. Neyrey ("Despising the Shame," 126) articulates the gravity of this command against Jesus in terms of honor and shame: "Rejection by one's ἔθνος and delivery to the Romans would be shame enough; now his own people call for his shameful death."

134. Duke, *Irony in the Fourth Gospel*, 133.

135. Koester, *Symbolism in the Fourth Gospel*, 214.

was based on Roman law (18:31b). They now turn to Jewish law and base their position upon their "Law" (ἡμεῖς νόμον ἔχομεν) to articulate their desire for capital punishment once again (ὀφείλει ἀποθανεῖν). The specific law they seem to be invoking is Leviticus 24:16, for this time the real charge of blasphemy that has arisen in the course of Jesus' public ministry (see 5:18; 8:58; 10:33) comes to the fore: "because he made himself the Son of God." Jerome Neyrey notes that "the public accusation that Jesus *makes himself* something functions as a *challenge* to a perceived empty claim."[136]

Jesus has encountered this sort of challenge throughout the narrative (5:18; 8:53; 10:33; here at 19:7; next at 19:12). The evangelist has defended that Jesus does not "make himself" anything and shown that Jesus truly is "King" and "Son of God" because these titles have been ascribed to him by God (5:19–29; 6:15; 13:31; 17:5, 24). The reader has thus been schooled as to how to interpret this new charge against Jesus and can reject any sense of a vainglorious claim by affirming the truth of the honor ascribed to Jesus.[137] The reader knows by now that the Law has a different word to say about Jesus, but the accusers are more correct than they know, for it is true that this Son of God must die (see 8:28; 12:23, 32–33).[138]

Nonetheless, it is this word (τοῦτον τόν λόγον) that gives Pilate pause, for when he heard it, he became very afraid (μᾶλλον ἐφοβήθη, v. 8). The adverb is puzzling since there is no prior reference to fear, but it seems to have the force of an elative and indicates that Pilate is "very afraid."[139] Unlike the previous implication of Jesus in sedition, this charge of "the Jews" is consonant with Jesus own self-identification as one who has come into the world to bear witness to the truth (18:37).

---

136. Neyrey, "Despising the Shame," 126.

137. Ibid., 127. He notes that Jesus rarely claims these titles himself. They tend to be ascribed to him by God or others (Son of God, 1:34, 49; Christ, 1:41; 10:24; king, 1:49; 6:15; 12:13; savior, 4:42; and prophet, 4:19; 6:14).

138. Duke, *Irony in the Fourth Gospel*, 133; Moloney, *John*, 495, 499; Pancaro, *Law in the Fourth Gospel*, 319–23. The fulfillment of Scripture in the death of Jesus will be emphasized in 19:24, 28, 36, 37.

139. Barrett, *St. John*, 542; Brown, *Death of the Messiah*, 1:830. This position contrasts that of others, including Bultmann (*John*, 661) and Schnackenburg (*St. John*, 3:260), who point to Pilate's previous attempts not to come to decision about Jesus as a manifestation of fear. However, the text gives no indication of Pilate's emotional state until here at 19:8.

Thus Pilate seems to become "very afraid" because it is becoming "clearer and clearer that he will not be able to escape making a judgment about truth."[140] This fear sends Pilate back inside with Jesus for another private interrogation.

Scene 6: Pilate and Jesus, Inside (19:9–11)

Pilate entered the praetorium again and asked Jesus, "Where are you from?" (πόθεν εἶ σύ, v. 9). Pilate's query arises directly from "the Jews'" charge that Jesus "made himself the Son of God." Therefore, Pilate must intend to elicit more than just the name of a town in Jesus' response.[141] The question of Jesus' origin has come up time and again in his encounters with others in his public ministry (see 7:27–28; 8:14; 9:29–30), so it is no surprise that it arises at this critical juncture.[142] Likewise, Pilate has come to understand that this is the real charge against Jesus, and thus Jesus' identity is a more profound issue than what he has done (18:35).[143] Readers have also come to know that the answer to this question is ἄνωθεν—from above, from God (3:1–36; see 19:11).[144] Indeed the whole Gospel has been answering this question of Jesus' origin and identity.[145] Jesus himself offered Pilate his revelation of the truth about his identity in their previous encounter (18:36–38), but that gift was soundly rejected. Accordingly, Jesus now offers only silence. The time when Pilate could have received Jesus' witness to the truth has passed. Jesus' refusal to answer is thus "a recognition that Pilate, who could not understand when Jesus explained about his being a king, will never understand his origins from above."[146] Jesus' silence, however, is not final. He does have more to say to Pilate about his destiny.

140. Brown, *Death of the Messiah*, 1:830.

141. Neyrey notes that "true honor is ascribed honor; and ascribed honor is a function of one's father and clan or one's place of origin." Hence Pilate comes to Jesus with this question now. See the detailed discussion of this question in antiquity in Neyrey, "Despising the Shame," 127–28.

142. Moloney (*John*, 495) calls this "the fundamental question of Johannine Christology." For more on the function of this question at this point in the narrative, see also Dewailly, "D'où es-tu."

143. Brown, *Death of the Messiah*, 1:840.

144. Lincoln, *Saint John*, 467.

145. Duke, *Irony in the Fourth Gospel*, 133.

146. Brown, *Death of the Messiah*, 1:841. On this, see also Bultmann, *John*, 661; Lincoln, *Saint John*, 467; Moloney, *John*, 496; Schnackenburg, *St. John*, 3:260.

Faced with Jesus' initial refusal to respond to him, Pilate indignantly reminds Jesus that his life is at stake, falling "into the false certainty of a man who is aware of his own power."[147] He presses, "Do you not know that I have the power to release you and I have the power to crucify you?" (v. 10). The dialogue "outside," however, has already made it clear that Pilate's "power" against the forces of the world is strikingly limited. He will soon overtly attempt to release Jesus and fail miserably (v. 12a).[148] Jesus articulates the limits and true origin of Pilate's power in his final response to the governor. Pilate would have no power over him, says Jesus, if it had not been given from above (εἰ μὴ ἦν δεδομένον σοι ἄνωθεν, v. 11a). The double entendre incorporates both Pilate's worldly superior, the emperor, and God who is "above" them all.[149] Jesus not only indicates what little power Pilate really has over him, he asserts his own agency in accepting his role in the divine plan.[150]

Jesus then concludes by making the outcome clear: "Therefore, the one who handed me over to you [ὁ παραδούς μέ σοι] has the greater sin" (v. 11b). There is only one sin in the Johannine story of Jesus: encountering the truth of Jesus and refusing to receive him. Therefore ὁ παραδούς has made the decision that has brought them here.[151] In this final dialogue between Jesus and Pilate, Jesus asserts once again that people are judged by their reaction to him (3:12–21); he will not be judged by them.[152] Jesus, the witness to the truth who has been put on trial, points to God the Father as the bearer of ultimate power, but also once again becomes judge himself (see 5:22, 27; 12:31) and hands down his own verdict of guilty upon those who have brought him to trial.[153] As Raymond Brown articulates so incisively, "Pilate, with all the power he thinks he has, is a secondary figure, only the man-in-between in a titanic battle between Jesus and the world (16:33)."[154] This characteriza-

---

147. Schnackenburg, *St. John*, 3:260.

148. Duke, *Irony in the Fourth Gospel*, 133.

149. Ibid., 134.

150. As Alan Culpepper observes, "Having been arrested by those less powerful than he, Jesus is tried by those with less authority than himself" (*Anatomy of the Fourth Gospel*, 174).

151. For a detailed discussion of the identity of ὁ παραδούς, see Carson, *John*, 600–602.

152. Brown, *Death of the Messiah*, 1:842.

153. Lincoln, *Saint John*, 468.

154. Brown, *Death of the Messiah*, 1:842.

tion proves fateful as Pilate exits the praetorium for the final time to face that world.

Scene 7: Pilate, Jesus and the Jews, Outside (19:12–15)

The narrator breaks into the direct speech of the Roman trial to explain that "consequently" (ἐκ τούτου) Pilate "sought to release" (ἐζήτει ἀπολῦσαι) Jesus. The phrase ἐκ τούτου refers both to temporal sequence and to result.[155] Therefore, based upon and directly following his final "inside" dialogue with Jesus where Jesus clarified the limits of Pilate's power, Pilate finally seeks overtly to let Jesus go. Jesus' accusers, now identified as "the Jews" (οἱ Ἰουδαῖοι), will not have it and threaten Pilate with his potential political vulnerability. Using a conditional sentence in the same contemptuous tone of the first scene of the trial, "the Jews" shouted (ἐκραύγασαν, 19:12; see 18:40; 19:6) that if Pilate releases this one (ἐὰν τοῦτον ἀπολύσῃς, 19:12; see 18:30) then he is "not a Friend of Caesar" (φίλος τοῦ Καίσαρος), because "everyone who makes himself king opposes Caesar." The term "Friend of Caesar" is a Roman honorific bestowed in recognition of service, so, if it was in use as such in the early first century AD and Pilate had received it, "the Jews" are accusing him of not being faithful to it, which would be politically disastrous to him.[156] The dramatic irony of this trial has intensified. "The Jews" have turned the tables on Pilate who tried to make them choose between Jesus and Barabbas, as they now put the choice to Pilate: Jesus or Caesar?[157] Since their charge of blasphemy has backfired, "the Jews" return to their initial charge of sedition and refer to Jesus as one who "makes himself a king." This time, it will work.

Pilate's hand is forced and now, and when he "heard these words" (ἀκούσας τῶν λόγον τούτον, v. 13) he acts in kind.[158] He has sought to negotiate with Jesus and bargain with his accusers to no avail. His attempts at neutrality have failed and now must end. The narrator explains that Pilate "brought Jesus outside" (ἤγαγεν ἔξω τόν Ἰησοῦν) for the last time

---

155. Ibid., 1:843.

156. Lincoln, *Saint John*, 468; Moloney, *John*, 500; Brown, *Death of the Messiah*, 1:843–44. For a more detailed discussion of the term as well as an argument for its usage in the early first century, see Bammel, "Philos tou Kaisaros."

157. On the dramatic irony of the scene, see Duke, *Irony in the Fourth Gospel*, 133–34.

158. The verb ἀκούω with the genitive implies "listening to."

and "seated him on the judge's bench [ἐκάθισεν ἐπὶ βήματος] in the place called the Pavement, in Hebrew 'Gabbatha.'"[159] This action has been the subject of extensive interpretive discussion, as commentators debate whether the verb καθίζω is used intransitively to denote that Pilate took the seat (as custom would expect) or transitively to describe that Pilate seated Jesus on the *bema* (as the syntax can also imply and as it is translated here). The former would indicate that Pilate sat on the *bema* to make his final ruling, while the latter would depict Jesus in a kind of enthronement for the purpose of mockery but with the ironic effect of portraying Jesus as the true judge of the proceedings.[160] Jesus has identified himself as a king whose role is to witness to the truth (18:37), and in Jewish scriptural tradition there is frequent identification of king and judge (see Ps 10:16–18; Isa 11:1–4; Dan 4:37).[161] Sitting on the judge's bench for this final scene of the Roman trial, and dressed as a king, Jesus witnesses the ultimate condemnation that will ironically depict the truth of his identity and facilitate his exaltation.

The narrator then provides the first temporal marker since the Roman trial began (19:14; see 18:28). More than the time of day, however, readers are told that the entire proceedings have been taking place on the day of preparation for Passover (ἦν δὲ παρασκευὴ τοῦ πάσχα).

---

159. For a survey of the scholarship on the location of the praetorium and the association of this "pavement," see Brown, *Death of the Messiah*, 1:705–10, 845–46. The two locations under discussion include the Antonia fortress and the Herodian palace. A Roman floor has been uncovered on the site of the former Antonia fortress, which is today the Ecce Homo Convent of the Sisters of Our Lady of Sion. See also P. Benoit, "Praetorium, Lithostroton and Gabbatha." What the evangelist terms the "Hebrew" translation "Gabbatha" is actually Aramaic from the root גבה or גבא which means "to be high," "to protrude," and is typically understood to indicate a hill. For those who understand theological symbolism behind this pointed designation, see Ehrman, "Jesus' Trial," 130; and Boismard, "Royauté Universelle du Christ," 39.

160. Scholars who read the intransitive include Brown, *John*, 2:881; Bultmann, *John*, 664; Lindars, *John*, 570; Moloney, *John*, 500; Schnackenburg, *St. John*, 3:305; Wead, *Literary Devices*, 58. For a comprehensive treatment of this position, see Brown, *Death of the Messiah*, 2:1388–93. Scholars who read the transitive include de la Potterie, *Hour of Jesus*, 108–11; Giblin, "John's Narration," 233; Haenchen, "History and Interpretation," 216; Lincoln, *Saint John*, 469; Meeks, *Prophet-King*, 73–76. For a comprehensive treatment of this position, see de la Potterie, "Jesus King and Judge." Several scholars suggest that the evangelist intended a meaningful ambiguity with this usage, including Barrett, *St. John*, 544; and Duke, *Irony in the Fourth Gospel*, 134. Brown notes that regardless of how the verb is translated, the *bēma* could include the entire platform, and not just the judge's bench proper. Therefore, they could have both been seated on the *bēma*.

161. Lincoln, *Saint John*, 470.

Further, the trial has taken up the morning and it is now about noon (ὥρα ἦν ὡς ἕκτη).[162] Therefore this Friday is the vigil day of preparation for the Passover. Further, the designation of noontime indicates that these final moments of the Roman trial, when it has already become evident that Jesus will not escape being handed over for crucifixion, took place during the very hour that the priests in the temple would begin slaughtering the lambs for the Passover meal to be eaten that evening. The evangelist gives several indications that relate Jesus to the paschal lamb motif: 1:29, 36 (Lamb of God); 19:29 (the hyssop branch); 19:36 (the affirmation that no bone of Jesus is broken). With this temporal designation, then, the evangelist indicates that Jesus, who has already been portrayed and proclaimed, however ironically, as the true king and judge, is also the Lamb of God who will be sentenced to death at the very hour when the lambs for the Jewish Passover began to be killed.[163]

For his part, Pilate clarifies his contempt for Jesus' accusers as the bearers of responsibility for the coming condemnation at this solemn moment with a proclamation that resonates with his earlier declaration (19:14b; see 19:5). On this occasion, however, he pronounces the claim for which Jesus will be convicted: "Behold, your king!" (ἴδε ὁ βασιλεὺς ὑμῶν, v. 14b).[164] Pilate finally ironically proclaims the truth about Jesus before his accusers.[165] In having Pilate utter this pronouncement to "the Jews," the evangelist also employs "his usual dialogue technique of statement, response, and further probing to accomplish his goal in this final episode of the Roman trial," which is to articulate how responsibility for

---

162. The Greek text delineates that "it was about the sixth hour," which is translated above in modern idiom as "noon." The designation of the sixth hour is attested by the vast majority of witnesses. However, several witnesses read "about the third hour." This minority reading must be understood as an attempt to harmonize the chronology with that of Mark 15:25. For a brief textual analysis, see Metzger, *Textual Commentary*, 216.

163. Brown, *Death of the Messiah*, 1:847.

164. Bultmann (*John*, 665), e.g., sees this scene as an exact repetition of the earlier scene. Schnackenburg (*St. John*, 3:265), e.g., sees this scene as continued mockery in a final attempt to convince "the Jews" to accept the release of Jesus as a harmless pretender. I concur with those such as Brown (*Death of the Messiah*, 1:848) who read this announcement as Pilate's indication that "he will yield to the threats of denunciation before Caesar and will condemn Jesus." However, Pilate will still "maneuver to clarify who has the responsibility for this condemnation."

165. Moloney, *John*, 496.

this condemnation should be assigned.[166] Pilate has made his statement; Jesus' accusers now shout their initial response to it.

"The Jews" (ἐκεῖνοι, v. 15a; see τοῖς Ἰουδαίοις in v. 14b) continue shouting their responses to Pilate (ἐκραύγασαν, v. 15a; see 18:40; 19:6, 12). Their response is similar to, though a progression of, their shouts in 19:6. Their double-imperative response to Pilate's request for their pity in 19:6 is made stronger when he indicates what is really at stake. Three imperatives mark their response, as they shout in response to Pilate's designation of Jesus as their king, "Take him away, take him away, crucify him!" (v. 15a).[167] Pilate takes this opportunity for continued dialogue to spell out the responsibility of the Jews as this Roman trial reaches its culminating point.[168] He asks, "Shall I crucify your king?" (τόν βασιλέα ὑμῶν σταυρώσω v. 15b). Pilate forces Jesus' accusers to confess the full implications of their decision. Ironically, the one who has just been urged to show fidelity to his own king now compels "the Jews" to consider their own.[169] On behalf of "the Jews," the chief priests answered with finality, "We have no king but Caesar!" (v. 15c). With these words they seal Jesus' fate as well as their own.

Israel is to have but one king (see Judg 8:23; 1 Sam 8:7; Isa 26:13). In the Passover haggadah that would be recited that very evening, the concluding hymn of the Greater Hallel, called the *Nišmat*, reads:

> From everlasting to everlasting you are God;
> Beside you we have no king, redeemer or savior,
> No liberator, deliverer, provider,
> None who takes pity in every time of distress and trouble.
> We have no king but you.[170]

By pronouncing that they "have no king but Caesar," "the Jews" commit the ultimate hypocrisy. In their fervor to reject and condemn Jesus, they renounce God as their one true king. With these final words of the

---

166. Brown, *Death of the Messiah*, 1:848.

167. Lincoln, *Saint John*, 470.

168. Brown, *Death of the Messiah*, 1:848.

169. Duke, *Irony in the Fourth Gospel*, 135. Giblin ("John's Narration, 233) notes that Pilate is "sardonically capitalizing on his own previous tactical error" of 18:40.

170. This hymn is cited with varying translations in Duke, *Irony in the Fourth Gospel*, 135; Lincoln, *Saint John*, 471; Meeks, *Prophet-King*, 76–77; Neyrey, "Despising the Shame," 130. Meeks acknowledges that it could be a second-century addition to the Seder, but suggests it was used quite early in Palestine. See also Brown, *John*, 2:895.

chief priests on behalf of their people, the evangelist culminates Jesus' relationship to "his own people" who "did not accept him (1:11).[171] With these same words, the narrative thus also portrays "the Jews" as judging and condemning themselves. As Andrew Lincoln observes, "They have accused Jesus of blasphemy but now they are shown to be guilty of apostasy by accepting Caesar's exclusive claim to kingship instead of God's."[172] The irony of the scene reaches its pinnacle as "the Jews" utter the ultimate blasphemy with the same breath they use finally to reject Jesus who they have accused of the same.[173] And with that they have the last word of the Roman trial.

Conclusion: Handing Over for Crucifixion (19:16a)

Now that "the Jews" have completed their self-condemnation in terms of apostasy, Pilate's turn arrives to complete his.[174] His attempts to remain neutral and rid himself of the challenges presented to him theologically by Jesus and politically by Jesus' accusers have failed entirely. He has garnered the chief priests' pledge of subjection to Rome, but he has also publicly avowed Jesus' innocence three times. Nonetheless the political gambit has cost Jesus his life. Pilate therefore articulates his final response to both parties, not by direct speech but by his action, as he "then handed him over to them [παρέδωκεν αὐτόν αὐτοῖς] to be crucified" (v. 16a). Thus far in the Gospel Judas has been characterized as "the betrayer," the one who "hands Jesus over" (6:64, 71; 12:4; 13:2, 11, 21; 18:2, 5). With the onset of the Roman trial, "the Jews" have also taken on that role (18:30, 35, 36; 19:11). Now Pilate too becomes one who hands Jesus over to his enemies in this world (παρέδωκεν). In so doing Pilate also reverses the process that was initiated in 18:28. "The Jews" handed Jesus over to Pilate, and now he hands Jesus over to them for crucifixion. Although it is certainly the Roman soldiers who actually implement the sentence of capital punishment, Pilate does hand Jesus over to "the Jews" insofar as he completes his own self-condemnation by betraying one he knows to be innocent to the desires of those who

---

171. Brown, *Death of the Messiah*, 1:849.
172. Lincoln, *Saint John*, 471.
173. Lindars, *John*, 572.
174. Lincoln, *Saint John*, 471.

perceive his threat and wish him dead.[175] Despite the intentions of both parties, readers know that what Pilate and "the Jews" have really facilitated is lifting up the Son of Man in fulfillment of his mission to the world (v. 16; see 3:14; 8:28; 12:32).

Conclusion: Jesus as the Covenant Gift of Truth before Pilate

In his study of the Roman trial and crucifixion of Jesus within his larger investigation of Mosaic traditions in Johannine Christology, Wayne Meeks notes the emergence in his analysis of four components that seem to undergird the entire narration.[176] First, Jesus' kingship stands "at the center of attention in the whole narrative." Second, Jesus' kingship is "inextricably connected with his function as judge, a function which is depicted by the deeply ironic 'exchange of roles' apparent in the dramatic structure of the narrative." Furthermore, Jesus' kingship expresses "*God's* kingship," and thus the rejection of Jesus by "the Jews" was equivalent to rejection of God. Third, the "King of the Jews" and the "Good Shepherd" are corresponding characterizations of Jesus, "having the same functions." Finally, the mission of Jesus which manifests his kingship is twofold: (1) Jesus' kingship "consists in bearing witness to the truth, which is equivalent to the Good Shepherd's 'call' to which 'his own' respond," and (2) Jesus' kingship is "inaugurated through his willing death. As the Good Shepherd is the one who 'lays down his life for the sheep,' so the 'exaltation' of the king consists in his being 'lifted up' on the cross."[177] Jesus thus performs various roles and functions across the Gospel that begin to coalesce in this Roman trial. The Son of Man whose kingship consists of giving and bearing witness to the truth takes his stand on behalf of "his own" by issuing his final challenge before the powers of the world (18:37; see 1:14–16). Pilate, the representative of the state and all worldly power dismisses his challenge and final offer of truth (18:38) and ultimately forsakes this truth for political security (19:12–16a). But this too is part of the mission of the Son of Man in

---

175. On uncertainty regarding the pronoun αὐτοῖς and its referent, see Schnackenburg, *St. John*, 3:266–67.

176. Meeks, *Prophet-King*, 80–81.

177. Ibid., 81. See chapter 2 for my discussion of the OT covenant text that relates to kingship and the messianic hopes for a son of David (2 Sam 7).

order that he be "lifted up" (18:32; see 12:32), and by dying "gather into one the scattered children of God" (11:52; see 1:12; 19:11).

"The Jews" and their representatives also have a major role in the process of the Roman trial. Throughout the Gospel, "the Jews" have been the evangelist's representative characters for "the world" and its rejection of God's revelation in Jesus, in general, and the Jewish opponents of later Johannine Christianity, in particular.[178] By this point in the Gospel "the Jews" have already proved themselves closed to the revelation of God in Jesus and have soundly rejected any covenantal challenge and offer of the gift of truth that the person and mission of Jesus brings.[179] In the Roman trial the evangelist "has used the political aspect of the charge against Jesus as a bludgeon against these opponents."[180] Their startling proclamation, "We have no king but Caesar!" (19:15), which brings the trial to its bitter end (19:16a) and is also uttered just as the observance of Passover begins (19:14), is not just a rejection of Jesus but a renunciation of the fundamental profession of Israel to have no king but God. Their failure, according to the evangelist, is both a religious and a political one as they reject Jesus (18:30–32; 19:6–7, 14–15) and choose Barabbas the λῃστής (18:39-40).[181] Their journey of rejection of the gift of truth that has spanned the Gospel is completed here before the Roman state.

The final character in the narrative of the Roman trial to be discussed is the only new character to the Fourth Gospel: Pontius Pilate, the Roman governor. Because he is a character just introduced to this Gospel narrative and his assumed authority renders his action decisive for the remainder to the story, it behooves readers to pay particular attention to his role in this act of the passion drama. Pilate's interaction with "the Jews" outside the praetorium is openly hostile, and the

---

178. Brown, *John*, 1:lxxi–lxxv; Martyn, *History and Theology*, 37–62.

179. See chapter 5 and the analysis of John 7–8 for a detailed exposition of this rejection.

180. Rensberger, "Politics of John," 406.

181. Meeks, *Prophet-King*, 76; and Rensberger, "Politics of John," 407. Rensberger suggests this reflects the evangelist's understanding both of what happened to Jesus as well as what is happening in and around his community: "John may thus be making his own way among ambivalent tendencies in the Jewish community between the two revolts. For him, once the true King of Israel had appeared both the continued expectation of a revolutionary Messiah and the accommodation of the emerging Pharisaic leadership to the kingship of Caesar were abhorrent."

two parties stand in clear opposition. However, his interaction with Jesus inside the praetorium is more complex. On the practical level, readers might understand Jesus' interviews with Pilate as a model for the Johannine community's dealings with Roman officials.[182] On the literary level, Pilate's characterization is often regarded as somewhat sympathetic: he is a man who wants to be fair and would acquit Jesus, but through political and moral vulnerability he falls to the pressure of Jesus' accusers and becomes the tool by which they achieve their malevolent ends.[183] By contrast, David Rensberger suggests that the figure of Pilate is a strong character rather than a weak one. Rensberger observes the irony woven through the passage and understands Pilate to be an operative agent of "the world" just like "the Jews." He claims that Pilate "is undeniably hostile to 'the Jews,' but that does not make him friendly to Jesus, for whose innocence he is not really concerned. Rather, his aim is to humiliate 'the Jews' and to ridicule their national hopes by means of Jesus."[184] The above exegesis supports Rensberger's understanding of the characterization of Pilate. However, when Jesus' interactions with his dialogue partners across the Gospel are also considered, we must go a step further and clarify not only how Pilate's dialogues with Jesus affect Jesus and where he stands in the Gospel narrative, but also how they affect Pilate and where he stands in relation to the gift of truth that forms the basis for the entire Gospel story.

In their first dialogue inside the praetorium (18:33–38a), Jesus reveals himself as a king whose kingdom is not of the world but is nonetheless in the world (v. 36). Jesus' role in establishing this kingdom is testifying to the truth so that all those who are of the truth may hear his voice and enter into and abide in relationship with him (v. 37; see 10:1–21; 13–17). He gives the gift of truth by giving himself both in his revelatory dialogues with those he encounters and, as the reader has come to understand, in the giving of his life. According to the prologue, those who receive him (who are of the truth) are empowered to become children of God (1:12). The narrator later clarifies for the reader

---

182. Rensberger, "Politics of John," 407. Rensberger further suggests this corresponds to the presentation of Jesus' interrogation by the high priest as reflecting the community's relations with Jewish authorities.

183. This reading correlates to the view that the evangelist's purpose is apologetic. See, e.g., Barrett, *St. John*, 531–46; Dodd, *Historical Tradition*, 96–17, 119–20; Schnackenburg, *St. John*, 3:241–67.

184. Rensberger, "Politics of John," 402.

that Jesus will further lay down his life to draw into one the scattered children of God (11:51–52). The imagery that accompanies Jesus' offer of relationship in truth and the language used in narration and direct speech is the language of covenant.[185] This self-revelation of Jesus to Pilate and the implicit gift of truth that accompanies it constitutes an offer of covenant to Pilate. Pilate has come in to question Jesus openly, and, as Jesus does in every dialogue across the Gospel, he engages Pilate in a dialogue in which he offers himself as the gift of truth. By responding to Jesus the way Pilate does, with the brusque rhetorical question "What is truth?" followed by an immediate exit (19:38), Pilate dismisses Jesus' challenge. Further, he shows that he does not really understand the question, i.e., the truth of relationship in covenant with God that is at stake. By not being open to the revelation of Jesus and the offer of truth, Pilate fails to recognize the gift of truth that is standing in front of him. Therefore his attempts to remain neutral, to act as if the person and fate of Jesus has nothing to do with him, also fail (18:38b—19:8). Eventually even his appeals to his own power before Jesus and his attempts to act decisively before "the Jews" fail as well (19:9–15).

The sheep that are of Jesus' fold hear his voice of truth and enter into abiding covenantal relationship with him as empowered children of God. There are others who, when challenged by Jesus' revelation of this gift of truth, not only reject the offer of relationship in covenant, but also use all human means to rid themselves of the perceived threat his person and offer constitute. In the Fourth Gospel, "the Jews" represent this group who oppose Jesus, and their rejection reaches its climax here at the Roman trial. Pilate, then, constitutes a third possible response to Jesus as the questioner who is given the revelation of truth and the challenge to accept relationship as a child of God that Jesus' offers. In the end he proves himself to be so committed to human endeavor and the powers of this world (including his own) that he cannot understand what is really being asked of him. He fails to see the truth when it is standing before him and thus, despite all efforts to exert his own will, hands the Truth over to its enemies to be crucified.

---

185. See chapter 2 for the discussion of truth as the language of living in covenant relationship with God (see e.g., Isa 10:20; 43:9; 65:16; Jer 2:21; 4:2; 5:1–3; 14:13; Zech 7:9; 8:16–19; Mal 2:5–6), and lack of truth as a breach of covenant with God (see, e.g., Isa 48:1; 59:14–15; Jer 7:28; 9:3–5; Hos 4:1).

The gift of truth that God has offered through Jesus does not come to an end with his earthly life and mission. Human response and failure cannot thwart God's plan and cannot negate God's covenantal action in the world. Indeed, the full glorification of the Son is perfected by his being lifted up on the cross. It is then that his mission is perfected and he can say, "It is finished" (τετέλεσται, 19:30), and "gather into one the scattered children of God" (τα τέκνα τοῦ θεοῦ, 11:52).

The Resurrection of the Word (John 20)

The post-resurrection narratives begin at John 20. These episodes can be broadly divided into two acts defined by their settings: at the empty tomb (vv. 1–18) and in the upper room (vv. 19–29). The activity at these locations is structured in two additional scenes each. At the tomb in the garden, the action centers first around Peter and the Beloved Disciple (vv. 1–9), then around Mary Magdalene (vv. 10–18). Mary's commission leads her to the disciples to give her message (v. 18). The following scenes take up the action in the disciples' room, first without the presence of Thomas (vv. 19–25) and then later with the presence of Thomas (vv. 26–29). The final verses conclude both these post-resurrection narratives and the body of the Gospel (vv. 30–31).[186] These early narratives present the evangelist's story of the resurrection of the Word of God through the lens of his concern for the members of the early Christian community.

John 20 begins with Mary at the empty tomb with no concept of a resurrection (v. 1). In these verses a number of divine passives reflect the agency of God in these empty tomb scenes. She runs away from the tomb to the disciples, and Peter and the Beloved Disciple run back to the tomb (vv. 2–3).[187] The Beloved Disciple runs faster but gives access to Peter to enter first (vv. 4–7). The Beloved Disciple then sees the signs of death overcome and believes (v. 8). Peter's response is not recorded. The disciples did not know the Scripture that details the events at hand,

---

186. For discussions of the structure of John 20, see, e.g., Brown, *John*, 2:965; Carson, *John*, 631–63; Moloney, *John*, 515–17; Matera, "John 20:1–18." See chapter 3 for a brief discussion of John 20:30–31.

187. For a detailed study of these initial verses in the post-resurrection accounts of the Gospel of John and how they affect both the conclusion of the Gospel as well as the community to whom the Gospel was written, see Mahoney, *Two Disciples*, esp. 228–85.

because the evangelist is writing that Scripture. They are characters within the Gospel story, and the Scripture will be written to privilege the reader so that those who do not see can believe (v. 9). The disciples leave the scene (v. 10) and Mary is left again to go through her own journey of faith with Jesus, the "gardener" (vv. 11–17). She thus becomes the apostle to the apostles as she fulfills the commission Jesus gives her (v. 18). She prepares the disciples so that when Jesus appears to them, they are overjoyed and receive both the Holy Spirit and their own commission.

The evangelist then provides Thomas's journey of faith through Jesus' encounters with the remaining disciples (vv. 19–25, 26–29). Thomas's journey within the story comes to completion when he sees Jesus for who he is and finally believes. His exclamation provides a profession of faith for all those who have made this journey: "My Lord and my God" (v. 28). Jesus rebuffs Thomas for the need to see in order to believe and blesses the next generation of readers who, like the Beloved Disciple, will believe without seeing (v. 29, see v. 8). Jesus' first words to potential disciples, and his first words of the Gospel, "What do you seek?" (1:38) and "Come and you will see" (1:39), are balanced by his blessing, his final words in the body of the Gospel to all disciples who live beyond his earthly ministry in his new covenantal community of believers: "Blessed are those who have not seen and yet have come to believe" (20:29).

John 20 comes to an end with the closing remarks through which the author makes his claim for writing Scripture (20:30–31). The rhetorical purpose behind this Gospel is to bring the narrative tradition of the Bible to a culmination in Jesus. The indication is that the next generation, the one that believes without seeing, is qualitatively better off. This is the sacramental catechesis of the evangelist to his struggling community.[188]

The Dialogue of Covenant in John 13–20

The dialogue of covenant—in terms of language, setting, characterization, and symbolism—in this second half of the Gospel according to John is subtle, though still extensive and complex. The evangelist continues to weave the language and symbolism of the OT covenant meta-

---

188. Moloney, *John*, 542–45.

phor through his presentation of the good news of Jesus Christ without overtly making covenantal claims insofar as the use of the term itself. Rather, the evangelist sets scenes, formulates characters, and recounts dialogue that resonate the OT covenant narratives, symbols, and themes so as to continue to present Jesus as the new covenantal gift that is also truth. In his encounters with people in John 13–20, Jesus continues to offer himself as the revelation of God, and relationship with himself as an abiding one that constitutes the children of God.

Jesus' final meal and last discourse with his disciples is recounted in John 13–17. This extended section was presented at length in terms of its covenantal overtones at the beginning of this chapter, and there is no need to repeat that discussion here. It is sufficient to restate the central claim that the action and dialogue of Jesus and his disciples narrated in those chapters reflects the covenantal renewal ceremonies of the OT, and particularly that of Joshua 24. Jesus' public ministry has come to a close. Throughout that time he engaged all those he encountered in dialogues in which he presented himself as the revelation of God and challenged his dialogue partners to enter into abiding relationship with him. The nature of this relationship is covenantal. Some rejected his offer completely, others showed a partial faith that could lead to acceptance or rejection, while still others move toward acceptance of Jesus' challenge to enter into relationship with him and thereby receive the power to become children of God. Those who received Jesus reconstitute "his own" in the world, and these he will love to the end (13:1) by renewing and sealing his covenant with them as he turns toward his glorification. The evening begins with Jesus washing the feet of his disciples. This action sets the stage for his lengthy discourse, which follows the general form of covenant challenge, promises, obligations, and consequences of a covenant renewal ceremony. The disciples respond to Jesus' discourse with the affirmation that they understand and accept him, his mission, and the future mission he has laid out for them. Jesus concludes the process with a lengthy prayer on their behalf that seals their covenant. At the close of his final words of prayer, Jesus' passion begins.

In a recent survey of the study of the Gospel according to John, Udo Schnelle articulates both the theology and Christology of the Gospel through the Fourth Evangelist's telling of the passion narrative, and in particular the locus of the cross. Schnelle observes:

Many Johannine texts point emphatically to an orientation of the Fourth Gospel around a theology of the cross (see 1:29, 36; 2:14–22; 3:14–16; 10:15, 17–18; 11:51–52; 12:27–32; 19:30). Above all the placement of the cleansing of the temple early in the gospel, the orientation of the foot washing toward a theology of the cross (13:1–3, 18–19), and Jesus' last words on the cross in John 19:30 demonstrate that the revelation of Jesus reaches its goal precisely at the cross. The cross is not only a transitory stage in the framework of a dominant sending Christology, but in John it is precisely the goal of the sending and thereby the place of salvation. At the cross Jesus receives the dignity of being raised up and glorified (see 12:27–33). The cross, especially for John, is the fundamental datum and abiding location of salvation; only from the perspective of the cross can Jesus' going to the Father be appropriately viewed.[189]

Everything that happens in John 18–19 first moves Jesus and those around him to the cross (18:1—19:16a) and then, after the Roman trial that concludes with the accomplishment of that end (19:16a), emanates from Jesus being lifted up on the cross (19:16b–42).

The dialogues of the Roman trial were the focus of the exegetical analysis above. The covenantal aspect of those exchanges focused primarily upon the question of truth, and the correlating question of kingship and the nature of the kingdom of Jesus. Although Jesus is fully in control of his destiny throughout the passion account, and certainly though this proceeding, it is Pilate and his vigorous movement between the truth of Jesus and security of the world that structures the dialogue of this act of the passion. Jesus extends the challenge of covenant to Pilate through the revelation of himself and his kingship as the gift of truth. Pilate's dismissive response "What is truth?" proves that not only does he not understand the fullness of the revelation that stands before him but further that he cannot endeavor beyond the human realm of political maneuvering and status-seeking. From this point forward, regardless of Pilate's efforts he is powerless to affect any real decision.

---

189. Schnelle, "Recent Views," 357. Schnelle therefore draws the following conclusion: "When Johannine dualism is seen not statically, but as a dynamic event resulting from the movement into the world of the one who reveals God, then incarnation and cross are no longer out of place but the center of Johannine Christology." For more detail on these observations, Schnelle cites Knöppler, *Theologia crucis*; Schnelle, *Antidocetic Christology*, 170–73.

Ultimately, as Jesus foretold, Pilate hands Jesus over to be crucified, and the lifting up is accomplished (19:16–37; see 8:28; 12:32–33).

The crucifixion proceeds swiftly and Jesus is indeed lifted up to die, with the inscription "King of the Jews" placed above him (19:19–21).[190] In his final moments, Jesus gazes upon his mother at the foot of the cross (19:26). Jesus' mother, the first to believe and to begin to live in covenant relationship with him (2:1–12), and "the disciple whom Jesus loved" stand before him.[191] Jesus gives to his mother, the model disciple before "the hour," a new son in the Beloved Disciple, the one who emerged as the model disciple during "the hour" of Jesus' glory, sealed in covenant relationship with Jesus.[192] Jesus then completes the family formation by giving to the Beloved Disciple his mother in kinship. By using performative language, Jesus' pronouncement accomplishes the new relationship that it declares.[193] By his declaration, Jesus constitutes a new family. The theological and dramatic significance of "the hour" of Jesus is affirmed when the narrator explains that "because of that hour" (ἀπ' ἐκείνης τῆς ὥρας) the Beloved Disciple takes his new mother into his own (εἰς τὰ ἴδια).[194] From the beginning, the evangelist has employed the language of kinship to characterize the believers' new relationship to God, in covenant with Jesus (see 1:12; 11:52). Here at the

---

190. The crucifixion scene can be understood as the fourth of five acts in the passion narrative (19:16b–37). Most scholars observe five scenes in this act, structured as follows: the crucifixion and title (vv. 16b–22), the seamless garment (v. 23–24), the mother of Jesus and the Beloved Disciple at the cross (vv. 25–27), the death of Jesus and the gift of the Spirit (vv. 28–30), and the aftermath: the gift of water and blood (vv. 31–37). Some find a chiastic structure (Brown, *Death of the Messiah*, 2:907–9; Stibbe, *John*, 193–94). Others focus on the forward motion of the story (Moloney, *John*, 502; Senior, *Passion of Jesus*, 99–100). Regardless, the gift of mother and son at the foot of the cross stands at the center of this act.

191. The covenant relationship between Jesus and his mother at Cana was established in chapter 4.

192. Alan Culpepper ("Theology of the Johannine Passion," 29) notes that this disciple is introduced as "beloved" at 13:23 where he reclined on the lap of Jesus (ἐν τῷ κόλπῳ τοῦ Ἰησοῦ/) just as Jesus reclined on the lap of the Father (εἰς τὸν κόλπον τοῦ πατρός, 1:18). He appears at all the key moments of the passion narrative and the narrator eventually affirms that, like Jesus before him, this disciple's testimony is true. He thus functions as the representative of the Johannine community; "he is their founder and their apostolic authority."

193. Ibid., 30.

194. Moloney, *John*, 503. Moloney appeals to BDF §210 for the reading of the preposition ἀπό followed by a noun in the genitive case as both temporal and causative.

foot of the cross, the formation of this new family "provides a nucleus for the community of believers."[195] A covenantal community of family that lives beyond the earthly life of Jesus is born and emanates from the evangelist's ecclesiology of the cross that culminates in Jesus' last words, "It is finished" (τετέλεσται).

The body of the Gospel then comes to a close with the post-resurrection narratives, which send this community forward with the memory of their encounters with Jesus, now the risen Lord (John 20). Jesus sends Mary Magdalene forth as the apostle with the message of his rising to his "brothers" (ἀδελφούς μου), the new family of his own (v. 17).[196] She fulfills her mission: she goes to the disciples and they, too, have their encounters. The final words of direct speech in the body of the Gospel come first from a witness to Jesus, as Thomas proclaims the truth he sees before him, "My Lord and my God!" His witness is true, but Jesus' response points beyond the first generation to the Johannine community and the community of readers who take the covenant of abiding in relationship with Jesus into the future: "Have you believed because you have seen me? Blessed are those who have not seen and yet have come to believe" (v. 29).

With these words the narrator can then conclude the body of the Gospel with the proclamation that this Scripture has indeed been written so that the community of readers may be affirmed in their belief and may go forward into the world of their future as the covenantal community of Christ (20:30–31).

---

195. Culpepper, "Theology of the Johannine Passion," 30. He concludes that what "Jesus accomplished on the cross is characterised in this pivotal scene as the constitution of a new community of 'his own.' The redemptive significance of the cross in John is therefore not merely individual but corporate. More than an underlying theory of atonement, John has an underlying ecclesiology of the cross" (31).

196. Ibid., 30.

7

Community and Covenant
Gift upon Gift

IN HIS SURVEY OF RECENT SCHOLARSHIP ON THE GOSPEL ACCORDING to John, Udo Schnelle identifies two primary reasons why both synchronic and diachronic hermeneutics must be employed in the study of the narrative. In other words, he articulates why the exegete must focus on the final form of the text produced by the evangelist and his community as well as the tradition that informs the evangelist and his hearers or readers.[1] He claims:

> Like the other New Testament authors, John the Evangelist stood in relation to tradition, so that the intention and reception of his work must be understood by considering how it both continues and differs from the prevailing traditions that provided its horizon of meaning.... If, using the genre of gospel, John recasts nineteen quotations from the Old Testament, each with characteristic introductory formulas and alterations, a Logos hymn, and a variety of miracle stories and sayings of Jesus; if he includes variations of synoptic texts and takes up Pauline thoughts; then our reading of John's Gospel can only be fully productive when done with an appropriate comprehension of its prehistory. Then we see that the literary achievement of the Fourth Evangelist is precisely the way he arranges heterogeneous material—some of which has its own lengthy prehistory—into a new text.[2]

Schnelle concludes this initial observation by noting that particularly with the Gospel of John, the present text cannot be fully appreciated apart from an understanding of its history. He goes on to articulate

---

1. Schnelle, "Recent Views."
2. Ibid., 254.

the second, correlative reason the inclusion of the tradition that informs the evangelist and his hearers or readers is essential:

> The reality to which the New Testament texts refer is not first and foremost constituted in their reception by the hearer or reader; these texts point to a reality outside of themselves. The Johannine texts in particular consistently exhibit this character of referring beyond themselves. This in no way excludes the meaning found by the individual hearer or reader, but it does make clear that this must always relate to a meaning already constituted by God in Jesus Christ. These considerations plead for a combination of diachronic and synchronic textual interpretation that considers not only the text's original situation and intended message but also the ways in which the present author intends to go beyond these. The interpretation of every text requires both an appropriate understanding of the text itself and a suitable model of communication that takes into consideration the author, the work, and the recipients.[3]

The preceding chapters of the present study focused on analysis of the final form of the narrative written for the evangelist's first-century readers. This chapter, the conclusion of the study, will build upon Schnelle's observations on the interpretation of the Fourth Gospel, by first examining John 21 as an epilogue to the body of the Gospel that presents the ongoing covenantal dialogue in the community of the church established at the cross in John 19:25–27. We will then be able to reappraise the methodological components of this study presented at the outset, including the evangelist's self-understanding as a writer of Scripture and the dramatic dialogical nature of the Gospel narrative he composed. We can then conclude by reflecting upon what the concepts of covenant and covenantal relationship with God meant for this community, how the OT covenant metaphor could be used effectively as the underlying literary fabric of the evangelist's Scripture for his community, and why the evangelist may have employed covenant as a guiding literary paradigm for his Christian community at the end of the first century AD in the subtle and nuanced manner he does.

---

3. Ibid., 354–55. For detailed study of the quotations and literary forms of the Fourth Gospel that he mentions as well as the reception of texts in antiquity, Schnelle cites Menken, *Old Testament Quotations*; Schnelle, *Antidocetic Christology*; Labahn, *Jesus al Lebensspender*; Lang, *Johannes und die Synoptiker*; Müller, "*Versteht du auch, was du liest?*"

Epilogue: The Covenant for the Community of Believers (John 21)

Scholars often ponder the existence of the final chapter of the Gospel according to John given the concluding sounds of 20:30–31. Yet no manuscript exists without the scenes of this chapter as the final act of the Gospel.[4] The present study suggests that John 21 can be understood as an epilogue insofar as it brings the Gospel story beyond its conclusion into the time of its readers and clarifies the form and mission of the community it engenders.[5] Further, this narrative episode can be contextualized in terms of the problems emerging with the Johannine letters. Broadly speaking, the covenant relationship made possible by Jesus in the Gospel of John leaves its community of readers with only two commands: *to love* and *to believe* (see 12:36; 13:19, 34–35; 14:1, 11, 15, 21, 23, 24; 15:9–10, 12, 13, 17). However completely these truths are revealed, living through them as a community can become problematic over time when members differ on what exactly to love and to believe. The resulting issues can be summarized as an ecclesial problem and an authority problem.[6] The former is handled in the first part of John 21 (vv. 1–14), and the latter in the second part (vv. 15–25).

The intricacy of the narrative is revealed in the introduction of the primary characters of the second scene in the setting and action of

---

4. Dwight Moody Smith has argued that any theory about the origin and function of John 21 is "the key and cornerstone for any redactional theory" of the Gospel (*Composition and Order*, 234). For more detailed discussion of the function of John 21, see Minear, "Original Functions." For the argument that John 21 is a proper conclusion to the Gospel, see Breck, "John 21." For the counter-argument that John 21, however ecclesiologically beneficial, actually undermines the Fourth Evangelist's original narrative thrust, see Moloney, "John 21."

5. John Breck distinguishes the various ways the chapter may be understood: "An 'appendix' adds supplemental information to a literary product, material that has no direct bearing on or consequences for the theme that work develops; while an 'epilogue' *carries forward* some aspect of the theme by describing consequences resulting from its dénouement, its solution or outcome. The 'conclusion' of a work . . . represents the dénouement itself; it presents the results or consequences of the actions or thought involved and is an integral part of the work as a whole. To be both complete and intelligible, a literary product must have a conclusion; it need not have an epilogue or an appendix" ("John 21," 27 n. 1). Breck argues that John 21 serves as a conclusion, while I understand it as an epilogue.

6. For this analysis of the issues at stake in John 21, see Moloney, *John*, 562–65.

the first scene.[7] Jesus manifested himself (ἐφανέρωσεν ἑαυτον) one final time to the disciples (v. 1). The double use of φανερόω in the first verse "provides the hermeneutical key for the readers to interpret the story as a theophany or manifestation of God's presence among the disciples."[8] Seven of Jesus' disciples go out fishing (vv. 2–3) following the lead of Peter, who last appeared as an agent in the Gospel warming himself by a charcoal fire (ἀνθρακία) with the enemies of Jesus in the court of the high priest (18:18, 25–27). There Peter denied Jesus three times as Jesus predicted he would (18:18, 25, 27; see 13:38). Peter had sworn that he would lay down his life for Jesus (13:37), but Jesus prevented him from doing so when Peter tried to defend him in the garden (18:10–11). Peter, the earnest, aggressive spokesman for the disciples (see 6:68–69; 13:6–10, 24, 36–37; 18:10–11), was thrown from his former self-understanding and found himself denying all knowledge of and relationship with Jesus (18:18–27). In the present scene, Peter has returned to the occupation of fishing, the covenant relationship he accepted from Jesus being broken. A primary focus of the remainder of the chapter is to reconstitute the covenant relationship between Jesus and Peter and set Peter in his role of pastoral authority over the community of Jesus' flock (21:1, 15–19; see 10:1–16). Before that happens the nature of the ecclesial community is affirmed.

After a long night of failure, morning breaks to reveal Jesus standing on the shore. He greets his disciples by addressing them as "children" (παιδία, v. 5). These are the same sentiments for the disciples expressed in the covenant renewal of the last discourse, where the disciples were characterized as "his own" (οἱ ἴδιοι, 13:1) and Jesus called them "children" (τεκνία, 13:33). This greeting of Jesus for his disciples recalls the identity of the covenant community as "children of God" (1:12; 11:52) and sets the stage for the wondrous catch and renewal to come (vv. 6–11, 15–17).[9] The Beloved Disciple, in keeping with his character established in John 13–20 as the one who witnesses and gives access to the

---

7. For a detailed study that supports the narrative unity of the chapter, see Wiarda, "John 21:1–23."

8. Chennattu, *Johannine Discipleship*, 169. Chennattu observes that this is a characteristic of the covenant community and regards this language as the initial indication that the covenant theme of the Gospel will continue into John 21. For more on the revelatory dimension of John 21, see Smalley, "Sign in John XXI."

9. Chennattu, *Johannine Discipleship*, 170–71. Chennattu suggests Jesus' address in this epilogue "furthers the covenant-discipleship motif of the gospel" as a whole (171).

other disciples, is the first to recognize Jesus: "It is the Lord!" (v. 7). Peter, likewise in keeping with the earnest zeal of his character, gets dressed and jumps into the sea in an effort to get to Jesus (v. 7). As they all reach the land, Peter returns to the boat on Jesus' command to haul ashore the wondrous catch of fish in the unbroken net. The abundance of fish, 153 in total, reminds the reader of the abundance of wine (2:1–12) and the abundance of food (6:1–14) provided by Jesus, and indicates the fullness and inclusiveness of the church. The universal character of the mission of the community consists of bringing into one the children of God scattered over the earth (see 11:52).[10] The unbroken net reflects the unity of the community in the new life given by Jesus. "The risen Jesus, the giver of new life, comes to make efficient and effective the work of the disciples. The abundance motif brings home the presence of the messianic era and signals the actualization of the new messianic covenant community."[11]

The ecclesial issue at stake is thus addressed by the sign Jesus performs for the disciples signifying the universal nature of the church and its mission. The second part of John 21 properly situates authority in this inclusive church (vv. 15–25): Peter is designated the leader, the head of the church; the Beloved Disciple is the witness, the paradigmatic disciple in the church. Jesus has brought Peter and the disciples around a new charcoal fire (ἀνθρακιά) and provided a meal of bread and fish (vv. 9–13). The charcoal fire is a narrative marker that calls to mind Peter's last scene of covenant breach with Jesus. The meal calls to mind their final meal together before Jesus' passion, and has been characterized as a covenant renewal ceremony similar to the ritual covenant meals of the OT (see John 13:1–11; Gen 26:26–30; 31:43–54; Exod 24:5–11; Deut 27:6–7). Although all seven disciples are involved in the meal and its aftermath, the narrative has placed a steady focus on Peter (vv. 3, 7, 11), and the reconciliation of Peter's relationship with Jesus will take center stage in the following verses (vv. 15–22). As Timothy Wiarda has noted, Jesus "confronts Peter at every stage in the narrative, upsetting

---

10. Brown, *John*, 2:1097; Moloney, *John*, 551; Schneiders, "John 21:1–14"; Talbert, *Reading John*, 260. Many interpretations of the number of fish have been suggested. For a survey, see Beasley-Murray, *John*, 401–4. For the argument that, using *gematria*, the 153 fish represents "the children of God" (בני האלהים) that make up the community of believers, see Romeo, "Gematria and John 21:11."

11. Chennattu, *Johannine Discipleship*, 171. For her discussion of the covenantal motif of the abundance of fish and the unbroken net, see 171–73.

his equilibrium and challenging him to make decisions and take new action."[12]

In this context of a covenant meal, Jesus asks Peter three times if he loves him (ἀγαπᾷς με; vv. 15, 16; φιλεῖς με; v. 17), reconstituting Peter's three-time denial into a binding relationship with the consequences of mission and leadership.[13] Jesus initiates the dialogue with the comparative "more than these" (πλέον τούτον, v. 15), a phrase that has generated much scholarly debate.[14] Understanding Jesus' question of Peter's love for him as a comparison to Peter's love for other things, including his former way of life, calls to mind the absolute claim for love and commitment that God makes on those who enter into covenant in the OT (see esp. Deut 6:5; 7:9; 10:12; 11:1; 13:3; 30:36), which is set over against everything else (see Josh 22:5).[15] Jesus' threefold question and Peter's threefold response reconciles their breached relationship and renews the covenant between them. Jesus' commands that follow from this renewed covenant articulate Peter's mission as action in service of the new covenant community. He is to "feed" and "tend" the flock (vv. 15, 16, 17). Peter's leadership is clarified pastorally as he is mandated as the new shepherd of the burgeoning flock of the children of God. Peter's journey then comes to an end as Jesus demands his obedience and implicates his eventual crucifixion in parallel to Jesus' own: "Follow me" (vv. 19, 22).[16]

Then what of the Beloved Disciple? The evangelist must speak to the destiny and mortality of the disciple whom Jesus loved, who has journeyed and abided with Jesus throughout the Gospel story. The narrator closes by describing the unique mandate of the Beloved Disciple

12. Wiarda, "John 21:1–23," 53.

13. For a detailed study of the diction of vv. 15–17 that suggests the evangelist's word choice is "gently significant" in the progression of the dialogue, see McKay, "Style and Significance."

14. Some scholars, including Barrett (*St. John*, 584) and Carson (*John*, 677), argue that the comparison is between Peter's love for Jesus and the other disciples' love for Jesus. Other scholars, including Chennattu (*Johannine Discipleship*, 174–75) and Wiarda ("John 21.1–23," 62–63), argue that the comparison is between Peter's love for Jesus and Peter's love for other things, including his former life of fishing. Still others, including Brown (*John*, 2:1104) and Bultmann (*John*, 711), argue that the comparison is not determinative in this dialogue at all. I take the second position.

15. Chennattu, *Johannine Discipleship*, 175.

16. On John 21 as the culmination of a series of physical and metaphorical journeys, see Segovia, "Journey(s) of the Word," 50–51; Staley, *Print's First Kiss*, 72–73.

(vv. 21–25). He is the paradigmatic disciple and witness. Already in the first century of the church, there is a concern for the recognition of the pastoral role in authority and the testimonial role of discipleship. These roles do not have to be incorporated in one person. They can be, but they usually are not. The best disciple is not necessarily the shepherd of the community. Therefore, in this Gospel these roles are embodied in two separate characters, Peter and the Beloved Disciple. The narrator then concludes his story by attesting to its limitless nature (v. 25). He speaks in the first person and sends his readers into the world and their shared future as the new covenant community of God, children living in the love and faith of Jesus.

Covenant as a Guiding Literary Paradigm

In these concluding sections, we will synthesize the narrative force of the literary and theological theme of covenant in the Gospel according to John. We can then close the present study by speculating upon the meaning of living in covenant relationship for the first-century Johannine community as well the impact of this underlying theme upon readers of the Fourth Gospel.

In the introduction to his work on the passion narrative in the Gospel of John, Charles Giblin claims that "as every Irishman knows, the meaning of a story lies largely in the way it is told. For each storyteller wants himself to be understood appreciatively through his own way of telling the tale, whether that tale is not as yet known or, and indeed preferably, if it already is. That is how the storyteller functions as a teacher."[17] Giblin's assertion is more pertinent for the Gospel of John than for the other canonical Gospels, and possibly more than for any other narrative in biblical literature. The Fourth Evangelist is the consummate storyteller, and his distinctive style has captivated readers and writers since his version of the good news of Jesus Christ first circulated. Therefore, to attempt to gauge the impact of this Gospel and the storytelling techniques of its author, we can begin with the basic fact that the evangelist chose to crystallize his experience of and catechism on the good news as a story. Narratives can be used to do a number of things, but there are three basic phenomena that narratives can be

---

17. Giblin, "Confrontations," 215.

understood to manifest well.[18] First, narratives encourage in their audiences a sense of affinity, or identification, with their central character or characters. Second, they are capable of indicating the rich interrelations among the many forces that help to shape human experiences in concrete situations. Third, narratives work to draw their audiences into their worlds so as to undergird shared values or to challenge the imaginations and views of their audiences as well as their thoughts and practices. The Fourth Evangelist composes his story of the gospel from his received traditions in his unique manner by using all the storytelling techniques at his disposal to build and bond his community. In this way he also shapes its self-understanding, mission, and practice as the true children of God living in covenant relationship through the received gift of truth and life in the name of Jesus.

In the first chapter of the present study we saw that the juxtaposition of historical narrative and theological discourse is so pronounced in the Johannine story of Jesus that a number of scholars over the past century have suggested a relationship between the Fourth Gospel and ancient drama. These studies on dramatic character all highlight one phenomenon in particular: speech is action in this story of the gospel event. Much of what *happens* in the Gospel according to John happens when Jesus of Nazareth is in dialogue with other characters in the story. Thus, much can be gleaned from studying the Gospel through the prism of dialogue. The image of the prism is particularly helpful here, as these dialogues are truly multifaceted. On the narrative level, the evangelist does indeed advance his story of Jesus through these dialogical interactions. At the same time, on the discourse or meta-narrative level, the evangelist employs these dialogues symbolically to present Jesus as the revelatory incarnate Word of God and to illustrate how the children of God are to respond in relationship with that Word. Working in conversation with scholars of dramatic criticism, as well as the Greek and Roman tragedies themselves, Jo-Ann Brant analyzes speech as action in the Gospel, observing that the "prominent role that dialogue and direct speech play in the Fourth Gospel calls for attention to the capacity of language to perform multiple functions in one literary context."[19] Language thus works in the Fourth Gospel in a manner comparable to

---

18. For these three basic attributes of narratives, see Achtemeier, Green, and Thompson, *New Testament*, 124.

19. Brant, *Dialogue and Drama*, 75.

theatrical discourse in terms of speech as gesture and speech as deed. The characteristics of these forms of indicative language and patterns of speech-action in John's plot, in concert with an appreciation of the overall dramatic flavor of the Gospel, augmented the examination of several key dialogues over the course of the narrative. Despite the fact that the term "covenant" does not appear, these analyses were able to focus on the evangelist's use of the OT covenant metaphor to underpin the theological fabric of the good news he writes for his community.

The primary manner by which the Scriptures of Israel render understandable the relationship between God and creation, in general, and Israel, in particular, is in terms of covenant. Chapter 2 of the present work focused on a literary reading of the covenantal narrative preserved in the OT. That study concluded by articulating five fundamental characteristics of the essence of biblical covenant texts and the covenantal relationship these texts emanate. The first and most fundamental characteristic is the aspect of *chosenness*. The second element characteristic of the OT covenant relationship is the offer of *covenantal promises*. Those chosen by God to participate in covenant relationship are made promises as part and parcel of establishing that particular obligation. The third characteristic that manifests from a literary rehearsal of the biblical narrative is the corollary human response to the first two characteristic covenantal moves on God's part: *covenantal obedience in action*. The first three articulated characteristics of the OT covenant relationship each build upon the former to establish the relationship itself. Taken together, these three characteristics and the resultant relationship they form make possible the fourth characteristic: *the abiding presence of God* in creation and in the lives of those who accept the covenantal offer. Articulating the final characteristic of the OT covenant relationship in many ways brings us to the purpose of the entire activity: making God known in creation. The fifth basic characteristic is thus *the knowledge of God*. This knowledge (דַּעַת) includes understanding God's binding loyalty (in terms of steadfast covenant love: חֶסֶד) and faithfulness (in terms of truth: אֱמֶת) in kinship with his people (see Hos 4:1–3).[20] The flourishing of this knowledge of God made possible through the dynamic of daily living in covenantal obedience breathes life into the relationship between God and his people. Likewise, however, the failure

---

20. For detail of this claim, see Cross, *Epic to Canon*, 3–20; and de Menezes, *Voices from Beyond*, 110–13.

or wearing out of this knowledge (see Isa 5:13) threatens the very existence of the covenantal relationship. To live in the truth of the love and knowledge of God, then, is the fundamental purpose and the overarching hope of the OT covenant relationship.

The OT covenantal texts and the celebrations that recall God's covenantal and saving action in the past and render that action present in the current community provide the symbolism for ongoing use of the covenant metaphor. The themes gleaned from a narrative review of the OT covenant texts provide the language used to articulate this hope and its resulting lived experience in the literary expression of this covenantal relationship between God and humankind. The language of knowledge, love, truth, and familial kinship in the context of Israel's Scripture is thus the language of covenant.

In the opening sections of chapter 3, we saw how recent scholarship on the Fourth Evangelist's self-understanding as a writer of Scripture, particularly that of Dwight Moody Smith and Francis J. Moloney, is crucial to the present study because it provides a response to the why question. The evangelist made use of the literary technique of weaving the OT covenant metaphor through the fabric of his Gospel, as a guiding narrative motif evinced through both symbolism and dialogue, as a key component of his established mission not only to continue but further to bring the biblical story to an end, even its *telos*, through his Scripture of the narrative of Jesus Christ. In the culmination of his argument, Moloney asserts:

> The use of "fulfillment" language in the second half of the Gospel, culminating in 19:28–30, shows that the author claims to have brought the story of Israel's Scripture to an end. As this is the case, the story the evangelist tells, heard and read by later generations, is ἡ γραφή: the completion of Israel's Scripture. Indeed, as he closes his Gospel account, he tells all who have heard and read the Scripture of the Johannine Gospel that it has been written precisely for that purpose (20:30–31).[21]

Since the metaphor of covenant is the primary concept that characterizes and unifies OT literature, particularly the biblical narrative of Israel, God's covenantal relationship with creation in general and the children of God (see 1:12; 11:52) in particular is the fundamental means by which the evangelist can resonate the word of Scripture and

21. Moloney, "John as Scripture," 466.

the Johannine community can be drawn into the sacred narrative of that Scripture.

This process is begun in the prologue to the Gospel (1:1–18). The bulk of chapter 3 presented an analysis of the prologue that focused on the covenantal underpinnings of this first page of the narrative. Jesus, the Word become flesh who dwelt among his own in creation, is revealed to be the gift which is truth (χάριτος καὶ ἀληθείας, v. 14) that follows and perfects the former gift (χάριν ἀντὶ χάριτος, v. 16) of the Law of the Sinai covenant, given through Moses (ὅτι ὁ νόμος διὰ Μωϋσέως ἐδόθη, ἡ χαρὶς καὶ ἡ ἀλήθεια διὰ Ἰησοῦ Χριστοῦ ἐγένετο, v. 17). Jesus Christ makes God known (ἐκεῖνος ἐξηγήσατο, v. 18), and all who receive him, who believe in his name, are given the power to become children of God (ἔδωκεν αὐτοῖς ἐξουσίαν τέκνα θεοῦ γενέσθαι, v. 12).

In the Gospel according to John, "children of God" is the operative designation of those who receive and believe in Jesus and thus of the Johannine community (1:12; 11:52; implied in 3:3, 5, 7, 8, and 8:31–44; see also 1 John). This term also describes those who are restored to new life in the Messiah based in the covenant story of Israel.[22] As such, the "children of God," as the objects of the empowering of the Word in 1:12 and the fathering and unification in 11:52, are the true covenant community. Both Alan Culpepper and John Dennis have shown that the language of family, and particularly "children of God," is an essential characterization of God's covenant people.[23] The Fourth Evangelist writes to place his community, despite any current hardship and alienation, in the genealogy of that family tree.

The life engendered by this process is not static; it is a dynamic relationship and by no means easy to achieve. Therefore, on the model of the Abraham narrative of Genesis 12–22, the evangelist characterizes the people in his Gospel story as walking a journey with Christ.[24] The Beloved Disciple is the character to appear to walk in union with Jesus throughout his mission. This is why he is understood as the paradigmatic disciple. Yet he is not the only one to respond to the challenge the Jesus poses, which the present study has argued is the challenge of

---

22. Dennis, *Jesus' Death*, 259.

23. See Culpepper, "Pivot"; and Dennis, *Jesus' Death*, 247–92.

24. See chapter 2 for more on Abraham's journey of faith in Gen 12–22. On journeys in the Fourth Gospel, see Segovia, "Journey(s) of the Word"; and Staley, *Print's First Kiss*, 72–73.

living in a new covenant relationship with God through Jesus. Some people respond positively and accept the gift of truth that Jesus gives. Others are not open to God's revelation in Jesus and respond negatively, rejecting Jesus and the gift he gives. Still others are characterized as either responding ambivalently or not understanding the relationship at stake and the gift of truth manifested in Jesus.

Chapter 4 presented the mother of Jesus as the representative figure of those who accept the covenantal challenge of Jesus. The story of her encounter and dialogue with Jesus at the wedding feast of Cana (2:1–12) was embedded in the symbolism of Pentecost and God's covenantal gift of the Law at Sinai. The mother of Jesus was presented as the first to receive the gift and believe as she inaugurated the public ministry of Jesus. Covenantal obedience in action was further portrayed as the servants participated in her faith by acting on the word of Jesus.

Chapter 5 presented the encounter and dialogues between Jesus and "the Jews" at the Feast of Tabernacles, to show how "the Jews" are representative of those who ultimately reject Jesus and God's ongoing covenant relationship revealed in Jesus. The symbolism of the abiding presence of God at the Feast of Tabernacles, associated with both the Sinai covenant and God's care and guidance during the wilderness experience, as well as hopes for the coming of the Messiah and messianic age, served as the backdrop for this encounter. The covenantal language that dominated the dialogues included that of abiding with Jesus, knowledge of God (reflecting the covenant lawsuit of the Prophets), and the identity of the true children of Abraham and thereby of God.

Chapter 6 presented Pilate as one who, through his dialogue with Jesus at the Roman trial, represents those who do not understand the gift of truth at stake in the mission and person of Jesus. Throughout the passion narrative, the language of knowledge and truth pervades the dialogues. The question of the truth revealed in Jesus reaches its pinnacle in the dialogues between Jesus and Pilate. Although beyond the scope of this study, the story of Nicodemus, which begins with his dialogue with Jesus at night in John 3 and ends in his open participation in the burial of Jesus in John 19, is representative of those whose response to Jesus is ambivalent, whose journey of faith is a lengthy process of finding their way. Interspersed across this Gospel narrative is also the story of the rest of the disciples, led by Peter, with whom readers identify and participate in their journey of becoming children of God in the faith, knowledge, and love of the truth of God's revelation in Jesus.

The symbolism and language of covenant are thus woven metaphorically throughout the settings and dialogical encounters of the Fourth Gospel as Jesus challenges all those whom he encounters to accept or reject the relationship he offers. Regarding the phenomenon of acceptance and rejection in the Gospel, Sharon Ringe notes:

> The entire Gospel narrative is the story of the interplay of the acceptance and rejection of Jesus. Those who follow him and "remain" with him (and he with them) constitute the insiders of the Johannine community, those born ἄνωθην as children of God (1:12; 3:1-10). Others reject him (and ultimately his followers as well, as in 15:18-24 and 16:1-4) and bear labels that in this Gospel identify outsiders (principally "the world" and "the Jews"). This dynamic is played out in virtually every segment of this Gospel, but it can be seen with particular clarity in 3:17-21, 31-36; 5:1-18, 39-47; 6:25-66; 7:1-13; 8:31-39; 9:1-41; 10:19, 24, 31; 11:45-53; 12:42-43; and, of course, the passion narrative (chapters 18-19).... Thus, Jesus as the incarnate λόγος ... serves as the point of discrimination between insiders and outsiders. In that way, [the evangelist] establishes the boundaries of the community to which this Gospel is addressed.[25]

This community to which the Fourth Evangelist addressed his Gospel in order to draw them into the sacred narrative of Scripture is made up of those who have accepted the gift of covenant made possible through belief in Jesus Christ. The evangelist writes to these children of God so that, despite any current experience of suffering and alienation, they can understand themselves as God's new covenant community firmly rooted in the story of the word and action of God in history and forged in the revelation of the glory of God in Jesus Christ. We can now conclude by reflecting upon how the covenant metaphor could be used effectively as the underlying literary fabric of the evangelist's Scripture for his community, and why he might have employed covenant as a guiding literary paradigm for his fledgling Christian community in the subtle and nuanced manner he does.

---

25. Ringe, *Wisdom's Friends*, 55.

Covenant through Word in the Gospel of John

> John told his story of Jesus for his community. This means that there are two fundamental levels in the communication process sought by the evangelist: (1) the level internal to the text, which portrays the ongoing periods of the narration from the preexistence to the post-existence of Jesus Christ; (2) the level of the Johannine community, external to the text, for which John conceived the story of Jesus in order to lead them to the knowledge and understanding of the saving work of God in Jesus Christ. The interpreter must always keep both levels in mind since John intends his story of Jesus for the community but at the same time binds the community to the story of Jesus.[26]

Udo Schnelle's observations are restated here as he articulates the narrative and discourse levels of the Gospel of John in terms of the evangelist and the community for which he composed his version of the good news of God's action in Jesus. Schnelle goes on to argue that the Gospel unfolds "as a post-Easter remembering (*anamnesis*) that is brought about by the power of the Spirit" that allows the evangelist to "translate theological insights into narrated history" for his community and simultaneously provides them with a direction for the future.[27] Schnelle then suggests that this process is what makes the form of the Fourth Gospel both understandable and effective for its readers. He explains:

> In comparison to the Synoptics, John clothes the story of Jesus for his hearers and readers in new concepts, symbols, and stories (see, e.g., John 2:1–11; 3:1–11; 4:4–42; 10:1–18; 13:1–20; 15:1–8; 20:11–18). He introduces new people, names, and groups into the Jesus story (the Beloved Disciple: 1:35–42; 13:23–26a; 18:15–18; 19:25–27, 34b–35; 20:1–8; Nathanael: 1:45–49; Nicodemus: 3:1, 4, 9; 7:50; 19:39; the "Greeks": 12:20–21; Malchus: 18:10, 26; Annas: 18:13, 24); creates surprising sequences of events (see, e.g., 2:12–13; 5–6; 7:9–10; 14:31—15:1); draws toward the front central events in the life of Jesus (cleansing of the temple: 2:14–22; plot to kill Jesus: 11:46–54; anointing at Bethany: 12:1–8; entry into Jerusalem: 12:12–19; Gethsemane: 12:27–36); expands individual scenes into narrative blocks (e.g., expanding the fare-

---

26. Schnelle, "Recent Views," 255–56.

27. Ibid., 256. For detailed exposition of this claim, see Schnelle, *Human Condition*.

well scene at the last supper into the farewell discourses); and provides the story of Jesus with an unexpected dramatic sense (see, e.g., John 7 and 8)—all done to make the tradition fruitful for a new time and a new situation.[28]

These observations lead to inquiries on the nature and context of the Johannine community as well as what the content and goal of the Johannine discourse might be.[29] In his study on the restoration themes in the Gospel of John, John Dennis suggests that, based on the entirety of the Gospel, "those who receive [Jesus] in Judea or elsewhere will become 'children of God,' for the designation 'children of God' stands for the totality of the Messianic community, the true Israel."[30] As far as the evangelist is concerned, the "who" of his community are the children of God, whatever their ethnic background and identity. This designation is crucial for understanding the intent of the evangelist but does not fully answer the question of what his catechetical goal in writing might be. In this vein Jo-Ann Brant observes:

> Instead of asking, "Who are the children of God?"—that is, inquiring about who is in and out—the question that the Fourth Gospel addresses seems to be, "What does it mean to be children of God?" The irony of the gospel made all the more pronounced by its allegiance to dramatic form, expresses an epistemology of hindsight. Knowledge is a privilege of vantage point. The action of the gospel leaves one with the impression that life lived as children of God, in truth, as opposed to children of a lie, will make clear the competing demands of life. Community may risk betrayal. Friendship may demand self-sacrifice. The righteous may suffer injustice. The certainty that it offers is not a retreat into the kind of false security offered by Caiaphas. Jesus' invitation to Simon Peter to follow him is an invitation to give up safety. It is not a denial of suffering and death. In order to become children of God, we must freely step into a world of

---

28. Schnelle, "Recent Views of John's Gospel," 256–57.

29. Moloney notes that "the 'story' is the sequence of events along a timeline, during which characters interact and develop as a plot unfolds, etc. 'Discourse' is the underlying meaning the storyteller wishes to communicate to a reader *by means of* the story" (see Brown, *Introduction to the Gospel of John*, 290 n. 26). For more on the relation of story and discourse, see Chatman, *Story and Discourse*. On implicit commentary in this Gospel, see Culpepper, *Anatomy of the Fourth Gospel*, 151–202.

30. Dennis, *Jesus' Death*, 258.

contingency in which we relinquish the security of associations and make ourselves vulnerable to death.[31]

For the Fourth Evangelist then, living life as the children of God is thus living a life of truth in the Word of God, but this is not to say that such a call is easy. This life includes knowledge of God, love, and community, but it also includes the potentiality and even eventuality of separation, alienation, and persecution. This is the evangelist's particular challenge, and the fruit of persevering as the children of God through this experience is his particular discourse for his readers. But why is this so?

The proposed influences on the religious thought of the Fourth Evangelist and the context of the Johannine community have been the focus of much discussion in modern Johannine scholarship. The three most frequently suggested contextual influences are Gnosticism, Hellenistic thought, and traditional Judaism.[32] As a result of twentieth-century archaeological finds at Nag Hammadi and Qumran, and following the groundbreaking work of J. Louis Martyn, a large number of scholars are coming to agree that the principal background for Johannine thought is the traditional Judaism of the first century AD.[33] The OT is the evangelist's essential literary backdrop throughout, and OT references and themes are woven into both the structure of the Fourth Gospel and the actions and words of Jesus it recounts, even when explicit OT citations are lacking.[34] In addition, some of the background of Jesus' thought can be found in the Pharisaic theology of his time, as known from the later rabbinic writings.[35] Further, the thought of Jesus in the

---

31. Brant, *Dialogue and Drama*, 231–32.

32. Brown, *Introduction to the Gospel of John*, 116. See 115–50 for Brown's full discussion of these influences with a summary avocation of traditional Judaism as the primary context of the Johannine community and influence on the religious thought of the evangelist.

33. Ibid., 132. I am following Brown's decision to use the broader term "traditional Judaism" in lieu of the more common "Palestinian Judaism." He uses the term "traditional" to describe "a Judaism that took its main inspiration from what we call the OT (including the deuterocanonical books) without conscious adoption of large amounts of extrabiblical Hellenistic philosophy/theology. After the Babylonian exile this Judaism had undergone Persian and Greek influence and had reacted in different ways, so that it was far from monolithic. Indeed, its very diversity helps to explain different aspects of Johannine thought" (ibid.). See also Martyn, *History and Theology*. For more on the relationship between the Gospel and the findings at Qumran, see the various studies in Charlesworth, ed., *John and the Dead Sea Scrolls*.

34. Hanson, *Prophetic Gospel*, 234–53. See also Barrett, "Old Testament."

35. Brown, *Introduction to the Gospel of John*, 138–39, 142.

Fourth Gospel "is expressed in a peculiar theological vocabulary and outlook" that is consonant with the Jewish Qumran group in Palestine.[36] Therefore, behind the Fourth Evangelist's theological conceptualization as well as the Johannine community's developing Christian context lies a complex combination of various forms of religious thinking and expression that were current in Judaism and Palestine during Jesus' lifetime and the generations after his death.

Traditional Judaism also forms a large component of the context of the Johannine community. The opponents of Jesus in the Gospel, identified as "the Jews," likely correlate with the opponents of the Johannine community. They "were doubtless ethnically Jewish people with a fierce commitment to the religion of Israel, especially as it was being established after the devastations of the Jewish War" (AD 66–70).[37] The Gospel indicates that these opponents are in a position of authority in the culture of Jewish society. This group casts out the man born blind from the synagogue (9:22, 34), and some of their number are afraid to confess that Jesus is the Messiah lest they too be cast out of the synagogue (12:42). Jesus explicitly warns his disciples that they will be thrown out of the synagogue and even killed by people who understand their own actions as giving praise to God (16:2). Across the Gospel, these opponents are portrayed as systematically rejecting Jesus and those who believe and follow him. The Fourth Gospel thus arises from a context in which those who believed and confessed that Jesus is the Christ were forcibly excluded from the synagogue.[38] Therefore, however diverse the Johannine community may have been, many of its members were ethnically Jewish and committed to the religion of Israel. As John Ashton has noted so eloquently, one must "recognize in these hot-tempered exchanges the type of family row in which the participants face one another across the room of a house that all have shared and all call home."[39] This is the context into which the Fourth Evangelist writes his Gospel.

The Gospel according to John states its purpose in the conclusion of the body of the narrative (20:30–31). It is devoted to confirming the faith of those who already believe and giving them further catechesis of

---

36. Ibid., 143.
37. Moloney, *John*, 10.
38. Ibid., 11.
39. Ashton, *Understanding the Fourth Gospel*, 151.

that faith. Raymond Brown notes that "the Gospel was written in good part to deepen the faith of believers so that they could understand that what they had gained by way of God's life more than made up for what had been lost in their former religious adhesion."[40] What we see in this Gospel is a strong emphasis on events in Jesus' ministry that foreshadow the sacramental life of the church. The evangelist speaks to a Christian audience that depends upon baptism and the Eucharist for that life. Thus, he does not mention these institutions, but presupposes them through references to living water and rebirth, as well as living bread and the wine of the new dispensation. Brown further suggests the entire theological basis for the sacramental system is found in this Gospel.[41] He states, "In general, John's theology of a divine Word who comes from a heavenly world and expresses himself in the language of this world is a highly sacramental approach if sacraments are understood as external signs that give God's grace."[42] And yet references to these community rituals are descriptive and symbolic, while direct identifications are not included or necessary. I suggest the Fourth Evangelist does something similar with the word "covenant," understood as the metaphor by which God's relationship with humankind is "expressed in the language of this world," though arguably for a different reason.

Arthur Dewey presents the concept of witness in the Johannine literature as "a revision through memory," an image of the past that combines recollections of Jesus with "both the Gospel story (viewed from the perspective of its conclusion) and the resources of Jewish scripture."[43] The Gospel according to John integrates witness to the Word of God in the written form of the Torah, the revelation of God in the incarnate form that is Jesus Christ, and the present reality and future hope of his community. Therefore, a corollary to the primary

---

40. Brown, *Introduction to the Gospel of John*, 182. For his full discussion on the purpose of the Gospel as encouragement to believing Christians, Gentile and Jew, see 180–83.

41. Brown, "The Johannine Sacramentary Reconsidered." For Brown's most recent survey of sacramentalism in the Gospel, see Brown, *Introduction to the Gospel of John*, 229–34. Brown suggests that these days "most scholars recognize some form of sacramentalism" and names explicitly Cullman, Corell, Bouyer, Vawter, Niewalda, Stanley, Hoskyns, Lightfoot, Barrett, Becker, Boismard-Lamouille, Lindars, Schnackenburg, Schneider, Schulz, and Moloney (229–31).

42. Ibid., 230.

43. Dewey, "Eyewitness of History," 68.

purpose of the Gospel, confirming the faith of the believing community, is connected to the location and cultural milieu of the community and their vision for the future. The larger Hellenistic world of the community and the Gospel it produced demanded a narrative that recast the Jewish story of Jesus in the language and style of the Greco-Roman world. The expulsion of the Christians from the synagogues also necessitated a telling of the story that explained how the one who claimed to be the Jewish Messiah became known as Messiah to Christians instead. George MacRae has suggested that the Fourth Evangelist consciously incorporated into his Gospel different attitudes, symbols, and traditions in order to reach out to as many religious backgrounds and experiences as possible, and so that his work would have appeal in the universalizing and transcendent Hellenistic religious world.[44] Ultimately, as a foundational document, the Gospel according to John attempts both to appropriate the traditions of Israel for the emerging faith and to reorient the movement away from the Israelite world of its past and toward the Greco-Roman world of its future.

In many ways the evangelist was doing exactly what the rabbis of post-AD 70 Judaism were doing. Facing new crises of life without the temple, for the rabbis, and life beyond the synagogue, for the evangelist, these community leaders had to reorient their teaching (including their terminology), their literature, and their community. This is why the evangelist uses the language and symbolism of covenant and the metaphor of fulfillment throughout the text in the subtle and nuanced manner he does. The term "covenant" will remain a part of the technical language of the synagogue and post-AD 70 Judaism. Life in the synagogue as well as celebrations of the Jewish feasts and the language and ritual associated with them are part of the Johannine community's past. The Fourth Evangelist is thus taking on the challenge of incorporating his community's need for being grounded in God's saving action of the past while reorienting his community members into the Greco-Roman world of the future. This process, however painful, is necessary for their survival. Therefore he uses the language and symbolism of covenant, while forgoing the term itself in favor of the language of knowledge,

---

44. MacRae, "Fourth Gospel." See also Brown, *Introduction to the Gospel of John*, 182. For more on historical references in the rhetoric of the Gospel, see Davies, *Rhetoric and Reference*, 242–315.

love, and truth, which is also consonant with the culture and society of their future.

The Fourth Evangelist, understanding himself to be writing Scripture, is articulating for his community the continuation of God's covenantal work in creation through the new community founded on truth and belief in the revelation of the Word of God. The Gospel according to John becomes the lifeline for the fledgling Johannine community to find their genealogy in the story of Israel and God's saving covenantal relationship with that chosen people of God. At the same time, the community is able to perceive its future in a world that is the perfection of that story, where the revelation of God in Jesus, God's gift of truth, has set all of humankind free to accept and believe in the Word of God and to live in covenant relationship with that Word as the true children of God.

Bibliography

Abbott, H. P. *The Cambridge Introduction to Narrative*. Cambridge: Cambridge University Press, 2002.
Achtemeier, P. J., J. B. Green, and M. M. Thompson. *Introducing the New Testament: Its Literature and Theology*. Grand Rapids: Eerdmans, 2001.
Alter, R. *The Art of Biblical Narrative*. New York: Basic Books, 1981.
———. *The David Story: A Translation with Commentary of 1 and 2 Samuel*. New York: Norton, 1999.
Alter, R., and F. Kermode, editors. *The Literary Guide to the Bible*. Cambridge, MA: Belknap, 1987.
Anderson, B. W., S. Bishop, and J. H. Newman. *Understanding the Old Testament*. 5th ed. Upper Saddle River, NJ: Pearson Prentice Hall, 2007.
Anderson, G. "The Interpretation of Genesis 1:1 in the Targums." *CBQ* 52 (1990) 21–29.
Ashton, J. *Understanding the Fourth Gospel*. Oxford: Clarendon, 1991.
Asiedu-Peprah, M. *Johannine Sabbath Conflicts as Juridical Controversy*. WUNT 2/132. Tübingen: Mohr/Siebeck, 2001.
Austin, J. L. *How to Do Things with Words*. Cambridge: Harvard University Press, 1962.
Bal, M., editor. *Anti-Covenant: Counter-Reading Women's Lives in the Hebrew Bible*. BLS 22. JSOTSup 81. Sheffield: Almond, 1989.
———. *Narratology: Introduction to the Theory of Narrative*. Translated by Christine van Boheemen. 2nd ed. Toronto: University of Toronto Press, 1997.
Baltzer, K. *The Covenant Formulary; in Old Testament, Jewish, and Early Christian Writings*. Translated by D. E. Green. Philadelphia: Fortress, 1971.
Bammel, E. "Philos tou Kaisaros." *TLZ* 77 (1952) 205–10.
———. "Joh 7:35 in Manis Lebensbeschreibung." *NovT* 15 (1973) 191–92.
Bampfylde, G. "John xix 28: A Case for a Different Translation." *NovT* 11 (1969) 247–60.
———. "More Light on John 12:34." *JSNT* 17 (1983) 87–89.
Bar-Efrat, S. *Narrative Art in the Bible*. BLS 17. JSOTSup 70. Sheffield: Almond, 1989.
Barnhart, B. *The Good Wine: Reading John from the Center*. New York: Paulist, 1993.
Barrett, C. K. "The Old Testament in the Fourth Gospel." *JTS* 48 (1947) 155–69.
———. *The Gospel according to St. John: An Introduction with Commentary and Notes on the Greek Text*. 2nd ed. Philadelphia: Westminster, 1978.
———. *The Gospel of John and Judaism*. London: SPCK, 1975.
———. *The Prologue of St John's Gospel*. London: Athlone, 1971.
Barrosse, T. "The Seven Days of the New Creation in St. John's Gospel." *CBQ* 23 (1959) 507–16.

Baum-Bodenbender, R. *Hoheit in Niedrigkeit: Johanneische Christologie im Prozess Jesu vor Pilatus (Joh 18,28—19,16a)*. FB 49. Würzburg: Echter, 1984.
Beasley-Murray, G. R. *John*. WBC 36. Waco: Word, 1987.
Belle, G. van. "Jn 4,48 et la Foi du Centurian." *ETL* 61 (1985) 167–69.
———. "The Meaning of ΣΗΜΕΙΑ in Jn 20,30–31." *ETL* 74 (1998) 300–25.
Benoit, P. "Praetorium, Lithostroton and Gabbatha." *RB* 59 (1952) 531–50.
Berlin, A. *Poetics and Interpretation of Biblical Narrative*. BLS 9. Sheffield: Almond, 1983.
Bienaimé, G. *Moïse et le Don de l'Eau dans la Tradition Juive Ancienne: Targum et Midrash*. AnBib 98. Rome: Biblical Institute Press, 1984.
Birch, B. C. *1 and 2 Samuel*. 2 vols. NIB. Nashville: Abingdon, 1998.
Blenkinsopp, J. *Ezra-Nehemiah: A Commentary*. OTL. Philadelphia: Westminster, 1988.
Boguslazwski, S. "Jesus' Mother and the Bestowal of the Spirit." *IBS* 14 (1992) 106–29.
Boismard, M.-E. *Du Baptême à Cana (Jean 1,19—2,11)*. LD 18. Paris: Cerf, 1956.
———. "La Connaissance de Dieu dans l'Alliance Nouvelle d'après la première lettre de S. Jean." *RB* 56 (1949) 365–91.
———. "Je ferai avec vous une alliance nouvelle." *LV* 8 (1953) 94–109.
———. *L'Evangile de Jean: Études et Problèmes*. RechBib 3. Bruges: Desclée de Brouwer, 1958.
———. *St. John's Prologue*. Translated by Carisbrooke Dominicans. London: Blackfriars, 1957.
———. "La Royauté Universelle du Christ (Jn 18,33–37)." *AsSeign* 88 (1966) 33–45.
———. "Les Traditions Johanniques concernant le Baptiste." *RB* 70 (1963) 5–42.
Booth, W. C. *The Rhetoric of Fiction*. 2nd ed. Chicago: University of Chicago Press, 1983.
Borgen, P. *Bread from Heaven: An Exegetical Study of the Concept of Manna in the Gospel of John and the Writings of Philo*. NovTSup 10. Leiden: Brill, 1965.
———. "Logos Was the True Light: Contributions to the Interpretation of the Prologue of John." *NovT* 14 (1972) 115–30.
———. "John 6: Tradition, Interpretation and Composition." In *From Jesus to John: Essays on Jesus and New Testament Christology in Honour of Marinus de Jonge*, edited by M. C. De Boer, 268–91. JSNTSup 84. Sheffield: JSOT Press, 1993.
———. "Observations on the Targumic Character of the Prologue of John." *NTS* 16 (1970) 288–95.
Botha, J. E. *Jesus and the Samaritan Woman: A Speech Act Reading of John 4:1–42*. NovTSup 65. Leiden: Brill, 1991.
Botterweck, G. J. "ידע." In *TDOT* 448–81.
Bowen, C. R. "The Fourth Gospel as Dramatic Material." *JBL* 49 (1930) 292–305.
———. "Love in the Fourth Gospel." *JR* 13 (1933) 39–49.
———. "Notes on the Fourth Gospel." *JBL* 43 (1924) 22–27.
Boyarin, D. "The Gospel of the Memra: Jewish Binitarianism and the Prologue to John." *HTR* 94 (2001) 243–84.
Brant, J. A. *Dialogue and Drama: Elements of Greek Tragedy in the Fourth Gospel*. Peabody, MA: Hendrickson, 2004.
Breck, J. "John 21: Appendix, Epilogue or Conclusion." *St. Vladimir's Theological Quarterly* 36 (1992) 27–49.

Brown, R. E. *The Death of the Messiah: From Gethsemane to the Grave. A Commentary on the Passion Narratives in the Four Gospels*. 2 vols. ABRL. New York: Doubleday, 1994.

———. *The Gospel according to John*. 2 vols. AB 29-29a. Garden City, NY: Doubleday, 1966-70.

———. *An Introduction to the Gospel of John*. Edited by F. J. Moloney. ABRL. New York: Doubleday, 2003.

———. "The Johannine Sacramentary Reconsidered." *TS* 23 (1962) 183-206.

———. "The Passion according to John: Chapters 18 and 19." *Worship* 49 (1975) 126-34.

———. "The Resurrection in John 20: A Series of Diverse Reactions." *Worship* 64 (1990) 194-206.

———. "Three Quotations from John the Baptist in the Gospel of John." *CBQ* 22 (1960) 292-98.

Brueggemann, W. *Genesis*. Interpretation. Atlanta: John Knox, 1982.

Bultmann, R. K. *The Gospel of John: A Commentary*. Translated by G. R. Beasley-Murray. Philadelphia: Westminster, 1971.

Byrne, B. "The Faith of the Beloved Disciple and the Community in John 20." *JSNT* 23 (1985) 83-97.

Campenhausen, H. *Formation of the Christian Bible*. Translated by J. A. Baker. London: A & C Black, 1972.

Carson, D. A. *The Gospel according to John*. Grand Rapids: Eerdmans, 1991.

———. "The Purpose of the Fourth Gospel: John 20:31 Reconsidered." *JBL* 106 (1987) 639-51.

———. "Syntactical and Text-Critical Observations on John 20:30-31: One More Round on the Purpose of the Fourth Gospel." *JBL* 124 (2005) 693-714.

Cassem, N. H. "A Grammatical and Contextual Inventory of the Use of Cosmos in the Johannine Corpus with Some Implications for a Johannine Cosmic Theology." *NTS* (1972-73) 81-91.

Charlesworth, J. H., editor. *John and the Dead Sea Scrolls*. COL. New York: Crossroad, 1990.

Chatman, S. B. *Story and Discourse: Narrative Structure in Fiction and Film*. Ithaca, NY: Cornell University Press, 1978.

Chenderlin, F. *"Do This as My Memorial": The Semantic and Conceptual Background and Value of Anamnesis in 1 Corinthians 11:24-25*. AnBib 99. Rome: Biblical Institute Press, 1982.

Chennattu, R. M. "The Good Shepherd (Jn 10): A Political Perspective." *Jnanadeepa: Pune Journal of Religious Studies* 1 (1998) 93-105.

———. *Johannine Discipleship as Covenant Relationship*. Peabody, MA: Hendrickson, 2006.

Clark, D. J. "Criteria for Identifying Chiasm." *LB* 5 (1975) 63-72.

Collins, A. Y. "Narrative, History and Gospel." *Semeia* 43 (1988) 145-53.

Collins, J. J. "Marriage, Divorce, and Family in Second Temple Judaism." In *Families in Ancient Israel*, edited by L. J. Perdue, 104-62. The Family, Religion, and Culture. Louisville: Westminster John Knox, 1997.

Coloe, M. L. *Dwelling in the Household of God: Johannine Ecclesiology and Spirituality*. Collegeville, MN: Liturgical, 2007.

———. "Like Father, Like Son: The Role of Abraham in Tabernacles—John 8:31-59." *Pacifica* 12 (1999) 1-11.
———. "The Structure of the Johannine Prologue and Genesis 1." *ABR* 45 (1997) 40-55.
Connick, C. M. "The Dramatic Character of the Fourth Gospel." *JBL* 67 (1948) 159-69.
Conway, C. *Men and Women in the Fourth Gospel: Gender and Johannine Characterization*. SBLDS 167. Atlanta: Scholars, 1999.
Cory, C. "Wisdom's Rescue: A New Reading of the Tabernacles Discourse (John 7:1—8:59)." *JBL* 116 (1997) 96-116.
Cross, F. M. *From Epic to Canon: History and Literature in Ancient Israel*. Baltimore: Johns Hopkins University, 1998.
Cullmann, O. *The Christology of the New Testament*. Translated by Shirley C. Guthrie and Charles A. M. Hall. Philadelphia: Westminster, 1959.
Culpepper, R. A. *Anatomy of the Fourth Gospel: A Study in Literary Design*. FFNT. Philadelphia: Fortress, 1983.
———. "The Death of Jesus: An Exegesis of John 19:28-37." *FM* 5 (1988) 64-70.
———. "The Johannine *Hypodeigma*: A Reading of John 13." *Semeia* 53 (1991) 133-52.
———. "John 5.1-18: A Sample of Narrative Critical Commentary." In *The Gospel of John as Literature: An Anthology of Twentieth-Century Perspectives*, edited by M. W. G. Stibbe, 193-207. NTTS 17. Leiden: Brill, 1993.
———. "The Pivot of John's Prologue." *NTS* 27 (1980) 1-31.
———. "The Theology of the Johannine Passion Narrative: John 19:16b-30." *Neot* 31 (1997) 21-37.
Danby, H., translator. *The Mishnah: Translated from the Hebrew, with Introduction and Brief Explanatory Notes*. Oxford: Oxford University Press, 1933.
Davies, M. *Rhetoric and Reference in the Fourth Gospel*. JSNTSup 69. Sheffield: Sheffield Academic, 1992.
de la Potterie, I. "Jesus King and Judge according to John 19:13." *Scr* 13 (1961) 97-111.
———. *La Vérité dans Saint Jean*. 2 vols. AnBib 73-74. Rome: Biblical Institute Press, 1977.
———. "Structure du Prologue du Saint Jean." *NTS* 30 (1984) 354-81.
———. *The Hour of Jesus. The Passion and Resurrection of Jesus according to John: Text and Spirit*. Middlegreen, Slough: St. Paul Pub., 1989.
Delebecque, E. *Evangile de Jean: Texte Traduit et Annoté*. CahRB 23. Paris: Gabalda, 1987.
Dennis, J. A. *Jesus' Death and the Gathering of True Israel: The Johannine Appropriation of Restoration Theology in the Light of John 11:47-52*. WUNT 2/217. Tübingen: Mohr/Siebeck, 2006.
Dewailly, L. M. "D'où es-tu (Jean 19:9)." *RB* 92 (1985) 481-96.
Dewey, A. "The Eyewitness of History: Visionary Consciousness in the Fourth Gospel." In *Jesus in Johannine Tradition*, edited by R. T. Fortna and T. Thatcher, 59-70. Louisville: Westminster John Knox, 2001.
Dodd, C. H. *Historical Tradition in the Fourth Gospel*. Cambridge: Cambridge University Press, 1976.

---. *The Interpretation of the Fourth Gospel.* Cambridge: Cambridge University Press, 1960.
Domeris, W. R. "The Confession of Peter according to John 6:69." *TynBul* 44 (1993) 155–67.
---. "The Johannine Drama." *JTSA* 42 (1983) 29–35.
Du Rand, J. A. "A Story and a Community: Reading the First Farewell Discourse (John 13:31—14:31) from Narratological and Sociological Perspective." *Neot* 26 (1992) 31–45.
---. "A Syntactical and Narratological Reading of John 10 in Coherence with Chapter 9." In *The Shepherd Discourse of John 10 and Its Context*, edited by J. Beutler and R. T. Fortna, 94–115. SNTSMS 67. Cambridge: Cambridge University Press, 1991.
Duke, P. D. *Irony in the Fourth Gospel.* Atlanta: John Knox, 1985.
Edwards, R. B. "*Charin anti charitos* (John 1.16): Grace and Law in the Johannine Prologue." *JSNT* 32 (1988) 3–15.
Ehrman, B. D. "Jesus' Trial before Pilate: John 18:28—19:16." *BTB* 13 (1983) 124–31.
Eichrodt, W. *Theology of the Old Testament.* Translated by J. A. Baker. 2 vols. Old Testament Library. Philadelphia: Westminster, 1961–67.
Elam, K. *The Semiotics of Theatre and Drama.* London: Routledge, 1980.
Ellis, P. F. *The Genius of John: A Composition-Critical Commentary on the Fourth Gospel.* Collegeville, MN: Liturgical, 1984.
Faure, A. "Die alttestamentlichen Zitate im 4. Evangelium und die Quellenscheidungshypothese." *ZNW* 21 (1922) 99–121.
Fee, G. D. "On the Text and Meaning of John 20:30–31." In *The Four Gospels 1992: Festschrift Frans Neirynck*, edited by F. van Segbroeck et al., 2193–2206. 3 vols. BETL 100. Louvain: Louvain University Press, 1992.
Feuillet, A. *Le Prologue du Quatrième Évangile: Étude de théologie Johannique.* Paris: Desclée de Brouwer, 1968.
---. "La Signification théologique du second miracle de Cana (Jn IV,46–54)." In *Etudes Johanniques*, edited by A. Feuillet, 34–46. MLSB 4. Bruges: Desclée de Brouwer, 1962.
Flusser, D. "What Was the Original Meaning of *Ecce Homo* [Jn 19:5]." *Imm* 19 (1984–85) 30–40.
Ford, J. M. "Mingled Blood from the Side of Christ: John 19:34." *NTS* 15 (1969) 337–38.
Freed, E. D. "Ego Eimi in John 1:20 and 4:25." *CBQ* 41 (1979) 288–91.
---. "Ego Eimi in John 8:24 in the Light of Its Context and Jewish Messianic Belief." *JTS* 33 (1982) 163–67.
---. "John IV:51, PAIS or HUIOS." *JTS* 16 (1965) 448–49.
---. *Old Testament Quotations in the Gospel of John.* NovTSup 11. Leiden: Brill, 1965.
---. "Who or What Was before Abraham in John 8:58." *JSNT* 17 (1983) 52–59.
Freedman, D. N. "Divine Commitment and Human Obligation: The Covenant Theme." *Int* 18 (1964) 419–31.
Fuente, O. de la. "El Cumplimento de la Ley en la Nueva Aleanza segun los Profetas." *EstBib* 28 (1969) 293–311.
Garland, D. E. "John 18–19: Life through Jesus' Death." *RevExp* 85 (1988) 485–501.
Gerhart, M. "The Restoration of Biblical Narrative." *Semeia* 46 (1989) 13–29.

Giblin, C. H. "Confrontations in John 18,1–27." *Bib* 65 (1984) 210–31.

———. "John's Narration of the Hearing before Pilate (John 18:28—19:16a)." *Bib* 67 (1986) 221–39.

———. "Structural Patterns in Joshua 24:1–25." *CBQ* 26 (1964) 50–69.

———. "Suggestion, Negative Response, and Positive Action in St John's Portrayal of Jesus (John 2:1–11; 4:46–54; 7:2–14; 11:1–44)." *NTS* 26 (1980) 197–211.

———. "Two Complementary Literary Structures in John 1:1–18." *JBL* 104 (1985) 87–103.

Gnilka, J. *Johannesevangelium*. 3rd ed. NEchtB, NT 4. Würzburg: Echter, 1989.

Goodman, P. *The Sukkot and Simkah Torah Anthology*. Philadelphia: Jewish Publication Society, 1963.

Graham, W. A. "Scripture." In *ER* 13:133–42.

Grassi, J. A. "The Wedding at Cana (John 2.1–11): A Pentecostal Meditation." *NovT* (1972) 131–36.

Grossouw, W. K. "A Note on John XIII 1–3." *NovT* 8 (1966) 124–31.

Haenchen, E. "History and Interpretation in the Johannine Passion Narrative." *Int* 24 (1970) 198–219.

———. *John: A Commentary on the Gospel of John*. 2 vols. Translated by Robert W. Funk. Hermeneia. Philadelphia: Fortress, 1984.

Hanson, A. T. *The Prophetic Gospel: A Study of John and the Old Testament*. Edinburgh: T. & T. Clark, 1991.

Harvey, A. E. *Jesus on Trial*. London: SPCK, 1976.

Harvey, W. J. *Character and the Novel*. Ithaca, NY: Cornell University Press, 1965.

Heil, J. P. *Blood and Water: The Death and Resurrection of Jesus in John 18–21*. CBQMS 27. Washington: Catholic Biblical Association of America, 1995.

Hermaniuk, M. *La Parabole évangélique*. Louvain: Louvain University Press, 1947.

Heschel, A. J. *The Prophets*. New York: Harper & Row, 1962.

Hillers, D. R. *Covenant: The History of a Biblical Idea*. Seminars in the History of Ideas. Baltimore: Johns Hopkins Press, 1969.

Hooker, M. D. *Beginnings: Keys that Open the Gospels*. Harrisburg, PA: Trinity, 1997.

———. *Endings: Invitations to Discipleship*. Peabody, MA: Hendrickson, 2003.

———. "Johannine Prologue and the Messianic Secret." *NTS* 21 (1974) 40–58.

———. "John the Baptist and the Johannine Prologue." *NTS* 16 (1970) 354–58.

Hoskyns, E. C. *The Fourth Gospel*. Edited by Francis N. Davey. 2nd ed. London: Faber & Faber, 1947.

Howard, J. M. "The Significance of Minor Characters in the Gospel of John." *BSac* 163 (2006) 63–78.

Howard, W. F. *The Fourth Gospel in Recent Criticism and Interpretation*. London: Epworth, 1931.

Howard-Brook, W. *Becoming Children of God: John's Gospel and Radical Discipleship*. B. & L. Maryknoll, NY: Orbis, 1994.

Huffmon, H. B. "The Covenant Lawsuit in the Prophets." *JBL* 78 (1959) 285–95.

———. "A Further Note on the Treaty Background of Hebrew Yada'." *BASOR* 184 (1966) 36–38.

———. "The Treaty Background of Hebrew Yada'." *BASOR* 181 (1966) 31–37.

Hull, W. E. *John*. BBC 9. Nashville: Broadman, 1970.

Iersal, B. M. F. van. "Tradition und Redaktion in Joh. i 19–36." *NovT* 5 (1962) 245–67.

Irigoin, J. "La Composition Rythmique du Prologue de Jean (I,1–18)." *RB* 98 (1991) 5–50.
Jakobson, R. *Language in Literature*. Cambridge, MA: Belknap, 1987.
Joubert, H. L. N. "'The Holy One of God' (John 6:69)." *Neot* 2 (1968) 57–69.
Kalluveettil, P. *Declaration and Covenant: A Comprehensive Review of Covenant Formulae from the Old Testament and the Ancient Near East*. AnBib 88. Rome: Biblical Institute Press, 1982.
Käsemann, E. "The Structure and Purpose of the Prologue to John's Gospel." In *New Testament Questions of Today*, 146–66. NTL. London: SCM, 1969.
Kelber, W. H. "The Birth of a Beginning: John 1:1–18." *Semeia* 52 (1990) 121–44.
Kelly, A. J., and Francis J. Moloney. *Experiencing God in the Gospel of John*. New York: Paulist, 2003.
Kennedy, H. A. A. "The Covenant-Conception in the First Epistle of John." *ExpTim* 28 (1916) 23–26.
———. "The Significance and Range of the Covenant-Conception in the New Testament." *Expositor* 10 (1915) 385–410.
Kermode, F. "St John as Poet." *JSNT* 28 (1986) 3–16.
Kierkegaard, S. *Fear and Trembling: Dialectical Lyric by Johannes de Silentio*. Translated by A. Hannay. London: Penguin, 1985.
Kilpatrick, G. D. "John IV:51, ΠΑΙΣ or ΗΥΙΟΣ?" *JTS* 14 (1963) 393.
Klauck, H.-J. "Geschrieben, erfüllt, vollendet: die Schriftzitate in der Johannespassion." In *Israel und seine Heilstraditionen im Johannesevangelium: Festgabe für Johannes Beutler SJ zum 70. Geburtstage*, edited by M. Labahn, K. Scholtissek, and A. Strotmann, 140–57. Paderborn: Schöningh, 2004.
Knöppler, T. *Die Theologia crucis des Johannesevangeliums: Das Verständnis des Todes Jesu im Rahmen der johanneischen Inkarnations- und Erhöhungschristologie*. WMANT 69. Neukirchen: Neukirchener, 1994.
Koester, C. R. "Messianic Exegesis and the Call of Nathanael (John 1.45–51)." *JSNT* 39 (1990) 23–34.
———. *Symbolism in the Fourth Gospel: Meaning, Mystery, Community*. 2nd ed. Minneapolis: Fortress, 2001.
———. "Texts in Context: The Passion and Resurrection according to John." *WW* 11 (1991) 84–91.
Korošec, V. *Hethitische Staatsverträge; Ein Beitrag zu ihrer Juristischen wertung*. Leipziger rechtswissenschaftliche Studien 60. Leipzig: Weicher, 1931.
Kruger, P. A. "Israel, the Harlot (Hos 2:4–9)." *JNSL* 11 (1983) 107–16.
Kruse, H. "David's Covenant." *VT* 35 (1985) 139–64.
Labahn, M. "Between Tradition and Literary Art: The Miracle Tradition in the Fourth Gospel." *Bib* 80 (1999) 178–203.
———. *Jesus als Lebensspender: Untersuchungen zu einer Geschichte der johanneischen Tradition anhand ihrer Wundergeschichten*. BZNW 98. Berlin: de Gruyter, 1999.
———. "Jesus und die Autorität der Schrift im Johannesevangelium." In *Israel und seine Heilstraditionen im Johannesevangelium: Festgabe für Johannes Beutler SJ zum 70. Geburtstage*, edited by M. Labahn, K. Scholtissek, and A. Strotmann, 185–206. Paderborn: Schöningh, 2004.
Lacan, M.-F. "Le Prologue de Saint Jean: Ses Thèmes, sa Structure, son Mouvement." *LV* 33 (1957) 91–110.

Lacomara, A. "Deuteronomy and the Farewell Discourse (Jn 13:31—16:33)." *CBQ* 36 (1974) 64–84.
Lagrange, M.-J. *Évangile selon Saint Jean*. EBib. Paris: Gabalda, 1936.
Lamarche, P. "Le Prologue de Jean." *RSR* 52 (1964) 529–32.
Lang, M. *Johannes und die Synoptiker: Eine redaktionsgeschichtliche Analyse von Joh 18-20 vor dem markinischen und lukanischen Hintergrund*. FRLANT 182. Göttingen: Vandenhoeck & Ruprecht, 1999.
Lategan, B. C. "The Truth That Sets Man Free: John 8:31–36." *Neot* 2 (1968) 70–80.
Lauterbach, J. Z., editor and translator. *Mekilta de-Rabbi Ishmael*. 3 vols. JPSLJC. Philadelphia: Jewish Publication Society, 1961.
Lee, D. A. *Flesh and Glory: Symbol, Gender, and Theology in the Gospel of John*. New York: Crossroad, 2002.
———. *The Symbolic Narratives of the Fourth Gospel: The Interplay of Form and Meaning*. JSNTSup 95. Sheffield: JSOT Press, 1994.
L'Hour, J. *La Morale de l'alliance*. CahRB 5. Paris: Gabalda, 1966.
Lincoln, A. T. *The Gospel according to Saint John*. BNTC 4. Peabody, MA: Hendrickson, 2005.
———. *Truth on Trial: The Lawsuit Motif in the Fourth Gospel*. Peabody, MA: Hendrickson, 2000.
Lindars, B. "The Composition of John 20." *NTS* 7 (1961) 142–47.
———. *The Gospel of John*. NCB. London: Oliphants, 1972.
———. "Slave and Son in John 8:31–36." In *The New Testament Age: Essays in Honor of Bo Reicke*, edited by W. C. Weinrich, 1:270–86. Macon, GA: Mercer University Press, 1984.
Lombard, H. A., and W. H. Oliver. "A Working Supper in Jerusalem: John 13:1–38 Introduces Jesus' Farewell Discourses." *Neot* 25 (1991) 357–78.
Lund, N. W. *Chiasmus in the New Testament: A Study in Formgeschichte*. Chapel Hill: University of North Carolina Press, 1942.
———. *Chiasmus in the New Testament: A Study in the Form and Function of Chiastic Structures*. Peabody, MA: Hendrickson, 1992.
———. "The Influence of Chiasmus upon the Structure of the Gospels." *AThR* 13 (1931) 42–46.
Maccini, R. G. *Her Testimony Is True: Women as Witnesses according to John*. JSNTSup 125. Sheffield: Sheffield Academic, 1996.
MacRae, G. W. "The Fourth Gospel and *Religionsgeschichte*." *CBQ* 32 (1970) 13–24.
———. "The Meaning and Evolution of the Feast of Tabernacles." *CBQ* 22 (1960) 251–76.
Mahoney, R. *Two Disciples at the Tomb: The Background and Message of John 20.1–10*. TW 6. Frankfurt: Lang, 1974.
Malatesta, E. *Interiority and Covenant: A Study of εἶναι ἐν and μένειν ἐν in the First Letter of Saint John*. AnBib 69. Rome: Biblical Institute Press, 1978.
Manns, F. *L'Evangile de Jean à la Lumière du Judaïsme*. SBF 33. Jerusalem: Franciscan, 1991.
Martyn, J. L. *History and Theology in the Fourth Gospel*. 3rd ed. NTL. Louisville: Westminster John Knox, 2003.
Matera, F. J. "Jesus before Annas: John 18,13–14, 19–24." *ETL* 66 (1990) 38–55.
———. "John 20:1–18." *Int* 43 (1989) 402–6.

Matthews, V. H. *Old Testament Turning Points: The Narratives That Shaped a Nation*. Grand Rapids: Baker Academic, 2005.

Maynard, A. "TI EMOI KAI SOI." *NTS* 31 (1985) 582–86.

Mays, J. L. *Hosea: A Commentary*. OTL. Philadelphia: Westminster, 1969.

McCarter, P. K. *I Samuel: A New Translation with Introduction, Notes, and Commentary*. AB 8. Garden City, NY: Doubleday, 1980.

———. *II Samuel: A New Translation with Introduction, Notes, and Commentary*. AB 9. Garden City, NY: Doubleday, 1984.

McCarthy, D. J. "Notes on the Love of God in Deuteronomy and the Father-Son Relationship between Yahweh and Israel." *CBQ* 27 (1965) 144–47.

———. *Old Testament Covenant: A Survey of Current Opinions*. Richmond: John Knox, 1972.

———. *Treaty and Covenant: A Study in Form in the Ancient Oriental Documents and in the Old Testament*. 2nd ed. AnBib 21. Rome: Pontifical Biblical Institute, 1978.

McKay, K. L. "Style and Significance in the Language of John 21:15–17." *NovT* 27 (1985) 319–33.

McKenzie, S. L. *Covenant*. UBT. St. Louis: Chalice, 2000.

McNamara, M. "Logos of the Fourth Gospel and Memra of the Palestinian Targum: Ex 12:42." *ExpTim* 79 (1968) 115–17.

Mead, A. H. "The Basilikos in John 4.46–53." *JSNT* 23 (1985) 69–72.

Meeks, W. A. *The Prophet-King: Moses Traditions and the Johannine Christology*. NovTSup 14. Leiden: Brill, 1967.

Mendenhall, G. E. *Law and Covenant in Israel and the Ancient Near East*. Pittsburgh: Biblical Colloquium, 1955.

Mendenhall, G. E., and G. A. Herion. "Covenant." In *ABD* 1:1179–202.

Menezes, R. *Voices from Beyond: Theology of the Prophetical Books*. Mumbai: St. Paul's, 2003.

Menken, M. F. F. *Old Testament Quotations in the Fourth Gospel: Studies in Textual Form*. CBET 15. Kampen: Kok Pharos, 1996.

———. "The Quotation from Isa 40:3 in John 1:23." *Bib* 66 (1985) 190–205.

Merwe, D. G. "The Historical and Theological Significance of John the Baptist as He Is Portrayed in John 1." *Neot* 33 (1999) 267–92.

Metzger, Bruce M. *A Textual Commentary on the Greek New Testament*. 2nd ed. New York: United Bible Societies, 1994.

Miller, E. L. "The Christology of John 8:25." *TZ* 36 (1980) 257–65.

Minear, P. S. "The Original Functions of John 21." *JBL* 102 (1983) 85–98.

Mlakuzhyil, G. *The Christocentric Literary Structure of the Fourth Gospel*. AnBib 117. Rome: Biblical Institute Press, 1987.

Moloney, Francis J. *Belief in the Word: Reading John 1–4*. Minneapolis: Fortress, 1993.

———. "Can Everyone Be Wrong? A Reading of John 11.1—12.8." *NTS* 49 (2003) 505–27.

———. "From Cana to Cana (Jn 2:1—4:54) and the Fourth Evangelist's Concept of Correct (and Incorrect) Faith." In *Studia Biblica 1978: Sixth International Congress on Biblical Studies, Oxford 3–7 April 1978*, edited by E. A. Livingstone, 2:185–213. JSNTSup 2. Sheffield: JSOT Press, 1980.

———. "The Function of John 13–17 within the Johannine Narrative." In *What Is John?*, edited by F. F. Segovia, 2:43–66. SBLSymS 7. Atlanta: Scholars, 1998.

———. *Glory Not Dishonor: Reading John 13–21*. Minneapolis: Augsburg Fortress, 1998.

———. *The Gospel of John*. SP 4. Collegeville, MN: Liturgical, 1998.

———. *The Gospel of John: Text and Context*. BIS 72. Boston: Brill, 2005.

———. "The Gospel of John as Scripture." *CBQ* 67 (2005) 454–68.

———. *The Gospel of Mark: A Commentary*. Peabody, MA: Hendrickson, 2002.

———. *The Johannine Son of Man*. 2nd ed. Rome: Libreria Ateneo Salesiano, 1978.

———. "John 18:15–27: A Johannine View of the Church." *DRev* 112 (1994) 231–48.

———. "John 1:18 'in the Bosom of' or 'Turned Towards' the Father." *ABR* 31 (1983) 63–71.

———. "John 6 and the Celebration of the Eucharist." *DRev* 93 (1975) 243–51.

———. "John 21 and the Johannine Story." In *Anatomies of the Fourth Gospel: The Past, Present, and Futures of Narrative Criticism*, edited by T. Thatcher and S. D. Moore, 237–51. SBLRBS. Atlanta: SBL, 2008.

———. *Mary: Woman and Mother*. Collegeville, MN: Liturgical, 1988.

———. "Narrative and Discourse at the Feast of Tabernacles." In *The Gospel of John: Text and Context*, 193–213. BIS 72. Boston: Brill, 2005.

———. "Reading John 2:13–22: The Purification of the Temple." *RB* 97 (1990) 432–52.

———. *Signs and Shadows: Reading John 5–12*. Minneapolis: Fortress, 1996.

———. "The Structure and Message of John 13:1–38." *ABR* 34 (1986) 1–16.

———. "Telling God's Story: The Fourth Gospel." In *The Forgotten God: Perspectives in Biblical Theology: Essays in Honor of Paul J. Achtemeier*, edited by A. A. Das and F. J. Matera, 102–22. Louisville: Westminster John Knox, 2002.

Montgomery Hitchcock, F. R. "The Dramatic Development of the Fourth Gospel." *Expositor* 4 (1907) 266–79.

Moody, D. "God's Only Son: The Translation of John 3:16 in the Revised Standard Version." *JBL* 72 (1953) 213–19.

Moran, W. L. "The Ancient Near Eastern Background of the Love of God in Deuteronomy." *CBQ* 25 (1963) 77–87.

Morrison, C. E. "The 'Hour of Distress' in Targum Neofiti and the 'Hour' in the Gospel of John." *CBQ* 67 4 (2005) 590–603.

Muilenburg, J. "The Form and Structure of the Covenantal Formulations." *VT* 9 (1959) 357–65.

Müller, P. *"Verstehst du auch, was du liest?" Lesen und Verstehen im Neuen Testament*. Darmstadt: Wissenschaftliche Buchgesellschaft, 1994.

Myers, J. M. *Ezra-Nehemiah*. AB 14. Garden City, NY: Doubleday, 1965.

Neirynck, F. "The Anonymous Disciple in John 1." *ETL* 66 1 (1990) 5–37.

———. "John 4,46–54: Signs Source and/or Synoptic Gospels." *ETL* 60 (1984) 367–75.

———. "Short Note on John 19, 26–27." *ETL* 71 (1995) 431–34.

Neyrey, J. H. "Despising the Shame of the Cross: Honor and Shame in the Johannine Passion Narrative." *Semeia* 68 (1994) 113–37.

———. "The Jacob Allusions in John 1:51." *CBQ* 44 (1982) 586–605.

———. "Jesus the Judge: Forensic Process in John 8:21–59." *Bib* 68 (1987) 509–42.

———. "The Trials (Forensic) and Tribulations (Honor Challenges) of Jesus: John 7 in Social Science Perspective." *BTB* 26 (1996) 107–24.
Neyrey, J. H., and R. L. Rohrbaugh. "He Must Increase, I Must Decrease (John 3:30): A Cultural and Social Interpretation." *CBQ* 63 (2001) 464–83.
Niccaci, A. "Esame letterario di Gv 14." *EuD* 31 (1978) 209–14.
———. "L'unita letteraria di Gv 13,1–38." *EuD* 29 (1976) 291–323.
Nicholson, E. W. *God and His People: Covenant and Theology in the Old Testament.* Oxford: Clarendon, 1986.
Nicholson, G. C. *Death as Departure: The Johannine Descent-Ascent Schema.* SBLDS 63. Atlanta: Scholars, 1983.
Obermann, A. *Die christologische Erfüllung der Schrift im Johannesevangelium: Eine Untersuchung zur johanneischen Hermeneutik anhand der Schriftzitate.* WUNT, ser. 2, 83. Tübingen: Mohr Siebeck, 1996.
O'Brien, K. S. "Written That You May Believe: John 20 and Narrative Rhetoric." *CBQ* 67 (2005) 284–302.
O'Connell, M. J. "The Concept of Commandment in the Old Testament." *TS* 21 (1960) 351–403.
O'Day, G. R. *The Gospel of John.* NIB 9. Nashville: Abington, 1995.
———. "'I Have Overcome the World' (John 16:33): Narrative Time in John 13–17." *Semeia* 53 (1991) 153–66.
Osborn, A. R. "The Word Became Flesh: An Exposition of John 1:1–18." *Int* 3 (1949) 42–49.
Pancaro, S. *The Law in the Fourth Gospel: The Torah and the Gospel, Moses and Jesus, Judaism and Christianity according to John.* NovTSup 42. Leiden: Brill, 1975.
Perry, M. "Literary Dynamics: How the Order of a Text Creates Its Meanings (With an Analysis of Faulkner's 'A Rose for Emily')." *Poetics Today* 1 (1979) 35–64, 311–61.
Pfitzner, V. C. "Coronation of the King: The Passion in the Gospel of John." *CurTM* (1977) 10–21.
Pickering, S. R. "John 7:53—8:11: The Woman Taken in Adultery." *NTTRU* 1 (1993) 6–7.
Potin, J. *La Fête juive de la Pentecôte.* LD 65. Paris: Cerf, 1971.
Powell, M. A. *What Is Narrative Criticism?* GBSNT. Minneapolis: Fortress, 1990.
Prickett, S. *Words and the Word: Language, Poetics, and Biblical Interpretation.* Cambridge: Cambridge University Press, 1986.
Pryor, J. W. "Covenant and Community in John's Gospel." *RTR* 47 (1988) 44–51.
———. *John, Evangelist of the Covenant People: The Narrative & Themes of the Fourth Gospel.* Downers Grove: InterVarsity, 1992.
———. "John 4:44 and the *Patris* of Jesus." *CBQ* 49 (1987) 254–63.
———. "John the Baptist and Jesus: Tradition and Text in John 3.25." *JSNT* 66 (1997) 15–26.
Rad, G. *Genesis: A Commentary.* Translated by John H. Marks. Rev ed. OTL. London: SCM, 1961.
Rankin, O. S. *The Origins of the Festival of Hanukkah: The Jewish Newage Festival.* Edinburgh: T. & T. Clark, 1930.
Reim, G. "John IV.44—Crux or Clue." *NTS* 22 (1975–76) 476–80.
Reinhartz, A. *The Word in the World: The Cosmological Tale in the Fourth Gospel.* SBLMS 45. Atlanta: Scholars, 1992.

Rensberger, D. K. "The Politics of John: The Trial of Jesus in the Fourth Gospel." *JBL* 103 (1984) 395–411.
Riesenfeld, H. "Zu den johanneischen hina-Sätzen." *ST* 19 (1965) 213–20.
Rimmon-Kenan, S. *Narrative Fiction: Contemporary Poetics*. London: Routledge, 1983.
Ringe, S. H. *Wisdom's Friends: Community and Christology in the Fourth Gospel*. Louisville: Westminster John Knox, 1999.
Rissi, M. "John 1:1–18 (The Eternal Word)." *Int* 31 (1977) 394–401.
Rius-Camps, J. "The Pericope of the Adulteress Reconsidered: the Nomadic Misfortunes of a Bold Pericope." *NTS* 53 (2007) 379–405.
Roberge, M. "Le Discours sur le pain de vie (Jean 6,22–59): Problèmes d'intérpretation." *LTP* 38 (1982) 265–99.
Robertson, A. T. *A Grammar of the Greek New Testament in the Light of Historical Research*. 4th ed. New York: Hodder & Stoughton, 1923.
Robinson, B. P. "The Meaning and Significance of 'The Seventh Hour' in John 4:52." In *Studia Biblica 1978: Sixth International Congress on Biblical Studies, Oxford 3–7 April 1978*, edited by E. A. Livingstone, 2:255–62. JSNTSup 2. Sheffield: JSOT Press, 1980.
Robinson, J. A. T. "Destination and Purpose of St John's Gospel." *NTS* 6 (1960) 117–31.
———. "Elijah, John and Jesus, and Essay in Detection." *NTS* 4 (1957–58) 263–81.
———. "The Relation of the Prologue to the Gospel of John." *NTS* 9 (1963) 120–29.
Romeo, J. A. "Gematria and John 21:11: The Children of God." *JBL* 97 (1978) 97–98.
Rowland, C. "John 1:51, Jewish Apocalyptic and Targumic Tradition." *NTS* 30 (1984) 498–507.
Sakenfeld, K. D. *Faithfulness in Action: Loyalty in Biblical Perspective*. OBT 16. Philadelphia: Fortress, 1985.
———. *The Meaning of Hesed in the Hebrew Bible: A New Inquiry*. HSM 17. Missoula, MT: Scholars, 1978.
Saxby, H. "The Time-Scheme in the Gospel of John." *ExpTim* 104 (1992) 9–13.
Schenke, L. "Joh 7–10: Eine dramatische Szene." *ZNW* 80 (1989) 172–92.
Schnackenburg, R. *The Gospel according to St. John*. Translated by Kevin Smyth. 3 vols. HTKNT 4.1–3. New York: Herder & Herder, 1968–82.
———. "Die situationsgelösten Redestücke in John 3." *ZNW* 49 (1958) 88–99.
———. "Zur Traditionsgeschichte von Joh 4,46–54." *BZ* 8 (1964) 58–88.
Schneider, J. "Zur Komposition von Joh 7." *ZNW* 45 (1954) 108–19.
Schneiders, S. M. "Death in the Community of Eternal Life: History, Theology and Spirituality in John 11." *Int* 41 (1987) 44–56.
———. "John 21:1–14." *Int* 43 (1989) 70–75.
———. *Written That You May Believe: Encountering Jesus in the Fourth Gospel*. New York: Crossroad, 1999; rev. ed., 2003.
Schnelle, U. *Antidocetic Christology in the Gospel of John: An Investigation of the Place of the Fourth Gospel in the Johannine School*. Translated by Linda M. Maloney. Minneapolis: Fortress, 1992.
———. *The Human Condition: Anthropology in the Teachings of Jesus, Paul, and John*. Translated by O. C. Dean Jr. Minneapolis: Fortress, 1996.
———. "Recent Views of John's Gospel." *WW* 21 (2001) 352–59.

Scholtissek, K. "'Geschrieben in diesem Buch' (Joh 20,30)—Beobachtungen zum kanonischen Anspruch des Johannesevangeliums." In *Israel und seine Heilstraditionen im Johannesevangelium: Festgabe für Johannes Beutler SJ zum 70. Geburtstage*, edited by M. Labahn, K. Scholtissek, and A. Strotmann, 207-26. Paderborn: Schöningh, 2004.

———. *In ihm sein und bleiben: Die Sprache der Immanenz in den johanneischen Schriften*. HBibS 21. Freiburg: Herder, 2000.

Schwank, B. "Exemplum dedi vobis: Die Fusswaschung (13, 1-17)." *Sein und Sendung* 28 (1963) 4-17.

Segovia, F. F. *The Farewell of the Word: The Johannine Call to Abide*. Minneapolis: Fortress, 1991.

———. "The Final Farewell of Jesus: A Reading of John 20:30—21:25." *Semeia* 53 (1991) 167-90.

———. "The Journey(s) of the Word of God: A Reading of the Plot of the Fourth Gospel." *Semeia* 53 (1991) 23-54.

———. "The Structure, *Tendenz*, and *Sitz im Leben* of John 13:31—14:31." *JBL* 104 (1985) 471-93.

Senior, D. *The Passion of Jesus in the Gospel of John*. The Passion Series 4. Collegeville, MN: Liturgical, 1991.

Serra, A. M. "Le tradizioni della teofania sinaitica nel Targum dello Pseudo Jonathan Es. 1.24 e Giov. 1:19—2:12." *Marianum* 33 (1971) 1-39.

Simoens, Y. *La Gloire d'aimer: Structures Stylistiques et Interprétatives dans le Discours de la Cène (Jn 13-17)*. AnBib 90. Rome: Biblical Institute Press, 1981.

Skinner, C. W. "Another Look at 'the Lamb of God.'" *BSac* 161 (2004) 89-104.

Skinner, J. *A Critical and Exegetical Commentary on Genesis*. 2nd ed. ICC. Edinburgh: T. & T. Clark, 1930.

Smalley, S. S. "The Sign in John XXI." *NTS* 20 (1974) 275-88.

Smith, D. M. *The Composition and Order of the Fourth Gospel: Bultmann's Literary Theory*. Yale Publications in Religion 10. New Haven: Yale University, 1965.

———. *John*. Proclamation Commentaries. Philadelphia: Fortress, 1976.

———. "When Did the Gospels Become Scripture?" *JBL* 119 (2000) 3-20.

Speiser, E. A. *Genesis*. AB 1. Garden City, NY: Doubleday, 1964.

Staley, J. L. *The Print's First Kiss: A Rhetorical Investigation of the Implied Reader in the Fourth Gospel*. SBLDS 82. Atlanta: Scholars, 1988.

———. "The Structure of John's Prologue: Its Implications for the Gospel's Narrative Structure." *CBQ* 48 (1986) 241-63.

Sternberg, M. *The Poetics of Biblical Narrative: Ideological Literature and the Drama of Reading*. Indiana Literary Biblical Series. Bloomington: Indiana University Press, 1985.

Stibbe, M. W. G. *John*. Readings. Sheffield: JSOT Press, 1993.

———. *John as Storyteller: Narrative Criticism and the Fourth Gospel*. SNTSMS 73. Cambridge: Cambridge University Press, 1992.

———. "A Tomb with a View: John 11:1-44 in Narrative-Critical Perspective." *NTS* 40 (1994) 38-54.

Strachan, R. H. *The Fourth Evangelist: Dramatist or Historian?* New York: Doran, 1925.

Strathmann, H. *Das Evangelium nach Johannes*. NTD 4. Gottingen: Vandenhoeck & Ruprecht, 1955.

Sturch, R. L. "The 'PATRIS' of Jesus." *JTS* 28 (1977) 94–96.
Suggit, J. "John 19:5: 'Behold the Man.'" *ExpTim* 94 (1982–83) 333–34.
———. "John XVII. 17, O LOGOS O SOS ALHQEIA ESTIN." *JTS* 35 (1984) 104–17.
Sylva, D. D. "Nicodemus and His Spices (John 19:39)." *NTS* 34 (1988) 148–51.
Talbert, C. H. "Artistry and Theology: An Analysis of the Architecture of Jn 1,19—5,47." *CBQ* 32 (1970) 341–66.
———. *Reading John: A Literary and Theological Commentary on the Fourth Gospel and the Johannine Epistles*. New York: Crossroad, 1992.
Thatcher, T. "Jesus, Judas, and Peter: Character by Contrast in the Fourth Gospel." *BSac* 153 (1996) 435–48.
Thomas, J. C. "The Fourth Gospel and Rabbinic Judaism." *ZNW* 82 (1991) 159–82.
Throntveit, M. A. *Ezra-Nehemiah*. Interpretation. Louisville: John Knox, 1992.
Tobin, T. H., S.J. "The Prologue of John and Hellenistic Jewish Speculation." *CBQ* 52 (1990) 252–69.
Tolman, H. C. "A Possible Restoration from a Middle Persian Source of the Answer of Jesus to Pilate's Inquiry 'What Is Truth?'" *JAOS* 39 (1919) 55–57.
Tolmie, D. F. *Jesus' Farewell to the Disciples: John 13:1—17:26 in Narratological Perspective*. BIS 12. Leiden: Brill, 1995.
Tovey, D. M. H. *Narrative Art and Act in the Fourth Gospel*. JSNTSup 151. Sheffield: Sheffield Academic, 1997.
———. "Narrative Strategies in the Prologue and the Metaphor of ὁ λόγος in John's Gospel." *Pacifica* 15 (2002) 138–53.
Trudinger, L. P. "The Seven Days of the New Creation in St. John's Gospel: Some Further Reflections." *EvQ* 44 (1972) 154–58.
Unnik, W. C. van. "The Purpose of St John's Gospel." *SE* 1 (1959) 382–411.
———. "The Quotation from the Old Testament in John 12:34." *NovT* 3 (1959) 174–79.
Vander Kam, J. C. "Weeks, Feast of." In *ABD* 6:895–97.
Vermes, G. "Jewish Literature and New Testament Exegesis: Reflections on Methodology." In *Jesus and the World of Judaism*, 74–88. London: SCM, 1983.
Waetjen, H. C. "Logos πρὸς τὸν θεόν and the Objectification of Truth in the Prologue of the Fourth Gospel." *CBQ* 63 (2001) 265–83.
Wallace, D. B. *Greek Grammar beyond the Basics: An Exegetical Syntax of the New Testament*. Grand Rapids: Zondervan, 1996.
Wead, D. W. *The Literary Devices of John's Gospel*. TD 4. Basel: Reinhardt Kommissionsverlag, 1970.
Weinfeld, M. *Deuteronomy 1-11: A New Translation with Introduction and Commentary*. AB 5. New York: Doubleday, 1991.
Wellhausen, J. *Prolegomena to the History of Israel*. Translated by J. S. Black. Scholars Press Reprints and Translations Series. Atlanta: Scholars, 1994.
Westcott, B. F. *The Gospel according to Saint John*. 2 vols. London: J. Murray, 1908.
———. *The Gospel according to St. John: The Authorized Version with Introduction and Notes*. London: J. Clarke, 1958.
Westermann, C. *Genesis: A Commentary*. Translated by J. J. Scullion. 3 vols. Minneapolis: Augsburg, 1984–96.
———. *The Gospel of John in the Light of the Old Testament*. Translated by S. S. Schartzmann. Peabody, MA: Hendrickson, 1998.

Wiarda, T. "John 21:1–23: Narrative Unity and its Implications." *JSNT* 46 (1992) 53–71.
Wikenhauser, A. *Das Evangelium des Johannes*. RNT 4. Regensburg: F. Pustet, 1948.
Willemse, J. "La Patrie de Jésus selon Saint Jean IV.44." *NTS* 11 (1964–65) 349–64.
Williams, R. H. "The Mother of Jesus at Cana: A Social-Science Interpretation of John 2:1–12." *CBQ* 59 (1997) 679–92.
Williamson, H. G. M. *Ezra, Nehemiah*. WBC 16. Waco, TX: Word, 1985.
Wilson, J. "The Integrity of John 3:22–36." *JSNT* 10 (1981) 34–41.
Winbery, C. L. "Abiding in Christ: The Concept of Discipleship in John." *TTE* 38 (1988) 104–20.
Witcamp, L. T. "The Use of Traditions in John 5.1–18." *JSNT* 25 (1985) 19–31.
Woll, D. B. "The Departure of 'The Way': The First Farewell Discourse in the Gospel of John." *JBL* 99 (1980) 225–39.
Wright, G. E. *Shechem: The Biography of a Biblical City*. Norton Lectures 1963. New York: MacGraw-Hill, 1965.
Wuellner, W. "Putting Life Back into the Lazarus Story and Its Reading: The Narrative Rhetoric of John 11 as the Narration of Faith." *Semeia* 53 (1991) 114–32.
Yee, G. A. *Jewish Feasts and the Gospel of John*. Zacchaeus Studies, New Testament. Wilmington, DE: Glazier, 1989.

www.ingramcontent.com/pod-product-compliance
Lightning Source LLC
Chambersburg PA
CBHW071243230426
43668CB00011B/1558